Old borders
new borders
no borders

Sport and physical education in a period of change

11th Conference
International Society
for Comparative Physical
Education and Sport
ISCPES
K.U.Leuven, Belgium
Faculty of Physical Education
and Physiotherapy
8th - 13th July 1998

J. Tolleneer & R. Renson (eds.)

Meyer & Meyer Sport

British Library Cataloguing in Publication Data
A catalogue record for this book is available from the British Library

J. Tolleneer / R. Renson (eds.):
Old borders, new borders, no borders: Sport and physical education in a
period of change/J.Tolleneer/R. Renson.
– Oxford : Meyer & Meyer Sport (UK) Ltd., 2000
ISBN 1-84126-052-5

© 2000 by Meyer & Meyer Sport (UK) Ltd.
Oxford, Aachen, Olten (CH), Vienna, Québec
Lansing/Michigan, Adelaide, Auckland, Johannesburg, Budapest

 Member of the World
Sportpublishers' Association

Typesetting: Sonja Teck
Cover design: Orientaliste, Roeland Kotsch, Lea Goovaerts
Cover and type exposure: frw, Reiner Wahlen, Aachen
Printed and bound in Germany
by Mennicken, Aachen
ISBN 1-84126-052-5
e-mail: verlag@meyer-meyer-sports.com

Contents

Preface
    Jan Tolleneer and Roland Renson   9

ISCPES president's address   13
    Shirley H.M. Reekie

Part A   Disciplines crossing borders   17

Chapter 1   Geography and comparative sports studies: 19
                a rapprochement ?
                John Bale

Chapter 2   The utility of the cross-cultural comparative method   31
                in the study of sport
                Garry Chick

Chapter 3   The uses of history in comparative physical culture   49
                Richard Holt

Part B   Countries getting closer   57

Chapter 4   The effects of American hegemony on the   59
                international sporting community
                Roy A. Clumpner

Chapter 5   Convergent process and diversified growth of national   71
                sport experience in this global village
                Walter King Yan Ho

Chapter 6   Fitness as cultural phenomenon   83
                Karin A.E. Volkwein

Chapter 7   Integration trend of western and eastern fitness   95
                exercises
                Hai Ren

Chapter 8   Ten years of China watching: present trends and   105
                future directions of sport in the People's Republic
                Robin Jones

Chapter 9   Football and nationalism. An analysis of spoken and   117
               written press comments of the football game between
               Belgium and the Netherlands at the World Cup 1994
               Philip Verwimp

Chapter 10   Globalization and localization in sport   137
               Paul De Knop and Sandra Harthoorn

Part C   The past explaining the present   145

Chapter 11   The evolution of physical education in Quebec: 147
               the history of two cultural solitudes (1875-1965)
               Rose-Marie Lèbe

Chapter 12   Sport in the French Colonies: comparative study.   157
               Guadeloupe and Réunion 1925-1950
               Evelyne Combeau-Mari and Jacques Dumont

Chapter 13   Introduction to a comparative approach to naturism   177
               in France and Germany (1800-1939)
               Sylvain Villaret and Jean-Michel Delaplace

Chapter 14   A comparative analysis of the training schools for teachers 185
               of physical education in Italy and Spain: 1860-1910
               Teresa Gonzales Aja and Angela Teja

Chapter 15   The English response to America's national pastime: 197
               American baseball tours to England, 1874-1924
               Daniel J. Bloyce

Chapter 16   Historical background of undergraduate professional   207
               preparation in the United States and Japan. Fragmentation
               between professional and academic disciplines
               Shunichi Takeshita and Kanji Watanabe

Chapter 17   The American invasion of the British turf: a study of   219
               sporting technological transfer
               Wray Vamplew

Chapter 18   Universiades 1959-1996: university games or inter-   227
               olympics ?
               Roland Renson and Line Verbeke

Chapter 19   Old Borders in Olympism the Presidency of Baron Henri   233
               de Baillet-Latour the Successor of Baron de Coubertin
               Karl Lennartz

Chapter 20   Coubertin, nationalism and the media: a case study of   241
             the Atlanta Games
             Catherine O'Brien

Chapter 21   The distinction between the English and American   247
             educational concept of amateurism and its influence
             on the formation of the Olympic Movement
             Stephan Wassong

Part D   Sports challenging the world   255

Chapter 22   Sport for All ! ? Variations of inclusion in Germany,   257
             France and Great Britain
             Ilse Hartmann-Tews

Chapter 23   The evolution of sport participation in Flanders :   269
             a comparison between cities and municipalities
             Lies Van Heddegem, Kristine De Martelaer and Paul De Knop

Chapter 24   The Canadian experience: federal government sport policy   275
             on the eve of the new millennium
             Darwin M. Semotiuk

Chapter 25   Regional divisions, pyramids and twin towers: a   287
             comparison of national football league structures in Europe
             Vic Duke

Chapter 26   Major issues of design for comparative research in sport   301
             sciences
             Herbert Haag

Chapter 27   Attitude towards fouls in German and Japanese rugby   311
             players
             Dieter Teipel and Akihiko Kondo

Chapter 28   Youth culture in New Zealand : the changing face of sport   317
             Rex W. Thomson

Chapter 29   The difficult path of the women in the Olympic Movement   327
             Edeltraud Odenkirchen

Chapter 30   Women's careers in sport and leisure sciences studies.   333
             A German-English comparison
             Karen Petry

Part E   The world confronting physical education   343

Chapter 31   Border guards in and of physical education   345
             Dawn Penney

Chapter 32   Health education as a part of the P.E. curricula in Sweden   355
             and Germany (State of Northrhine-Westphalia) within the
             last ten years
             Annette Fouqué

Chapter 33   The role of physical education and sport in nation building   363
             March L. Krotee and David J. Waters

Chapter 34   A comparative analysis of physical education programs in   373
             Puerto Rico, the United States and Europe
             Ilia N. Morales-Figueroa, March L. Krotee and
             Laurence E. Myeres

Chapter 35   To move with a different view   383
             Winston A. Kloppers

Chapter 36   Sport education at the University of Ljubijana   391
             Bumik S., M. Doupona and M. Bon

Chapter 37   Harmonization of the Physical Education Teacher   401
             Education (PETE) in Europe. A challenge for comparative
             studies
             Willy Laporte

Chapter 38   PE teaching, ageing and the working environment.   411
             The view of female and male PE teachers
             Kroch Christensen Mette, Else Trangbæk and
             Per Fibæk Laursen

Chapter 39   Olympism in the classroom: partnership sponsored   421
             educational materials and the shaping of the school curriculum
             Kimberly S. Schimmel and Timothy Chandler

Chapter 40   Selling the "Spirit of the Dream": olympologies and the 431
             corporate invasion of the classroom
             Tara Magdalinski and John Nauright

Preface

At the turn of last century, a 'fin de siècle' mentality seems to appear. The same happens *a fortiori* when the transgression into a new millennium approaches. It is a period for reflection on change and continuity, on local identity and globalization. Every day the map of the movement culture is drawn and redrawn. How far is western movement culture being enriched by Asian martial arts and physical activities? Should physical education place more emphasis on traditional and local games? Can soccer be an integrative force in the Balkans? The title of this volume *Old borders, new borders, no borders* should not only be understood in its geographical meaning but also in its broader sense.

Old borders, new borders, no borders also applies to the relationship between different disciplines, which embraces the phenomena of movement culture. Comparative and cross-cultural studies are of great significance when the world is becoming smaller and when changes are accelerating. Similarities and differences in the movement cultures of the world should be completed by the study of their historical roots and their evolution. Comparative research, cross-cultural studies and historiography can learn a lot from each other and should not be isolated one from the other. The same applies to their relationship with geography. To date, the overlap between sports geography on the one hand and comparative physical education and sport on the other hand, has been insufficiently explored. These methodological issues are addressed in the first part of the book, *Disciplines crossing borders,* which encompasses the keynote lectures by John Bale, Garry Chick and Richard Holt.

In part two, *Countries getting closer*, researchers from different continents focus on international and intercontinental developments. The concept of the so-called 'global village' also seems useful for sports studies, but there is a need for a sound conceptual framework and methodology to analyse movement culture as a specific text in a specific socio-cultural context. Market forces, technology and communication are significant factors in the convergence of movement forms on a world-wide scale. This dialectic between convergence and divergence is not only driven by an economic rationale but is also affected by value orientations, beliefs and local traditions. The proponents of post-modernism and inter-culturalism expect an attractive variety of forms in the movement cultures of the 21st century. History, however, teaches how difficult it is to protect 'couleurs locales' and regional characteristics against forms of national control and international hegemony.

The third part, *The past explaining the present*, offers a number of case studies of a comparative-historical nature. Sport and physical education are not developing in a socio-historical vacuum but rather they are mirrors as well as vehicles of socio-cultural systems. The acculturation and assimilation process of modern sports in former colonies shows the impact of supra-local networks. Pierre de Coubertin located the origin of modern sports in the elitist British public schools, but the Olympic movement since its origins in 1894 has spun a world-wide net in the industrialised countries; although Africa produces runners 'en masse', it does not appear on the list of Olympic Games organizers. The major gymnastics systems, which dominated physical education in the 19th century and in the first half of the 20th century, were ideological strongholds which rivalled each other with semi-scientific arguments. The bicultural situation of Québec in Canada may be considered as an interesting case in this respect. The physical education history of the English speaking community differs considerably from the Franco-phone community: the first was receptive to new developments from abroad, especially from the United States; the latter was characterised by a conservative approach in line with tradition and with religion.

In the fourth part, *Sports challenging the world*, active sport participation appears as a cultural phenomenon with its own dynamics. The number of sport participants increased considerably because of the promotion campaigns of the Sport for All movement during the 1960s and 1970s. In the 1980s and 1990s, the democratisation process continued in various respects. Nowadays, men and women, young and old, and rural and urban populations are exposed to an ever increasing variety of sports and leisure activities. This creates a number of organisational, financial, ecological and ethical challenges. Contributions in this part depict different sports policies in different countries. They show clearly that the challenges have both a global and local nature.

What does all this mean for the theory and the practice of physical education? This question is answered in the concluding part, *The world confronting physical education*. In almost all countries, physical education is today put to the test at two levels. The first level regards 'quantity' and 'strategy': an adequate number of hours of physical education per week within the curriculum must be guaranteed. In order to obtain this objective the specific pedagogical objectives of physical education must be clearly stated and explicated. These range from general motor competence to a healthy and safe lifestyle, and the development of proper body concepts, self-concepts and social relations. There are enough arguments for the defence of the field. What the field needs in the first place is strategic and political action on the local, national and international levels. A second level, where physical education is confronted with challenges can be summarised by the concepts 'quality' and 'content'. The world's movement culture is becoming so rich and varied that physical education curricula need to be constantly revised and adapted in flexible ways. Tradition and renewal should go hand in hand because immobility will undoubtedly lead to sclerosis. Many studies reveal that physical education has gradually put an over-emphasis on modern sports. The Olympic movement certainly has specific connotations with striving for excellence as a powerful pedagogical driving force. However, standardised competitive sports are only one of the components of movement culture. Other equally important components of the movement panoply are traditional games, physical exercises, and dance forms.

Is the concept of physical education still adequate enough to cover these rich possibilities? Is it not referring to a kind of mental block or political immobilism? The manifest achievements of modern sports must be blended with the rich patrimony of play and games, gymnastics and dance and with new phenomena of the movement culture scene. Is the time ripe for a change of name, as a leverage for a change of mentality and a new world-wide application in the 21st century? Is the term "physical education" *passé* and are neologisms such as "sport education" or "movement culture" better alternatives? The American Academy of Physical Education, for instance, changed its name in 1993 to the American Academy of Kinesiology and Physical Education. Comparative and cross-cultural research, as presented in this volume, can help to identify the objectives of this renewal and can show the way to actualize it on all educational levels, including the teacher education level.

The eleventh conference of the International Society for Comparative Physical Education and Sport (ISCPES) offered an excellent opportunity to discuss these issues and to set out new perspectives for further research. The Katholieke Universiteit Leuven and especially its Faculty of Physical Education and Physiotherapy were pleased to act as host for this international conference. The roots of this Faculty only go back to 1937, whereas the University was founded in 1425. The Faculty is now a dynamic centre focusing on the study of 'homo movens' from a bio-cultural, educational and therapeutic perspective. Two research units of the Department of Sport and Movement Sciences had a close affinity with the content and context of the ISCPES Conference: Socio-cultural Kinesiology and Movement Education and Sport Psychology.

Like other Physical Education Faculties worldwide, the Leuven Faculty strives to cover a wide variety of sub-disciplines and to undertake fundamental research as well as applied research in these areas. By doing so the Faculty in a way mirrors, on a smaller scale, what happens in the entire University. This diversity is enriching, but also sometimes threatening to the status of Faculty of Physical Education and Physiotherapy. In his welcome address on 8th July 1998 in the historical City Hall of Leuven, the K.U.Leuven Vice-rector Guy Mannaerts, stressed that the Faculty offers some excellent examples of inter-disciplinary research and co-operation beyond the borders of research units, faculties and universities. The conference itself was a co-production between the Faculty and the other K.U.Leuven Campus in Kortrijk. Furthermore, this conference was organised in collaboration with two other universities in Flanders (Belgium): the Universities of Ghent (RUG) and Brussels (VUB), which have similar Faculties of Physical Education and Physiotherapy.

The ISCPES 11th Biennial Conference in Leuven (Belgium) started on Wednesday 8th July 1998. The Society's President, Prof. Shirley Reekie, delivered her welcome address during the opening ceremony in the Leuven Town Hall, which at the time of the Conference was celebrating its 550th anniversary. The Chièvres House in the Leuven 'Begijnhof' was an appropriate location for the plenary and parallel sessions and also for the General Assembly of the International Society for Comparative Physical Education and Sport and the special session *Quo vadis: where do you go to ISCPES?* In total, 27 countries and all continents were represented. Brett Hutchins from Australia received the C. Lynn Vendien Award and John Bale from the United Kingdom the John E. Nixon Award. Freddy

Thielemans and Roland Renson gave addresses in the Brussels Town Hall on the occasion of an excursion to the Belgian capital on Saturday 11th July, the Flemish national holiday. The closing session on Sunday 12th July took place in the Faculty of Physical Education and Physiotherapy. Afterwards the participants were invited to the Brasserie Waaiberg for 'panem et ludenses'. This consisted of a cocktail of participating in traditional Flemish folk games, exploring local dishes and beers and ... watching the Soccer World Cup Final 1998 on a huge TV screen.

Jan Tolleneer and Roland Renson

The members of the honorary committee were Prof. em. Michel Ostyn (chairman), Rector Prof. André Oosterlinck, Rector Prof. Marcel Joniau, Honorary rector Prof. G. Maertens, Vice-rector Prof. Guy Mannaerts, Dean Prof. Jan Pauwels, Mr. Luc Van den Brande, Jacques Rogge and Geneviève Ostyn. The scientific committee was composed of Prof. Roland Renson (chairman), Prof. Jan Tolleneer, Prof. Bart Vanreusel, Prof. Richard Holt, Prof. John Nauright, Prof. Roland Naul, Prof. Willy Laporte, Prof. Paul De Knop and Prof. Marc Depaepe. Keynote lectures were given by Prof. Richard Holt, Prof. John Bale, Prof. Garry Chick, Prof. Ilse Hartmann-Tews and Prof. Willy Laporte.

A large number of persons and institutions gave support and encouragement to this conference: the International Council of Sport Science and Physical Education ICSSPE, the City of Leuven, the City of Brussels, Interbrew, the Flemish Folk Games Center, Brasserie de Waaiberg, the Belgian Olympic and Interfederal Committee, the Philatelic Department of the Belgian Post Service, and finally also the Printing Company Orientaliste which produced the conference brochures and website. Furthermore we mention Roland Kotsch, Lea Goovaerts, Jan Creuwels, Ivo Peeters, Lieve Tielemans, Marc Maes, Marleen Vertommen and Hilde Vertommen.

The members of the organizing committee were Prof. Bart Vanreusel (chairman), Prof. Jan Tolleneer, Prof. Marijke Taks, Caroline Gevaert, Paul Meugens, Jeroen Scheerder, Raymond Serrien, Jean-Marc Silvain and Marijke den Hollander. Thanks also to Cedric Ballestrin, Hilde Dewachter, Lotte Vanreusel and Marieke Tolleneer and especially to assistant-coordinator Liesbet Trimpeneers. At more than one occasion Richard Holt, Susan Reed and Ken Hardman were helpful with language control. Sonja Teck played a special role both in the conference coordination and in the preparation of these proceedings.

ISCPES President's address

Shirley H. M. Reekie
San Jose State University, U.S.A.

Thank you to K.U.Leuven, and to the people of Leuven, for this wonderful opening session, and may I add my welcome to this, the 11th biennial conference of the International Society for Comparative Physical Education and Sport, with past conferences having been held in Israel, Canada, the USA, Germany, Hong Kong, Great Britain, the Czech Republic, and Japan.

With regret, I must start my brief remarks on a sad note. Many of you will already know that in March of this year, we lost the Society's Honorary Life President, Dr. C. Lynn Vendien. Lynn was 87 years old; after teaching physical education in her home state of Michigan, she joined the faculty at the University of Massachusetts in 1951 where she remained until her retirement in 1980. A devotee of music, horseback riding, golf, and skiing, Lynn's contribution to the field of physical education was centred on her pioneering efforts in comparative physical education and sport. In 1968, she wrote, with Dr. John E. Nixon, the foundation text of this new field, *The World Today in Health, Physical Education, Recreation and Dance*. Ten years later, she was a leader in the founding in 1978 of what became this International Society for Comparative Physical Education and Sport. Since that inaugural meeting in Israel, Lynn never missed one of these, our biennial conferences, including the last one in Japan in 1996. She was totally committed to international sport and physical education, and to international students, as many of us here can attest to. Dr. Ken Wall, of Springfield College, Massachusetts, was kind enough to represent the Society at the memorial service in April. Lynn has given the Society a generous bequest to enable us to continue awarding the scholarship which bears her name, and this year's scholar will be presenting later in the week. I know that the theme of this conference, "Old Borders, New Borders, No Borders", is one of which she thought highly, and I ask you to stand for a moment of silence in memory of Dr. C. Lynn Vendien, founder, honorary president, international scholar, and friend. Thank you.

Borders - do they keep people, things, ideas out or in? Are they a safeguard or a restriction? A dividing line or meeting point? We can of apply the concept of borders in a geographical sense but also temporally, to borders (or lack thereof) between past, present, and future. I often explain the comparative field to students in this way - whereas history compares across time, our field compares across place. We may also think of the lack of borders in the ether, as in the Internet, which internationally connects, and ask what are the implications for teachers of physical education, for example, of international distance learning?

International connections and borders falling rapidly - as well as being built - are certainly illustrated in modern Europe and it is so fitting that a conference with this theme should be held so close to Brussels. This rapid change is reflected in international sport: two World Cups ago, who would have predicted that Croatia would do so well? Indeed, how many of us would have predicted Croatia? One looks also at the hockey players who grew up under Soviet restrictions but who today earn, and keep, vast salaries earned in the National Hockey League of North America. A similar situation is seen in the National Basketball Association, with the best players in the world being lured to play in the US. On the eastern shore of the Atlantic, some of the best soccer players in the world may leave the country of their birth to play here in Europe. Is there a danger that US professional soccer will always be second rate and that European basketball may suffer the same fate? Or how soon will it be before there are truly international leagues, crossing many borders, as those in the sports marketing business seek to broaden the financial bases of their operations.

In a geographical sense of borders, sport has long been a leader in breaking down barriers. One immediately thinks of the so-called ping pong diplomacy that led to the establishing of political links between China and the US. With last month's soccer game between the US and Iran, and the general goodwill created, will this game be seen as having been a catalyst in improving US/Iranian links? Geographical borders may never have seemed more open than if one had recently clicked on the Jamaican soccer team's home page. After Jamaica qualified for the World Cup, that country 'imported' four English-born players of Jamaican heritage and put on their Website the question, "Do you know of any other players with Jamaican heritage overseas? If so, click here."

And yet, one is also mindful that just as we hear that all politics is local, so is much of sport. You may well, like me, while in another country, have tried in vain to find out the results of a cherished sports event in your homeland. In a way, nothing is more parochial than club sport. With the general move toward internationalisation of so much in the modern world, will unique traditional sports be lost in the mass of big name sports, or will people strive to preserve their sporting idiosyncrasies?

We have probably each experienced the tremendous power of sport in bringing people together, and breaking down barriers. In the eight-oared shell in which I compete in California, we have one Australian, two from Great Britain, one New Zealander, one Canadian, one Frenchwoman, and three from the US. We would likely never have come together but through rowing. This bringing together of peoples through sport is of course seen on a much grander scale between, for example, Northern Ireland and the Irish Republic, and within many newer nations striving to build an identity.

Seasons and even climate in the past have been borders. The concept of the Jamaican bobsled team amused us because it was so unlikely. In winter, we may play field hockey or rugby and then cross the border into summer tennis and cricket. With increasing use of indoor facilities, however, there can be sheets of ice in the desert or track and field during a snowstorm. Thus, even natural borders are being blurred.

Borders are being increasingly broken down in sport between the able bodied and those with disabilities; likewise, highly competitive sport is not just for youth anymore with the huge growth of masters events; and distinctions in sport between the genders are also undergoing rethinking with women competing in pole vault and men in synchronised swimming, to give but two recent examples.

Sometimes an event that seems to cross borders may be seen very differently by those on either side. For example, the Boston Marathon, which has been won by Kenyan men for the past eight years, has even served as the Kenyan Olympic trials, largely because all the runners were in the US anyway on track scholarships. As a result of this dominance, some US road races have sought to exclude foreign runners in a variety of ways. Likewise, some colleges have awarded so many athletic scholarships to foreign athletes that resentment has built within the local community that home-grown athletes are losing out. Protectionism is alive and well in areas other than world trade, it seems. And should foreign athletes be allowed or excluded entrance into a country's national championships, or does it depend on the level of sport?

Are athletes' passports today any more than flags of convenience? Zola Budd is one name which springs to mind here. Of course, the International Olympic Committee accepts entrants only through National Olympic Committees, thus ensuring that teams cannot be truly multi-national. Fortunately, grand slam tennis does not do the same or we would have been denied seeing the Belarussian/US and Czech/Swiss combinations of Zvereva and Davenport, and Novotna and Hingis in the recent Wimbledon final. Rules about borders are different everywhere, of course, and many a Yorkshireman has driven his pregnant wife at great speed along Britain's roads so as to have their child born inside the borders of the county of Yorkshire, thus ensuring the opportunity to be considered for that county's teams. Does all this make a mockery of county, or national, representative status, and how long before nationality is an outdated concept to be replaced by some other category, such as corporate affiliation, in top level representative sport?

And for our own Society, what ought to be our borders? What is our subject matter and how broadly or narrowly should we draw it? When the Society was founded, there were few international physical education and sport associations. Now there is the International Society for Sport History, for Sport Sociology, for Biomechanics, and many others. Are they really international, or just multi-nationally constituted? If the former, how are we different and what, precisely, is our focus? I invite you to be part of the Society's discussions on this topic at the plenary session entitled "Quo Vadis?" which precedes the General Assembly on Friday.

Over the course of the next few days, our Society can look forward to hearing about topics central to our purpose, as in addition to those I have already mentioned, we will discuss sport and geography, cultural anthropology and sport, globalisation and localisation in sport, and fitness and sport in cultural contexts. I know that we will all be challenged in our thinking about many facets of sport and physical education and their various borders. I hope we can have our own borders open to new ideas while still retaining our personal idiosyncrasies. Thank you.

Part A

Disciplines crossing borders

Chapter 1

Geography and comparative sports studies: a rapprochement? [1]

John Bale
Keele University, U.K.

Sports share the characteristics of being the same but also different. All sports must share certain characteristics for them to be sports. [2] Football played in London is the same sport as football played in Leuven. Because the rules of sports like football are standardized and the specifications of the playing area laid down are explicated in the rules, peoples from quite different backgrounds and localities are able to join in a common cultural convention. Sports make national borders permeable and provide common cultural currencies. Furthermore, it can be argued that there is a tendency for individual sports to become more and more similar over time so that regional and national differences become increasingly reduced. Indeed, we could not engage in sports like football and tennis unless each game or match was played according to the same set of rules - though it is likely that they would be more entertaining and laughable if players from different teams did play with different sets of rules! Sameness in sport is obvious at the level of the site on which it is 'played'. The synthetic running track has to be same in terms of its length and composition - 'has to', that is, for records to be validated. This requirement - that sports places must be the same - has led to the term 'placelessness' being applied to them. Such placeless locales are reflected in the concrete stadium, the rectangular swimming pool, the synthetic running track and the regular ice hockey rink and basketball court. [3]

Yet despite the fact that achievement sports *per se* possess the same ideology of seeking optimal performance and the 'production' of records, it is clear that for any individual sport, differences in it can be recognized from time to time and from place to place. Serious, achievement-oriented football was not the same in 1900 as it is today; nor is football - the technique or the tactics of players or spectators - quite the same in, say Brazil as they are in Belgium. And even in the most sanitized spaces where sports take, people and their behavior can claim them back as unique places - making them 'placeful' rather than 'placeless'. It is the delicate balance between sameness and difference - between space and place - which makes sport such an ambiguous - but eminently geographical - phenomenon.

The concern with similarity and difference between sports characteristics of places - be they cities, regions or nations - forms a concern for both comparative sports studies and the geographical study of sports. I would go so far as to say that such common concerns almost dissolve the borders between the respective 'fields of study'. Consider figures 1 and 2. Each of these shows a map - one found in a book on comparative sports, and the other from a book on the geography of sport. It is not immediately obvious which map came from which book. [4] The 'comparative method' is known in geography as 'areal differentiation'. Basically, they mean the same thing. This implies that that there are benefits to be gained from inter-disciplinary links and this paper seeks to explore potential benefits that might be gained from such a *rapprochement*. Rigid disciplinary allegiance both enables a specific 'way of seeing' but at the same time may constrain a broader view. The growing recognition that disciplinary borders may serve to obfuscate, rather than enlighten the search for understanding has led to exhortations for greater interdisciplinarity in the social scientific and humanistic study of sports. [5] Maguire quotes the Dutch sociologist Johann Goudsblom who noted that 'the divorce of history and sociology is detrimental to both'. [6] The same might be said of sports geography and comparative sports studies. The recognition of the arbitrariness and restrictions of academic boundaries has increasingly led to a softening of such boundaries (borders) and the emergence of fields such as 'cultural studies'. But I acknowledge that interdisciplinarity can lead to partially digested content as well as to the grand synthesis.

Geography, like comparative sports studies 'does not have either a universal or a unique method of approach'. [7] Nevertheless, the various approaches that have been employed in the geographical study of sports would seem to me to be relevant to students of comparative sports. [8] Coming from geography myself, I am barely qualified to discuss the ways in which geographers might benefit from comparative sports studies. On the other hand I hope that I may be able to provide some insights which reveal the benefits to comparativists of at least an awareness of a 'geographical' approach. My paper is structured around four brief summaries of quite different geographical approaches to the study of sports. My intention is to illustrate their inherently 'comparative' nature and, at the same time, a relative lack of respect for disciplinary borders.

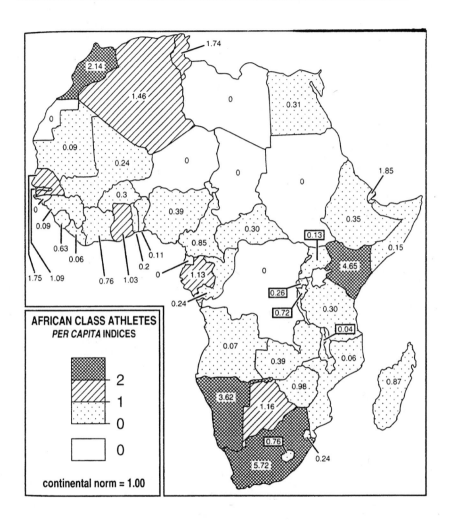

Figure 1 : African class athletes (Bale & Sang 1996)

\\\\: games of strategy
////: games of chance

Figure 2 : Games of strategy and games of chance (van Mele & Renson
          1992)

Where they come from

It has been suggested that comparative sport and physical education is
concerned with the establishment of 'reliable data on each country and
system'. [9] A traditional geographical approach to sport is to do just that. [10]
Consider the problem of identifying geographical variations in the
'development' of track and field athletics in Africa. It is, after all, in its mission

to convert Africa to achievement sports, the objective of the IAAF is to 'help remove cultural and traditional barriers to participation in athletics'. [11] How successful has the IAAF been? Using data for 1993 it is possible to explore the geographical variations in the 'production' of African class athletes in each nation of that continent. Consider the example where a per capita index is used to show national variations in per capita production of 'African class' athletes. [12] An index of 2 indicates that the country is producing twice the continental average; and index of 0.5 that is producing at half the continental norm. From such analysis it can be shown that South Africa is the national per capita leader with an index of 5.72. The map also reveals a periphery-center model - with countries at the periphery generally out-producing those at the continent's center. However the map of athletics in Africa (figure 1) ignores gender and when we look at respective maps for male and female athletes we notice some major differences. The map of male athletes shows that Kenya is the major producer at nearly six times the African norm, even though nearly all those of African class come from a relatively small number of events. On the other hand, in the case of women athletes South Africa is the major 'producer', at a level over seven times the continental average. [13]

This approach is a popular genre with the geography of sport and it the most obviously comparative. However, like many such studies it suffers (not only from 'merely' describing what appears to be a static pattern, but also) from the fact hat the data are contained by national borders. The nation-state 'contains' the data and this can be very misleading. In the case of Kenya, for example, the production of elite athletes occurs in a relatively small part of the country and is far from representative of the country as a whole. Having said that, this approach is valuable in exploring the comparative nature of the success of national systems of sport talent 'production', especially in view of the wealth of statistical data which are readily available. [14]

Not in my back yard

Sport and its effects are also differentiated at the local scale. It would be erroneous to think that sports only impact positively on local communities. Negative spillovers from sports are also consumed, especially by those who live in proximity to sports stadiums. How do the effects of football effect people living within various distances from the stadium? And what are the comparative effects of the nuisances generated by sports? This subject has attracted a number of geographical studies in Britain where, during the 1980s especially, football hooliganism and other negative 'spillovers' from professional football, were seen to be a problem for those who lived near football arenas. One study illustrates the kinds of results generated by such surveys.

A study by geographers Colin Mason and Andrew Moncrieff addressed the question of the benefits of a suburban location for a football club, compared with the traditional inner city location, characteristic of many UK clubs. [15] They took St. Johnstone FC, in the city of Perth in Scotland, as an example. In the early 1990s the club relocated from it's inner city ground to a new stadium at the edge of the urban area. The nuisances generated by football matches, as perceived by local residents, were identified and ranked for each stadium. It was revealed that it was around the new suburban stadium, McDiarmid Park, that nuisances were scored highest. This was contrary to planners' expectations. What is more, the worst nuisances, again as perceived by local people, were car parking and traffic congestion. Hooligamism as a nuisance barely featured in the findings. Maps were constructed to compare the geographical extent of perceived football nuisance ('football pollution'). It is clear that the new stadium was far from innocent in the generation of football nuisances.

Comparative landscapes of sport: real and imagined

The third and fourth approaches are of a more humanistic in nature and draw on (perhaps) two unlikely figures for comparative studies of sports. These are Roland Barthes and Edward Said. Little work by students of sports has applied the semiotic approach of Roland Barthes. Using Barthesian language, the game of cricket can, in Britain, be often seen to *signify* a mythical landscape or rural peace and harmony. Landscape is a recurring theme in geography and geographical studies of the sports landscape have been approached from a number of directions. [16] In England, the sport of cricket is mainly played in the northern countries of Yorkshire and Lancashire. It is also widely played in the industrial towns of those countries with major cricket grounds being located, for example, at Manchester and Leeds. Many of the greatest cricketers have come from the north of England. Yet when represented in writing, poetry and art it is almost invariably taken to represent rural, southern England. Indeed, using the semiotic approach of Barthes, it could be said that the sign 'cricket' is used to signify a mythical rusticity of 'merrie England'. Consider the signs of one of the most extravagant descriptions of the English cricket idyll:

> *"It was a hot summer's afternoon. There was no wind, and the smoke from the red-roofed cottages curled slowly up into the golden haze. The clock on the flint tower of the church struck the half-hour, and the vibration spread slowly across the shimmering hedge rows. ... Bees lazily drifted. White butterflies flapped their aimless way among the gardens. Delphiniums, larkspur, tiger-lilies, evening primrose, monk's hood, sweet peas, swaggered brilliantly above the box hedges, the wooden palings and the rickety gates. The cricket field itself was a*

> *mass of daisies and buttercups and dandelions, tall grasses and*
> *purple vetches and thistledown, and great clumps of dark red sorrel,*
> *except, of course, for the oblong patch in the centre - mown, rolled,*
> *watered - a smooth, shining emerald of grass, the pride of Fordenden,*
> *the Wicket."* [17]

The tranquil myth of English cricket has been recognized by Fred Inglis (and others) as being deeply ideological. 'In such unfettered providence, men and women dissolve the division of labour and hateful class divisions which follow them and live lives of joyful, cooperative praxis and poesis'. [18] The conventional, essentialized image of English cricket is one which deflects or covers up opposed class interests through collective memories of particular landscapes of nature. It represents an arcadia, set in some past time when the living was easy and somehow, 'natural', unscathed by technology. As a comparativist, however, I know that the images represented above are belied by cricket's industrial, quantitative, scientific and technological character.

Imaginative geographies of sport

In this final section I am inspired by the work of another cultural critic, Edward Said, whose book *Orientalism* placed considerable emphasis on what he termed 'imaginative geographies' and focuses on ways in which Europe 'constructed' the orient through the use of a variety of literary modes. [19] Here, the comparative approach is reflected in the difference between (a) the 'reality' of early colonial African body culture and (b) how the European saw and constructed - often for Europe - alternative body cultural practices in the rhetorics which were employed. I will take my examples from European representations of indigenous peoples of Kenya during the first half of the present century. The sources of my information come mainly from travel writing. In these texts, as in others deriving from international forms of cultural contact, the Europeans 'took their pre-texts with them' in which their 'dreams of the fantastic were captured'. [20] David Spurr has suggested that twelve rhetorical modes of writing have been used in colonial discourse to describe non-western people. [21] The variety of these modes reflects the ambiguity of colonialist representations of the 'new worlds' which they sought to re-present. Here I will use three of these modes, surveillance, idealization and appropriation, and apply them to the representation of the physicality of members of various Kenyan ethnic groups in the early twentieth century. I want to concentrate on a number of written and visual texts in order to illustrate not only how Africa was communicated to the West but also, and specifically, how the body-culture of the African was transformed by a western imagination into familiar and reductive cultural forms. Specifically, non-sportised cultures were transformed into sportised ones. Bringing back images of Africa provided not only evidence of conquest but also a permanent medium for the voyeuristic gaze. Exotic landscapes and exotic/erotic bodies could be commodified and consumed by a variety of representations of the Other. But *how* the new realities of Africa were (re)presented was more problematic.

The basic question posed by Spurr is how the Western writer constructed a coherent representation of the 'strange and (to the writer) often incomprehensible realities confronted by the non-western world'. [22] I am mainly concerned here with the body cultures that preceded the formalization of modern sports in Kenya. But modern sport was far from unfamiliar to many of the British migrants and travel writers who journeyed to East Africa. Many of the District Officers, schoolteachers and soldiers were products of the private schools and the ancient universities - the homes of the English sporting ethos. It was through the gazes of these kinds of people that the African physicality was captured in texts of various kinds.

I now want to take the three rhetorical modes and use these show how Europe 'captured' textually, the African body.

Surveillance

The European record of pre-sportized Kenyan body culture can be interpreted as a form of surveillance through its use of quantification. Many examples reflect the European desire to record the African's athleticism in western terms. Members of the Turkana were said to be able to throw their spears 210 feet (64 meters). [23] It was noted that among the Waukaufi a club could be hurled 'with the greatest precision'; 'at a distance from fifty to seventy paces they can dash out the brains of an enemy'. [24] Allusions to 'astonishing weight carrying feats' are typified by the case of an old woman who was said to have walked 11 miles with a load of wood weighing 115 pounds. [25] Performances of pre-sportized walking and running were also subject to the quantitative gaze. It was noted, for example, that the Turkana 'thinks nothing of walking fifty or sixty miles in one day'. [26] One colonist's 'favourite runner' was recorded as having covered 92 miles in 28 hours - a perfectly plausible claim but meaningless in terms of the indigenous culture on which the record was imposed. 'The African's body was as much an object of examination, commentary and valorization' as the landscape. [27] It was valued for its aesthetic, economic - and athletic potential.

Such quantification was part of the longer-term European project of the systematization of nature. Measurement was central to the European description of the non-European world; it reflected a European 'way of seeing'. It imposed the record and achievement orientation of the western sports enthusiast on the image of the pre-sportised oral world of the Masai, Nandi and other ethnic groups. In its own small way the measurement of the African thrower's performed the same function as the mapping of the broader empire.

Idealization

Although African customs - notably dancing - were often presented in late nineteenth and early twentieth century travel writing as negative, bizarre or freakish, the ambivalence of colonial discourse is reflected by the frequent willingness to describe the physical characteristics of the African in idealized terms. The Masai were often projected as fantastic runners. The nineteenth century geographer, Elisée Reclus noted that 'the men of pure Masai blood ... have slim, wiry figures, admirable for running'. [28] Of a Masai shepherd it was observed that 'his gait, as he strides, is an example of what human carriage is at its best'. [29] The Nandi were described as being 'agile, athletic, and able to travel long distances without fatigue ... they exhibit considerable powers of endurance and great reserves of strength'. [30] This was not the lazy, indolent African native as displayed in the environmentally deterministic writings of early twentieth century geographers. [31] What is more, it was implied that the body-cultural performances were 'natural'; that is, the athletes had not previously trained for them. The English athletics coach F.A.M. Webster, for example, noted that while serving in the King's African Rifles in the 1910s, he 'saw a number of *untutored*, bare footed natives who could jump anything between 6 ft. (1.829 m.) and 6 ft. 5 ins. (1.956 m.) with *the greatest ease*'. [32] Here idealization is imbricated with tropes of surveillance (or quantification) and naturalization.

Idealization suggests the Rosseauian view of the 'noble savage'. An interesting interpretation of this is suggested by Spurr who suggests that it provides compensation on the symbolic level for the political and economic processes that destroyed the traditional fabric of non-western societies. By representing individual instances of courage, beauty, and athleticism, western representations of Africa offered a kind of 'substitute gratification for what would otherwise be an overwhelming sense of loss'. [33]

Appropriation

Europeans saw the natural (including human) resources of colonized lands as rightfully belonging to 'civilization' and 'mankind' rather than to the indigenous peoples. The notion of Africa - and the African body - as the colonizer's inheritance is reflected in the way in which African culture was recorded and perceived. For example, Henry Morton Stanley's description of the terrain around Lake Tanganyika included its transformation into an Anglicized landscape inhabited by church spires and herds of cattle. [34] In the case of the Kenyan athletes, the writings and photographs of those who witnessed them also transformed them into familiar cultural terrain. The measurements used to describe it were, literally, Imperial. They only meant anything when compared with the records of the west - a comparison which was itself an imposition.

The comparison with western athletic performance was common in western writing about the Kenyan athletes. This is perhaps most graphically illustrated by Ernest Hemingway who, in one encounter with Masai runners, noted that the best of the runners were moving 'at the pace of a fast miler, and carrying their spears as well'. [35] The Africanist, Joy Adamson, while spectating at what she perceived as some remarkable Masai high jumping, found it necessary to claim that a Masai high jumper had easily broken the existing world record.[36] Whereas Stanley had constructed the English country village out of the East African landscape, those who viewed the Masai constructed the 'cultural landscapes' of the mile race and of the world record. They were seen as available bodies waiting to be sportized. Applying comments made in a quite different context by the geographer, Derek Gregory, [37] the European witnesses of the Masai high jumper and runner found in their athleticism the possibility of bridging the African past and the global present. While in many situations the differences between the African and the European was vast, in African body culture the European observers saw a kind of 'meeting ground'. The athletics statistics 'provided the cultural equivalent of a universal currency'. [38]

Conclusion

The four geographies of sport noted above reflect the eclecticism of geographical research. But what does it say to the 'field' of Comparative Sports Studies? In a world of increasingly permeable borders, it implies that there is surely a strong case to be made for the creation of stronger links between those engaged in the geographical study of sport and those in comparative sports studies. What form these links might take requires further discussion but they could include collaborative research, publishing in each others' journals,[39] and hosting joint conferences. One of Geography's main traditions has been the examination of regional differences in terrestrial phenomena. And what is the study of comparative sport if it is not the study of place-to-place differences in sporting characteristics and performances?

Notes

[1] My *Shorter Oxford English Dictionary* tells me that *rapprochement* means "a coming together, an establishment of harmonious relations".

[2] Guttmann, A. (1978). From ritual to record. New York: Columbia University Press. However, the very notion of '*comparative*' studies of sport (and geographical 'variations' in sport) raises a fundamental philosophical - and, indeed, a semantic - problem. It can be argued that comparativists have failed to consider the difference in meaning between 'compare' and 'contrast'. To compare something with something else is to look for differences *and* similarities. To contrast is to look for differences. If, therefore, regional *differences* in sports are being considered we should be exploring 'contrasting' rather than 'comparative' sports.

[3] See Bale, J. (1994). Landscapes of modern sport. London: Leicester University Press.

[4] Figure 1 is taken from Bale; J. & Sang, J. (1996). Kenyan running: movement culture, geography and global change. London: Cass; figure 2 is from van Mele, V. & Renson, R. (1992). Traditional games in South America (Sport Science Studies 4, ICSSPE). Schorndorf: Verlag Hofmann.

[5] See, for example, Maguire, J. (1995). Common ground? Links between sports history, sports geography and the sociology of sport. Sporting Traditions, 12(1), 3-25.

[6] Ibid.

[7] Bennett, B., Howell, M. & Simri, U. (1983). Comparative physical education and sport. Philadelphia: Lea and Febiger, p. 9.

[8] I should add that some of the best geographical writing on sports has been authored by non-geographers. Three examples are: Jokl, E. et al. (1956). Sports in the cultural pattern of the world, Helsinki: Institute for Cultural Health; Eichberg, H. (1988). Leistungräume: Sport als Umweltproblem. Münster: Lit Verlag; Springwood, C. (1996). Cooperstown to Dyersville: a geography of baseball nostalgia. Boulder, Co.: Westview Press.

[9] Anthony, D. (1996). Comparative physical education. Physical Education, LVIII, p. 71.

[10] This approach was popularised by the American geographer Rooney, J. (1974). From Cabin Creek to Anaheim: a geography of American sport. Reading, Mass.: Prentice Hall. Overviews of the geography of sport are found in Bale, J. (1989). Sports geography. London: Spon, and Augustin, J.-P. (1995). Sport, géographie et aménagement, Paris: Édition Natan.

[11] Abmayr, W. (1983). Analysis and perspectives of the project in Kenya. In Women's track and field in Africa (Report of the first IAAF congress on women's athletics), Darmstadt: Deutscher Leichthathletik Verband, 532-538.

[12] These are defined as athletes who were ranked in the top 50 in Africa in 1993.

[13] See Bale & Sang (1996).

[14] Ibid.

[15] Mason, C. & Moncrieff, A. (1993). The effect of relocation on the externality fields of football stadia: The case of St. Johnstone FC. The Scottish Geographical Magazine, 109(2), 96-105. Other such studies are reviewed in Bale, J. (1993). Sport, space and the city. London: Routledge.

[16] These are reviewed in Bale (1994).

[17] Macdonnell, A. England, their England. London: Macmillan.

[18] Quoted in Bale (1994).

[19] Said, E. (1975). Orientalism. London: Penguin.

[20] Gregory, D. (1995). Geographical imaginations. Oxford: Blackwell, Oxford.

[21] Spurr, D. (1993). The rhetoric of empire. Durham: Duke University Press.

[22] Ibid, p. 3.

[23] Barton, J. (1920). Notes on the Turkana of British East Africa. Journal of the African Society, 19, 107-115. This, and the other examples presented below, are taken from Bale & Sang (1996).

[24] Krapf, L. (1968). Travels, researches and missionary labours during an eighteen year's residence in Eastern Africa. London: Frank Cass, [18..].

[25] Browne, S. (1925). The vanishing tribes of Kenya. London: Seeley, Service and Co., London.

[26] Barton (1920).

[27] Spurr (1993, p. 22).

[28] Reclus, E. (1876). The universal geography (vol. 13). London: J.S. Virtue, p. 364.

[29] Ross, W.M. (1927). Kenyan from within. London: Allen and Unwin.

[30] Matson, A. (1922). Nandi Resistance to British Rule 1890-1906. Nairobi: East African Publishing House.

[31] Livingstone, D. (1992). The geographical tradition. Oxford: Blackwell.

[32] Webster, F.A.M. (1927). Athletics of today: history, development and training. London: Warne, emphasis added.

[33] Spurr (1993).

[34] Pratt, M.L. (1992). Imperial eyes. London: Routledge.

[35] Hemingway, E. (1954). Green hills of Africa. London: Cape, (emphasis added).

[36] Adamson, J. (1967). The peoples of Kenya. London: Collins and Harvill.

[37] Gregory (1995).

[38] McClintock, Imperial leather, p. 123.

[39] It is not clear if the journal Sport Place: an International Journal of Sports Geography, is still in existence. Published at the Department of Oklahoma State University, it appeared sporadically between 1987 and 1996.

Chapter 2

The utility of the cross-cultural comparative method in the study of sport

Garry Chick
University of Illinois at Urbana-Champaign, USA

The field of anthropology developed during the second half of the 19th century from the recognition that the cultures of people to be found in the various corners of the world are both similar and different in many ways. As such, anthropology has long had an important comparative tradition, in addition to its descriptive, ethnographic tradition. Nevertheless, only a few modern anthropologists conduct explicitly comparative research while ethnographic description has come to be regarded as the defining characteristic and core of the discipline. Further, the ethnography of sport, leisure, and expressive culture has always taken a back seat to the description of the more utilitarian aspects of culture, including social organization, economic systems, political systems, and the like (Chick 1998a). It is no surprise, therefore, that comparative studies of sport, leisure, and other expressive systems are relatively rare in the anthropological literature.

The rarity of such studies does not mean that they are without value, however. Indeed, I believe that cross-cultural comparative studies of sport, leisure, and expressive activities, more generally, have immense potential for informing us about the place of such phenomena in human culture. Comparative research has several clear virtues. First, such studies permit data exploration. A survey of the cross-cultural literature shows, for example, that a variety of expressive phenomena, such as games, music, art, and casual leisure are all but ubiquitous in human cultures (Roberts & Barry 1976; Chick 1998a). Second, examinations of the cross-cultural literature permit the formulation and testing of hypotheses. Later in this essay I will describe several tests of hypotheses that deal with aspects of leisure, recreation, or sport in cross-cultural samples of societies. Third, cross-cultural comparative studies permit the systematic testing of hypotheses generated from case studies or wider consideration of the ethnographic record. Fourth, because cross-cultural researchers sample from societies around the world, they are able to examine the widest possible range of human variation in culture traits. Finally, in the case of comparisons where secondary data is used, cross-cultural comparative studies, whether used for data exploration or hypothesis testing, tend to be extremely cost efficient. That is, a relatively large number of cases can be included in a relatively inexpensive study.

Both the cross-cultural comparative method and existing cross-cultural data have been underutilized by researchers interested in recreation, sport, leisure, and expressive culture. Therefore, the purpose of this paper is to provide a brief history of cross-cultural comparative research and to provide a couple of examples that give evidence for the value of the approach. Before I do so, however, I think that it is necessary to distinguish "cross-cultural" research from "cross-national" research.

As the name implies, cross-cultural research involves the comparison of two or more presumably distinct cultures or, put another way, two or more societies that possess distinct cultures. Cross-national research, such as a comparison of sport policies in Belgium and The Netherlands, involves distinct political entities but not necessarily distinct cultures. Political boundaries are not always, or even usually, coterminous with cultural boundaries. Large countries, such as the United States, China, or Brazil, may contain numerous more or less distinct cultural entities and even smaller nations, such as Belgium, often encompass two or more distinguishable cultural traditions. In Belgium, one could conduct a cross-cultural study of traditional folk games as played in the Flemish speaking and French speaking parts of the country, for example. In this paper, I will not be directing my attention at cross-national research although that does not mean that I believe that there is anything wrong with such research. It is simply the case that, from an anthropological perspective, cross-cultural and cross-national research are not the same and should be distinguished.

Cross-cultural comparative research deals, obviously, with two or more societies that possess relatively distinct cultures (though they may share many cultural traits, such as each having patrilineal descent and each having some form of wrestling). That brings up the problem of what culture is, on one hand, and how one determines how one culture is distinct from another, on the other. There are many different definitions of culture but, fortunately, nearly all involve three key concepts. First, many definitions of culture are based on the idea that it is something in the heads of members of a particular society. That is, culture is the knowledge, beliefs, attitudes, and other mental traits that characterize a particular group of individuals and guide their behavior. Second, some add behavior to the mental component of culture. This is because many behavioral characteristics, such as the distances people keep between themselves in both public and private encounters or the way in which they handle knives, forks, and spoons at the dinner table, are culture specific and learned, but largely unconscious. Third, certain material objects are peculiar to particular cultures so material objects may be included as part of the definition of culture. For example, mention of the boomerang immediately brings native Australian cultures to mind while the computer chip would not. So, definitions of culture may involve only its ideational components, its ideational and behavioral components, or its ideational, behavioral, and material components (Chick 1997).

The problem of how cultures may be distinguished also remains problematic. Societies existing in close physical proximity to one another may have shared cultural traits at some point in their histories. Further, unlike political boundaries, cultural boundaries tend to blend one into the other at the edges. So, cross-cultural researchers have typically adopted sampling strategies that permit them to claim that the cultures in their studies are historically autonomous so that any shared traits developed independently. As will be discussed later, this is a major bone of contention in cross-cultural comparative research.

A brief history of cross-cultural comparative research

The first cross-cultural comparative study was presented at the annual meeting of the Royal Anthropological Institute of Great Britain and Ireland by Edward B. Tylor in 1889. Tylor's paper, which pioneered what has become known as the cross-cultural survey, was titled "On a method of investigating the development of institutions applied to the laws of marriage and descent." In the paper, Tylor examined the associations among marital residence and kinship with other aspects of culture, including kin avoidance and joking relationships among xx societies that he culled from the then-extant ethnographic literature. Sir Fancis Galton, the president of the society at the time, asked the first question of Tylor from the audience, as was the tradition. His question to Tylor was, in essence, how did he (Tylor) know that the traits in which he was interested developed independently in the cultures sampled when it was possible that they could have diffused from one to the other? The assumption of the independence of the sample units is fundamental for statistical tests and the question posed to Tylor has since become known as *Galton's Problem* in cross-cultural research. It has attracted more methodological attention than any other concern with cross-cultural comparative research (Levinson & Malone 1980). Naroll, Michik, and Naroll (1974) succinctly summarized Galton's Problem:

> "... if cultures are interdependent with respect to the characteristics being studied, the actual number of independent observations may be less than the number of cultures the investigator examined. The effect of interdependence on the significance tests of a study might be similar to systematic error. The spuriously high number of cases involved in

> the computation of statistical significance would tend to decrease the
> probability of chance occurrence indicated by those tests.
> ... In addition, the inclusion of interdependent cases can produce
> spuriously inflated or deflated) coefficients of association ..." (p. 127).

The effect of Galton's question was to suppress cross-cultural comparative
research for more than 30 years. Though a few such studies were produced
between 1890 and 1920 (e.g., Steinmetz 1896; Hobhouse 1906; Nieboer
1910; Hobhouse et al. 1915) they had relatively little impact on the field and
were often not highly regarded. Evans-Pritchard (1965), for example,
dismissed Hobhouse, Wheeler, and Ginsberg's (1915) attempt to explain the
existence of slavery as demonstrating only that slaves were kept where they
were useful. Moreover, the father of American anthropology, Franz Boas,
who was originally enthused over the potential of the cross-cultural
comparative method, later rejected it completely. Naturally, Boas left a lasting
impression on American anthropology.

Galton's Problem was not the only reason for the rejection of the comparative
method, however. Tylor was one of several proponents of a form of cultural
evolution in the late 19th century (others included Herbert Spencer, Sir James
Frazer, and the American attorney-anthropologist Lewis H. Morgan) who used
what they termed as the "comparative method" to discover the steps through
which social evolution had progressed. But Boas and Kroeber in the United
States and members of the *Kulturkreislehre* school in Germany, for example,
dogmatically rejected their evolutionary position. The problem was that Tylor
and the other evolutionists held that cultures changed over time through
basically a linear pattern of stages that were determined by fixed "laws" of
social evolution. This "unilinear evolution" did not accord with the
ethnographic record which showed that, in fact, societies change in
individualistic ways and do not necessarily evolve though any prescribed set
of successive stages. So, more historically oriented schools of anthropology
rejected the idea of cultural evolution by the turn of the 20th century and the
concept was held in disfavor until its revival in the United States in the late
1940s and 1950s by Leslie White, Julian Steward, and others.

Cross-cultural comparative studies were reborn in the US largely under the
tutelage of George Peter Murdock (1897 – 1985). Murdock received his Ph.D.
in the Department of the Science of Society (later, Sociology) at Yale
University in 1925. He was trained by Albert G. Keller who, in turn, had been
a student and, later, a colleague of William Graham Sumner, a social
evolutionist in the tradition of Tylor. Sumner had compiled extensive
ethnographic materials on cultures around the world and conducted
comparative studies on them (e.g. 1906). But his data base was idiosyncratic
and his studies involved only societies in which he had a special interested.

Murdock realized that for comparative research to be successful, a representative sample of the cultures of the world was required. He aspired to create such a sample, along with a comprehensive bibliography for each society, verbatim information for each, and a set of uniform codes for cultural subjects. Further, all similarly coded materials should be filed together for easy access. With such a data base, he felt that the theoretical orientation of the researcher would be unimportant. If they were evolutionists, they could seek cross-cultural patterning and if they believed that forces of cultural diffusion were critical, they could search for geographical distributions of traits.

Murdock began to implement his plan with the publication of *Our Primitive Contemporaries* in 1934. In that book, he summarized information about 18 societies that he had selected to be geographically representative as well as representative of varying levels of cultural complexity. More important, he created a series of topics that he presumed to cover all aspects of cultural life, including subsistence, technology, social and political organization, games and recreation, and religion. These topics served to keep the summaries comparable (Goodenough 1996) and would permit additional summaries to be added in a systematic fashion. This initial series of cultural topics would itself evolve into the *Outline of Cultural Materials* (Murdock et al. 1938).

The second step of Murdock's agenda was realized with the development of the Cross-Cultural Survey at Yale University in 1937. Housed at Yale's Institute of Human Relations, this ethnographic filing system was funded by the Rockefeller Foundation. Murdock planned to have a sample of 200 societies in the Survey. After World War II, the Survey was reorganized under Murdock's direction as the Human Relations Area Files, Inc., (HRAF) a not-for-profit corporation supported by a consortium of universities. This was the third step in Murdock's agenda. Fourth, Murdock established the Cross-Cultural Cumulative Coding Center at the University of Pittsburgh, where he had moved in 1960. This purpose of this center was to code specific culture traits on cross-cultural samples, rather than the subject matter of entire cultures as with the HRAF, in order to allow quick comparative studies on large numbers of precoded traits (Goodenough 1996).

Fifth, and finally, Murdock helped found the Society for Cross-Cultural Research in 1972. When the society was established, it began to publish *Behavior Science Notes* (later, *Behavior Science Research*, and now, *Cross-Cultural Research*) as its official journal. As a result of the work of Murdock, and others, there are now more than 1,000 published cross-cultural comparative studies, compared with only 80 or so in 1964 (Ember 1997).

Organization of the human relations area files

The HRAF was developed in order "to faciliate the comparative study of human society, culture, and behavior by collecting, organizing, and distributing ethnographic materials on the cultures of the world" (Ember 1997: p. 5). This mission was originally served by the distribution of annual installments of paper files that contained copies of pages of original ethnographic materials to member institutions. These copies were on 5 inch by 8 inch slips of paper with the text indexed in the margins with *Outline of Cultural Materials (OCM)* code numbers. All pages, from all sources, for each society in the files that contained material indexed by a specific *OCM* number were then filed together for easy and rapid retrieval. Hence, individual pages were usually reproduced several times since each typically had several different *OCM* categories indicated in the margins. A researcher who was interested in sport among the Thonga, for example, simply had to go to the file drawer (or drawers, as the collections for some societies required several) for that society and pull out the bundle of pages grouped together under the *OCM* category 517, Leisure Time Activities. Each page will have at least one instance of 517 written in the margin, indicating the a mention or discussion of some sort of leisure activity or aspect of leisure.

The HRAF greatly simplified the retrieval of information on the range of topics indexed using the *OCM* categories (of which there are more than 700). The HRAF renders it unnecessary for researchers to develop bibliographies of the societies that they wish to study and then find the books or articles in their bibliographies. Further, since HRAF ethnographies are already indexed with the *OCM* categories, it is not necessary to read every page of every source in order to find the desired information (Ember 1997). From 1949 through 1957, the annual installments to "sponsoring members" (of which there are 21) were on paper only. Between 1958 and 1993, sponsoring members of the HRAF and "associate members" (of which there are more than 300) also received micofiche copies. Beginning with installment 43 in 1994, the *HRAF Collection of Ethnography* arrived on computer compact discs and is now available on the World Wide Web, as well. This version is now known as the eHRAF.

The eHRAF is radically superior to either the paper or microfiche versions of the HRAF. According to Melvin Ember (1997), President of HRAF, Inc., researchers

> *"can scroll backward and forward through the texts in eHRAF to get the full context of your search "hits." You can also click on icons that call up full citational information, footnotes, tables, and images; and you can call up a cultural summary to give you an overview of the culture. And, of course, search and retrieval is now much faster, as well as more sophisticated, with eHRAF. "(p. 6)*

Searching the eHRAF can be accomplished in three ways (Ember 1997). First, one may use the *OCM* categories, as with the paper and microfiche files. The virtue of using the *OCM* categories is that desired topics that contain few or no standard terms can be accessed. Second, searches can be based on key words in the texts, either singly or in Boolean combinations. Finally, searches can involve both *OCM* categories and key words. It should be remembered that the eHRAF still does not provide precoded data but, as with both the paper and microfiche versions, indexed full-text data.

At present, the HRAF cover approximately 370 societies, or about 30% of the world's well described cultures (Ember 1997). For the future (starting in the year 2000), the HRAF board of directors has approved a plan designed to accomplish three tasks: (1) catching up on world ethnography, (2) improving the sampling strategy, and (3) updating existing cases and adding new ones (Ember 1997). With respect to the second goal, files on cultures not previously in the collection will be added on a random basis from a newly designed sampling frame. In addition, the *HRAF Collection of Ethnography* is to be augmented by the *HRAF Collection of Archeology*. The HRAF Collection of Archeology will permit testing of causal hypotheses for cultural variation and evolution as it will provide researchers with time-series data (Ember 1997).

Doing a cross-cultural study

Cross-cultural studies can differ along several dimensions (Ember & Ember 1998). First, studies may be primarily or wholly descriptive; that is, the researcher may only be interested in trait frequencies in his or her sample of societies. Or, the researcher may be interested in relationships among traits/variables. Second, studies can also differ in terms of their geographical scope: they may be worldwide or regional. Third, the samples in cross-cultural studies can range from 2 to many. Fourth, data can be primary, collected by the researcher in the field, or secondary, gleaned from existing data sources, such as censuses, ethnographies, or other documents. Fifth, the study can be either synchronic, where the data on each case pertain to only one time period, or diachronic, relevant to several time periods. Most existing cross-cultural studies involve both the description of trait frequencies and their associations with other variables. Most are also worldwide, use samples with many cases, and are based on secondary data. Nearly all are synchronic.

Sampling in cross-cultural research

There are two basic questions in sampling for a cross-cultural study. First, how many cases should be in the sample and, second, how should the cases be selected ? The minimum number of cases is obviously two but the scientific value of two-case comparisons is questionable (Ember & Ember 1998). This is because any *particular* difference between two cases can be explained by *any other* difference or differences between them (Campbell 1961; Ember & Ember 1998). Munroe and Munroe (1991) indicate that the minimum number of cases necessary for meaningful statistical testing is four, and that assumes unbiased sampling and errorless measurement, both of which are unattainable in practice. Naturally, the number of cases to be included in a sample also depend on whether the study will use primary or secondary data. The cost of conducting field research is so high that studies based on primary data will necessarily have much smaller samples than those that use secondary data. With secondary data, the size of the sample depends on the statistical power of the tests to be used, along with the strength and confidence level of the associations sought. If strong associations are expected, smaller samples (on the order of 30 at the minimum) may be used while larger samples are needed if weaker associations are anticipated.

Major considerations with respect to the choice of primary over secondary data include whether or not the variables of interest are available in secondary sources, cost, political considerations (field research is not possible in many places around the world), and the particular interests of the researcher. Because of these factors, the samples for cross-cultural studies using primary data have generally relied on purposive, rather than random, samples (Ember & Ember 1998). For secondary data, other choices must be made. First, the research must denote a sampling frame; that is, what is the list of societies (or nations) from which the sample is to be selected ? Second, is the sample to be worldwide or regional ? Third, will the sample include only distinct cultures ? Or will it include nation-states, which may not be coterminous with cultures ?

Several cross-cultural samples already exist. These include the *Ethnographic Atlas* (Murdock 1967), with 862 cases, the HRAF Collection of Ethnography, with about 370 cases, the Standard Ethnographic Sample (Naroll & Sipes 1973), with 273 cases, the Standard Cross-Cultural Sample (Murdock & White 1969), with 186 cases, and the HRAF Probability Sample (Lagacé 1979), with 60 cases. Beginning in 2000, HRAF, Inc. will begin the development of a true random sample of the world's well-described cultures. Of the samples noted above, the Standard Cross-Cultural Sample (SCCS) is by far the most commonly used and more than 1,200 coded variables are available for it in the cross-cultural literature. Each of these samples is purposive in some way or another and only the HRAF Probability Sample uses random sampling as part of the selection procedure: one case was randomly selected from within 60 "culture areas" although the culture areas were determined purposefully. Culture areas were selected to insure that the chosen societies would not be located near each other, a way to deal with Galton's Problem.

While the SCCS has the great virtue of having many variables already coded for it and, thus, available for use by researchers, it also has drawbacks. First, it is a purposive sample in that 3 societies were selected (judgmentally, not randomly) from within 62 culture areas from around the world. Because the culture areas were equally weighted, each case in the ethnographic literature did not have an equal chance of being selected, an assumption for most statistical tests. Moreover, there is good evidence to indicate that the 62 culture areas lack ethnographic validity (Burton et al. 1996). Finally, the SCCS includes no modern industrial societies, a truly significant and meaningful deficiency. Unfortunately, until the truly random HRAF Collection of Ethnography is available, the SCCS will continue to be the most-used sample for cross-cultural comparative research.

Measurement of variables in cross-cultural research

Measurement concerns for cross-cultural comparative research are similar to those for other sorts of research. It is important for the measurements of variables to be both valid and reliable. Unfortunately, there are several points at which error can occur in cross-cultural comparative research. First, informants themselves may give erroneous information, either out of ignorance of their own culture or because the topic they are addressing is sensitive. Illegal activities or issues such as sexual behavior and witchcraft may elicit error (for an example, see Freeman's (1983) analysis of how Margaret Mead's Samoan informants lied to her regarding sexual mores). Second, ethnographers may introduce error. They may over-report (idealizing behavior to fit preconceived typologies, for example) or under-report (not report the number and types of leisure activities in a community because social organization, for example, was thought to be more important). Third, the coders who analyze ethnographic materials may introduce error through their interpretations of what the ethnographers reported. Finally, error may be introduced through sampling (i.e., Galton's Problem).

A major form of ethnographic error is under-reporting. American ethno-graphers who were concerned with studying Native American cultures before they vanished spent considerable effort on describing games, sports, and other recreational activities. In contrast, British ethnographers working in Africa during the colonial period were much more concerned with social and political organization and their descriptions of games, sports, and recreations were less thorough. Coders of ethnographic materials, therefore, must be cautious not to assume that a "presence of absence" means an "absence of presence." That is, simply because something is not reported does not mean that it was not there. This situation also raises the difference between random and systematic error. Random error has the effect of depressing the strength of relationships (Ember & Ember 1998).   Since social scientists have traditionally been more concerned about accepting hypotheses that are, in fact, false (Type I error) than rejecting hypotheses that are, in fact, true (Type II error), Naroll (1962) termed random error "benign." Systematic error, on the other hand, is "malignant" (Naroll 1962) in that it can create apparent relationships where none, in reality, exist (Ember & Ember 1998).

Ember and Ember (1998) discuss numerous ways in which both random and systematic error in cross-cultural research can be minimized. In particular, they suggest that multiple coders work independently so that their codes can be compared for inter-rater reliability. They further suggest that direct, low-inference variables should be preferred over indirect, high-inference variables. Demographic variables, for example, tend to be low-inference—it is fairly easy to count village populations, sex ratios, or the number of different kinds of children's games—while "unconscious fear of witchcraft" requires substantial inference and is much more difficult to measure reliably.   Further, are mentions of witchcraft in folk tales valid measures of fear of witchcraft, for example? Ember and Ember (1998) also suggest that researchers be very explicit with both the theoretical and operational definitions of their variables. Explicit definitions that indicate clear empirical referents simplify coding. They also recommend that coders rate the degree to which they believe that the ethnographer has supplied reliable information. In this way, data for cases that are deemed untrustworthy can be eliminated from analyses.

Galton's problem

As noted earlier, Sir Francis Galton asked a question regarding Edward B. Tylor's first cross-cultural comparative study that essentially terminated such research for some 30 years. Over the years, cross-cultural researchers have suggested a variety of approaches to Galton's Problem. These have taken three basic forms. The first is the "sampling response" wherein a sample is designed so that the societies in it are relatively distant or are separated by geographical obstacles, thus minimizing the possibility of culture trait diffusion. The SCCS and the HRAF Probability Sample are examples of such efforts. The second type of approach to Galton's Problem is the "historical connections response." Here, it is assumed that there are always historical connections among societies. These connections are then controlled for statistically by means of techniques such as spatial autocorrelation, wherein the proximity of cultures are measured in terms of variables such as distance or language similarity (Ember & Ember 1998).

As it turns out, most studies that have employed statistical controls for Galton's Problem have relatively little evidence that it affects obtained correlations. Hence, Ember and Ember (1998) suggest that the problem is really much less important than has been claimed in the past. Indeed, as they point out, if the diffusion of information among cases in a sample was a problem, then psychological research that samples university students (who obviously share a common history, geography, and language) would be deeply suspect. Therefore, the Embers advocate the third response to Galton's Problem and it is nothing more than adherence to pure random sampling, the method adopted for the eHRAF.

Time and place focus

In past cross-cultural studies, it was common for researchers to mix data from different communities from the same society or from different time periods for the same society. This practices was, at least in part, based on the 19th century idea that cultures are homogenous and relatively stable over time. Modern anthropologists recognize that neither of these beliefs are accurate. Culture traits within different communities of the same society may vary somewhat and, clearly, even technologically simple societies do change over time. Hence, cross-cultural comparative researchers who use secondary data must insure that the data they use for particular cases are all from the same community and from, more or less, the same point in time. Otherwise, error is introduced into the study.

Examples of cross-cultural research on sport

As indicated earlier, cross-cultural comparative studies on sport are rare. There are several probable reasons for this. First, anthropologists have been much more interested in the utilitarian aspects of life, basically how people go about making a living, than in the expressive aspects of life, or how they enjoy themselves and attribute meaning to what they do. Second, sport, as a category, has not had much meaning for anthropologists, whose focus has traditionally been on technologically simple societies (see, Blanchard 1995, for an exception, however). So, when anthropologists have studied sport, these activities have most often been referred to as games of physical skill. Around the turn of the last century, Stuart Culin, for example, produced several books wherein he compared games of physical skill in various cultures (e.g., Culin 1895, 1899, 1907). More recently, two cross-cultural comparative studies of games of physical skill/sport have achieved the status of anthropological classics. In the first of these, "Games in culture," John M. Roberts, Malcolm Arth, and Robert Bush (1959) developed a three-category classification of games (i.e., physical skill, strategy, and chance) as well as a definition of games (games must involve competition, have two or more sides, agreed upon rules, and criteria for determining winners and losers). Both of these have become anthropological standards. Roberts et al. found that most games are of combined types, primarily involving either physical skill and strategy (e.g., football, basketball, hockey, or tennis) or strategy and chance (e.g., most card games, dice games, etc.). Games of only a single type or of other combinations (such as physical skill and chance, but not strategy) are much less common. Roberts and his colleagues also found that several variables correlated with the presence or absence of various game-types. The most interesting of these relate to games and cultural complexity, defined primarily in terms of technological complexity and degree of social and political stratification. Though in their initial study, Roberts et al. found 5 societies, all of which were extremely simple, for which no games were reported, later research (Roberts & Barry 1976) suggests that all known human societies, both past and present, have or have had games of physical skill. Ethnographic reports that indicate their absence may either be in error or societies that once had games may have lost them due to contact with other, dominant, societies.

In 1998, I replicated the study by Roberts et al. with a larger sample (107 societies versus 50) and somewhat more sophisticated methods. In general, my results replicated those of Roberts et al. (1959) and Roberts and Barry (1976), especially the finding that the presence of games of strategy is strongly and positively associated with cultural complexity (Chick 1998b). My examination of the cross-cultural record also indicated that, among games of physical skill, wrestling, in one form or another, is probably the most common, though most cultures also have running games (races). Moreover, if a game is institutionalized in any way, such as being played at a certain time during the year, during festivals, played by some individuals and not others, or formally organized by community members, it is most commonly wrestling. So, if institutionalization is included as part of a definition of sport, wrestling may be the first and most common sport.

In 1973, Richard G. Sipes published the second classic cross-cultural comparative study of sport, "War, sports and aggression: An empirical test of two rival theories." In this paper, he used a small (N = 20) cross-cultural sample to examine the relationship between the presence or absence of what he termed "combative sports" and the presence of absence of warfare in culture. For Sipes, a combative sport is one wherein there is real or potential body contact between opponents (either individuals or teams) and where one of the objectives of the sport is to inflict real or symbolic injury to or gaining playing field territory from the opponent. Sports that lack these characteristics but which involve "patently warlike activity," such as the use of "actual or simulated combat weapons against an actual or simulated human being" were also defined as combative (Sipes 1973, p. 70).

Sipes tested two alternate hypotheses. First, the "drive discharge model," which was based on ethological theory prevalent in the 1960s. Basically, the model held that aggressive behavior was an innate human drive and that aggressive feelings built up over time and had to be discharged. This could be accomplished in varying contexts, such as warfare or combative sport. Hence, the drive discharge model predicted an inverse relationship between warfare and combative sport. The "culture pattern model" suggests that aggressive behavior is learned, not innate, and that societies wherein aggression is valued and taught should show evidence of it in multiple forms. Hence, the culture pattern model predicts that societies that have high levels of warfare should also have combative sports.

For his sample, Sipes selected 10 "extremely warlike" and 10 "extremely peaceful" societies from the ethnographic literature (he found it very difficult to find 10 extremely peaceful societies, in fact). He then scored each of the 20 societies on presence or absence of combative sports. The results strongly supported the culture pattern model. Of the 10 extremely warlike societies, 9 had combative sports and only 1 did not. Of the 10 extremely peaceful societies, 2 had combative sports and 8 did not. Sipes (1973, p. 71) concluded that his result "clearly supports the validity of the Culture Pattern Model and as clearly tends to discredit the Drive Discharge Model."

Two of my colleagues and I (Chick et al. 1997) conducted a reanalysis of Sipes hypotheses using a much larger data set (the SCCS). We also divided combative sports into those involving only individuals (such as wrestling), those involving teams (such as lacrosse), and what we termed "sham combats." Sham combats are activities that may involve either individuals or teams and have sportlike characteristics but which seemed to lack winners and losers (except in the sense that individuals might be injured or killed). These activities often appear to be informal mechanisms for combat training. We counted the number of each of these types of activities reported by ethnographers (we used the HRAF as the source for our data, coding from OCM categories 524 [games] and 526 [athletic sports]).

In general, our findings supported the culture pattern model, though the relationships that we found were much weaker than those reported by Sipes. The weaker relationships were to be expected since his sample included only the two tails of the "warlike" distribution (extremely warlike and extremely peaceful) while our sample had three values for warfare (1= absent or rare; 2=occasional or seasonal; 3=almost constant). In a direct comparison with Sipes' figures, we found that 13 of the 33 societies wherein war was absent or rare lacked combative sports, while 20 had them. Of the 18 societies where war was almost constant, only 3 societies lacked combative sports while 15 had them. While this relationship is in the same direction as that found by Sipes, it is not statistically significant. Further, we found no relationship between the presence or absence of individual combative sports (e.g., wrestling or boxing) and frequency of warfare. Similarly, there was no relationship between the presence or absence of team combative sports and the frequency of warfare. However, we did find a strong positive relationship between the presence or absence of sham combats and the frequency of warfare. Finally, we found a strong positive relationship between the presence or absence of individual combative sport and the frequency of homicide within societies (a variable not examined by Sipes).

In related research, Loy, Miracle, and I have examined possible relationships between combative sports and sexual aggressiveness, particularly rape, in cross-cultural comparative context (Chick et al. 1995, 1996; Chick & Loy 1998; Loy & Chick 1993). Basically, we have found that the presence of rape seems to be positively correlated with the presence of what we termed "sham combats" but not with sport, not even combative sports. Sham combats are activities that appear to be very much like military training but otherwise have game-like characteristics in the sense that no real hostile intent is involved, though injuries are fairly common. Mock combats with spears or clubs between young men or between fathers and sons are examples of sham combats. The purpose of such activities appears to be both training for real combat and instilling aggression in young men. However, we also indicated our concerns about both the reliability and the validity of existing cross-cultural codes on rape. Unfortunately, these problems render any results questionable.

These examples indicate some of the values of cross-cultural comparative studies on sport but many other kinds of possible relationships could also be examined. For example, the relationship between cultural complexity (for which there are several published measures; see Chick [1997] for a review) and the presence or absence of combative sports remains unexamined. A student of mine is currently working on a cross-cultural comparative study of sport type (whether it is combative, involves a ball, racing, etc.) and other cultural variables, including cultural complexity. The possibilities for cross-cultural comparative research on games and sport seem to be limited only by the imaginations—and the levels of interest—of researchers.

Summary and conclusions

A large quantity of descriptive material on sport, games, exercise, and other forms of recreation exists in the ethnographic literature. Despite this fact, only a few cross-cultural comparative studies of sport have ever been undertaken. This may be because the advantages of the cross-cultural comparative method are not well known to those with interests in sport or because researchers perceive some disadvantages with both the method and available. As with most things, there are distinct advantages, disadvantages, and issues for consideration with cross-cultural comparative research..

Advantages of cross-cultural comparative research

The major advantage of conducting worldwide cross-cultural comparative studies is that they probably generalize to the entire ethnographic record, unlike the case with regional studies. As such, they maximize the possible range of variation in the variables under study while within-region studies tend to minimize variation. A significant virtue of comparative studies that utilize secondary data is that they are extremely cost efficient. Compared to collecting primary data on as few as 4 societies (and even that number assumes unbiased sampling, errorless measurement, and a hypothesis that is true), the use of secondary data sources is extremely inexpensive.

Disadvantages of cross-cultural comparative research

Most of the disadvantages of the cross-cultural method have already been discussed. These include Galton's Problem, sampling problems, and the problems of informant, ethnographer, and coder error. All of these problems can be dealt with, to some extent (see Ember & Ember 1998). A problem for which there is no solution is inadequate (or no) ethnographic coverage of pristine (pre-Western contact) or extinct societies. The effects of contact with imperialistic and/or proselytizing outsiders (who also often carry diseases for which native peoples have no resistance) have typically been devastating, both biologically and culturally. The cultures of societies that have either been extinguished or Westernized are gone; their contribution to the pool of variance of human cultures is irretrievable and lost to the purview of cross-cultural comparative researchers.

Other disadvantages are occasionally suggested. One is that cross-cultural comparative research ignores context and denies the individual uniqueness of cultures. First, as for uniqueness, I am unaware of any cross-cultural researcher who claims that individual cultures are not unique. But that does not mean that they cannot be compared. Every person is unique, as well, but that does not mean that their heights or weights cannot be measured and compared, or that they cannot be tested in terms of how fast they can run or how far they can throw a ball. Researchers must always be sensitive to context, as well. Lacrosse among Native Americans may have been played for fun, for gambling, for divination, or for other ritual purposes and researchers should be sensitive to those meanings. Nevertheless, to the extent that the rules remain constant, it is the same game, whenever or wherever it is played. Finally, if every culture was truly unique and knowledge of the total context for every cultural act was always necessary for understanding, cross-cultural communication would be impossible. It would be inconceivable for anyone to enter another culture and function in even the most rudimentary way. We know that this is not the case.

Issues in cross-cultural comparative research

For cross-cultural comparative research to improve as a method in the future, several issues should be addressed. First, most research in the past has been correlational, though cause and effect relationships have often been implied. Future research should make use of statistical techniques, such as path analysis and LISREL, that are more appropriate than correlational methods for testing causality. At the same time, the data are available for diachronic research that would permit tests of causal models but such studies are rare (Ember & Ember 1998).

Two goals of the Human Relations Area Files, Inc. are to improve its collection of ethnography and to develop a truly random sample of societies (Ember 1997). To the extent that these goals are realized, cross-cultural comparative research will improve, as well. Good methods and a good sample are of no value, however, if there are no researchers interested in cross-cultural comparative research. The recent turn away from science and toward the humanities in American anthropology has been to the great disadvantage of cross-cultural research and relatively few young anthropologists are pursuing cross-cultural studies. But if anthropology abandons cross-cultural comparative research, that does not mean that others cannot take it up. Since data on sport in several hundred societies from around the world exist, and appropriate methods to take advantage of such data are available, there is no good reason why intensive and extensive cross-cultural comparative analyses of sport should not be undertaken.

References

Blanchard, K. (1995). The anthropology of sport. Westport, CT: Bergin & Garvey.
Burton, M.L., Moore, C.C., Whiting, J.W.M. & Romney, A.K. (1996). Regions based on social structure. Current Anthropology, 37, 87-123.

Campbell, D.T. (1961). The mutual methodological relevance of anthropology and psychology. In F.L.K. Hsu (ed.), Psychological anthropology: Approches to culture and personality. Homewood, IL: Dorsey Press, 333-352.

Chick, G. (1997). Cultural complexity: The concept and its measurement. Cross-Cultural Research, 31, 275-307.

Chick, G. (1998a). Leisure and culture: Issues for an anthropology of leisure. Leisure Sciences, 32, 1-15.

Chick, G. (1998b). Games in culture revisited: A replication and extension of Roberts, Arth, and Bush (1959). Cross-Cultural Research, 32, 185-206.

Chick, G., Miracle, A.W. & Loy, J.W. (1995, November). "Rape, sport, and war." Presented at the annual meeting of the American Anthropological Association. Washington, DC.

Chick, G., Miracle, A.W. & Loy, J.W. (1996). Rape, sport, and war. Human Peace, 11, 1, 3-13.

Chick, G., Loy, J.W. & Miracle, A.W. (1997). Combative sport and warfare: a reappraisal of the spillover and catharsis hypotheses. Cross-Cultural Research, 31, 249-267.

Chick, G. & Loy, J.M. (1998, February). "Making men of them: male socialization for warfare, combative sports, and sexual aggressiveness." Presented at the annual meeting of the Society for Cross-Cultural Research, St. Petersburg, FL.

Ember, C.R. & Ember, M. (1998). Cross-cultural research. In H. R. Bernard (ed.), Handbook of methods in cultural anthropology. Walnut Creek, CA: AltaMira Press, 647-687.

Ember, M. (1997). Evolution of the Human Relations Area Files. Cross-Cultural Research, 31, 1, 3-15.

Evans-Pritchard, E.E. (1965). The comparative method in social anthropology. In E.E. Evans-Pritchard (ed.), The position of women in primitive society and other essays in social anthropology. New York: Free Press, 1-22.

Freeman, D. (1983). Margaret Mead and Samoa: The making and unmaking of an anthropological myth. Cambridge, MA: Harvard University Press.

Goodenough, W.H. (1996). Murdock as bridge: From Sumner to HRAF to SCCR. Cross-Cultural Research, 30, 3, 275-280.

Hobhouse, L.T., Wheeler, G.C. & Ginsberg, M. (1915). The material culture and social institutions of the simpler peoples. London: Chapman and Hall.

Hobhouse, L.T. (1906). Morals in evolution. New York: Holt.

Lagacé, R.O. (1979). The HRAF probability sample: Retrospect and prospect. Behavior Science Research, 14, 211-229.

Levinson, D. & Malone, M.J. (1980). Toward explaining human culture. New Haven, CT: Human Relations Area Files.

Loy, J.W. & Chick, G.E. (1993, February). "A cross-cultural test of the cultural spillover theory of rape." Presented at the annual meeting of the Society for Cross-Cultural Research, Washington, DC.

Munroe, R.L. & Munroe, R.H. (1991). Comparative field studies: methodological issues and future possibilities. Behavior Science Research, 25, 155-185.

Murdock, G.P. & White, D.R. (1969). Standard cross-cultural sample. Ethnology, 8, 329-369.

Murdock, G.P. (1934). Our primitive contemporaries. New York: Macmillan.

Murdock, G.P. (1967). Ethnographic atlas: A summary. Ethnology, 6, 109-236.

Murdock, G.P., Ford, C.S., Hudson, A.E., Kennedy, R., Simmons, L. W. & Whiting, J.W.M. (1938). Outline of cultural materials. New Haven, CT: Human Relations Area Files.

Naroll, R. (1962). Data quality control—a new research technique: prolegmena to a cross-cultural study of culture stress. New York: Free Press.

Naroll, R. & Sipes, R.G. (1973). Standard ethnographic sample, 2nd edition. Current Anthropology, 14, 111-140.

Naroll, R., Michik, G. & Naroll, F. (1976). Worldwide theory testing. New Haven, CT: Human Relations Area Files.

Nieboer, H.J. (1910). Slavery as an industrial system, 2nd ed. The Hague: Nyhoff.

Roberts, J.M., Arth, M.C. & Bush, R.R. (1959). Games in culture. American Anthropologist, 59, 579-605.

Roberts, J.M. & Barry, H.C. III. (1976). Inculcated traits and game-type combinations. In T.T. Craig (ed.), The humanistic and mental health aspects of sports, exercise, and recreation. Chicago: American Medical Association, 5-11.

Sipes, R.G. (1973). War, sports and aggression: an empirical test of two rival theories. American Anthropologist, 75, 64-86.

Steinmetz, R.S. (1896). Endokannabilismus. Mitteilungen der Anthropologischen Gesellschaft in Wien, 26, 1-60.

Sumner, W.G. (1906). Folkways. Boston: Ginn.

Tylor, E.B. (1889). On a method of investigating the development of institutions applied to the laws of marriage and descent. Journal of the Royal Anthropological Institute of Great Britain and Ireland, 18, 245-272.

Chapter 3

The uses of history in comparative physical culture

Richard Holt
De Montfort University, U.K. and K.U.Leuven, Belgium

Why should a researcher working on the comparison of contemporary systems of physical culture be concerned with the past ? Most current research in this area is concerned with the present and tends to follow a fairly well-defined pattern : papers begin with a section on methodology and proceed to examine survey data, possibly incorporating interviews and a restricted 'literature search' using 'key words'. Of course, there are other approaches, though the collection and comparison of data is usually at the heart of the matter. The sociology of sport is full of papers based on statistical evidence of differential age and sex participation rates, varieties of leisure management systems, contrasting educational, sporting and social structures. Such information may be necessary and useful. But what does it *mean* ? How does such work connect to related areas of mainstream knowledge, for example, the study of nationalism ? Collecting data can raise as many questions as it answers. Whose data, which data and why bother ? Research may reveal differences without explaining *why* such differences exist.

Fortunately physical culture seems to have largely abandoned the attempt to find neat conceptual solutions. Invoking social theory whether in the form of Marxism or western liberal 'big ideas' like the 'civilising process', 'scientific rationality' or 'modernisation' can easily produce work based on a closed system of reasoning. Critical and eclectic use of 'big ideas' can be most valuable but narrowly sticking to 'sacred texts', which do not permit refutation, is fatal. [1] On the other hand, the mere collection of data without any general framework for its interpretation may seem pointless. Methodology is not a replacement for thinking and interpretation. Finding a reliable way to collect data does not ensure that such data is worth collecting. The key issue is what questions we ask. As social science sets itself more limited objectives and adopts a more self-critical perspective, the idea of taking an historical as opposed to a conceptual or methodologically determined 'approach' seems increasingly attractive.

Most historical work has been undertaken within the national framework. How then how can this help researchers committed to working comparatively ? The answer is that it can greatly deepen the knowledge of the societies to be compared. If comparative physical culture has an overwhelming fault it lies in the understanding of the nations involved in the comparison. Historians, however, know a great deal about national histories, about national patterns of economic growth, social structure, power relations and ideologies. To try to understand why one society has a sharply differing system of physical culture from another without making use of this knowledge is most unwise. The best historical work when properly used can provide the means to construct better explanations by understanding the underlying forces at work.

In the widest sense history is the totality of past events and attitudes. As such it can seem either inaccessible or irrelevant to someone working on a specific contemporary project. Very advanced or technical historical research is less important than a firm grasp on the broad consensus of recent historical interpretation. Good historical explanation provides proper context for specific issues. In fact, one way of understanding the historical approach is to see it as a technique for locating a phenomenon within a wider range of forces and explaining the relationship between the particular and the general. History denies essential or inherent meanings and seeks to construct accounts which 'explain' events by placing them alongside related phenomena to create patterns over time.

Good history books acquire a 'cumulative plausibility'. This is not a matter of being right or wrong. There are accounts which are more convincing and those which are less convincing. The most convincing accounts tend to be those which are not only most firmly based in the historical sources but which draw together as many aspects of the period as possible. A good book about the origins of the First World War, for example, will not simply look at diplomatic alliances and armaments; it will examine the role of public opinion, the press, the economic and imperial dimensions and finally the particular role and character of key individuals. History is very useful for general social investigation simply in terms of providing an approach which is based upon the notion of the multiplicity of factors and the nature of their interaction at specific moments.

Good history requires clarity and complexity. It may be possible to isolate quite simple themes but the way these themes interact in specific historical circumstances to produce particular changes shows how complex the real world can be. Historians understand societies partly by looking at their blend of common and special features. Most western societies experienced a process of industrialisation, urbanisation and nationalism which profoundly influenced patterns of physical culture. But no two nations did this in quite the same way. No single 'social theory' nor any 'research methodology' can explain the distinctiveness of national cultures, let alone regional and local ones. The usual way for historians to make comparisons is to take a phenomenon and locate it first within the wider culture of one nation and then within the different historic traditions and circumstances of another. [2] Once this is done, a judicious and carefully qualified comparisons can be made between the two. In this way the differences of fact or meaning emerge from the material itself rather than from a rigid application of theory and arbitrary selection of data.

What does this mean for the busy working researcher into comparative physical culture ? Take, for example, the case of two broadly comparable western industrial societies like Germany and Britain. The great popularity of football in both countries would seem to confirm convergence in the field of physical culture. Hartmann-Tews noted in her comparative study of the 'Sport for All movement' that there were around 4.6 million footballers in the UK and 4.8 million in Germany in 1989/90. But appearances can be deceptive. For Germany had 3.9 million in the 'turnen' movement whilst Britain did not even have a proper category for such activity. [3] This is a huge difference. No present-centered explanation about leisure preferences, facilities or policies could begin to explain it. The reasons are rooted in the sharply different general histories of Britain and Germany. The defense of a Prussia, a militarist state without natural frontiers, which had to rebuild its national army after defeat by Napoleon, largely explains the success of 'turnvater Jahn' and German gymnastics. Britain, on the other hand, long established within natural frontiers, had a liberal tradition of limited state power based upon a constitutional monarchy and a system of naval defense. This did not require or permit the maintenance of a large domestic army. The British state did relatively little for the para-military training of the young on a large scale. Such differing traditions of physical culture became rooted in national behaviour and still persist.

There is a wider issue here which has implications for the general history of physical culture, whose development arose from the complex relationship between traditional games, gymnastics and modern sports. [4] It was not until after the First World War that English-derived sports supplanted German and Swedish gymnastics as the dominant form of physical culture in the western world. The quarrel between sport and gymnastics is easily overlooked today. Yet in a conference devoted to the idea of 'old borders/new borders' this historic confrontation of opposing forms of body culture is most instructive. Supporters of sport claimed it stood for liberty and competition – the classic nineteenth century liberal values – and saw gymnastics as authoritarian and militarist. Gymnasts, on the other hand, thought sport was vain, trivial and individualistic. The triangular relationship between traditional games, gymnastic and sports was, of course, partly transformed by the success of team games, especially football, which proved far more attractive to young men than repetitive group exercise. But this was not the whole story. Gymnastic exercise was insidiously changed from within into a competitive and more individualistic form of 'sporting' activity. This process of 'sportification' offers a particularly striking and important example of how apparently rigid divisions can shift or dissolve over time as new definitions of what is physically desirable emerge.

Such points, though important, are of a general order. How can an historical approach illuminate specific projects. Consider a recent article in *The Journal of Comparative Physical Education and Sport* on 'A comparative study of the development of elite young soccer players in England and Belgium' by Richard Fisher and Martin Dean. [5] I select this purely because I am familiar with the history of both countries and with the history of football. This article is based on a very narrow literature review (only in English – a striking shortcoming in itself when comparing anglophone and non-anglophone cases), two short field trips to Belgium and some interviews. Its 'methodology was evolved from Holmes' suggestions for comparative study in PE and sport in which contemporary problems are analysed with a view to proposing solutions'. [6] The authors describe their approach as mainly 'qualitative'. It is certainly narrowly policy based and entirely ahistorical. They want to compare English selection and training of outstanding young players with Belgian methods. They find that in Belgium 'clubs are deemed responsible for producing excellence' and have 'their own policy objectives'. Belgium has no 'national school' of excellence unlike England but England has its own problems and 'the greatest barrier to change ... is that of tradition'. [7]

The authors, however, seem to know nothing about 'tradition'. For history is required to understand traditions. National traditions are indeed of great importance, especially in Belgium which is a single state composed of two linguistic nations. The relative influence of each language community in the national team is a controversial issue. If FIFA permitted the Flemish to have a national team (as Scotland, for example within the UK), there is little doubt many would support the idea. Hence it is hardly surprising there is no Belgian 'national school' for producing top players. There is no agreement about what the nation is and selecting a Belgian team is hard enough. Nor is it surprising French and Flemish clubs insist on running their own affairs. On the English side, the historic working class structure of professional football, which has had profoundly negative implications for the training and education of players, is ignored. Middle class boys have been virtually excluded by making higher education and professional football effectively incompatible. [8] The chance to say something interesting about football in both societies is lost despite assembling some potentially useful information.

I do not want to suggest the authors are anything less than competent within their own narrow terms. On the contrary, it is precisely that they are representative of a wider reluctance to look beyond the immediate 'facts', which is important. This example – and there are plenty of others – illustrates what can happen to comparative research when it is cut off not only from general history but from sports history as well. The latter is a particularly serious omission. It is surely *not* acceptable that anyone doing serious work on a sport should be unaware of the history of that activity. Over the past twenty or so years sports history has emerged as a sub-discipline of history with its own journals and a significant number of research monographs and articles in mainstream academic journals. Sports history has moved from being a mere collection of stories about past performances to a proper historical discipline where sports are placed in their wider social context. Letting the trained sports historian do some of the groundwork can be a relatively quick and painless way for the sociologist to get a grip on more general history, though it would be a serious mistake only to read sports history and neglect the best relevant general work.

History teaches many things : it instills caution about dogmatic generalisation and theorising; it stresses the interplay between change and continuity; it underlines the necessity of understanding what makes individual societies distinctive. Most obviously it teaches that any social survey is simply a 'snapshot' of the moment, which cannot be understood without reference to what went before to produce this configuration. It makes little sense to look at the emergence of women and ethnic minorities into sport without understanding why they were absent in the past and how they were portrayed. Media representation is a crucial dimension. Increasingly historians – and this includes sports historians – are shifting from the social to the cultural, from 'facts' to symbols, from 'reality' to the construction of that reality. Nations as 'imagined communities' has been a powerful theme of much of the best new work on nationalism. This in turn has to be set against the theme of 'globalisation', which has dominated so much recent discussion of economic and social change. Material change does not translate into cultural change in a simple way. National attitudes mediate the relationship between consumption and values.

Hence the importance – and the difficulty – of comparing nations. Those involved in comparative physical culture should reflect upon this when identifying global trends and their impact on different cultures. Existing comparative work is largely restricted to what is happening (the 'facts') and ignores what people *think* is happening. But self-perception is highly significant. Some peoples see themselves as much more 'sporting' than others. Why is this and what does it mean ? Comparative work on sport and identity is a promising field which links up with a mass of more general recent research around nationalism. This has given rise to a new interest in individuals as national symbols. [9] The individual sporting hero carries the weight of national expectation and comes to stand for the national image. The body of the athlete is much more than bone and muscle. Styles of performance, physical appearance and posture, clothing, gesture and language all play their part in creating the hero, onto whose life we can project – or allow others to project – all manner of virtue, real and imagined. These lives are interpreted to us through the media. Heroes are made in the press and on television. We need comparative studies of this heroic process in different cultures. Such new topics await investigation and the current preoccupation with institutional comparison, especially education and administration, is too limiting.

However, the relationship between history and comparative physical culture is not all one way. Historians also have much to learn. First of all, there is the commitment to comparative work itself. Historians frequently hold forth about the benefits of comparative work but rarely attempt it. Economic historians have been more willing to cross national frontiers, following capital flows and labour migration, but social, political and cultural history has been locked into the nation state. Urban history, for example, which seems like a prime candidate, has not produced much in the way of comparative work. Take a simple example, such as Paris and London. These two great west European capital cities have dozens of historians but few comparative studies. In sports history there is very little work on London and Paris and no comparative work at all. Social historians and sports historians have similarly been very slow to exploit the possibilities of transatlantic comparison despite sharing a common language. British, European and American systems of sport remain historically isolated from each other. Work on contemporary physical culture is far ahead of history here, especially when it comes to comparing African or Asian societies with the western world.

Sports history has been overwhelmingly concerned with establishing the context under which sports could develop. There has been much less interest in the sporting performance itself. Yet sport without the body is like Hamlet without the Prince. The centrality of bodily form and display within physical culture has been neglected by historians until recently. Those working within physical culture have been more sensitive to the need to understand movement and technique in its own terms. How the activity and appearance of the body is interpreted is finally commanding wider historical interest. For example, the use of body images to represent different ideas of the nation has become a major area of historical research. This was brilliantly developed in Pierre Nora's influential three volume collection, *Realms of Memory* ('Les lieux de memoire'), which includes a brilliant essay by Georges Vigarello on the Tour de France and the cyclist as national symbol and physical type. [10]

In conclusion, the relationship between history and comparative physical culture is more complex - and more reciprocal - than one might suppose. History has important lessons for those working on contemporary research projects in terms of defining problems and understanding context. Without this there is a danger that 'sports' research can seem limited and of low quality. Physical culture researchers must engage with serious research in the humanities and social sciences in a way that those working in the mainstream can understand and appreciate. Otherwise it will remain marginal. There is a good book waiting to be written here. What we need is an elegant synthesis – not *another* text book, still less a book of readings - which will draw together contemporary work in such a way as to convince academics in other disciplines of the value of looking at physical culture from a cross cultural perspective.

Notes

[1] This is discussed this at much greater length in 'Some observations on social history and the sociology of sport' in Holt, R. (1989). Sport and the British : a modern history. Oxford: Oxford University Press, 358-367.

[2] There are distinguished exceptions such as European historical work of Eric Hobsbawm.

[3] Hartmann-Tews, I. (1996). Sport für alle *!?* Cologne: Verlag Hoffman, 102-105.

[4] I am grateful to the research group at the K.U.Leuven on comparative physical culture for expanding my awareness of the relationship between gymnastics and sports; E. Weber's 'Gymnastics and Sports in fin-de siècle France', American Historical Review, Feb. 1971, is a brilliant example of how to treat physical culture historically and required reading for anyone wishing to pursue this subject seriously.

[5] See International Journal of Comparative Physical Education and Sport, 20 (2), 44-51, 1998.

[6] *ibid.* p. 44

[7] *ibid.* p. 51

[8] Mason, T. (1979). Association football and English society, 1863-1915. Brighton: Harveste, is the classic account of the formation of English football values; the most recent account is Russell, D. (1997). Football and the English. Preston: Carnegie; I discuss English football, class and education in 'La tradition ouvrieriste du football anglais' in Actes de la Recherche en Sciences Sociales, 103, June 1994, 36-41.

[9] For example, Dawson, G. (1994). Soldier heroes : British adventure, empire and the imagining of masculinities. London: Routledge; see also Lanfranchi, P., Mangan, J.A. & Holt, R. (eds) (1996). European heroes : myth, identity, sport. London: Cass.

[10] Vigarello, G. (1997). The Tour de France. In Nora P. : <u>Realms of memory :
the construction of the French past.</u> New York, Columbia UP, vol. 2, 469-
500

Part B

Countries getting closer

Chapter 4

The effects of American hegemony on the international sporting community

Roy A. Clumpner
Western Washington University, U.S.A.

This paper concerns itself with a discussion of several trends taking place in American sport and focuses on recent unsettling practices which are occurring. Since American trends often are exported, strategies which may be implemented to prevent or at least deflect the adoption of unsettling practices are explored.

Background

Cantelon and Murray (1993) in their review of globalization and sport define globalization as the internationalization of the market economy. The assertion is that as the marketplace becomes more technologically and industrially developed the actions of those who operate within this marketplace become undifferentiated with the result that according to Weber (1947) the world will lose all its uniqueness in the drive to maximize production in the most efficient manner. Sport has not been immune to globalization and among sport sociologists discussion has centered on whether the term should be globalization or Americanization and what effects these two practices have been on sport in various cultures. For the most part, sport sociologists agree (Guttman 1991; McKay & Miller 1991; Wagner 1990) it is not specifically an American process but more of a globalization process of blending or homogenization of world sports and many sporting traditions which is taking place.

For this paper the distinct term "Americanization" is used to connote the transmission of practices occurring in American sport (primarily merchandizing and game play) rather than the transmission of a particular sport to a country. America is a global trendsetter so it would behoove those in the world sporting community to be cognizant of such trends in the United States so if these trends which might be undesirable should appear, strategies are in place to thwart their adoption.

American capitalism

At the center of America is capitalism, its greatest export, and while Americans might not have invented it, they certainly have refined it to a finite science. The media play a central role in all of this by the systematic blurring of the lines between information, entertainment, and promotion (Sklair 1995) and America campaigns to make "consumer culture" universal through its domination of the global film, television and radio broadcasting industries. By and large it is successful to the extent that it does persuade people that this system is best (Sklair 1995).

At the heart of this is the drive by Americans for amusement and excitement; something not lost to merchandisers and marketers. Today, even super-markets have been built like theme parks while restaurants have clowns and play equipment, all indicative of the American obsession with amusement (Ritzer 1993). This penchant for amusement has carried over into sport with the result that the game is often altered from its original product in order to amuse or excite.

Maintaining this system of dependency on amusement and excitement are the multinational corporations, a significant number of whom have interest in international sport, leisure wear, and sports equipment and who market these products through television and other media (Houlihan 1994). Recently, American professional sport teams have embarked upon promotion and merchandizing of their own products globally, on their way toward becoming multinational corporations themselves, particularly through the media; the effects have not gone unnoticed on the international community. In describing the impact of American football on the landscape of English sports culture, Maguire (1990) highlighted the interweaving of interests of media and multinational corporations in the creation of a market not simply for the game of American football but also for the merchandising, sponsorship, and endorsement operations associated with it. McKay and Miller (1991) described the format of the Americanization of Rugby League, Australian Rules and basketball as that of showbiz with cheerleaders, mascots, live bands and spectacular displays before, during, and after events. It is not the merchandizing, sponsorship or endorsement of the sport that is of concern. Rather it is this continued rush to market and change the nature of the game and the negative behavior of the participants which is worrisome and detracts from the true meaning and nature of sport. This American obsession with amusement, entertainment and merchandizing a product has directly affected American sport at all levels and has the potential of spreading globally if it has not already done so.

Trends in American sport

Americans have been major contributors to the development of sport in the 20th Century. In one way or another, whether by invention or refinement, Americans have added numerous changes in sport, for better or worse. Among other things we can be thankful (sic) for are:

- The merchandising of sport.
- Interscholastic and intercollegiate sport.
- College athletic scholarships.
- Instant Replay
- The television time out.
- Pay television for sport.
- Global sportswear.
- Salary caps.
- The draft.
- Stacking players
- The event promoter.
- The sports franchise evaluation expert.
- Stadia blackmail.
- Luxury boxes.
- Affirmative action.
- Sponsorship.
- The sports agent.
- Ultimate Frisbee.
- The sex marketing sport of Beach Volleyball

The current direction of American sport is not well established but five trends will be discussed which the global community should take notice if they have not already done so.

Integration of entertainment delivery systems

There is a continued move toward an integrated entertainment delivery system in which entertainment companies control everything from programming to distribution and sport is an integral part of this integration. This trend is best displayed in Disney's ownership of the Mighty Ducks National Hockey League (NHL) [1] team which produced a very successful Disney movie prior to the team playing its first game. The result was not only a box office hit but a merchandizing coup the first year as the team lead the NHL in merchandize sales (Ozanian 1994). This commercialization of sports on a very American scale is likewise spreading across Europe, with everything from emblazoned merchandize for fans to theme restaurants with of course, rising ticket prices (Europe Enters the Big Leagues 1997).

Targeting youth in the global promotion of American sport

There is a concerted effort in the global marketplace to target youth in merchandizing products. According to Joseph Quinlan, senior economist at Dean Witter Reynolds Inc. of New York, there is out there "... a global MTV generation... They prefer coke to tea, Nikes to sandals; chicken McNuggets to rice, credit cards to cash" (Wysocki 1997). What is being marketed is not simply a soft drink but a style of life, specifically a North American style of life (Sklair 1995). Not only is the global teenage market being targeted, but it turns out that sport is a central focus. Coca Cola for example, conducted a nine country study and discovered that the three parameters of the global teenage market were clothing, consumer electronics and sport (Tully 1994) and, in a study of 24,000 teenagers around the world, a unit of New York advertising giant D'Arcy Masius Benton and Bowles Inc. found that in these youths eyes, basketball edged out soccer as the world's most popular sport. (Wysocki 1997).

Indications are that major professional American sports are making inroads. Maguire (1990) noted that American football has been used in Britain as a vehicle for the merchandizing operations of the National Football League (NFL) and a range of companies and, as such, has spread out beyond the conventional boundaries of sport. By 1996, broadcast rights outside North America grossed $10 million for the NFL, $25 million for the National Basketball Association (NBA) and $20 million for professional baseball (Copetas 1996). Merchandising proved more lucrative, with $250 million in gross receipts for the NFL and $70 million for major league baseball. The previous year, the NHL grossed over $1 billion in merchandize sales (Copetas 1996). In order to increase overseas marketing share the big four's (NHL, NBA, NFL & Major League Baseball) strategy is to educate potential fans on their sport.

For example, 1997 Major League Baseball spent $200,000 on a pitch, hit and run program at 300 schools in Britain and 600 schools in Germany, while the NFL promoted flag football and the NHL in-line skating (Ibid.). Meanwhile, the NBA was more active. In addition to sponsoring basketball programs in schools in Britain, France and Germany it conducted a survey of 28,000 teenagers in 44 countries and found that in Western Europe 98% recognized the league's loge and 93% that of the Chicago Bulls (Europe Enters the Big Leagues 1997).

Game tampering

By altering or creating new rules or not enforcing rules, overseers in sport hope to develop a more marketable product to the un-educated would-be fan.

Evidence of this recently took place in June of 1998 when the NHL, in order to increase scoring (excitement for the game), moved the net out several feet and changed line markers. Attempts to change from three, twenty minute periods to four, fifteen minute periods were not successful. These changes were in addition to the changes previously made to increase the American viewing audience whereby glowing pucks were used during FOX network telecasts so that American viewers could discern the puck more clearly (Canadians were in disbelief).

In Europe, Americans playing basketball already have affected the structure of the game with the advent of rules designed to speed up play. The result has been a glitzy, media sporting spectacle based on the American model, to be marketed and sold as part of a consumer-oriented package with success based not on outcome but en the game's marketability (Chappell et al. 1996; Maguire 1994).

Similarly, bending rules (allowing handchecking, travelling and carrying the ball in basketball) the preferential treatment in games of star players (they seldom have the same rules applied as other players) and allowing rough play in order to draw fan interest, at the expense of the sport, deserve attention.

Finally, and somewhat related to rule changes are the movements to create sports spectacles (American Gladiators) and even the emerging development by one corporation (Pepsi) to create and market its own sport. Americans it seems, just can't leave well enough alone.

Continued recruiting of foreign athletes by American colleges

American colleges annually recruit foreign athletes primarily in basketball, hockey and track and field. In 1989 it was estimated that over 6,000 foreign athletes graced American college campuses (Bale 1991). Surprisingly, the results of Bale's research (1991) indicated the experience by and large was a positive one for most foreign athletes.

Violence, disrespect and showboating

This trend is the most disheartening and will be a focus of the remainder of this paper. Recently, there has been a spate of incidents which have undermined the true meaning of sport and the belief in fair play not only by professional athletes, but intercollegiate, and interscholastic athletes as well. What follows are selected examples of behaviors recently exhibited at all three levels of American sport.

Interscholastic sport
- In January of 1996, a referee with 20 years of experience was head butted unconscious by a 17 year old high school wrestler after the wrestler was disqualified for an illegal mount (Lipsyte 1997).
- The Florida Interscholastic Athletic Federation reported a dramatic increase in high school players thrown out of football games from 212 in 1994 to 333 in 1996 (Lipsyte 1997).
- In a Penn State study, it was reported that as many as 175,000 high school girls have used steroids to become leaner or to build more muscle (Study: Girls Steroid Use Up 1997).

Intercollegiate sport
- Two model female athletes at the University of Texas were arrested on robbery and assault charges (Two Model Citizens Arrested 1997).
- A Washington State University basketball player stepped on the throat of an opposing player and wouldn't let her up (Huntington 1997).
- Numerous instances of criminal activity by football players including sexual assault and robbery.

Professional sport
- September, 1996, Roberto Alomar spit in an American League umpire's face. (His five game suspension was delayed to the following season to allowing him to continue playing in the playoff games).
- Dennis Rodman of the NBA kicked a photographer during the 1996-1997 season.
- Numerous brawls in baseball and basketball including a brawl in the summer of 1997, when a womens' professional baseball player charged the mound (Huntington 1997).

This aberrant behavior is being reinforced by professional athletes appearing in commercials which extol deviant behavior and non-compliance with community standards and rules. In addition, negative messages such as "You don't win silver, you lose gold" by Nike, which were in evidence at the Atlanta Olympic games indicate a troubling trend in sport.

Some attribute it to an overall deterioration of respect for authority, which seems to be permeating American schools. To what extent will this influence the global community if it already hasn't ? According to Houlihan (1994) for most of the world, western sports and the western definition of sport reign supreme. If this is the case, then the global village needs to take immediate notice.

Strategies/solutions

The task of reversing or deflecting some of these negative practices will not be easy and Sklair (1994) and Houlihan (1994) have painted a bleak picture of thwarting the influence of a major economic power such as the United States and its extensive marketing abilities.

All is not hopeless however, for there are numerous forms of resistance [2]. Guttman (1991) notes that the rise of Islamic fundamentalism should be enough in itself to remind us that such processes can be reversed.

State interference

One method is for the state to step in. In the case of violence in American high school sports, legislation bas been enacted in 11 states which bring violent episodes on the athletic fields into the courts (Lipsyte 1997). More and more, violence which occurs in sport is being turned over to the courts for action.

The state has also been used in non-violent situations as well. The Canadian federal Government, in order to temper the flow of athletes going south to scholarship schools in the US, instituted with moderate success, a federal Athletes Assistance Program which makes living and training grants to outstanding athletes (Kidd 1991).

Local culture determination

Local cultures as well can have a large say in what goes on within their sphere. In Ireland, for example, in order to combat the English sporting tradition, the Gaelic Athletic Association was established in 1884 to rescue traditional Gaelic sports such as hurling and Gaelic football from obscurity by restricting members to playing Irish/Gaelic sports and prohibited contact with clubs subscribing to English sports, a strategy that maintained Irish sporting traditions (Houlihan 1994). Israel likewise made a strong stand to include sport to forge links between Jews throughout the world and not be taken up into the sport culture. Likewise, Japan has managed to systematically import ideas and world sporting views with relatively little "contamination," These examples indicate that others too can replicate the practice of local culture determination (Houlihan 1994).

Domestic sport organizations

Domestic sport organizations can also play a role in deflecting unwanted practices and traditions. In Los Angeles stringent codes of conduct have been drawn up and enforced together with intensive monitoring and increased adult supervision (Lipsyte 1997).

League restrictions on the number of foreign players allowed per professional team as practised in Canada and Europe is becoming much more common globally. Even the NBA has etiquette classes for athletes from the proper way to speak to the press to the way to held a knife and fork and in the NFL, referees doing pre-season games eat with players in training camp and discuss calls made during the games as a way to diffuse emotions (Lipsyte 1997).

Domestic sport organizations in poorer countries have a much harder time insulating their practices and traditions from external pressures and this is where the role of the international sports governing bodies have an important role to play as they are often treated with a high degree of respect by the states in recognition of their status as significant actors in the international system (Houlihan 1994). The role that these agencies have been playing will be discussed in another section of this paper.

Human agencies

Guttmann (1991) and Wagner (1990) make the case that human agency plays an integral part in embracing, acquiescing or resisting cultural formations (Cantelon & Murray 1993). Houlihan (1994) notes that athletes themselves have a role to play in this as they and their supporters and administrators flow between countries. This presumes that athletes are taking with them and demonstrating appropriate modeling skills. If the modeling is a debasement of the ideals of sport then this strategy is ineffective.

Individuals, especially when formed into pressure groups, can force change. At first, when faced with the seemingly insurmountable power of the media, change seems impossible. But this is far from true for the lessons of the Soviet Union tell us that total control of the mass media does not ensure that people can be controlled (Dyer 1998). Besides, today there is an additional media medium at our disposal which is not controlled (as yet) and offers a truly remarkable rallying and information dissemination vehicle: the internet.

Another human agency strategy is the use of a social movement to thwart penetration of unwanted practices. Lessons can be learned from the Green Movement, which managed to turn the transnational class into adopting sustainable development (Sklair 1995).

There are numerous examples of courageous individuals who linked with others to form pressure groups and made dramatic change. Who would have thought that in the United States attitudes behind drinking and driving could be changed, but one woman brought pressure to bear and through her organization, MADD (Mothers Against Drunk Drivers) reversed attitudes.

Sport has its own share of success stories of individuals pressuring for change. As a result of embarrassing news reports of using young children to stitch soccer balls and pressed by thousands of soccer-playing children and their parents in North America and Europe who wrote letters and signed petitions voicing concern, and bolstered by the threat in September 1996 by FIFA, the International Soccer Federation, who indicated they would not endorse soccer balls unless manufactures certified they were not made by children, sports equipment manufacturers in 1997 pledged to combat the sale of such balls (Greenhouse 1997). As of February, 1998, 56 companies had made the pledge.

Because of a consumer led pressure movement and the aggressive actions of sports governing bodies, Nike has changed numerous policies. Reacting to the numerous negative Nike ad campaigns Seth Blatter, FIFA's general secretary, condemned Nike's advertising trend that glorified violence or bad taste and noted that their campaigns did nothing to promote values, especially among impressionable youngsters (Thurow 1997). FIFA was joined by the International Olympic Committee (IOC) in condemning the campaigns and when Nike was stung by a barrage of criticism that it exploited Asian labor, corrupted athletic role models and filled kids heads with unrealistic notions about huge sneaker endorsement deals, the company adjusted its battle plan toward more of a sensitivity training and a global marketing strategy to reverse criticism (Thurow 1997). The result, Nike pledged it would play down its rebel image outside the US (Goll-Beatty 1997). In addition, Nike announced that they would pay homage to the history of the game (soccer), work with grassroots organizations and famous sport clubs and federations in each country, tone down their violent images in ads and connect with the global language and passion of the sport of soccer, and take American sport icons and mix them with icons from foreign countries with their sports.

Nike has also demonstrated more sensitivity to various cultures. For example, in June of 1997, it pulled an ad which depicted Nike shoes resembling heat rising from blacktop after a chorus of protests from Muslims who noted that the image resembled "Allah" in Arabic script (Goll-Beatty 1997). In addition, Nike is using more local people in its ads. Nike ads in China now herald Chinese basketball stars performing with captions such as: "China also has sharpshooters" and " American cowboys are not the only ones who can make great shots" rather than Americans (Goll-Beatty 1997). Most recently the company announced a series of initiatives to improve factory working conditions worldwide and to provide increased opportunities for people who manufacture Nike products (National Press Club 1998). Finally it continues to fund PLAY (Participate in the Lives of America's Youth), a program it initiated in 1994 which awards $500 towards tuition to any college student who coaches children in youth organizations such as Boys and Girls Clubs (CORPS Meltdown 1998).

Conclusion

In conclusion, there are strategies which can be implemented to thwart the negative practices that are occurring in the United States. What is disturbing however, is that few if any agencies exist which protect sport itself and the sport consumer. Who is looking out for the betterment of sport ? Where does the sport consumer receive an opposing point of view other than that promoted by the multinational controlled media or the sport governing body ?

To its credit, one international sport federation, FIFA has taken the torch and instituted a worldwide "Fair Play" campaign to strengthen the ethical basis for football, and sport. All players in the 1988 World Cup finals and other FIFA events have been obliged to sign a Fair Play Declaration (FIFA 1998). However, it too has vested interests in its own survival and cannot be counted on to make decisions based on what is best for the game itself.

While a few international sport governing bodies have taken the initiative to focus on maintaining the integrity of the game, business still has considerable leverage over sports organizations (Houlihan 1994). Those sports under the umbrella of education have at least some protection, in that their decision is supposed to be based on educational outcomes, however they too have built in conflicts with making money, keeping the stands filled and developing a marketable product. The negative messages being sent by sport, particularly professional sport, as discussed in this paper continue to need deflection. Perhaps it is time for the creation of a union for the protection of sport itself and its consumers, unaffiliated with any sports organization. A "Greensport" if you wish (organic of course).

The challenge, as is the case with everything else in the free market place will lie in the hands of consumers themselves. The current disheartening trends do not have to be. Will consumers be like the Soviet people and read between the lines of televised propaganda and demand that negative practices cease ? As Wagner (1990) notes "... it is the people who modify and adapt the cultural imports, the sports, to fit their own needs and values (p.402). We shall see ! "... such is the power and magnetism of the American way of sport." (Eale 1991, p.203).

References

Bale, J.(1991). The braun drain. Urbana, Ill.: University of Illinois Press.

Cantelon, H. & Murray, S. (1993). Globalization and sport, structure and agency: the need for greater clarity. Society and Leisure, 16 (2), 275-292.

Chappell, R., Jones, R. & Burden, A. (1996). Racial participation and integration in English professional basketball 1977-1994. Sociology of Sport Journal, 13, 300-310.

Copetas, C. (1996). Europe is U.S. sports' new classroom. Wall Street Journal, Nov. 29, B. 7: 1.

CORPS Meltdown (1998). PLAY brochure from Nike. Summer 2, (7). Beaverton: Oregon.

Dyer, G. (1998). Is there an emerging global culture ? Surrey Teacher's Association Annual Convention, May 8, Surrey, British Columbia, Canada.

Europe Enters the Big Leagues (1997). New York Times, Sept. 10, D, 1-2.

FIFA (1998). On Line, http://www.fifa.com/index.html.

Goll-Beatty, S. (1997). Bad boy Nike is playing the diplomat in China. Wall Street Journal, Nov. 10, B 1:3.

Greenhouse, S. (1997). Sporting goods concerns agree to combat sale of soccer balls made by children. New York Times, Feb. 14, A 12, 1.

Guttman, A. (1991). Sports diffusion: a response to Maguire and the Americanization commentaries. Sociology of Sport Journal, 8, 185-190,.

Houlihan, B. (1994). Sport and international politics. London, Harvester Wheatsheaf.

Hugh-Jones, S. (1992). A survey of the sports business. The Economist, July 25, 324.

Huntington, A. (1997). Sugar and spice and everything nice ? New York Times, Dec. 7, VIII, 13:2.

Kidd, B. (1991). How do we find our own voices in the "New World Order"? A commentary on Americanization. Sociology of Sport Journal, 8, 179-184.

Klein, A. (1991). Sport and culture as contest terrain: Americanization in the Caribbean. Sociology of Sport Journal, 8, 79-85.

Lipsyte, R. (1997). When 'Kill the Ump' is no longer a joke. New York Times, Jan. 19, VIII, 1:2.

Maguire, J. (1990). More than a sporting touchdown. The making of American football in England 1982-1990. Sociology of Sport Journal, 7, 213 -237.

Maguire, J. (1994). American labour migrants, globalization and the making of English basketball. In: Bale, J. & Maguire, J. (eds.): The global sports arena: athletic talent migration in an interdependent world (pp. 226-255). London: Frank Cass.

McKay, J. & Miller, T. (1991). From old boys to men and women of the corporation: the Americanization and commodification of Australian sport. Sociology of Sport Journal, 8, 86-94.

National Press Club Conference with NIKE Chairman and CEO Philip Knight. (1998), May 12.

Ozanian, M. (1994). The $11 billion pastime. Financial World, May 10, 163 (10) 50-64.
PLAY Corps Update (1998). Summer. Nike Inc., Beaverton, Oregon.
Ritzer, G. (1993). The McDonaldization of society. Newbury Park, CA: Pine Forge Press.
Sklair, L. (1995). Sociology of the global system. Baltimore, Md.: John Hopkins University Press.
Study: Girls Steroid Use Up (1997). New York Times. Dec. 15, C, B-1.
Thurow, R. (1997). Shtick Ball. Wall Street Journal, May 5, 1-6.
Tully, S. (1994). Teens: the most global market of all. Fortune, May 16, 129 (10), 90-97.
Two 'Model Citizens' Arrested (1997). New York Times. March 13, B, 12:6.
Wagner, E. (1990). Sport in Asia and Africa: Americanization or mundialization ? Sociology of Sport Journal, 7, 399-402.
Weber, M. (1947). The theory of social and economic organization. New York: Oxford University Press.
Wysocki, B. (1997). The global mail. Wall Street Journal, June 26, A 1:6.

Notes

[1] While the NHL originally was controlled by Canadian teams, this is no longer the case and for this paper it is considered an American controlled business.

[2] For a discussion on resistance to globalization and modernizaton the reader is referred to Cantelon and Murray (1993), Houlihan (1994) and Klein (1991).

Chapter 5

Convergent process and diversified growth of national sport experience in this global village

Walter King Yan Ho
Curriculum Development Institute, Hong Kong, China

Convergent process and diversified growth of national sport experience

Globalization occurs as a result of the complex dynamics of political, economic and cultural practices (Maguire 1993). Although these practices do not aim at the development of globalization, they nonetheless produce it. The process arises when people share similar thoughts, actions and ideas. More frequent trade activities, strong financial links and most importantly the growth of telecommunication links notably through the Internet foster Greater integration between people. Today such globalization tendencies are seen in political, economic, cultural, educational and recreational spheres. For example, computerized data flow across borders allows a Chinese businessman to conduct trade activities with his American partners through electronic means. Similarly, the development of the Internet allows teachers and students from different countries to meet and discuss their educational ideas through a cider space tube. The improved circulation of educational materials and resources might encourage the development of similar curriculum content for basic mathematics, physics, chemistry, biology and even sport learning for our young children (Goonatilake 1995).

The ongoing processes of globalization however onset the tendency to wipe out local cultural identities and leading towards the loss of genetic diversity of human race (Goonatilake 1995). The development of such paradox is possible because cultural coherence of nation-states might be weakened by such globalization tendencies. The integrated and dependent ecological, socio-economic and political structure promotes the establishment of global village and fosters the development of global consensus between nations (Briggs 1994). Nevertheless, such optimistic viewpoint may overstrung on the strength of globalization development and miscalculates the limit of it. In reality, people do not melt together for the formulation of any global or universal race. The pursuit of regional and differentiated experience is more accurate to describe the ongoing process of globalization (Castells 1996).

For example, harmony is always regarded as the goal for development. Nations are well aware of it and different methods are adopted but the effectiveness of their methods is questionable. In America, the "melting pot" concept was initiated and regarded as an important progress in putting the multi-cultural society together. However, after years of development, the American still "remain strangers to each other" (Takaki 1995, p. 173). The 1992 Los Angeles riot would be an indicator to show that racial problem could be a time bomb for our society, if it is not managed properly. In England, racial prejudice towards the Black children has alleviated attention from education authority and measures are introduced. However, they are still discriminated in school. Many of them fail in their academic study and, as a result, turn into sports as a compensation for their personal success (Partington 1985). These social problems actually host a question to the strength of globalization. On one hand, it induces an universal establishment of global consensus but also encompasses the fragmented growth of regional, racial and national experiences in this global world.

The fragmented growth of regional experience is related to the various processes involved in the global movement. For example, many international sports companies such as Nike, Reebok and Rawlings Sporting Goods Co. have established their manufacturing plants in many developing countries such as Thailand, South Korea and Mexico. They sought for an export-process strategy from these off-shore bases because of their cheap labor, favorable tax abatements and sub-normal safety and environmental standards. Their products were then sold back to America and Europe and markets in those developing countries (Sage 1994). Moving plants to the developing countries provided a way to boost their profit. However, for American workers and their communities and even workers of the developing countries, a huge hidden social cost was entailed. Firstly, the increasing rate of suicide, alcoholism, domestic violence and family breakup in America are directly linked to the stress arising from unemployment when plants are closed to off-shore base because of their globalization strategy in production. Many people are unable to find new employment despite the expanding of American economy. Millions of American workers lost their job as a result of the relocation of production to low-wage nations such as South Korea, Mexico and Thailand.

For the developing countries, a chorus of protest in response to unjust and inhuman working condition, sexual exploitation, social disruption and distorted economic development is commonly heard (Sage 1994). Although cooperation and friendship are often claimed, the benefit of globalization is being abased by exploitation, domination and colonization. It creates a dependent economy where the global system is characterized with a pattern of unequal flow of partnership and relationship between the developed and developing countries (Maguire 1993). Despite globalization, Blacks remains

Blacks, Chinese remains Chinese and Japanese remains Japanese. It seems that there is a natural drift towards diversity development. Although globalization tends toward universal development, it cannot extinguish local practice and establishment.

These phenomena highlight a number of objections to the viewpoint of Kerr et al. (1960) that "industrialization will eventually lead us all to a common society where ideology will cease to matter" (p. 12). It is because convergent processes are covered with puzzled scenery which sometimes goes against any deal of cooperation and understanding. Globalization is a convergent process that creates dependent structures within our global system. Within this system, nations are held together because of different interests but the interests are conglomerated by force, coercion and subtle manipulation. The concern of the leaders is more often on the distribution and use of power than the promotion of common values and natural integration (Coakley 1996). Although some of the countries may benefit from this conglomerated structure, the overall gap between the developed and developing countries keeps widening (Sage 1994).

The movement of cultural products, knowledge and invention from one society to another is unavoidable and undeniable but it does not necessarily lead to the creation of a common society which is covered with same attitudes, thinking, expectations and behaviors. Ours is a diversified world with different colors and practice. Each individual is a product of their social setting and all human are captives of their culture. Thus, it is common for us to interpret the behaviors of others according to our own social background rather than their own. Often misunderstandings arise since we tend to assume other's behavior will be much the same as our own and interpret the others culture as if they are the same as ours (Hall and Hall, 1994). Culture and ethnicity are always the primary determinant of the meanings we apply to all the stimuli (Samovar & Porter 1995; Snyder & Spreitzer 1989; Takaki 1995). And there is no exception to the modern sports development.

Modern sports development becomes more standardized than before through the influence of international sports associations, the similarly of sports education content at schools and the control of commercialized activities, international sports competition and festivals. Yet we must also acknowledge the effects of social and cultural factor during its process of development. Modern sport is also a cultural product in which different cultures have different sports practice. Even though they are in an international sports festival, they still "Think Globally but Act Locally" (Renson 1997). The many soccer matches between the French, German and British have not lead to the lessening of hostility between their fans. Football, for example, can become one of the most important expressions of collective cultural identity which is more than just an uniformed game showed on TV (Galeano 1997). The

Olympic spirit of cooperation is being dissipated before racism, nationalism, commercialism or ethnicity (Lucas 1984a; 1984b). Modern sport is a showcase of different and diversified experience because this is a decade with mixed experience and thinking in between. On one hand, this is a global village that no country is an island. On the other, the reaction to globalization is to bolster diversified practice so as to develop national dignity before this common world. Nevertheless, the success of the diversified and localized experience relies on how the cultural properties are synthesized within the global development. The aim of this paper is to investigate how such processes can best be synthesized and to consider the strategies as adopted for the diversified growth of our modern sport experience in this global village.

Strategy one - functional perspective - purposive selection of the function of modern sports

According to this perspective, each part of society performs certain functions for the society as a whole. Although all the parts are independent to each other but their relationship is bounded by a network of choice and mutual exchange. Sport, as one of the parts of society, performs certain social function and meaning to the society. Its influence and relationship to other parts of society is related to the behavior of playing, choice of practice, cultural values, meaning and function to any person and society. Diversified sport experiences occur because there is no fix pattern of choice between nations. It is subject to the needs of a society and how the needs are synthesized into the national, social and cultural practice.

For example, when Korean was under the Japanese colonial rule, they were looking at the intrinsic value of the sport games. They started a war of resistance with the Japanese, not on the street but in the gymnasium and their weapon was a basketball. Their victory in the 1936, 1938, 1939 and 1940 All-Japan Basketball Tournament were vital to the national development of the Korean during the colonial period because sport served as a means of national integration and it built "people's consciousness of togetherness" (Lever 1988, p. 86). Although sport was promoted as a means of enhancing health and fitness, it was also a means to tie the people together and inculcate certain key social values (Wagner 1989). For Koreans during the colonial time, sport competition was seen as a direct confrontation between Koreans and Japanese, but it was a war fare without weapons.

Mulling (1989) believed that these victories spurred Korean nationalism. It is because national prestige can be enhanced by victories in the international sporting arena and each sport performance can influence a nation's image and each success may increase national vitality, strength and development. Such perceived benefits undoubtedly formed part of the motivators for many former communist and developing countries to enter international competition, particularly the Olympic Games (Bennett et al. 1983). Assisting nation building is also the ambition that motivates many Asian countries and cities like Hong Kong, Taiwan and Japan to establish sports' schools and scientific institutes specifically for the development of elite athletes (Speak 1991). For many Asian countries, the progress development of sport and politics are intertwined and sport education serves as the means of attaining national goals. Sport then is a commodity that benefits the nation because sport carries special functions and meanings.

For some societies, sport has taken on a strong competitive nature, while others are likely to be less competitive (Riordan 1993). The selective nature helps to construct and develop different sports behavior. Sport was seen in many former communist states as a product of bourgeois culture. Sports events were intended to help break down resistance to official recognition of the Soviet state and help to give it legitimacy in the eyes of the Western nations (Peppard 1988). In China, it was recorded that Den Xiaoping used sport as a tool to improve the country's image through achievements in international competitions. He and his administration believed that success in sports was an important contributor to obtaining greater international recognition (Hoberman 1987; Luo 1995). For the Western states, contemporary sport, such as American football and European soccer express those industrial societies' competitive and aggressive features in their stress on mainly physical proficiency and strength and individual fame and prosperity (Krawczyk 1996).

Such motives of participation transfer the functions of sport from the primary focus of play, leisure and physical improvement to an expression of a participant's individual personality as well as the fundamental aspirations of the nation. Sport is then turned into a symbol of ideology, utopia, ethnic, art form and a sacred cultural element for an individual and nation to follow. The various theoretical and social viewpoints on sports decorate the homogeneous-nature of sport rules with a diversified structure. Sport is then transformed from a matter of emotional enjoyment through simple participation to the development of diversified experiences through a purposive, selective and rational decision making process. Because of the differing emphases, sport does not stand as a homogeneous product that applies equally in all nations but exhibits with diversified functions and meanings in different tribal villages. It is because nations stress on its function selectively and purposively. As a consequence sport globalization turns into a myth and the actual practice of the myth in different nation is colored with diversified sports functions and experience.

Strategy two - hybridized perspective

Heider (1983) described a programme initiated by the Indonesian Government
to change the Dani minority into proper Indonesians. Although the Dani
children adopted the introduced game, they adapted it and translated the
game from Javanese to Dani. Heider (1983) concluded that

> *"... play was part of culture and consistent with the rest.*
> *... a game which was totally inconsistent with a culture would have a*
> *hard time. If it did not actually alter the culture, it would be rejected or*
> *itself altered (p. 497). "*

In the transmission and adaptation of a game to a culture, the game
undergoes a process of change that is being examined by the intellectual,
emotional, cultural and physical factors of a society. This is a form of
challenge and the consequence of it may leads to the development of a new
game or new sport behavior especially when there are lacking of rewarding
experiences. Actually, the extinction of any game is related with continued
failure, criticism, embarrassment and other forms of negative reinforcement
(Snyder & Spreitzer 1989). However, when a person is able to make a free
choice, the individual can either decide on an active involvement or withdrawal
from the game. For the Dani, they could not resist the "foreign invention"
because it is part of their national policy. They choose to alter it so that the
game is well suited to the needs of their society.

A similar experience happened in Japan when American occupied their
territory after the World War II. After her defeat, Japan was forced to accept
social reform during this period. Sports education in school adopted a more
humanistic approach (Hardman 1996). Western sports are taught and the
Japanese students are encouraged to choose their own choice. The changing
pattern of participation does not mean that the Japanese are going to lose her
cultural way of practice. Although the students are free to choose their sport,
their choices are related to their cultural practice. They are still required 'to
behave as part of the club, to accept the social norm shared within the
members explicitly, rather than to behave as an individual who has one's own
opinion and principles of behavior' (Ichimura 1989, p. 128). In Japan, it is very
rare to hear differing opinions among students, and their social norms require
them to seek for group homogeneity. Such group behavior is also an evident
in the daily life of Japanese (Ichimura 1989). Although western sports
education was borrowed, it was still not independent of its cultural and social
environment. Cultural factors reshaped it so that a new kind of sport behavior
emerged which was decorated with Japanese tradition over Western sport
games (Ichimura 1989).

American football is another classic example where the players reinvented the game so that it exhibited with unique forms of American culture. This is a common strategy when a particular game is adapted to a society. Games, although adopted, are reinvented and adapted to fit our own personal needs and cultural identity (Renson 1997). Diversity paradoxically arises from a convergent process.

Strategy three - rationalization and legitimization

For those sports which exceed a nation's tolerance, one possible strategy is to minimize its effects by rationalizing the sport activities through the process of reinventing, renaming and redefining. As a consequence, an intrinsic sport practice is legitimized within the cultural and social practice. For example, equality in sports is commonly cited by many European countries as a landmark of their social modernity. However, different values are established where in rural Greece, the participation in sports activities by women in a public arena is prohibited. They are expected to fulfill a strict feminine roles and participate only in approved public and religious activities (Harahousou 1989). Dishonor occurs when they transcend their domestic limits or do not exhibit an appropriate feminine manner (Petronoti 1980). Even in the urban cities, public places are unsafe for women and men still exercise their control over places where women are allowed to (Deem 1987). Women constrain their lives by behaving in accordance with certain expectations which are embedded within their daily routine and, as a result, seen a less constrained experience in the fields of sport and leisure (Harahousou 1989; Petronoti 1980). Such practice is justified by stressing the importance of the "sacred" mother and that sexuality must be captured and regulated so as to prevent any harm to society.

Actually, sports equality is a common ideal for this modern world but it seldom overcomes the dominance of masculinity culture, elitism and nationalistic sentiments. The issues of equality, elitism, nationalism and masculinity sport culture have been well canvassed (Evans & Davies 1993). Equality usually loses out to masculine culture, elitism and nationalistic sentiments (Katz 1996). Thus, China legitimizes the key point schools by citing social needs as their justification. Children subsequently receive a prescribed education that encourages them to sustain sexist, racist and elitist attitudes. Japan adopted a strong militaristic emphasis in their sports programmes during wartime. Sport reinforced nationalism by focusing attention on elitism and competitiveness. In England, the compulsory PE curriculum has often been skewed in favor of the physically talented. Pedagogical practices favor the privilege access for certain groups while oppressing and alienating others. The teaching of PE in England has not been a neutral activity and has benefited most those who are strong, fast and physically able (Thomas 1993).

The selective nature gradually transfers any global trend with other meanings. With the process of rationalization, there is a gradual adaptation of a calculating attitude towards certain aspects. Through the process of legitimization, sport practice is being synthesized into the social practice. The final outcome is the creation of a diversified sport experience towards any global trend of development. The consequence is the turning of a convergent experience into an ideal and diversified practice is what it really creates.

A concluding remark

In this modern world mass sport culture is characterized by convergent experience. The origins of such a process are hard to identify but there is no doubt that colonization marks one of the major causes. It is furthered by modern media and information technology to the point where the mass sport experience becomes a reality. Nevertheless, such a process is usually fragmented, disjointed and discontinuous. Although TV and global commercial activities tend to synchronize the development of popular sport culture, it is a two-dimensional context only. It becomes a three-dimensional experience after each nation processes the materials to suit their own cultural and national values. No nation is able to escape its background or entirely free itself from national bias. Diversified sport experience is the developmental trend that undermines a global collective identity. Sport globalization is a myth, an illusion and a misconception. In reality, we inhabit a world of heterogeneous and ever-changing pattern that provokes the development of an innovative and transitory society where diversity is the norm and practice.

The convergent hypothesis assumes that "industrialization will eventually lead us all to a common society" (Kerr et al. 1960, p. 12) and modern developments in communication and technology seems to provide strong evidence for such an assumption. Such an assumption suggests that nations will be drawn together into a common modernity when they are given sufficient time for the diffusion of technology, transfer of capital and the training of labor. However, such a notion misunderstands and miscalculates the impact of local factors that are unique to every nation. It is these differences that draw nations apart even if they actively borrow foreign ideas for development. They choose to accept some but decorated them with their emphases so as to establish internal harmony, consistency and congruity along with their national needs. The foreign materials are adapted and modified to meet local needs. As far as sport development is concerned, the convergent process as created through colonization or other electronic, commercial and international means does not necessarily lead to the creation of a common sport society. However, it has profound effects on the diversified growth of our social and national sport experience in our global village.

References

Biggs, A. (1994). The media and sport in the global village. In Wilcox, R.C. (ed.), Sport in the global village. Fitness Information Technology, INC., 5-20.

Benett, B.L., Howell, M.L. & Simri, U. (1983). Comparative education and sport. Lee and Febiger.

Castells, M. (1996). The rise of the network society. Blackwell.

Coakley, J.L. (1996). Sport in society: an inspiration or an opiate? In Eitzen, D.S (ed.), Sport in contemporary society, an anthology (5th ed.). St. Martins Press, 32-49.

Deem, R. (1987). The politics of women's leisure. In Horne, J. et al. (ed.): Sport, leisure and social relations. London: Routledge and Kegan Paul, 210-228.

Evans, J. & Dvies, B. (1993). Equality, equity and physical education. In Evans, J. (ed.), Equality, education and physical education. Falmer Press, 11-27.

Galeano, E. (1997). Football myth and reality (Paper presented at the international press seminar on Sport, Media and Civil Society; Vingsted, Demark), June.

Goonatilake, S. (1995). The self wandering between cultural localization and globalization. In Pieterse, J.N. & Parekkh, B. (eds.), The decolonization of imagination, culture, knowledge and power. Zed Book Ltd. 225 238.

Hall, E.T. & Hall, E. (1994). How cultures collide. In Weaver, G.R. (ed.), Culture, communication and conflict. Simon and Schuster Custom Publishing, 5-14.

Hrahousou -Kabitsi, Y.E. (1989). Sociocultural influences on women's participation in physical recreation in Greece. Unpublished Ph.D thesis, Department of Sport and Exercise Science, University of Birmingham.

Hardman, K. (1996). Physical and sporting activity in international and cross-cultural context: diversity or congruence? (Paper presented at the 10th ISCPES Conference; Tokyo, Japan), August.

Heider, K. (1983). From Javanese to Dani: the translation of a game. In Harris, J.C. & Park, R.J. (eds.), Play, games and sports in cultural context. Human Kinetics , 491-501.

Hoberman, J. (1987). Sport and social change: the transformation of Maoist sport. Sociology of Sport Journal, 4, 156-170.

Ichimura, S. (1989). Metamorphoses of western sport in the Japanese education system. In Fu, F.H., Ng, M.L. & Speak, M. Comparative physical education and sport Vol.6. Physical Education Unit, The Chinese University of Hong Kong. Condor Publication Ltd., 127-131.

Katz, J. (1966). Masculinity and sports culture. In Lapchick, R.E. (ed.). Sport in society, equal opportunity or business as usual. Sage Publications.,101-106.

Kerr, C., Dunlop, J.T., Harbison, F.H. & Myers, C.A. (1960). Industrialism and industrialize man: the problems of labor and management in economic growth, London: Heinemann.

Krawczyk, Z. (1996). Sport as symbol. International Review for the Sociology of Sport, 31, 429-435.

Lever, J. (1988). Sport in a fractured society: Brazil under military rule. In Arbena, J.L. (ed.). Sport and society in Latin America. Westpoint, Conn.: Greenwood Press.

Lucas, J. (1984). The survival of the Olympic Idea. JOPERD, January, 29; 32.

Lucas, J. (1984). No more amateurs - only nonprofessional athletes at the Olympic Games. JOPERD, February, 22-23.

Luo, P. (1995). Political Influence on physical education and sport in the People's Republic of China. International Review for the Sociology of Sport, 30, 47-57.

Maguire, J. (1993). Globalization, sport development, and the media/sport production complex. Sport Science Review, 2(1), 29-47.

Mulling, C. (1989). Sport in South Korea: Ssirum, the YMCA, and the Olympic Games. In Wagner, E.A. (ed.). Sport in Asia and Africa - a comparative handbook. Greenwood Press, 83-99.

Partington, G. (1985). Blacks, sport and schools. ACHPER, June, 18-21.

Peppard, V. (1988). A comparative analysis of early East-West sport diplomacy. In Broom, F., Clumpner, R., Pendleton, B. & Pooley, C.A. (eds.). Comparative physical education and sport Vol. 5. Human Kinetics, 149-155.

Petronoti, M. (1980). The economic autonomy of rural women: a survey of the Mediterranean with specific reference to three Greek islands. University of Kent at Canterbury.

Renson, R. (1997). The reinvention of tradition in sports and games. Journal of Comparative Physical Education and Sport, 19(2), 46-52.

Riordan, J. (1993). Sport in capitalist and socialist countries: a western perspective. In Dunning, E., Maguire, J. & Pearton, R. (eds.). The sports process: a comparative and developmental approach. Human Kinetics, 245-264.

Sage, G.H. (1994). Deindustralization and the American Sporting Goods Industry. In Wilcox, R.C. (ed.). Sport in the global village. Fitness Information Technology, INC., 39-51.

Samovar, L.A. & Porter, R.E. (1995). Communication between cultures (2nd ed.). Wadsworth Publishing Co.

Snyder, E.E. & Spreitzer, E.A. (1989). Social aspects of sport (3rd ed.). Prentice Hall.

Speak, M. (1991). A comparative study of three centers of excellence in East Asia. In Standeven, J., Hardman; K. & Fisher, D. (eds.). Sport for All: into the 90s, comparative PE and sport Vol.7. Meyer and Meyer Verlag,181-190.

Takaki, R. (1995). Culture war in the United States: closing reflections on the century of the color line. In Pieterse, J.N. & Parekkh, B. (eds.). The decolonization of imagination, culture, knowledge and power. Zed Book Ltd. 166-176.

Thoms, S. (1993). Education reform: juggling the concepts of equality and elitism. In Evans, J. (ed.). Equality, education and physical education. Falmer Press, 105-124.

Wagner, E.A. (1989). An overview of sport in Asia and Africa. In Wagner, W.A. (ed.). Sport in Asia and Africa – a comparative handbook. Greenwood, 3-11.

Chapter 6

Fitness as cultural phenomenon

Karin A.E. Volkwein
West Chester University, U.S.A.

During the last two decades, the influence of sport and the quest for physical fitness has grown tremendously in the Western world. According to a recent survey, Americans annually spend more than $10 billion on health and fitness products (Lellnes & Nation 1996). "The proliferation of exercise equipment and fitness facilities and the emergence of personal trainer and home gym have generated a new vocabulary of fitness terms and greater public awareness of the importance of exercise" (Bryant & McElroy 1997). The popular success of televised sports and the ever increasing participation of men and women of all ages in organized and unorganized sport and fitness activities attest this importance. This development has led to changes in the relationship between sport/fitness and society; it has also brought into focus the relationship of body and culture. There are many indications that changes in the area of sport or physical culture, including fundamental forms of human movement and physical activity, go hand in hand with changes in the way of life in highly industrialized societies (Coakley 1990).

Although culture is experienced personally, it represents a shared system, "a program for behavior" (Hall & Hall 1990). Traditions, values, and world views differ from culture to culture.
Culture is an ever changing process, which crosses national boundaries. Individual differences within each culture are reflected by race, ethnicity, gender, social class, education, and personality. In the United States and Germany, for example, regional differences have their own "mini-cultures." Furthermore, as a result of migration and globalization (or more specifically Westernization), cultural values and traditions are shared, exchanged, changed, and transformed. Thus, within a given country numerous cultures can be represented and exist simultaneously.

The fitness movement can be described as a phenomenon that is experienced primarily by a select group of people from a particular social class (middle and upper middle class). Income, gender, age, race and ethnicity have also been identified as variables that determine who is participating in fitness activities and why they are participating. Reasons for the rise of fitness movement are culture specific as well as global or transnational. A cross-cultural comparison of two advanced nations with close historical links, here Germany and the USA, will shed light onto the complexity of the issue. This investigation is based on the premise that the fitness movement, although a globalized phenomenon, is still rooted in the context of specific cultural codes and meaning.

Definition of terms

Fitness and health

The scientific literature in kinesiology (performance and human movement related sciences) distinguishes between two forms of physical fitness, one related to health and the other to performance. In this paper I will focus more on the relationship of fitness to health. The concept of fitness not only refers to exercise and its effects, but also to the general state of a person's psychophysical well-being (Glassner 1990, 216). Although some fitness enthusiasts distinguish between fitness and health, in everyday usage the two words have become generally synonymous. Both terms incorporate exercise, diet, lifestyle, and more (see definition by U.S. Department of Health and Human Services 1996).

Fitness and health also reflect the underlying concept that both are essential to the development of individuals, for the soma as well as the psyche (Uhlenbruck 1992). Indeed, both are associated with the quality of life, with life satisfaction and fulfillment, as well as the ecological and social parameters of each individual. That is, fitness and health are major determinants of how well people master their lives and adapt to new situations and requirements.

Cultural variations of the term sport

The word "sport" is derived from the Latin *deportare* , which means to divert. In the *German* language, the term "sport" has an all-inclusive meaning, incorporating a variety of human movements, including sport, recreation and leisure activities, as well as exercise and physical fitness. The term sport is used in the broadest sense of human movement and exercise. In *North America*, on the other hand, the term sport is generally used only in reference to competitive sporting endeavors. Other forms of human movement and exercise have their specific terminology, i. e. fitness or health exercise, leisure and recreational activities, dance, play, games, etc. Thus, the concept of sport in the North American context is essentially much narrower and only used when the main objective is competition.

Historical roots of the fitness phenomenon

To understand the fitness movement, one should examine its historical roots. Originally, *fitness* - although the term was created much later - was regarded as being "fit for fighting." In different time periods as well as different countries physical fitness has always been an important component for the military. In order to provide national security and fight in the wars, young men (today, also women) had to be strong and fit to defend their countries. Thus, fitness was seen as a useful tool for serving political purposes.

In the 18th century an important fitness movement was started by "Turnvater Jahn" (Friedrich Ludwig Jahn 1778-1852) in Germany. This movement later spread to other European countries and the USA. Although Jahn's ideas of *turnen* and fitness were still connected to the physical fitness ideals of the military, fun and enjoyment were new components added - as exemplified in the slogan *"frisch, fromm, froehlich, frei"* (fresh, pious, happy, free). Also, for the first time, women had access to these sporting activities called *turnen* and were allowed to improve their physical fitness levels.

A new understanding of fitness became associated with industrialization. This perspective connected physical fitness with work and an increase in productivity. Workers were expected to keep in shape so that they could perform better and stay healthy. Employers began to support worker's sports clubs much like the military incorporated fitness training at the work place. And the Third Reich exploited fitness during WW II by promoting ideas such as *"fit fuer den Krieg"* (fit for the war, or better 'funeral').

Another shift in the meaning associated with fitness developed after World War II. Physical fitness now was believed to positively enhance the quality of life for the individual. The focus was to derive pleasure and enjoyment from engaging in fitness and other sporting activities, which in return will benefit not only the physical aspects of a person, e.g. a more pleasurable sex life, but also the social and psychological well-being.

While the previous fitness movements were dictated and supported from the outside, e.g. the military, national leaders, and employers, it could be argued that this new fitness development is driven by the individuals from within. This might be a major reason why this latest fitness movement has been much more influential than its predecessors and is on the brink of becoming a "global" cultural phenomenon.

Today, individuals themselves assume responsibility for their health and well-being, partly because the costs of treating an illness are not fully paid by health insurances any longer. People engage in various activities to enhance the quality of life, to stay healthy, fit, youthful and attractive. Fitness now is marketed as means of achieving these goals and aspirations. As can be expected, the social and personal pressures to stay fit, healthy, beautiful, and thin (that go along with this fitness ideology) have had some detrimental effects as well. An increase in eating disorders and the rise of dangerous and unnecessary cosmetic surgery are only some of these consequences affecting both men and women. However, women have disproportionately been distressed more than men, as women traditionally have faced more pressure to adhere to certain beauty standards and body ideals (for further details see McConatha, Pfister, Behm in Volkwein 1998).

These changes in the way of life are directly related to the socio-economic developments of the latter part of the twentieth century. For example, the enormous progress in the medical sciences have effected large segments of the population in both the USA and Germany. However, not everyone has been able to benefit from these advancements. National leaders again are interested in the health and well-being of their people. Fitness has become a vital part in keeping overall health care expenditures down. Consequently, this latest fitness movement may be characterized by an overlapping of national, economic and personal interests.

The development of the various meanings of fitness accumulated during the period of the Third Reich, where military power, labor power and "power through joy" *(Kraft durch Freude)* reflected the fatal hegemony of the Third Reich. Today's fitness ideology is characterized by "joy through power" (e.g. in body building, (see chapters by Klein and Bolin in Volkwein 1998). People who do not fit the current body and fitness ideals, that is being fit, beautiful, and muscular (muscular *and* thin for females), become marginalized. They become second class citizens, whose accomplishments do not get the same recognition (e.g. being selected for a job), - much like Jessie Owens when his accomplishments during the 1936 Olympics in Berlin were not recognized by Hitler because he did not represent the Arian ideal. Thus, one could argue that an overemphasis on fitness to these extremes does not represent a *cultural* phenomenon but rather stands for "anti-culture," where the non-fit are discriminated against.

The current fitness movement with its positive and negative contributions represents the ethos of life in highly industrialized societies. Like other social phenomena in the post-modern world fitness is characterized by contradictions. For example, on one hand, one could argue that fitness can pave the way to emancipation, - as music, oral and written language, as well as cinema have done in the past -, and on the other hand, fitness is simply another form of hegemonic social practice.

This cross-cultural analysis of the fitness movement in Germany and North America (see Volkwein 1998) sheds light on the complex development of human movement culture, its export and import during the time of global expansion of Western values and traditions. However, it is important to acknowledge that the contemporary fitness movement is not a world-wide phenomenon - not yet - and not everyone is participating - only a select class of people. The fitness phenomenon is a production of the so-called Western world, unique to industrialized societies. The fitness phenomenon, as we know it today, has its roots in the USA. Many people associate Kenneth Cooper as the "father of the modern fitness movement" that started in the USA in the late 60s. One could argue that from there it has been imported into other highly industrialized nations, such as Germany.

It is important to analyze the fitness movement in its country of origin with its specific values and cultural dimensions. This movement has not only been imported to Germany, but rather has also undergone a specific process of adaptation, which reflects the German culture and its value system. The movement has demonstrated significant similarities and differences with each cultural adaptation; however, there is no doubt at the end of the 20th century that fitness has established itself as an important cultural phenomenon in the (post-)modern world.

Conditions of the (Post-)Modern

Weber characterizes modernity as the collapse of religious authority and the rise of a rationalized, bureaucratic social order with increased specialization. In *The Protestant Ethic and the Spirit of Capitalism (1904)* Weber observed that the whole "mighty cosmos of the modern economic order" is seen as "an iron cage." Marx, Nietzsche, Kierkegaard, Tocqueville, Mill and other great thinkers have further extrapolated on the forces that modern technology and social organizations exert over humankind. "But they all believed that modern individuals had the capacity both to understand this fate and, once they understood it, to fight it" (Berman 1988, p. 27).

Twentieth century social critics, on the other hand, seem to lack this empathy and faith in a better tomorrow. For example, Herbert Marcuse describes in *The One-Dimensional Man* (1964) that the masses have no egos, no ids, their souls are devoid of inner tension or dynamism: their ideas, their needs, even their dreams, are "not their own"; their inner lives are "totally administered," programmed to produce exactly those desires that the social system can satisfy. "The people recognize themselves in their commodities; they find their soul in their automobiles, hi-fi sets, split-level homes, kitchen equipment" (Marcuse 1964, p. 9). Here modern men and women are described as objects, as "beings without spirit, without heart, without sexual and personal identity, ... without being" (Berman, p. 27). Berman characterizes this lost hope of people as the postmodern condition.[1]

The result of modernity, the post-modern condition, is not necessarily more happiness for people but rather a loss of control over nature, which is characterized by the occurrence and increase of health problems such as heart disease, cancer, AIDS, and more. The disappointments associated with modern culture started to be expressed in America in the 60s, in the arts and in leftist politics. The fitness movement which followed in the 70s is described by Glassner (1990) as a reaction by the general public "to disengage the negative effects of life in modern culture" (p. 219). This reaction is described as an attempt by the individuals, mainly people from the middle and upper class, to counterbalance the deficiencies of the modern era. An interpretation of this trend may be that given that people have lost the hope to change the social conditions, they are focusing inward to change themselves and their bodies.

As societies change so does the role of the body[2], which today is becoming a source for happiness and a provider for meaning in people's lives. We are bombarded daily with countless images of idealized bodies on television, in newspapers, magazines, and billboards. "[These images] channel capital and serve as a common resource for judging the adequacy of self and others" (Glassner 1990, p. 215). Cultural economy arguments (see Featherstone et al. 1991), which state that the economy can simply not afford the increase in health expenditure due to sedentary life style, where bodies become commodities, will not get to the heart of the fitness furor. It is true that a general commodification of society and the bodies within it has taken place; but the question, "why fitness", still remains to be answered.

The end of the 20th century is characterized by de-colonization and de-Europeanization of the world; the complex process of post-traditional and post-national identification has given rise to the modern fitness movement. Traditional hierarchies and status based on income and education has been extended to the body. We are living in a world of body culture, where the body and taking care of one's body make a social statement (see Gebauer and Penz in Volkwein 1998). As major determinators for shaping the body, exercise and fitness activities have become means to acquire social status.

The concept of fitness is "sold" to the American people in many ways, not only in relation to improving the health status of the population. Fitness promises range from general health improvement, to relief of stress and depression, and the achievement of happiness in life. Fitness is also said to offer an intimate and holistic marriage between the self and the body. The body is experienced as an important dimension of the self. The physique becomes a sign of the self in a way that fashion and cosmetics no longer can. Fitness enthusiasts turn inward and avoid social problems (Glassner 1990, p. 225). The fitness movement can be described as a personal response to the aspirations and failings of modernist culture. Values and value changes are an important part of this development.

Value changes and the rise of the fitness movement

Research on changes in values in middle class adults (20-50) asserts that the public's emphasis has shifted from more socially oriented values, e.g. equality or national security, to personal values such as freedom, comfort, and excitement (Inglehart 1985). This shift indicates a change from materialistic to post-materialistic values. Klages, et al. (1992) state that the value change is characterized by processes of individualization; they acclaim value changes due to the process of 'functional differentiation of modern industrialized societies.' That is, Klages, et al. explain value change not as much as a shift but rather as an expansion, as 'value pluralism' (see also Tetlock 1986). Thus, the traditional value orientation does not vanish, it is extended. The 'old' achievement ethic is loosing its significance. 'Post-industrialized society' is described by Klages, et al. as one with decreasing achievement ethics, increasing expectations of the state, and an increased orientation and interest in leisure activities.

Value changes can be attributed to the increasing process of secularization that occurred after WW II: the rise in the standard of living, the resulting increase in consumption, the relative freedom of choice of behavior, the increased mobility, the expansion of the educational system, the ecological problems, the changes in family structures, the extended use and influence of mass media, as well as a number of other factors (see Digel 1986, pp. 25-29). Politics, economics, and personal values are all inextricably linked.

Changes in the ways in which sport, physical fitness, and health are perceived are a reflection of changes in society - in a microscopical dimension. New offerings in the movement culture are described as a reflection of dramatic value changes (Heinemann 1989). Changing values in sport are identified by Digel (1986) as part of the general process of value change in society, especially in the area of leisure. Society and the subsystem, sport, have an inter-relationship: society influences the world of sport (- e.g. through an increase in leisure time) and sport influences society (- e.g. through body worship, fitness, and new body ideals).

The following value changes that are characteristic for post-modern USA are also relevant for the furor of the fitness movement[3]. According to Schulze (1992), people in modern societies direct their actions toward the potentially challenging experiences or "thrilling" feedback an action may provide

(*Erlebnischarakter*). That is, the decision for or against a certain action is not simply determined by its pragmatic character or durability, but rather by the adventure (*Erlebnis/Abenteuer*) that goes with the action. For example, millions of "Sport 4x4" cars and off-road vehicles have been sold in the last 10 years to Americans and Germans because of the association with adventure, but very few people take these cars off the highway.

Furthermore, modern society is increasingly characterized by the process of secularization, where traditional religious values are losing their significance. That is not to say that people are not interested in religion anymore; rather an increasing number of members of the middle and upper middle classes are searching for meaning providers outside traditional religions. Elsewhere, I have argued that sport, including fitness activities, have often become the "new religion of the new world" (see Volkwein 1997). The place and function of religion increasingly becomes replaced by worldly endeavors, such as the focus on the body: "the body as heaven."

People's daily activities are often focused on the present, a subjective sense of happiness, satisfaction through a sense of adventure, and the maximization of excitement and exhilaration. Sport provides people a promise of such experiences; and therefore, it has gained importance as a provider of meaning in people's lives through their bodies. The question arises as to how people in modern societies solve their existential problems. They may focus on the body as a source of satisfaction and happiness. Rittner/Mrazek (1986) characterize this phenomenon as *Glück aus dem Körper* (happiness through/from the body).

One of the most important problems of people in contemporary societies is their concern for health. Since the focus on the here and now (rather than the afterlife) has gained more importance, people are striving to live a comfortable and fulfilling life.   This development is also related to the increasing automation and technological advancement, which resulted in a decrease of bodily labor and human movement in general. Thus, people in advanced societies need some kind of physical compensation in order to balance their rather inactive life style. If they fail to get it, they are more likely to develop health problems, such as obesity, heart and bone structure diseases, and more. Health has become a precious commodity. The responsibility for one's health and well-being has become focused on the individual. People turn to the various forms of sport and exercise in order to take better care of themselves.   Thus, programs that are offered in health and fitness studios have become extremely popular in the USA since the 70s and in Germany since the 80s.

Although the positive relationship between an active lifestyle and healthy living has been well documented for quite some time, sport/exercise just recently has experienced a tremendous boom in the areas of health promotion and illness prevention (see US. Department of Health and Human Services 1996). Today, health seems to be commodified in various forms, not only in health/fitness studios, but also in drug stores, hospitals, health and grocery stores, and more. Sport and exercise have become a catapult for health. Thus, the development of sport and fitness activities in highly industrialized societies is directly related to the quest for health. That is, sport has lost its unity and its primary focus on competition. Rather, the general social processes of differentiation have also influenced the world of sport leading to a variety of diverse offerings in the area of physical activity. The focus of contemporary "sport" has expanded from a traditional focus on competition to an emphasis on enjoyment, fitness and health, rehabilitation, prevention, and adventure, as well as to help cope with disabilities. The majority of physically active people today engage in the various activities for health and fitness reasons (Rittner 1994).

The changes in human movement culture in modern societies are reflected in greater differentiation. New dimensions in the areas of rehabilitation, leisure, adventure, fitness and relaxation have been developed; new sports such as jogging, aerobics, walking, bungy jumping, hang gliding, surfing, and body building have been created; and engagement in sport activities today serves as meaning provider in people's lives. The traditional achievement principle, *citius - altius - fortius* (faster, higher, further), governing mainly top-level sport, is substituted for fun, fitness, health and happiness.

Lifestyle changes are directly linked to a different interpretation of health and the body. New body ideals have been formed. Since the 70s, the ideal body image is one of being fit, sporty, young, dynamic, and so on. In highly industrialized societies, where physical labor becomes more and more obsolete, the body becomes suppressed and the mind becomes elevated. At the same token, almost paradoxical, bodily behavior becomes more important. Goffman (1974) in this regard speaks of the "best self" people aspire to, which includes the perfect body, e.g. no bodily odors, no dandruff, no hair on female legs. This movement can even be characterized as a clinical fight against the body's natural functions. What is interesting about this shift in the body ideal is that now people are using their body to represent the self. The ideal of the fit, slim, dynamic body represents a revolution in dealing with the body.

Conclusion

Given the social and cultural context of physical activity, modern human movement can best be understood from a multi-disciplinary perspective. In the book *Fitness as Cultural Phenomenon*, Volkwein (1998) and contributors aim to explain the role sport/exercise has played in society; how the opportunities of engaging in sports have varied from one group to another; how sport/exercise reflects the interests and values of the participants in their culture; when and how sport can be used as a catalyst for change in society as a whole. A phenomenon such as the fitness movement can not be explained using empirical data analysis alone (see contribution by Mielke/Uhlenbruck/Volkwein), rather it has to be understood from a socio-historical and cultural perspective.

It is of vital importance to attempt to understand these social and cultural changes in order to adequately serve and address the needs, expectations, and goals of people. These changes will also impact the curricula development of sport and physical education programs, health and wellness education, as well as our body culture in general. The book *Fitness as Cultural Phenomenon* addresses these issues from a multi-disciplinary as well as a cross-cultural perspective. The social sciences - history, philosophy and sociology - are integrated with the natural sciences, such as medicine, behavioral and cognitive psychology.

References

AAHPER Research Council (1996). <u>Health related physical fitness test manual</u>.

Airhihenbuwa, C. (1995). <u>Health and culture. Beyond the western paradigm</u>. Thousand Oaks.

Barney, R. (1991). "The German-American Turnverein Movement: its historiography. In R. Naul (ed.). <u>Turnen and sport - the cross-cultural exchange</u>. Muenster/New York.

Beckers, E. (1988). "Körperfassaden und Fitness-Ideologie - Wiederkehr des Körpers in der Fitness-Bewegung?" In N. Schulz & H. Allmer (eds.) <u>Fitness-Studios. Anspruch und Wirklichkeit</u>. Brennpunkte der Sportwissenschaft, 2, pp. 153-175.

Berman, M. (1988). <u>All that is solid melts in the air. The experience of modernity</u>. Harmondsworth.

Bryant, J. & McElsroy, M. (1997). <u>Sociological dynamics of sport and exercise</u>. Englewood, CO.

Bouchard, C.; Shepard, R.; Stephens, T.; Sutton, J.; McPherson, B. (eds.) (1990). <u>Exercise, fitness, and health</u>. Champaign, IL.

Coakley, J. (1994). <u>Sport in society</u>. St. Louis/Toronto/ Boston/Los Altos.

Council of Europe (no year). European Sport for All Charter.

Digel, H. (1986). Über den Wandel der Werte in Gesellschaft, Freizeit und Sport. In K. Heinemann & H. Becker (eds.). <u>Die Zukunft des Sports</u>. Schorndorf.

Featherstone, M. (1982). The body in consumer culture. Theory, Culture, and Society, 8, 18-33.

Featherstone, M., Hepworth, M. & B. Turner (1991). The body - social process and cultural theory. London.

Glassner, B (1990). Fit for post modern selfhood. In H. Becker & M. Call (eds.) Symbolic interaction and cultural studies (pp. 215-243). Chicago.

Goffman, E. (1974). Gender advertisement. New York.

Hall, E. & Hall, M. (1990). Understanding cultural differences. Germans, French, and the Americans. Yarmouth.

Heinemann, K. (1989). Der "nicht-sportliche" Sport. In K. Dietrich & K. Heinemann (Eds.). Der nicht-sportliche Sport: Beiträge um Wandel im Sport. Schorndorf.

Inglehart, R. (1977). The silent revolution. Changing values and political styles among western publics. Princeton.

Inglehart, R. (1985). Aggregate stability and individual level flux in mass belief systems: The level of analysis paradox. American Political Science Review, 79, 97-116.

Klages, H., Hippler, H.-J. & Herbert , W. (1992). Werte und Wandel. Ergebnisse und Methoden einer Forschungstradition. Frankfurt.

Lellness, A. & Nation, J. (1996). Sport psychology. Chicago.

Marcuse, H. (1964). One-dimensional man: studies in the ideology of advanced industrial society. Boston.

Postman, N. (1992). Technopoly - the surrender of culture to technology. New York.

Rittner, V. & Mrazek, J. (1986). "Neues Glück aus dem Körper." Psychologie Heute, November, 54-63.

Rittner, V. (1994). "Die 'success-story' des modernen Sports und seine Metamorphose: Fitneß, Ästhetik und individuelle Selbstdarstellung." Das Parlament, May, 3-11.

Schulze, G. (1992). Die Erlebnisgesellschaft - Kultursoziologie der Gegenwart. Frankfurt/New York.

Tetlock, P. (1986). A value pluralism model of ideoligical reasoning. Journal of Personality and Social Psychology, 50 (4), 819-827.

Turner, B. (1984). The body and society. London.

Uhlenbruck, G. (1992). Sport und Fitness - ein Leib-Seele-"Problem." Natur- und Ganzheitsmedizin, 5, 50-52.

Uhlenbruck, G. (1996). "Bewegungstraining verbessert Lebensqualität." TW Gynäkologie, 9, 345-351.

US Department of Health and Human Services (1994). Healthy People 2000 Review. Centers for Disease Control and Prevention.

U.S. Department of Health and Human Services (1996). Physical acitivity and health: a report of the surgeon general. Pittsburgh, PA: Superintendent of Documents.

Volkwein, K. (1995). Fitness in the context of the North American health and sport system. In J. Mester (ed.). Images of sport in the world - Congress Proceedings. Koeln.

Volkwein, K. (1997). "Living faith: sport - the new religion in the 'New World'." In: R. Mahlke, R. Pitzer-Reyl, & J. Süss (eds.) Living faith - Lebendige religiöse Wirklichkeit - Festschrift für Hans-Jürgen Greschat (pp. 461-470). Frankfurt/Berlin/Bern/New York/Paris/Wien.

Volkwein, K. (1998). Fitness as cultural phenomenon. Münster, New York

Weber, M. (1904). The protestant ethic and the spirit of capitalism. Translated by Taslcott Parsons in1930. Scribner.

Notes

[1] Post-modern discourse started in France in the late 1970s with Michel Foucault, Jacques Derrida, Jean-Francois Lyotard, Jean Baudrillard, and others, and established itself first as literary criticism in the 1980s in the USA.

[2] Nietzsche already remarked that the body is crucial to understanding the dilemmas of modernity.

[3] For a more detailed description of value changes in post-modern America see Volkwein (1995).

Chapter 7

Integration trend of western and eastern fitness exercises

Hai Ren
Beijing University of Physical Education, China

One of the most magnificent phenomena of our time is the spectacle of sport for all. Since 1960s this world wide movement, aimed at preventing diseases and enhancing quality of life, has quickly swept through the western industrial world and now spread over some countries in Southern America, Asia and Africa.

Undoubtedly, to deal with today's health problems the most serious attention has been given and unprecedented efforts have been made. Various measurements have been taken to increase the participation rate. A survey made nine years ago already indicated that the goal of sport for all has been formulated in 87 countries of the world. [1]

Taking a global view of the patterns of fitness exercises used by the fitness enthusiasts we can easily find that those western patterns mainly characterized as the energy consuming physical exercises like jogging, walking, swimming, circling, aerobic dancing ant others are still enjoying the greatest popularity. At the same time the number of participate in some eastern fitness exercises such as Tai Chi and Yoga has rapid increased.

It may be reasonable to ask, do these western or eastern exercises meet our needs? What exercises can best serve our purpose?

To answer these questions, we have to look at the health problems in our times first and then followed by a cross cultural study in the depth of the western and eastern fitness excises.

Today's health problems and their requirements to fitness exercises

Health is not an unchangeable concept beyond all time and space limits. health problems are always closely related to a particular natural and social environments in which a person lives. So the health problems are in a changing process along with the natural and social evolution and presented in various forms and characteristics.

All physical exercises are designed explicitly to deal with health problem so they have to be updated quite often in order to keep themselves relevant to deal with the health problems in a given social context. So before examining the validity of the exercises to be used we have to look at the dominant health risks in our days so as to make argument realistic.

Having observed the current health related problems, many specialists have pointed out that the dominate health risks are shifting rapidly from the acute diseases caused by infectious ones to the noncommunicable chronic ones associated with changed lifestyles. Indeed, the rapid and sweeping industrialization in the 20th century has tremendously changed the entire world and one of those social changes directly influenced millions of people on their daily lives is urbanization. In 1955, 68% of the global population lived in rural areas and 32% in urban areas. Forty years later in 1995 the ratio was 55% rural and 45% urban; by 2025 it will be 41% rural and 59% urban [2].

The shift from a traditional rural pattern to an "artificial world" has unprecedented impacts on the lifestyle of city dwellers, as the table 1 shows.

Table 1 : A comparison of rural and urban lifestyles

	Rural life	Urban life
	Rural life	Urban life
Environment	Natural	Artificial
habitation	Scattered	Concentrated
Energy resources	Man power and animal	Oil, electricity
Labor division	Low	High
Living rhythm	Slow	Fast
Social roles	Simple	Complex
Social competition	Lower	Higher
Inter-personal relations	Intimate	Aloof
Main health risks	Infectious and acute diseases	Noncommunicable and chronic diseases.

With this great social change, the dominant causes for ill-health are no longer the infectious diseases, but the unhealthy lifestyle accompanied with the advanced industrialization and modernization. While city dwellers have enjoyed many wonderful things they have to face serious challenges physically, mentally and socially.

Insufficient physical activities

One feature of the modern society is more and more labor works being substituted by machine, so "work and physical exertion were no longer synonymous". [3]

A study on groups of bus drivers and conductors of England in 1953 indicated the relationship between the risk of heart attack and physical activities. [4] More studies of the Cooper Clinic show the relationship between low physical fitness and poor health status [5]. In 1997 there were over 15 million deaths due to circulatory diseases, of them 7.2 million were caused by coronary heart disease, 4.6 million by stroke, 500 000 by rheumatic fever and rheumatic heart disease, and 3 million by other forms of heart disease. [6]

Mental distress

As physical activities are dropping down all sorts of mental problems have rapidly increased due to accelerating working rhythm, sophisticated social roles and tense social competition.
The World Health Organization reported in1997, more than 40 million people suffer from different types of epilepsy, an estimated 29 million people suffer from dementia; 200 000 died of it in 1996, and there were 2.6 million new cases, an estimated 45 million people are affected by schizophrenia. There were 4.5 million new cases of schizophrenia and other delusional disorders last year. Some turned to smoking, alcoholism, even drugs for help, an estimated 28 million people worldwide incur significant health risks by using psychoactive substances other than alcohol, tobacco and volatile solvents [7]. Tobacco alone is calculated to cause 3 million deaths a year mainly from lung cancer and circulatory diseases [8].

Social alienation and deviation

A industrial society, to some extent, may be referred as the society to produce, consume and pursuit material benefits, and the society in which material wealth would determine everything. The widespread materialism has led the material enjoyments over the spiritual ones, the external purposes super than the internal ones, and the material gains prior to the values of mankind itself. The very human rights and values have been suppressed. This generates considerably negative impact on one's well being as a social creature.
Being reciprocal causation, all these problematic dimensions are interwoven one another in a synthetic complex, formed big challenge to the wellness of human beings in our times. Consequently, the World Health Organization correctly defines the term, Health, as "*a state of complete physical, mental and social well-being and not merely the absence of disease or infirmity*" [9].
The conceptual development of health and the inability of the conventional medical means in dealing with today's health problems set up a much higher goal and difficult tasks for today's fitness exercises, requiring them to play more comprehensive active roles in health promotion movement, not only physically but also mentally and socially. The goals are explicit and urgent. However, neither the western fitness exercises nor their eastern counterparts alone can meet today's fitness requirements due to their inherent limits.

Comparison of western and eastern fitness exercises

Comparing the fitness exercises like jogging, swimming, circling, aerobic dance, which are enjoyed the greatest popularity in the western world and Qi-Gong and Yoga, the typical eastern fitness we will be interested in seeing that these two categories follow quite different philosophic ideas as well as practical methods in dealing with the health problems.

Physical versus mental

It is true that all fitness activities involve both the physical and mental aspects, but they treat the two fundamental dimensions often differently due to different understandings of the body and mind (soul) and their interrelationships.

In general, the Western fitness exercises focus directly on the physical side of the human being and correspondingly to emphasize on muscular movement, especially the vigorous ones. What the fitness exercises work on, to the western thinking, is undoubtedly the physically tangible body so they may be referred to musculoskeletal activities,

While the eastern exercises treat the intangible mind prior to the tangible body due to emphasizing the extraordinary roles of the mind in giving a positive influence on the entire organ system as a Yoga master said that there was nothing more important to one's health than a healthy and normal nervous system [10]. So mental training is the main focal point of the eastern fitness exercises, and those physical activities are used mainly for forming up a proper "environment" to the optimization of mental status. Guided by this philosophy Tai-Chi, Qi-Gong and Yoga have complicated sets of methods physically to adjust body postures and promote the growth of vital energy. They specially emphasize the mind concentration and breathing control. So the eastern exercises may be referred as mentally concentrated fitness activities. The physical health is regarded merely its natural result.

In dealing with mental health the western and the eastern seem to reverse their positions. The western type turns to be indirect, that is to discharge the negative mental energies or stresses accumulated in daily life, through physical movement as some scholars refer sport participation as a "safety valve" or a "social cathartic".

While the eastern exercises try to solve the problem in a direct way: since the negative mental energy is harmful, especially when they accumulated, it would be better and easier to deal with them in their early stage, and no allow them to grow up. Therefore the primary concern is to keep mind in a proper state. By a variety of subtle mental training methods assisted by certain body postures and breathing to get rid of all interruptions of negative emotions. So the eastern approach is aimed right at the corn of the mental status.

External versus internal

Closely related to their ideas on the interrelationship between the body and mind as the above-mentioned. The western exercises put the emphasis on external aspect, trying to use muscle solve everything. Here all measurements adopted seem to be logical and explicit: to deal with the lack of physical activity, the amount of energy surplus occurred between nutrition intake and physical activity is precisely counted and "burned out" with the same amount of the macular activities; to keep the cardiorespiratory system normal three times of 30 minute exercises of large muscle groups /week are prescribed. to rehabilitate injuries or dysfunctional parts of the organ, the injured or dysfunctional parts are precisely located and corresponding physical therapies are given.

While the eastern hold that health is rooted internally as long as the person keeps the vital energy smoothly circulated along the Jin Luo (the network channels of the vital energy) and the Yin and Yang balanced he/she will in a health status. The external physical health is no more than natural result of the internal cultivation. Health is not necessarily to be the tremendous muscular development, in stead, it tends to be harmonious status of all internal body elements.

Analytic versus synthetic

The western exercises are aimed at the tangible physical structure so they follow the analytic principle in practice. That is to break down the whole system into various parts by certain criteria then give each part corresponding physical training separately, as the table shows.

Table 2 : Criteria of fitness exercises

Criteria	Anatomy dimension	Fitness qualities	Energy supply
Exercise	Up body	Speed	Aerobic
Exercise	Low body	Endurance	Non-aerobic
Exercise	Trunk	Strength	...
Exercise	....	Flexibility	...
Exercise	...	...	...

A human being is the most complicated organism in the world, it is hard to deal it as a whole so it is more operational to train it separately with hope that the entire body will be exercised when all the partial effects are added together. This way also provides exercisers with a precise and quantitative idea for their workout. However, a potential shortcoming is that under this analytic principle some conflicts among various parts may occur with some being overdeveloped and other underdeveloped.

The eastern fitness exercises emphasize on the holistic integrity, not only the integrity of human being and also the integrity of man and the natural environment. Even those exercises aimed at particular parts of the body also have to be based on the grasp of entire human organism. The Chinese Qi-Gong has a concept of "the heaven and man integrated into one", and Yoga holds that "Buddhist and I are the same". So the eastern fitness activities, following the synthetic principle, seem to lead a more harmonious result.

In addition, the synthetic principle and holistic view let fitness exercises intimately interconnected with one's lifestyle, including spiritual nourishment, body movement, proper diet and every aspects of one life. So adopting such exercises like Yoga, Qigong and Taichi, is often accompanied by overall improvement of one's entirely lifestyle. when one determines to follow strictly the requirements of these exercises, which will have profound influences on the person' social behaviors, morality, attitude towards life and even certain fundamental changes may occur in one's basic philosophy

Doubtlessly, the eastern exercises are more efficient in improving one's lifestyle due to their holistic view and approaches. But at the same time they also tend to be vague, objective and difficult in quantification.

Modern versus tradition - anatomy, physiology vs. acupuncture channels

Western approach is clear in the relation between the tools and end, logical in and explicit to interpretation in the light of modern theories such as physiology, biochemistry.

Since all fitness practices are based on certain theories, the fundamental mechanism for western fitness exercises is known based the fundamentals of modern sciences, such as anatomy, physiology, biochemistry etc.

While their eastern counterpart mainly follow the Jin Luo (network channel of vital energy) theory constituted with the traditional philosophies and medical theories. It considers that one's health status depends on an unlocked Jin Luo through which the most important nourishing elements, vital energy is delivered. As the Yellow Emperor's Canon states, the Jin Luo must be unblocked, which determines live and death, all sorts of diseases [11]. In other words, health is the status in which the networks of Jin Luo are not jammed. Guided by this theory, the eastern exercises are designed to promote the vital energy to circulate smoothly along the invisible channel [12].

Integration of western and eastern approaches

Compensative potentials

The above discussion shows whatever lacks in the western fitness exercises are sufficient in their eastern counterparts and vice versa so there is a great possibility for their compensation.

Table 3 : Characteristics of western and eastern fitness exercises

	Western exercises	Eastern exercises
Principles of exercise	Analytic Separable treatments based on various criteria(anatomy, fitness quality, energy supply, etc.) (accurate but conflict potential possible)	Synthetic and holistic Entire treatment, the entire body regarded as an inseparable system. (Harmonious but vague)
focal point	physical, external	Mental, internal
Energy consumption	High	Low
Effect evaluate	More accurate and objective	More subjective and vague
Space and facilities	Certain spatial space and facilities are required	Flexible with space and facilities
Scientific bases	Modern sciences(anatomy, physiology, biochemistry etc.)	Traditional Jin Luo(Network of vital energy) theory
Motive inspiration	Effect may show in short time Easier to motivate	Effect may show in long time Difficult to motivate
Internal and external environment	Separated	Integrative
Organization	Team and individual	Individual

Since none of them alone cannot meet the demands to maintain people's health in the contemporary times, and these two are potentially mutual benefited each other, some sorts of their integration seem to be expected and this will not only beneficial to the western and eastern fitness exercises themselves but more importantly, may open a new path to the mass sport participation by providing more relevant practicing tools to them.

Possibilities of integration

Even the compensation of the western and eastern fitness exercises has been potentially existed for a long time but this process has been really initiated only in recent years. What made it possible is the powerful trend of globalization. Globalization has set up a unprecedented favorable social conditions for the western and eastern to meet each other. It provides a vast and fast communication network we have ever had to disseminate all sorts of information so people know each other much better, including their fitness exercises. In addition, the sense of "global villager" has gradually been accepted, which transferred the cultural barriers and resulted in impartiality towards one's own and others' cultural patterns. People are getting aware of their owe advantages and limits and ready to learn and share one another. All these are in favor of integration of the two forms of fitness exercises.

Some signs have indicated this development, we have already seen that the number of participants in Yoga, Qi-Gong and Tai chi have increased in the western world. The Time magazine selected Andrew Weil as one of America's most influential people because he proposed a great idea so called integrative approach consisting of both the western and eastern medical ideas in his books - *Health and Healing* and *Spontaneous Healing* - which have spent more than 22 weeks on the New York Times bestseller list [13].

Possible forms of integration of the two

Assembling pattern. Perhaps it is the easiest way to benefit the advantages from both western and eastern exercises. One can set up a fitness program consisting of the two types of the exercises according to ones needs. It may be called a functional compensation, for example, jogging - Tai chi, aerobic dance - Qi-Gong or Yoga to let the internal and external training interact each other functionally.

Combinative pattern. In this form, both fitness exercises take certain essential elements from each other, in order to enrich the effects of the existing exercises. For example, when jogging, walking or circling the doer may add some eastern internal training methods with mind concentrated and vital energy network being concerned. While exercising Qi-Gong Tai-Chi and Yoga, some quantifiable measurements may used to lead the doer more consciously step by step towards the advanced level.

Integration pattern. This is a new created form with features of both the western and eastern fitness exercises. One of the excellent example is the Tai-Chi gentle ball which came into being recent years in Chin by combining Tai-Chi movements with badminton and tennis. It has enjoyed a good reputation as an attractive fitness activity.

Conclusion

Today's health problems have endowed fitness exercises with multi-dimensional tasks in promoting people's wellness not only physically but also mentally and socially. This comprehensive goal cannot be fulfilled by neither the western nor the eastern approaches alone. But these two have great potentials to compensate each other to meet the challenge. The trend of integration of the western and eastern fitness exercises has already come into being and will make further progress in the process of globalization.

Notes

[1] Palm, J. Sport for All as a challenge of sports organizations in the 1990s. In Oja, P. & Telama, R. (eds.): Sport for All. Amsterdam: Elsevier Science Pub., 509.

[2] WHO (1998). World Health Report .

[3] Naisbitt, J. (1986). Megatrends. NY: Warner Book, 147.

[4] Fox, E. & Mathews, D. (1981). The physiological basis of physical education and athletics, 3rd ed. NY: Saunders College Pub, 399.

[5] Blair, S. & Kohl, H. What are the benefits of occupational exercise promotion programs ? In Oja, P. & Telama, R. (eds.) : Sport for All. Amsterdam: Elsevier Science Pub., 225.

[6] WHO (1997). World Health Report.

[7] WHO (1997). World Health Report.

[8] WHO (1997). World Health Report.

[9] WHO, Health for all for the 21 Century.

[10] Zhongyan, B. & Zhang Huilan (1986). Yoga-Qi-Gong and meditation. Beijing: People's Sport Press, 22.

[11] Nei-Jing.

[12] Xinchun, H. (1989). History of Indian philosophy. Beijing Commerce Press, 328.

[13] Rae, B. (1998). An American physician talks about health, 6. English World, 87.

Chapter 8

Ten years of China watching: present trends and future directions in sport in the People's Republic

Robin Jones
Loughborough University, U.K.

Returning regularly to China, frequently to the same location(s), on an annual basis, the author has witnessed both the gradual, and sometimes the rapid developments, that have come about in China over the last ten years. Increased material wealth is transforming the lives of a few citizens, but has not reached the majority. The remnants of the earlier rigidity in the system have been replaced by pragmatism and enterprise that are subsumed within the phrase "socialism with Chinese characteristics", but what does this mean for sport? The official relationship between sport and the state, including moves towards greater provincial autonomy, may be seen in the Chinese government's new regulations covering sport, which show that, whilst espousing a market economy, there remains considerable government control over sport. Contraction in the numbers of state sports officials and departments has not eliminated state influence; the arrival of sponsorship and commercialism has not swept away links with government agencies; the emergence of the sports superstar has not replaced the state athlete. Is the search - or scramble - for the pot of gold a distant illusion or an imminent reality? The situation is dynamic, and further substantial changes are afoot.

On March 2nd 1998, sweeping changes to the structure of Chinese government were announced at the Ninth National People's Congress in Beijing. Eleven out of forty ministries and other offices of the State Council were to be closed, including the State Physical Culture and Sports Commission. It was also announced that provincial Sports Commissions would close, and the number of employees in government offices would be reduced by fifty per cent by the end of 1998 [1].

Whilst the pattern of reform was evident at the beginning of 1998, it was certainly not the start of the process, nor was it complete. Table 1 gives a simple chronology of some of the changes identified.

Although the last ten years have been remarkable in many ways for China, perhaps the most remarkable fact is that in those ten years, China's population has increased by approximately one hundred million, and so strikingly obvious are the implications of this, that further comment is probably unnecessary.

It has been a decade of reform, but "why"? What has driven the reform process? After all, the insular policies of the early years after 1949, resulted in China being isolated from the West. It is only twenty years ago that the door started to open, and then only gradually. Several reasons are evident for this:

Table 1: Chronology of change in the period 1979 to 1998

1978/79	Deng Xiao Ping comes to power. Start of the reform era; open door policies and modernisation programme take root.
1980s	The collapse of communism and the decade of change in eastern Europe.
1990s	Re-alignment of policies with free market under the banner "Socialism with Chinese characteristics".
1995	New government regulations for sport; new professional soccer leagues formed; soccer management centre planned.
1996	Soccer management centres established; basketball and volleyball management offices follow suit.
1997	Sports Commission re-structured; management offices for all major sports planned. Provincial Regulations appear in some provinces.
1998	Major government restructuring announced by State Council; State Sports Commission to close; closure of provincial sports commissions also announced. All China Sports Federation to become the government's sports office, listed directly under the State Council, with loss of ministerial status.

The collapse of the former USSR was a warning against early political reform - but at the same time clearly signalled that change was almost inevitable. If communism was unable to survive in Eastern Europe, it was because, de facto , it simply wasn't providing the improvements to living standards that might have been expected to attract popular support. Sport today, in the former Soviet Union is far less prominent as an instrument of the state, and has lost most, if not all, state financial support.

Deng Xiao Ping (the late, former leader of China), was a reformer by nature, and his determination drove the government to take a reformist line - the open door policy of 1979 / early 80s, the four modernisations programme (of agriculture, industry, science and technology, and defence), and the establishment of Special Economic Zones (e.g. Shenzhen in southern China) are testimony to this. China under Deng first accepted, and has since built on, some measure of co-operation with the West, but although communism has subsided elsewhere, it still under-pins the official policies of the country.

Basic reform began in 1986 - and the USA, UK and Germany were examples of countries that were looked at, and by 1992/3, structural reform was under way.

The pattern of reform was evident - sport was being separated from government, and was adopting, broadly, a western approach. However, the separation was not total. Under reforms to the training system, different levels of funding emerged, notably, parents contributing towards their children's involvement in sport at the introductory level (payment for coaching sessions), followed by government help at medium level (coaching payed for; and special sports schools), and finally at the top level, government funding only for those sports unable to attract major sponsors, leaving sponsors to fund the rest. For competitive sport, the government will now only fund the Olympic sports programme, thus making national priorities quite transparent.

To analyse what China expects from sport, reference is made to government regulations published in 1995 [2], the key features of which are: (1) the move towards market forces and commercialism; (2) the separation between government agency and sport agency; (3) concern for mass sport, leisure and free time; (4) sport management issues - as opposed to simply sport provision; (5) the active promotion of sponsorship; (6) retention of State concern for nationalism, socialism, morality and discipline; (7) recognition of international concerns over substance abuse in sport; (8) the rights of athletes to careers after sport and the State's duty to provide opportunity for job training; (9) importance given to school physical education - compulsory, daily PE, evaluation alongside academic performance, national standards, school sports clubs and health and fitness checks.

The regulations were relatively clear about policy, but less clear about implementation, and as the following examples show, retained the hallmarks of sports policies in communist countries, as well as marking the change towards a free market .

Regulation 3. "Sport is valued for its contribution to the economic, social and military development of China...."

Regulation 24. "China promotes the development of competitive sport and encourages athletes to improve the level of their sports skills, in order to raise the standard of sports competition, and gain honour for the country"

Regulation 17. "Schools must include Physical Education to develop the moral, intellectual, and physical qualities of the students".

Regulation 42. The departure from the traditional pattern of State provision lies in this regulation: "Sports organisations are encouraged to raise money through sponsorship by business companies and individuals".

Here was a clear sign that reform was part of an ongoing, planned process, rather than an end product in itself. This process is still unfinished, and by 1997, a number of provinces were formulating local versions of these regulations, that spelled out in greater detail the responsibilities of local authorities in sports planning and provision [3].

The regulations represent the sporting aspirations of China, and focus constructively on past traditions, present realities and future possibilities. International recognition, almost automatically, follows Olympic success, and by reaching fourth place in the medal tables at Atlanta in 1996, China undoubtedly attracted much acclaim for its success in events such as diving and gymnastics. But China has also attracted negative publicity as its sportsmen and women have been found guilty of drug abuse on a number of occasions. Of course, it is true to say that no country has solved the problem of substance abuse in sport, and China, by Article 50 of the 1995 Regulations recognises the problem, "...athletes found guilty will be punished according to the rules; people in charge will also be held responsible. Wu Shao Zu, the head of the Sports Commission emphasises that there should be a strict ban on drugs, with rigorous testing, management and enforcement of the laws [4].

The 1995 Chinese regulations thus display a measure of real concern on the part of the government, but as the government relax their control of sport, and commercialism rushes in, any reduction of the problem seems likely to become more difficult.

The demise of the USSR left a gap in the Olympic merry-go-round, that hitherto had been eagerly exploited by the media. The symbolic portrayal of the east-west "cold war" in the sporting arena was regularly highlighted by the media, but after the changes in eastern Europe of the 1980s and early 90s, this lost much of its credibility, and instead switched to metaphors about "the sleeping dragon", as China began the push for Olympic success.

Olympic sport and key international sports are the sharp edge of China's sporting profile, with the exception of their martial arts, wushu. From beyond the Olympic arena, surrounding the martial arts of China, there is still an aura of mystery, a sense of something different. Sports science does not dominate the training and practice of these ancient forms of exercise. International Federations have not sanitised the activity by chopping away tradition and replacing it with "Competition Rules". Westerners, keen to become "masters of the craft", turn to China for the deepest level of understanding and the highest level of teaching, and whereas Olympic sport is regularly associated with drugs, such scandals do not pervade wushu. But even the long traditions of wushu are not exempt from evidence of change, and starting in 1998 a "Dan" system[5] is being introduced in order to standardise the various levels of achievement amongst practitioners "both at home and throughout the world", and this "after a thousand years being without such a system" [6].

China's re-entry into the Olympic Games in 1980, and their agreement to take part alongside Chinese Taipei, marked the end of their sporting isolation, which had lasted since 1949. By the late 1980s, preparations for the Asian Games (Beijing, 1989) were at an advanced stage. A new stadium had been built for the Asian Games, together with a competitors' village, and the intention to bid for the 2000 Olympic Games was clear (the bid was to be finally decided by September 1993). This chain of events demonstrated China's long term commitment to world sport. The Chinese National Games, (i.e. those under the People's Republic of China, post-1949, not to be confused with National Sports Games that took place in China pre-1949) started in 1959, and, held every four years (with some breaks between 1966 and 1976), have become a very important part of the national and international sporting effort of the country.

Brownell (1996)[7] suggests that the Chinese National Games, held in Guangzhou, Southern China, in 1987, already displayed strong moves towards a western pattern. At the next National Games (1993, held partly in Chengdu, Sichuan province and partly in Beijing), sports leaders were saying [8] that future Games would be further trimmed back, in line with the Olympic programme, and by the time of the 1997 National Games (held in Shanghai) this had happened. With the exception of wushu, the programme of events in Shanghai was Olympic.

Although cuts to the programme of the National Games were not matched by cuts in financial investment (see earlier comment on government support for the competitive sports programme), sponsorship of the National Games had become essential to their future. Shanghai spent around US$ 850 million on the 1997 National Games, refurbishing 38 stadiums, pools, fields, training centres and gymnasiums, as well as building a new, 80,000 seater stadium at a cost of US$ 155 million, but the stadium included 104 executive boxes, available for 50 year leases at a cost of US$ 600,000 [9].

All the changes to the administrative and legislative structure of Chinese sport - government policy, regulations, streamlining of the State Sports Commission - that occurred in the 90s, signalled that substantive change was also to be expected in the practice of sport. Jones (1996) [10], outlined the emergence of professional soccer in China in the early 90s, and today, the game is firmly established as the most popular spectator sport in the country. Soccer was the first sport to go down the professional route, to achieve a large measure of independence from State control, to gain substantial sponsorship and generate a sport culture in China that, hitherto, was more associated with western sport. The management of sport in China was under review, and by 1996, first basketball and then volleyball, adopted a similar structure. Soccer had been the guinea pig for the experiment, and the management centres for soccer that were established, focused on the grass roots development of the sport. The professional game lacked the sort of infrastructure that would nurture new players: junior leagues, competitions, training / coaching programmes, soccer sports schools and links with clubs. The management centre's task was to provide these. The centre received three million yuan (about US$ 350,000) from the State Sports Commission in 1997, and as part of the re-structuring of the Commission itself, some of the staff switched employment to the soccer management centres. Significantly, however, in contrast to the government money, around 30 million yuan (about US$ 3,500,000) in sponsorship money flowed into the soccer management centre [11]. Currently the soccer centre managers are given no specific management training, and in China there are few, if any, sports management courses available outside Beijing Sports University.

Until the beginning of 1998, the planned restructuring of the State Sports Commission continued, with the extension of the management centre system to twenty sports, but the reduction of the Commission to 380 staff and twelve departments, for the overall administration of the country's sport (see figure 1). Autonomy for sport was increasing by every move, but just three months later, came the announcement, in March 1998, of the closure of the Sports Commission. Part of a whole package of government re-structuring designed to lead the drive for a more efficient system, the changes were sweeping in their extent and profound in their potential for the future of China (see figure 2).

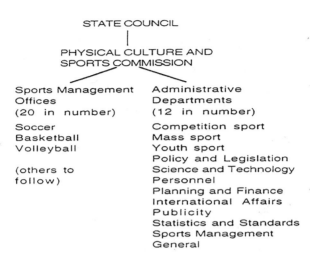

STATE COUNCIL
|
PHYSICAL CULTURE AND
SPORTS COMMISSION

Sports Management	Administrative
Offices	Departments
(20 in number)	(12 in number)
Soccer	Competition sport
Basketball	Mass sport
Volleyball	Youth sport
	Policy and Legislation
(others to	Science and Technology
follow)	Personnel
	Planning and Finance
	International Affairs
	Publicity
	Statistics and Standards
	Sports Management
	General

380 Staff

Figure 1 : Administrative structure of the State Sports Commission, January
1998

Before March 2	After March 2
40 Ministries	29 Ministries
State Physical Culture and Sports Commission	State Commission closed
Provincial Sports Commission in all Province	Provincial Sports Commission to be closed
	50% reduction in government officials
	Sports Office with All China Sports Federation to oversee sport; responsible directly to State Council
	Sports Management Centres to be responsible for their particular sport

Figure 2 : Closure of the State Sports Commission, March 2nd 1998

A gap was created between government and sport that, for the first time since 1949, was tantamount to the partial de-politicisation of sport. In conclusion, five possibilities for the future of Chinese sport are located in a macro and micro model of "government control over sport" and "type of economy" (see figures 3 and 4).

(1) Reforms remain in place, based on the 1995 regulations and the March 1998 announcement, together with the "With Chinese characteristics..." clause. The strength of the economy gives political stature and international credibility to the government, which can claim much credit for setting the agenda for the reforms of the last decade, reducing inflation and achieving rising living standards. "With Chinese characteristics" would suggest that some control of, and support for sport will remain a government objective, while at the same time creating a degree of separation between government and sports agencies. With the announcement of the closure of the Sports Commission, came the parallel announcement that a Sports Office would be created, based upon the All China Sports Federation, and listed directly under the State Council[12]. Although its functions were not made clear at the time, there are obviously sporting issues which would require government approval, such as funding for international events, that would appropriately be dealt with by such an office, but the status of the Sports Office would seem to be at a lower level in the government hierarchy than the former Commission, whose minister held cabinet level rank [13].

(2) Reforms continue, but become dominated by commercialism. With a growth in GDP of 8.8% in 1997 (which has been the trend throughout the 90s) and inflation down to single figures (targetted as 3% for 1998) [14], China has experienced spectacular development, especially in cities such as Shanghai. The government has positively encouraged foreign investment. Commercialism and sponsorship in sport have already been referred to and as long as the economic market remains buoyant, the pressure for further moves towards a free market will grow, subject to the government allowing it, or being unable to stop it! A gradual withering away of the State was supposed to be one of the eventual outcomes of a communist state, so there would be some irony in the process of reform if "With Chinese characteristics" began to lose its relevance, and commercialism allowed sport to become independent.

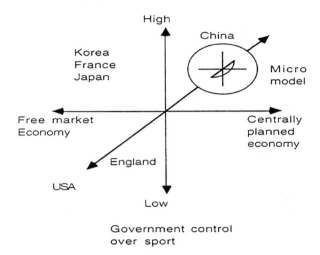

Figure 3 : Macro-model of the relationship between government control over sport and type of economy

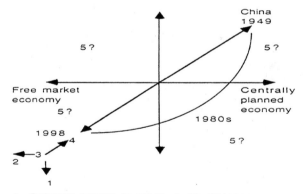

1. Reforms remain in place, "with Chinese characteristics"
2. Reforms continue, dominated by commercialism
3. Reforms come to a halt because of stagnation
4. Reforms are reversed, eg new leadership
5. Total collapse because of crisis, eg world recession

Figure 4 : Micro-model of the relationship between government control of sport and type of economy

(3) Reforms come to a halt. A slowing down of the Chinese economy may lead to a period of austerity and stagnation. Other Asian economies such as the Japanese, the Korean, and the Indonesian, are currently suffering economic decline, but the Chinese government declared in March 1998 that it was determined to avoid the pitfalls that trapped other Asian economies in the 90s: "We must put a stop to irrational, redundant construction, and never launch projects for which there is not sufficient capital or whose products are not marketable". (Chen Jinhua, Minister in Charge of the State Planning Commission[15]) The reforms are predicated on the expectation that sponsors will invest in sport, but a stagnant economy would be unattractive to commercial investors, and might leave the government unwilling or unable to rescue sport. Starved of sufficient State support and unable to attract sponsors, Chinese sport would struggle to fulfil its potential as a world sporting superpower.

(4) Reforms are reversed. Although the present leaders have affirmed the government's intention to continue on the reformist road, there is no absolute guarantee that future changes to the Chinese government will not alter those policies. Natural change, the death of a leader, a rethink of policy or a response to outside events, could conceivably see China steering a new path, but whether the reform process reaches some sort of "escape velocity", which would make it impossible to reverse, is difficult to say. However, when events merit it, governments around the world have been known to reverse their policies. China is no different in this respect, and withdrawing from the international sports arena could be one outcome, if reversal did happen.

(5) Total collapse. In a deep crisis (as was the case in the USSR and eastern Europe in the late 80s), then sport, too, would be unlikely to survive. A world recession, for example, could lead to an exodus of foreign investors from China, a total withdrawal of sponsorship, and the inability to fund sport from the public purse. This would leave China marginalised and unable to build on the successes of the past. Riordan [16] suggests that sport in the former Soviet Union is now subject to criminal abuse because the re-structuring of the country has left sport with little support and exposed to commercial exploitation. There is no suggestion here that China will follow the same path, indeed there is much that separates the two, but the interdependence of countries today in the global economy means the delicate balance between sport and international events is critical to a country like China.

At a time when Asian economies are weakening, but commercial interest in Chinese sport is still strong; when Chinese government policies are relaxing, but the sporting framework is still tightly defined by regulations, the conclusion is drawn that the axis of reform will revolve around the retention of "with Chinese characteristics" against the lure of "commercialism".

Notes

1   Announced by Luo Gan, Secretary General of the State Council at the Ninth National People's Congress, Beijing, People's Republic of China, March 2,1998. The People's Congress is the supreme legislative body of the Chinese government.

2   Regulations published under President's Order (PRC) Number 55, signed by President Jiang Zemin, 29th August 1995.

3   Sichuan province, in central south west China was amongst the first to publish its own provincial regulations.

4   Wu Shaozu (1995). Regulations, op cit, page 9.

5   The system of grades used in Judo and other martial arts to signify the level of the participant. First Dan in judo is the lowest grade of black belt, for example.

6   The Messenger, 9(4), 3, 1998 (The Messenger is the overseas newsletter of Radio Beijing).

7   Brownell, S. Training the body for China, op cit, 117-119.

8   Author's conversation with sports leaders at the National Games in 1993.

9   Shanghai Today, September 1997, Shanghai Today Magazine Company, Number 1, page 27.

10   Jones, R. (1996). The emergence of professional sport in China, paper presented at the ISCPES Conference, Hachi Oji, Tokyo, Japan, July 1996.

11   Author's conversation with Sports Commission, January 1998

12   China Daily, 7th March 1998.

13   Wu, Z.Y. & Que, Y.W. (1990). Organisation of China's physical culture. In Knuttgen, H. et al. (eds) : Sport in China. Human Kinetics, 47.

14   Report on the Implementation of the 1997 Plan for the National Economic and Social Development, Ninth National People's Congress, 6 March 1998. Reported in China Daily, 24 March 1998.

15   Chen Jinhua, Minister in Charge of the State Planning Commission. Report on the Implementation of the 1997 Plan for the National Economic and Social Development, Ninth National People's Congress, 6 March 1998. Reported in China Daily 24 March 1998.

16   Author's discussion with Professor Jim Riordan at Loughborough University, April 1998.

Chapter 9

Football and nationalism.
An analysis of spoken and written press
comments of the football game between
Belgium and the Netherlands
at the World Cup 1994

Philip Verwimp
K.U.Leuven, Belgium

The World Football Cup is the event which attracts world wide the most attention from people and media of all events on the planet. For about a month every four years the media cover this event on a level that is not reached by any other event. The peoples of the countries that participate in the World Cup are far from indifferent spectators. If their team wins a game, the countries cities experience an outburst of joy. A lot of people are emotionally involved in their teams successes and failures. This is not only true for ordinary people, but also for politicians. After the team of Iran won the game against the team of the USA at the 1998 Cup in France, the Iranian leader Khamenei told the world that his team has beaten the enemy. The political use of football games is not restricted to leaders of undemocratic states, politicians all over the world have an outspoken interest for football games.

In this paper, I want to find our if one can find empirical evidence for the relationship between the media, football and politics. More specifically, I will analyse the relation between football and nationalism as it occurs in the spoken and written press comments of the game between the Belgian and the Dutch national teams at the World Cup football, June 25, 1994.

The outline of this paper is the following. The second part presents the theoretical background of the research and the third part describes the methodology that was used in the empirical research. The results and their interpretations are presented in the fourth part. The analysis of TV comments and newspaper articles are each given a separate treatment in parts three and four. Conclusions are drawn in the final part with a short note on the 1998 game between Belgium and the Netherlands.

Theoretical background

Literature on this topic suggests a whole set of relations between football, politics and national identity. According to Duke and Crolley, the extent of overlap between *the state* and *the nation* in a given country is crucial for the understanding of these relationships [1]. *The state* is a political unit, having the monopoly of legitimate force on a given territory. The government of a state collects taxes and has relations with other states managed by a foreign ministry. States usually have a football team to represent them in international competitions. *The nation* is a sociological entity, involving common sentiments and a shared identity. Nation is often associated with a feeling of community and belonging. This distinction allows one to describe two political situations

(1) When the state and the nation overlap to a large degree : in this case, nationalism becomes loyalty to the state. International football competitions offer an ideal opportunity to raise support for the state and its leaders. The emotions that are expressed towards the football team and which rely on the concept of nation, national identity and a sense of belonging are transferred to the political arena and can be interpreted as support for the political leaders and the regime.

(2) When several submerged nations exist within a state : in this case, international football competitions are an opportunity for ethnic groups to show their discontent with the political situation. If these ethnic groups want more autonomy, they refuse to accept the association the football game makes between the state and the nation. Political leaders can use international competitions to create political debate on the status of an ethnic group in the state.

Belgium and the Netherlands form two interesting cases, since the first has undergone a profound transformation towards a federalist country. One therefore has the specific situation of competition between different kinds of nationalism, meaning the Belgian, Flemish and Walloon nationalism. And the second, the Netherlands are a case in point where the state and the nation almost coincide.

In both cases, an international football competition between two teams can have an integrating effect on the peoples of both countries. In these settings, nationalism and in-group feelings are likely to grow, be it towards the state or/and towards the nation. Political personalities like to identify themselves with success in sports. A winning team comes from a strong state/nation with talented leaders. Politicians like to identify themselves with winners, so they can take part in their success. [2] The media is not a neutral player in international football competitions, a major football event is an opportunity for the media to stress the values that are considered to be the core of the countries national identity. Sports represents basic values such as courage, discipline, and perseverance. The media will stress the character of a sports hero as a model for society.

Methodology

TV- analysis

The game between Belgium and the Netherlands was observed on both channels (not at the same time, but with the help of a video-recorder). I used seven items as indicators for the overall concept of nationalism. It is quite hard to find adequate indicators for 'nationalism' that are at the same time useful in the analyses of a running football commentary. My question is : " Can I find traces of nationalism in the comments of the football game ?" These seven items should therefore be seen as operational statements that are attempting to make the broad concept of 'nationalism' ready for empirical research.

These seven Items are : (1) negative judgement about a Belgian player; (2) negative judgement about a Dutch player; (3) positive judgement about a Belgian player; (4) positive judgement about a Dutch player; (5) call upon 'we'-'them' feelings; (6) confirmation of order and hierarchy; (7) disturbance of order and hierarchy.

Items 1 to 4 are value-judgements about a players performance. These questions want to indicate a kind of 'love for one's own', in the sense that they are measuring the frequency of approval or disapproval of a players performance. The items were used for both the Belgian and the Dutch channel. It is then possible to compare the approval or disapproval of the players of one's own team and the players of the opponent's team. These items measure the number of times the commentator expresses his approval or disapproval of a players performance, e.g. for item 1 'that was a bad assist from Scifo'.

I realise this way of operationalising our concept is debatable and open to criticism. When watching a football game, it is very difficult to distinguish between a 'nationalist' comment and a comment that is just describing what is happening on the field. I hope to find out whether or not the comments have a nationalist bias. Do commentators objectively describe what is happening o the field or do they interpret and filter what they see ?

Item 5 measures the frequency of the call upon nationalist feelings of 'we' against 'them'. It only measures the frequency of a commentator's appeal to the 'nation' or to a 'national identity'. It measures the number of times that the commentator, during the game, links the football game with the 'national identity' of the Belgians or the Dutch, e.g. 'this is a wonderful day for Belgium' or 'our country can be proud of its players'.

Items 6 and 7 try to indicate the function of the football game as a mirror of one's own society. There is no direct link to 'nationalism', these Items are looking for expressions of obedience versus rebellion. The question is whether or not I can associate them with the commentator's own society and whether this association is allowed. These items measure the frequency of the commentator's approval or disapproval of the order of the game, e.g. of item 6 'the referee is right'.

However, measurement of frequencies of expressions does not tell us all. Therefore, next to these measurements, a more qualitative type of analysis is used. I tried to get an overview of the choice of vocabulary the commentator used and of the atmosphere he wanted to build by means of his comments during the game as well as in his studio during the break.

Newspaper analysis

I analyzed 12 newspapers (6 Flemish (Dutch-speaking Belgian) and 6 Dutch). They are all nation wide daily newspapers. I omitted the newspapers with a strong regional approach. For Belgium, I used 6 Flemish newspapers, *Het Nieuwsblad* (HN), *Gazet van Antwerpen* (GVA), *De Morgen* (DM), *De Standaard* (DS), *Het Volk* (HV) and *Het Laatste Nieuws* (LN). The Dutch newspapers were *De Volkskrant* (VK), *NRC Handelsblad* (NRCH*), Het Parool* (PA), *Trouw*, *De Telegraaf* (Tel) and *Algemeen Dagblad* (AD). I took the newspapers from June 22 through June 28. I had 6 editions of each newspaper, with the game right in the middle of this period. To enable a comparison to the TV commentaries, I used the same approaches. This means that I analyzed all articles concerning the Belgian-Dutch football game in the 12 journals by means of the seven items listed under (3.1). In each article dealing with the Belgian-Dutch game, I noted the frequencies of written expressions for the seven Items.

In addition, descriptive statistics of each newspaper were gathered by counting the following items each day for all journals: (1) the total number of sport articles; (2) the total number of World Cup articles; (3) the total number of articles dealing with the Belgian-Dutch game; (4) the total number of photographs of World Cup events; (5) the size of the newspaper; (6) the surface on the front page devoted to World Cup news; (7) the presence of a sport readers' letters section (letters to the editor); (8) the presence of a separated sports section.

This way of collecting information is standard in newspaper analysis. One measures, so to say, the degree of importance of the football game in each newspaper. How much attention is paid to the game in the newspapers ? One could, of course, collect more quantitative data, but for this approach it would not teach us that much more. For Items (1), (2) and (3), I counted all articles, independent of their length. Afterwards, I counted averages for each newspaper and for all data.. I also related some pieces of data with others. In the end, I had 13 numbers, averages and relations: the 8 items mentioned above plus the following : (2) (a) relative number of World Cup articles to total number of sports articles; (2) (b) average of World Cup articles per day; (3) (a) relative number of articles about the Belgian-Dutch game to total number of WC articles; (3) (b) average of number of articles about the Belgian-Dutch game per day; (6) (a) relative number of average square centimeters of WC news on the front page to the total size of the front page

I also used a more qualitative approach, equivalent to the second approach used in the TV analysis. Here, I observed the style of the newspapers. Are they using colours ? What kind of vocabulary do they use ? Do they make direct associations to politics? I will also quote coaches or players a few times.

Results and interpretation

TV- analysis : quantitative approach

Table 1 : Frequency of expressions of the Flemish and the Dutch commentator

Comments - Items		Frequencies		Percentages	
		Dutch	Flemish	Dutch	Flemish
Item 1	- Belgian	11	20	8.4	19
Item 2	- Dutch	9	20	7	19
Item 3	+ Belgian	43	29	33	27.6
Item 4	+ Dutch	46	11	35.3	10.4
Item 5	we-them	8	14	6	13.3
Item 6	obedience	7	4	5.3	3.8
Item 7	disturbance	6	7	4.6	6.6
Totals		130	105	100	100

Using the Chi-square distribution to test for significance :

$$\chi^2 = \sum_{i=1}^{r} \sum_{j=1}^{k} [(f_{ij} - F_{ij})^2 / F_{ij}]$$

where r =2 and k = 7 ; f_{ij} are the observed frequencies and F_{ij} are the theoretical frequencies

yields the following result : $\chi^2 = 31,15$

This needs to be compared to χ^2 (α = 0,05 ; d = 6) = 12,59

Where α = 0,05 is the level of significance and d=(r-1)(k-1)= 6 are the degrees of freedom.
Since 31,12 > 12.59 we can say that the observed frequencies do not originate from the same distribution, χ^2 is large enough to be significant.

I will first discuss items 1 to 4. Independent of the nationality of the player, the Dutch commentator makes a lot appreciating comments. Of a total of 109 Dutch comments (which is also a lot more then the Flemish), 89 comments (81,6 %) positively comment on the players' performances, independent of the nationality of the players. Out of a total of 80 Flemish comments, 40 (50%) positively comment on the players' performances. However, when the nationality of the player is considered, another discrepancy between the two commentators needs to be discussed : the Flemish commentator is scarce with his appreciation of Dutch players. The majority (72,5%) of his appreciation is reserved for the players of his own team, whereas the Dutch commentator 'divides' his appreciation more equally over both the teams.

The results on Item 5 show that the Flemish reporter appeals more to national feelings than the Dutch reporter. Compared to the total number of expressions, the Flemish percentage of statements captured under this item more than doubles the Dutch one. The amount of expressions dealing with Items 6 and 7 are quite low in comparison to the other items.

How can we interpret these first observations ? The fact that the Dutch commentator, in comparison to the Flemish, made a lot more comments and a lot more approvals of a player's performance, independent of the player's nationality, tells something about the commentator. In his comments, the Dutch commentator did not differentiate between the Belgian and the Dutch players, both were commented upon equally, good or bad. Of course, the Belgian team won the game (1-0), but it is not obvious at all that the result of the game explains the difference in positive and negative comments by both commentators. The Dutch players created many chances as well and played a very good game. I do not think there are 'objective' reasons for a big difference in the judgement of the players of both teams. Given the abundance of his comments (and their appreciative content), I interpret the Dutch commenting as a characteristic of Dutch TV-reporting in general : the Dutch commentator is very talkative and tries to see things in a positive way. It looks like his frequent appreciations boost the game to a higher level, they serve as 'pep talk' for the public. Is this way of reporting a metaphor for Dutch society ? The same question could be asked for the Flemish comments: is the relatively low number of comments (in comparison to the Dutch) and the relatively high percentage of expressions of disapproval (independent of nationality) a metaphor for Belgian society ? The same scene on TV is indeed reported in different ways on the two channels. What the Dutch reporter often sees as 'a nice try', 'a good opportunity' , 'well done' , the Flemish reporter often sees as 'wrong play' , 'a lost ball' , 'a next time better'.

From a first analysis, these observations seem to indicate the following : the Dutch reporter made a lot more comments and a lot more appreciating comments then the Flemish reporter. This way of commenting on a running football game is a metaphor of (the cultural habits, norms, values of) both societies : Dutch society is more positively oriented towards a players' performance, more encouraging whereas Belgian society is more discouraging ones performances, more sceptical of ones actions. Further analysis has to prove if this provisional interpretation holds.

Next to this interpretation, which is not a direct proof of nationalism, one also observes the scarce number of positive comments of the Flemish commentator concerning the performance of the Dutch players. I would consider the absence of appreciating comments towards players of the other team, who 'objectively' perform very well, as an (hidden) indication towards nationalism. The interpretation then could be 'the Flemish reporter is more nationalist than the Dutch'. Nationalism is understood here as ' love for ones' own '. This observation is confirmed by the results of Item 5 : during the game, the Flemish reporter links the players' performance no less then 14 times with the national identity of the Belgians, e.g. 'Van der Elst is a real Belgian, a man with a strong character.' The Dutch reporter performs this link only 6 times. These observations I believe are an empirical proof of the way football reporters try to link the football game and the players performance to the national identity of their country.

TV-analysis: qualitative approach

What about the overall comments, the choice of vocabulary, and the reporters studio ? A more qualitative approach of the matter, suggests the following :

(1) Both the Dutch and the Flemish commentators try to appeal to the 'derby' atmosphere when they praise the long history of football games between the two countries. These games are called 'derby of the low countries'.

(2) I noted a remarkable difference between both channels during the break. Dutch TV first showed commercials and then asked professionals to comment on some actions which took place during the first half. Flemish TV had a live audience in the studio. Supporters from both teams were present and seemed to have a lot of fun. The reporter in the studio spoke with the supporters and let them have their fun. I would like to categorise this behavior as formal (Dutch) and informal (Belgian).

(3) I would like to point out one scene in detail : the Belgian player Degryse approaches the goal of the Dutch keeper. He just had to pass him to score. Instead of shooting the ball towards the goal, he passes the ball on to a fellow player. This player, however, stands 'off-side' (a position in football where a player stands between the goalkeeper and the last defensive player of the opponent's team). In this position this player cannot get the ball. When he gets the ball, the ball is ruled out. Exactly that happened at that moment. The attempt to make a goal thus ended unsuccessfully. The Flemish comment on Degryse's performance was 'unselfish ' , the Dutch comment, 'stupid'.

(4) Both reporters mention the other 'competition' that is taking place at the same time between Belgium and the Netherlands, a struggle personalized in the two Prime Ministers of both countries. Both are competing at the same time for the position of President of the European Commission, the highest and one of the most influential political positions in the European Community. The 'mentioning' of this competition, which in fact has by far nothing to do with football, is a good example of the attempts of the reporters to link the football game with national interests. 'It is not only the players that compete, our Prime Ministers our doing the same thing'. It is this association of football, national identity and politics that occurs explicitly in the comments of both reporters. I want to stress here the Flemish reporting, because Flemish TV had installed a camera in the living room of the Prime Minister Jean-Luc Dehaene. He himself, a big football fan, took a special plane home from the European summit to watch the game at home. Flemish TV especially wanted to register the Prime Minister's reaction in case of a goal. The entirety of TV- watching Flemish-speaking Belgium could therefore watch the Prime Minister cheering, laughing and throwing his arms in the air at the moment of the Belgian goal. A direct association between football, politics, and emotions is made.

I understand this as follows : in this more qualitative approach, the associations between football, the players' performances, politics, and national identity are more pronounced than in the former, more quantitative approach. The informal behavior in the Flemish studio, together with the clearcut association towards the Belgian Prime Minister and his emotions, create an ideal setting for the proliferation of feelings of Belgian nationalism. Whether or not it is meant like this, the whole construction is very appealing to nationalist emotions. One must feel like a real Belgian while watching this game.

This analysis would further strengthen my interpretation that Flemish reporting is more nationalist than Dutch reporting. I do not think remark (3) in this qualitative approach weakens my first interpretation. 'Stupid' indeed is not an approval of a player's performance; on the contrary, it is a hard negative judgement. But the Flemish reporter never uses the word 'stupid' to describe an action; that is too direct, too hard. I am certain that the Dutch reporter would also have used 'stupid' in the case of a Dutch player doing the same thing. Dutch reporting is more spectacular and more direct than Flemish reporting. From a Flemish perspective, Dutch reporting exaggerates and in this doing so it represents Dutch society. Flemish reporting is more modest, on the positive as well as on the negative side. Its approach is more discouraging and disapproving than the Dutch one.

Table 2 : Quantitative look at Flemish journals

Journals	HN	DS	DM	DGV	LN	HV
Items						
(1) total number of sports articles	514	257	221	575	357	514
(2) total number of World Cup articles	200	143	138	273	187	227
(2))(a) item (2) as percentage of item (1)	39%	56%	62%	47%	52%	44%
(2)(b) Average World Cup articles per day	33	24	23	45	32	38
(3) total n. of articles dealing with B-D game	56	32	23	59	58	38
(3)(a) item (3) as a percentage of item (2)	28%	22%	17%	22%	31%	17%
(3)(b) Average n. of B-D game articles per day	9	5	4	10	10	6
(4) total n. of photographs of WC events	79	17	50	74	88	81
(5) the size of the newspaper (in sq. cm.)	2100	2100	1610	2067	1715	1666
(6) the surface of WC news on the front page	196	131	245	558	369	297
(6)(a) item (6) as a percentage of item (5)	9%	6%	15%	27%	22%	18%
(7) the letters to the editor section	6	0	1	1	6	6
(8) the presence of a separate sports section	6	0	0	0	3	1

Table 3 : Quantitative look at Dutch journals

Journals	VK	NRCH	Trouw	AD	PA	Tel
Items						
(1) total number of sports articles	144	134	109	196	101	162
(2) total number of World Cup articles	79	68	73	121	56	68
(2)(a) item (2) as percentage of item (1)	55%	51%	67%	62%	55%	41
(2)(b) Average World Cup articles per day	13	11	12	20	9	11
(3) total n. of articles dealing with B-D game	20	15	17	22	16	19
(3)(a) item (3) as a percentage of item (2)	25%	22%	23%	18%	29%	28%
(3)(b) Average n. of B-D game articles per day	3	2	3	4	3	3
(4) total n. of photographs of WC events	21	22	17	33	14	38
(5) the size of the newspaper (in sq. cm.)	1815	2200	2067	2200	2200	2200
(6) the surface of WC news on the front page	151	109	171	334	247	225
(6)(a) item (6) as a percentage of item (5)	8%	5%	8%	15%	11%	10%
(7) the letters to the editor section	2	1	1	0	0	0
(8) the presence of a separate sports section	0	0	0	0	0	0

Newspaper analysis: descriptive statistics

Tables 2 and 3 present descriptive statistics for 6 Flemish and 6 Dutch newspapers.
Results for each newspaper separately will be discussed in a later section, I first present an overview of the averages for the newspapers in table 4.

Table 4 : Overall figures (averages) of Flemish and Dutch newspapers

Country	Dutch	Flemish
Items		
(1) Average number of sport articles	141	406
(2) Average number of WC articles	77	195
(2)(a) item (2) in percentage of (1)	55%	48%
(2)(b) Average of WC articles per day	13	32
(3)Average of B-D articles	18	44
(3)(a) item (3) in percentage of (2)	23%	23%
(3)(b) Average of B-D articles per day	3	7
(4) Average number of pictures	24	24
(5) Average size of newspaper	2113sq cm	1876sq cm
(6) Average surface of WC on front page	206sq cm	299sq cm
(6)(a) item (6)in percentage of (5)	10%	16%

Since we can observe large differences among the Flemish and among the Dutch journals, average numbers must be handled with caution. Nevertheless, the average numbers paint a clear-cut difference between the group of Flemish journals and the group of Dutch journals. In all Items considered, the averages of the Flemish journals *more than double* the averages of the Dutch journals. This is true for Items 1, 2 and 3. For Item 6 we also observe a significant difference between the two groups.

The conclusion is quite obvious here : The World Cup football and the game between the Belgian and the Dutch teams received much more attention in the Flemish journals than in the Dutch journals. What does this mean ? Is football more important for Flemish journals than it is for Dutch ? Based on this quantitative analysis, one would say yes, no doubt about it. Why is football so omni present in Flemish journals ? Two interpretations stand out : (1) if journals print what people want to read, then the importance of football in the Flemish journals is due to the fact that Flemish want to read about football. In other words, football is very important to them, more important than it is to Dutch people; (2) if journals write what people should read, then the Flemish opinion makers give high priority to football articles. Flemish publishing-houses and journalists 'overload' the Flemish reader with football news.

It is not difficult to opt for interpretation (1). If (2) were true, then the Flemish journals who pay the least attention to football would be the most successful. The contrary is true : The Flemish journals who pay most attention to football (measured by Items (2) and (3)), are also bought the most. These are *Het Laatste Nieuws, Gazet van Antwerpen*, and *Het Nieuwsblad*. Journals who pay little attention to football are also sold the least. These are *De Morgen* and *De Standaard*. I am not saying that one factor causes the other. I am just pointing on the importance of football news for the Flemish newspapers and the readers of these newspapers. Much more than the Dutch reader, the Flemish reader wants football news in his journal. This explains the omni presence of World Cup news, articles about the Belgian-Dutch game and the high amount of football pictures in the Flemish journals. This is also confirmed by the fact that *Het Laatste Nieuws, Gazet van Antwerpen* and *Het Nieuwsblad* each published a special Sunday football newspaper on Sunday, June 26. These special editions were full of articles and pictures about the Belgian-Dutch game and the Belgian triumph.[3] I did not analyse these special editions in detail. Not all Flemish journals published a special edition and none of the Dutch journals did. A comparative analysis would therefore be impossible.

Newspaper analysis: quantitative approach

For each article dealing with the Belgian-Dutch game, I counted the frequencies of expressions relevant to Items (1) to (7) which I used in the quantitative approach of the TV comment analysis.[4]

Table 5 :   Comments in Flemish newspapers dealing with the Belgian-Dutch game

	Journals	HN	DS	DM	GVA	N	HV
Items							
Item 1	- Belgian	13	9	1	2	7	5
Item 2	- Dutch	30	21	8	15	12	2
Item 3	+ Belgian	40	21	10	26	33	17
Item 4	+ Dutch	38	25	3	10	10	2
Item 5	we-them	45	29	8	27	29	18
Item 6	obedience	45	26	10	18	22	13
Item 7	disturbance	20	12	19	10	14	3
	Total	231	143	59	108	127	60

Table 6 : Comments in Dutch journals dealing with the Belgian-Dutch game

	Journals	VK	NRC	Trouw	AD	PA	T el
Items							
Item 1	- Belgian	6	7	5	10	4	2
Item 2	- Dutch	8	8	18	21	12	14
Item 3	+ Belgian	14	6	9	10	1	9
Item 4	+ Dutch	15	9	9	9	6	15
Item 5	we-them	19	6	5	18	7	19
Item 6	obedience	8	2	1	3	4	8
Item 7	disturbance	8	10	10	3	6	6
	Totals	78	48	57	74	40	73

Table 7 : Comparison of Flemish and Dutch journals by means of the seven items (averages)

		Frequencies (Averages)		Percentages	
	Comments	Dutch	Flemish	Dutch	Flemish
Items					
Item 1	- Belgian	6.1	6.6	9.8	5.4
Item 2	- Dutch	13.5	14.6	21.9	12
Item 3	+ Belgian	8.1	24.5	13	20
Item 4	+ Dutch	10.5	14.6	17	12
Item 5	we- them	12.3	26	20	21.6
Item 6	obedience	4	22.8	6.4	18.3
Item 7	disturbance	7	13	11.3	10.7
	Totals	61.5	121.3	100	100

Applying the same Chi-square test for significance as in (4.1.1) yields the following result

$$\chi^2 = 9,87 \quad < \quad \chi^2 (\alpha = 0,05 \; ; d = 6) = 12,59$$

which means that the observed frequencies originate from the same distribution, the calculated χ^2 is to small to be significant. This is also the case for $\alpha = 0,1$ where $\chi^2 = 10,64$. One could say that the results here are almost significant at the 10% level.

On average, the total number of Flemish comments, relevant to Items 1 to 7 doubles the number of Dutch comments. This is because the average number of Flemish articles is much higher than the average number of Dutch articles (44 to 18). There is a difference in the total number of relevant expressions per article. The Dutch articles score here 3,4 and the Flemish 2,7. This is because the Dutch articles are a bit longer than the Flemish, they contain more words then Flemish articles (I did not measure this separately, but it is quite clear when reading the newspapers). This difference, nevertheless, is small compared to the overall attention given to football in the Flemish journals.

Knowing that the overall results of the quantitative newspaper analysis are not significant, we can look at the individual items to see what is going on. This might teach us something about our former interpretations. My first interpretation was built on the results obtained for Items 1 to 4 in the TV analysis. This interpretation concluded that Dutch reporting was more spectacular and positive than Flemish reporting. This interpretation cannot explain the results of the newspaper analysis. The Dutch journals make as many negative as positive comments (19 to 18). This contradicts with our TV results where the Dutch comment had a strong 'appreciating bias'. The Dutch comment does not have a 'nationalist bias' , they give positive and negative comments to both Belgian and Dutch players. However, the Dutch players get more (positive and negative) comments. Another fact that contradicts this interpretation is the low number (relatively, compared to total expressions) of expressions of disapproval in the Flemish articles (21, or one-third of the expressions in Items 1 to 4) .This is in contrast to the TV results, where half of the Flemish comments were 'negative ' regarding a players performance.

My interpretation from the TV analysis, that Flemish reporting is more 'nationalist' than Dutch does not find new significant support in the newspaper analysis. Looking at Item 3, the Flemish comments are more positive towards Belgian players than towards Dutch players. Dutch players receive as many approving as disapproving comments, while Flemish players receive four times more approving than disapproving comments. The percentage difference between Items 3 and 4 in the Flemish newspapers is twice as large as in the Dutch journals. But, as indicated before, the results are not strong enough to be significant.

This does not mean however that newspaper reporting does not spread nationalist feelings during international football games. Looking at item 5, we can observe the contrary, newspapers in both countries do their best to boost nationalist feelings. Compared to the other items, the relative frequencies of relevant expressions is high. More than in the TV analysis, the newspapers in both countries appeal to national feelings. They make many associations between football, national identity, and politics. There is however no clear distinction between the Dutch and the Flemish newspapers. I will discuss this more in our qualitative approach of each newspaper.

Items 6 and 7 allow a more pronounced viewpoint than in the TV analysis. The relative number of expressions sized under Item 6 in the Flemish newspapers is three times higher than in the Dutch journals. The Flemish journalists often quote a Belgian player saying 'the coach will decide' or 'the coach is always right', whereas the Dutch journalist often quote a player saying 'I will discuss this with the coach' or 'our strategy is wrong'. The aim of these Items was to learn something about the journalist's society (see above). Does the strong obedient element in Flemish football articles reflect a key point in Flemish society ? According to the literature, sports journalism indeed reflects the core values of the journalist's society. Are Belgian citizens, just like the football players obedient towards their boss and modest in their demands and do Dutch citizens, just like the football players criticize their boss and articulate their demands ?

Newspaper analysis: qualitative analysis - the Flemish journals.

<u>Het Laatste Nieuws</u>   is one of the most popular Dutch-language Belgian newspapers. It had a market share of 24% in 1992 and is published by the families Hoste and Van Thillo. The newspaper stands in the Flemish humanistic tradition. It advocates free enterprise and a market economy. As we see in Table 2, the journal publishes many sports articles, but not as many as the three leading sports newspapers. It printed the most pictures of the World Cup and has the highest percentage of articles concerning the Belgian-Dutch game among its World Cup articles. It has an own sports section and publishes letters of its readers. Table 5 doesn't reveal anything spectacular about *Het Laatste Nieuws*, it is the newspaper which best fits to the Flemish averages (table 7). Its articles dealing with the Belgian-Dutch game were easy and pleasant to read. The journal mentioned the other 'competition' going on between the Belgian and the Dutch prime ministers. It wrote about the presence of Belgian companies in the lounge of the hotel of the Belgian national team, trying to do business with American firms. It had a special Sunday edition. It was the newspaper for persons who wanted to enjoy the sports event in all its colours and clichés. Its readership did not want its favorite game and team to be criticised.

<u>Gazet van Antwerpen</u> Had a market share of 14,6% in 1992. The newspaper describes itself as catholic and Flemish and is conservative in ethical topics. Its readership is mainly the settled middle class. It published on average 45 World Cup articles per day, the most of all newspapers. This is also true for the number of articles on the Belgian-Dutch game. It dedicated by far the most attention to the World Cup on its front page (Table 2). It had the largest discrepancy between positive and negative comments of Belgian players among all Flemish journals.(Table 5)
The articles made an amusing impression with a lot of humor and self-mockery. The journalists attempted to get the reader in the mood for 'the derby of the Low Countries' and associate the game often with 'our nation' and 'our country'. The example shows once again the rivalry between the Prime Ministers at the European Summit.

<u>Het Nieuwsblad</u> Together with *De Standaard* and its regional edition *De Gentenaar*, this newspaper holds 32% of the market. It is meant for the general public and addresses a lot of sports and entertainment. Its editors want to present a newspaper that is christian, Flemish, for democracy and the market economy. The World Cup and the Belgian-Dutch game received plenty of attention; as demonstrated by the number of articles and pictures (Table 2). Compared to 'GVA' and 'LN' which had about the same amount of articles dealing with the Belgian-Dutch game, this newspaper had a very high number of comments (Table 5). The journalists 'overloaded' their readers with value judgements; the articles were full of comments, associations and viewpoints. They often quoted players and attempted to create a 'derby atmosphere'. They

linked the game to the Dehaene-Lubbers competition. I had the impression that they wanted to create an artificial sense of nationalism.

Het Volk   This newspaper has always been the mouthpiece of the organised Flemish catholic workers. It holds 14,2% of the market. The journal addresses many sports events (begins to sound monotonic, doesn't it?), as seen in Table 2. Sport articles appear in an own sports section, also on weekdays. Compared to the overall attention to sports and the World Cup, the number of articles concerning the Belgian-Dutch game was very low. Relative to the number of articles, the frequency of relevant expressions was also very low (60, see table 5). Dutch players very rarely received comments. I found the articles quite boring and unpleasant to read. When the journalists gave any comment, it was likely to be affirmative for the game's rules and protective for societal order in general.

De Morgen was formerly closely associated with the Socialist Party which funded for the newspaper. It had a market share of 2,5% in 1992. The newspaper attempts to be open, progressive and independent. It paid little attention to football and the World Cup compared to the other Dutch-language Belgian journals (table 2). The results in table 5 suggests a strong 'chauvinist bias' : positive comments for the Belgian players and negative comments for the Dutch players.
The newspaper often published critical articles about the World Cup event, ranging from the hotel organisation and soccer in America to the salary of the players. The reader received the image of an over-commercialised football event and of the stupidity of many fellow countrymen who participated in it.

De Standaard is the leading newspaper in Dutch-language Belgium concerning politics, economics, and international news. It has a high standing and reaches the Flemish, catholic intellectual community. It reserved little space for sports articles (table 2). Despite its small number of sports articles, *De Standaard* scored high on frequency of expression (table 5). This is because the published sport articles are a selection of the sports articles appearing in *Het Nieuwsblad*. As I previously stated, in this newspaper I read more opinions, comments and judgements relevant to items 1 to 7 than in any other newspaper.
The newspaper stressed the 'football madness' of the Dutch and associated the Belgian-Dutch game with Dehaene and politics.

Newspaper analysis: qualitative analysis - the Dutch journals

Trouw   is a protestant newspaper, which was committed to the Dutch Resistance in World War II. It pays much attention to religious and population topics. Sports are of minor importance to the newspaper (see table 3). The newspaper criticised order and hierarchy strongly; table 6 shows a large discrepancy between item 6 and 7. This position is very clear in the articles : players openly discussed the coach and his tactics. They give their opinion about the way things develop. The newspaper reported professionally and critical on the World Cup : What goes wrong ? Why ? What is the background ? The only similarity   to the Flemish newspapers is the link made to the 'competition' between Dehaene and Lubbers.

Het Parool is considered a social-democratic, worker-oriented newspaper and has its readership among students and in the cities as well. It had the lowest number of World Cup articles of all newspapers. In these articles however, the Belgian-Dutch game was given a prominent place (see table 3). The space devoted to World Cup events on the front page, indicates that the newspaper considered this event as 'news', earning the same attention as other 'news'. In contrast to the Flemish newspapers, the World Cup did not get mass attention. In table 6   the very low number of positive comments towards the Belgian players' performances was remarkable. This was an exception in Dutch reporting. In general, I found few 'useful' expressions for the purposes of this paper in this journal, which for me had a sober and critical approach of the World Cup and the Belgian-Dutch game.

NRC Handelsblad is the Dutch quality-newspaper comparable to *Le Monde* and *The Times*. It has a high standing and wants to reach the established, successful professional. Sports news belongs in the last pages of the newspaper. The main pages are reserved for political comments, economic affairs and international news. Among the sports articles, the World Cup received 50%. The Belgian-Dutch game received little attention.
Table 6 suggest a rather equal distribution of all expressions over the different Items.
The newspaper reduces the 'event ' to more normal proportions in a business-like style of writing, 'football players are just human beings'. It nevertheless associates football with politics as it mentions the ongoing struggle between Lubbers and Dehaene.

De Volkskrant was formerly a catholic newspaper. It has a rather high standing. Its readers are democrats from the political centre of Dutch society. Its quantitative characteristics are very close to the Dutch average (table 3). Table 6 however, shows another picture : the newspaper here resembled the Dutch TV comments : many comments, and among them many positive ones, independent of nationality of the player. This was an exception in Dutch newspaper reporting.
In this newspaper the difference in mentality between Belgian and Dutch players and citizens was discussed extensively. Football is considered a good opportunity to talk about the people's mentality and national identity. Dutch maturity and arrogance versus Belgian modesty and obedience was the outcome of its articles.

The newspaper relates the football game to politics, personalized in the struggle of both prime ministers.

De Telegraaf is the most popular newspaper in The Netherlands. Compared to Flemish newspapers, it did not pay a lot of attention to football and the World Cup. Compared to other Dutch newspapers it printed a lot of color photos (table 3). Belgian players receive many appreciating comments in its articles (table 6).
The newspaper used war vocabulary to comment on the game: 'opponent', 'torpedo', 'war'.
It quoted foreign players playing in the Belgian league : , We are treated as slaves'. It quoted players saying that the rivalry with Germany is much more intense than with Belgium. The newspaper described the Belgian coach Van Himst in his beloved role as 'underdog' and linked the game with the struggle between Lubbers and Dehaene.

Algemeen Dagblad is a Rotterdam-based newspaper with a nation wide readership. It is among the most popular Dutch newspapers. It had the highest number of articles on the World Cup and the Belgian-Dutch game. 15% of its front page was devoted to World Cup news, which was the highest among Dutch newspapers. The journalist often criticised the Dutch players' performances (Table 6). The newspaper tried to create a 'derby atmosphere ' with headlines like ' een lesje krijgen' (to teach one a lesson) and 'pak'm '(get him), and the use of a lot of photos. It published the comments of other Dutch coaches on the tactics of Dick Advocaat, the coach or the Dutch team.

We conclude this qualitative analysis with some remarkable quotation in Dutch newspapers :

> *"The culture in this country does not allow one to oppose a national coach, who is just like his predecessors Thijs and Goethals, fosters the underdog feelings towards the 'arrogant' Dutch".*
> (Het Parool, *Saturday, June 25, page 33, (my translation))*

> *"...the Dutch establish here a disgusting mass behaviour, not to say mass hysteria. This nonsense of going to the game on wooden shoes. To enter an air conditioned hotel with orange sunglasses, in orange underpants, everything is orange. The cackling, the one who follows the other, this whole imitation, this behavior as a bunch of starlings that grows and lands on Koeman and the stand. It is not good, even frightening. I think it is ridiculous ..."*
> (*Trouw* , Saturday, June 25, page 15, interview with Hugo Camps, (my translation))

"... Van Himst was spoiled by the rococo-atmosphere at Anderlecht, where he was the star player for several years. As a player he was more like a young lady than a general. And what is never talked about : Van Himst has always had a problem with Dutchmen. Jan Mulders carefully preserves the friendship myth with Van Himst. This friendship, or better, the good communication, was established after his career at Anderlecht. In the team, both players fought a prestige battle. Van Himst was an introverted, fragile boy. Jan Mulders, on the contrary, criticised everything. Jan Mulder also introduced another vocabulary at Anderlecht with which he broke with the intimacy of the familial idyll ..."
(*Trouw* , Saturday, June 25, page 15, interview with Hugo Camps, (my translation))

Conclusions and comparison to the 1998 game

I wanted to find out what the relation is between football and nationalism as it occurs in spoken and written press comments. I analysed press comments dealing with the Belgian-Dutch game at the World Cup football, June 25, 1994.

The interpretation that most fits the analysed TV comments is that Flemish reporting has a 'nationalist bias' and Dutch reporting does not. More than Dutch nation wide TV, Flemish TV uses the World Cup football game as a nation-building opportunity for Belgium. This strong result was not found in the newspaper analysis.

For the Flemish media, the quantitative approach, as well as the more qualitative approach both for the TV and newspaper comments, suggest a strong relation between the football game, politics and the national identity of the Belgians. It appeared as the Belgians received an injection of nationalistic feelings and comments during the period of this World Cup game. The media in Belgium used this game to unite the Belgians, to strengthen the in-group feelings. The mixture of emotions, the Prime Minister and an 'arrogant ' opponent was an excellent setting for these in-group feelings. Being a Belgian national, the author is not surprised by this result : in a country where politics is often a scene of conflict between the Flemish and the Walloon communities, there are practically no other opportunities in Belgium or Flanders to raise Belgian nationalism in Flanders. The football game is used to unite an otherwise divided country.

For the Dutch media, I observed a difference between TV and newspaper comments. TV comments were spectacular and enthusiastic whereas newspaper comments were sober and of high professional standing. Dutch newspapers dealt with the World Cup as 'news' and did not overload its readers with football articles. The Dutch do not need a nationalistic injection ?

The football comments also teach something about the reporter's society. The Flemish reporters often quote the Belgian players as saying, 'the coach is right;

I will do what he says' (item 6 doubles item 7). The Dutch reporters often quote the Dutch players as saying 'the coach is wrong; I will talk with him this afternoon' (item 7 doubles item 6). The relation coach-player-press thus represents the obedient and closed Belgian attitude on the one hand, and the critical and open Dutch attitude on the other hand.

I have not undertaken the same in depth analysis for the 1998 game between Belgium and the Netherlands, but a superficial observation shows some very remarkable similarities between the 1994 and the 1998 game. Media coverage in Flemish journals is all over, with special editions after every game. Dutch journalists, players and the audience are convinced that their team will become World Champion. The coach of the Belgian Team sees his team as the underdog compared to the Dutch team. Flemish TV involves the Belgian Prime Minister Dehaene in an analysis of the game. During his 30 min TV-interview the day after the game the journalist switches 4 times between the strategy of the team and the political agenda of the Belgian Government. Questions of the quality of a player are followed by questions on a new law accepted by the Flemish parliament concerning the payment of a pension to world war II collaborators. This topic is again abandoned by new questions about the game and so on.

Notes

[1] Duke, V. & Crolly, L. (1996). Football, nationality and the state. Longman, England.

[2] Gruneau, R.S. (1975). Sport, social differentiation and inequality, in Ball, D.W. & Loy, J.W. (eds.), Sport and social order: contributions to the sociology of Sport. Reading; Petrie, B.M., Sports and politics, in Ball & Loy, ibidem; Listhaeghe, E. (1992). Sport, nationalisme en de rol van de media, Eindverhandeling K.U.Leuven; Clarke, A. & Clarke, J. (1982). Highlights and action replays, ideology, sports and the media. London.

[3] The publication of a special edition was not because of the Belgian triumph, but because of the game itself as can be derived from the special publications after each Belgian game in the 1998 World Cup.

[4] The number of articles that were analysed for each journal can be traced under item 3 in tables 2 and 3.

Chapter 10

Globalization and localization in sport

Paul De Knop and Sandra Harthoorn
Free University of Brussels V.U.B., Belgium

The world of sports is growing apart. We notice the polarization of on the one hand the ever more commercial and international top-class sport and on the other the revival of local recreation sport and local traditions. In this contribution we indicate, exemplify and explain the globalization and localization of sport and their consequences on the organization of sport. As far as research method is concerned, we have conducted a literature study in the field of sport sociology in order to investigate the significance of globalization in the context of sport. The examples used are abstracted from recent press articles to indicate the topicality of this development. Let us refer to Giddens as far as definitions are concerned.

> *"Globalization can be defined as the intensification of world-wide social relations which link distant localities in such a way that local happenings are shaped by events occurring many miles away and vice versa. This is a dialectical process because such local happenings may move in an obverse direction from the very distanciated relations that shape them. Local transformation is as much a part of globalization as the lateral extension of social connections across time and space"* (Giddens 1990, p. 64).

The world of today is the village of tomorrow. As a consequence of the increased mobility, new communication technologies, exploding information networks, mass media, the all-embracing economy,... we are now experiencing a mondialization in different areas. We are living in a world whose national borders are becoming ever more porous and in which different globalizing processes are occurring (Horsman & Marschall 1996).

Globalization

Sport is experiencing a globalization as well. This can be concluded from the following facts.

(1) Universalization of Western sports, Eastern combat sports, ... Research in twenty different countries world-wide (De Knop et al. 1996) has found that there are hardly any "large" sports which are practised by youngsters exclusively in one (or a few) countries

(2) The presence of international "sport heroes" such as Lewis, Jordan, ... who are functioning as universal models. Some sport forms contribute to globalization, not by contributing to the development of a metaculture, but rather through a fragmented and segmented culture, regrouping individuals independently from the national level. Such is the case, to a certain extent, for high-performance athletes whose identities are linked more to a network of training and competition than to any element of their national belonging, such as language or religion (Harvey & Houle 1994).

(3) (World) trade in sportswear and -material : especially the large multinationals / sport brands such as Nike, Adidas and Reebok have gained from the increased significance of sport. These three brands are undoubtedly the largest distributors of sportswear and -shoes. It is striking however that a large majority of the people buying these sport brands hardly ever or never practises sport. Sports goods have become world-wide fashion articles by means of world-wide promotional campaigns and sponsoring.

(4) Fragmentation of the production of sport products due to the extended specialization. Reich (1991) provided an example of economic, technological, and industrial globalization and interdependence in connection with sport : "Precision hockey equipment is designed in Sweden, financed in Canada, and assembled in Cleveland and Denmark for distribution in North America and Europe, respectively, out of alloys whose molecular structure was researched and patented in Delaware and fabricated in Japan." (p.112). The sports goods industry does not only aim at growing shares of a world market but also adopt global strategies of production, such as delocalization. A growing portion of the population in developing countries is engaged in the production of goods for the reproduction of the lifestyles of those living in developed countries (Andreff 1988).

(5) Increasing power of the international sports organizations (IOC, AGFI, FIFA, ...). This is shown for example by the fact that the IOC decides upon the admission of the Olympic venues, but also upon the Olympic status of a sport and therefore indirectly upon the popularity of a sport. According to the Olympic charter, in order to be an Olympic sport, a sport must comply with the

following criteria: only sports widely practised by men in at least seventy-five countries and in four continents and by women in at least forty countries and on three continents.

(6) International networks. This is where public sports policy is discussed (e.g. the Council of Europe).

(7) The international (European) legislation has sometimes major consequences for sport (e.g. the Bosman case).

(8) There is an increase in economic and political importance of the Olympic Games, the Commonwealth Games, different world championships, and other uni- or multisporttournaments on world level.

(9) The competition between cities to organise mega-sporting events with a view to becoming a "world-class" city; sporting facilities and major sporting events are important instruments in this context. The mega-sporting facilities and events are however designed according to homogenous concepts which make the local specificity fade away. "Many kinds of ex-urban leisure developments ... that were once distinctive have become internationally ordinary (Whitson & Macintosh 1993, p. 235-236). The final result is a diffusion of a strongly capitalized consumer culture, in other words a kind of "global culture".

(10) The media-globalization in sports: e.g. the World Cup soccer final or an important event of the Olympics will be watched on television by approximately one quarter of the adult world population. Not just the size of the audience, but also the way in which the media cover the programs, are characteristic for globalization. For example, most Africans watch a version of the Olympics and the Soccer World Cup in which the European Broadcasting Union decides what is worth watching and knowing. Even the images of African successes are being selected and shown by Europeans.

(11) The migration of players and coaches. East-European athletes and coaches started striving for contract with foreign clubs on a large scale after being confronted with an indifferent attitude of the new governments to sports, the media and the population in general. For example the tenfold world and triple Olympic champion figure-skating, I. Rodina, has become a coach in the United States. At the beginning of the open-borders policy, in 1989-1990, Soviet coaches and athletes became the largest migrating population in international sport. In hockey for example the migration from the Eastern countries was enormous. Around 1991 106 high-performance players moved abroad to compete, of which 11 to Northern America and 95 to European clubs. Also other sports, chess in particular witnessed a large scale exodus in the top ten ranking (Zilberman 1994);

(12) Transnational teams. Athletes representing countries different from their country of birth also represent a growing trend in international sport. Peter Medved, born in the Czech Republic, represented the Canadian team which won a silver medal during the Lillehammer Games. In 1986 82 foreigners played at the core of the 18 first class soccer clubs in Belgium. Ten years later this number evolved to a total of 157 (a doublation). Also in the Belgian national soccer team some no longer recognise their own national colour : Scifo (Italy), Weber (Croatia), Vukovic (Croatia), Czerniatinski (Russia), Oliveira (Brazil), Mpenza (Congo), Medved (Hungary), etc. During the major tournaments top-class tennis players no longer represent a nation, but in first instance themselves and in second instance their sponsor. Top-class tennis - and in particular the Grandslam-circuit can be understood in terms of a "third culture" characterized by a transnational current of money, goods, people, images and information (Featherstone 1991).

(13) The fact that sport is a part of world's number one industry, tourism : the "S" of "sport" can be added to the four traditional "s-es" of tourism, namely sun, sand, sea and sex (De Knop & Standeven, 1999).

(14) A universal consumer sovereignty which is gaining more and more importance (this global consumer culture is sometimes referred to with terms such as Americanization, Coca-colonization, Mc Donaldization ...) and manifests itself in consumer directed activities such as fitness, aerobics etc.

(15) Social movements. The fact that sport was influenced by and also contributed to social movements, such as feminism, pacifism and ecologism. The fight of women for equality in the Olympic Games and in sport, the anti-apartheid movement in sport and sport as a key element in the spread of these movements, the ecological trend in mass sport participation, etc. are typical examples (Harvey & Houle 1994).

Localization

As indicated above in the world of sports we notice the growing apart of, the polarization of on the one hand the ever more commercial top-class sport and on the other the revival of local recreation sport and local traditions. The revival of local popular sports (folk games, traditional sports and games, etc.) are examples of this (Reich 1991; Renson 1997).

Another development undeniable in the world of sports is that performances of top-class athletes on European or world level strongly increase the interest in active sport participation in the local and recreational sphere, partly due to the attention of the media.

Further more we also notice that within sport a lot is being done for the promotion and talent stimulation in the local sphere. The Flemish Tennis Association for example started an action "youth friendly Tennis Club" in 1995, with the aim to reward those clubs making special efforts towards youth tennis (Jaarverslag VTV 1996). Also the Tennis Cup of Flanders, an initiative of the Flemish Tennis Association, aims at helping the Belgian top-class players and upcoming talented players by means of gaining ATP-points in their own country and with their home audience. This gravel tournament functions internationally as an entry tournament for young Flemish professional players (*De Morgen* 28/7/1997).

Another manifestation is the desire expressed recently by the Flemish sports federations to participate in international competitions in analogy with Wales, Scotland, England, San Marino, etc.. Or in other words sport is also subject to the paradox of globalization versus localization.

Consequences on the organization of sport

Top-class sport is being more and more organized in competitions on a European or even an international level. Large tournaments and competitions (Roland Garros, Champions League, World Cup Soccer) are becoming ever more important at the expense of the smaller national competitions. Top-class athletes often *refuse participation in national competitions* and even the Olympic Games are sometimes passed over because of other interests. In tennis for example it seems to be more important to collect ATP-points and cash prizes that to participate in national competitions. Last year the Belgian top-class tennis players Sabine Appelmans and Filip Dewulf were absent during the Belgian Championships because they were not contracted to participate due to their high ranking. They preferred competing themselves in WTA- and ATP-tournaments (*De Morgen* 23/7/1997).

Because of this polarization, with top-class sport growing to be a mondial phenomenon on the one hand and, the increasing interest in sport on a recreational level on the other, the *national competition* seems to be *marginalized*. The national sports pyramid seems to be disappearing. The flight of the television amounts and merchandising in most West-European countries has seriously damaged the financial strength of the national flagbearers in comparison with the international opposition. The Bosman decree has completely faded the soccer barriers and accentuated the unequal battle. Never before did so many players leave the country. The "Red Devils" Belgian national soccer team can escape a crisis because of the many players in foreign employment, but in the European club competitions a strong step back is inevitable. Even the powerful Ajax has been squeezed dry completely last year. Quite logically the top-class players go were the most money can be earned and that is automatically to large countries, with large audiences and many potential television watchers. The smaller countries will experience even more difficulties in the future.

Moreover it is often a difficult or even an *impossible* task for the coach to *select a national team* because the top-class athletes have sponsor obligations or are playing abroad for large amounts of money. So commercialization weakens the nationalism in sport. Yet a certain form of nationalism will keep existing. A motor raceteam can for example be managed by a Frenchman, use a German racecar with a Japanese engine, but if the driver is Brazilian, a possible victory will primarily be felt as Brazilian. In this sense as well , despite their substantial input, the Dutchmen playing soccer in Italian super clubs rather accomplish an Italian than a Dutch victory (Houlihan 1994).

At the same time more and more small clubs are experiencing *financial difficulties*, partly due to the fact that the local players are making financial demands under the influence of the media.

The world of sports needs *the media* in order to survive. Without the media sponsoring would not have developed to the present level. On the other hand, the media need sport to fill in their programs and obtain high ratings. In some cases the media even put pressure on the sports federations to adjust the rules of their sport. Charaterizing is that these adjustments are in the interest of the spectators and/or the media and not in that of the sportsmen.
Some examples of "rule adjustments" in order to make the sport more attractive for television: boxing (decrease in the number of rounds from 15 to 12 to make commercials possible), squash (another scoring system), cricket (increase in "one-day" cricket games). In some cases the media tries to influence the place and time of the competitions in their interest. It is often stated that top-class athletes have become entertainers. A typical example of this development can be found in tennis, where the players adjust their game to the broadcasting time. The players divide the first two sets and then play an honest third set. Moreover the media is making a selection of the most amusing sports and the fragments which ensure a maximal interest from the audience, namely drama, the spectacular and theatrical - the knock-out, the winning goal ... (Sewart 1995).

On the other hand, due to globalization, the small and local sport threatens to become anonymous. Theoretically, the emergence of local television stations could bring a solution, but we notice that this has not happened so far.

The fact that the media are controlling the scenery of sports does not only have an impact on the watching of sport (television offer) but also on the *participation*. The recreational runner wants to and can climb the Mount

Ventoux ... This way new forms of sport emerge next to the traditional club sports.

On the other hand, due to the marginalization of the national competition and selection, sponsors are looking for *new and unique events* instead of sponsoring teams and individuals. For example the organization of competitions where two or more athletes compete. The top moments of athletics in the Olympics in Atlanta scored very high in every way and smart promoters smelled the gold. By means of sponsorship companies/brands are associated with certain sportsmen, certain sports or certain events. This association naturally also counts in connection with the negative aspects of the sport such as drug use, hooliganism, violence of the athletes themselves and bribery scandals (e.g. RSC-Anderlecht).

Moreover, we notice an increased interest in unique events with a *concentration of talent* such as the Champions League, where the best teams compete. Within soccer there is also talk of a Be-Ne league (Belgium - The Netherlands).

Sports sponsorship has grown rapidly over recent years. High-level athletes are increasingly appealing to international companies who wish to expand their brand name and image. After all sport is an outstanding means to attract the attention of the audience. But is this why there is a *shift* taking place from the interests of the sportsmen to an increasing promotion of the *interests of the sponsors* ? We can say yes. After all sponsors are more and more determining the organization of events and competitions, thus interfering with the place, the time, the rules of the game, etc. ... Sportsmen have become dependent on the powerful sponsors.

Conclusion

We conclude that the scenery of sports is growing more and more apart. On the one hand top-class sport has developed into a full time profession. These professionals are ever more to be found in an international arena, sponsored by multinationals and observed by an international audience. Players and clubs are more and more resilient to participating in national competitions. Both the media and the audiences show also less interest in this level. On the other hand, the participation on the recreational level has increased explosively and here sport is practised in a more local and individual setting. In other words, we can distinguish a *polarization* in the world of sports: an international/global direction where (top-class) sport is becoming ever more internationally oriented and a local direction where (recreational) sport is being practised on a local level. *Globalization versus localization* thus. Both globalization and localization are a manifestation of an ever increasing differentiation in sport, with great impact on the organization of sport.

References

Andreff, W. (1988). Les multinationales et le sport dans les pays en développement: Ou comment faire courir le tiers monde après les capiteaux [Multinationals and sport in developping countries: How to make the third world countries run after capital]. Revue Tiers Monde, 29(113), 73-100.

De Knop, P., Engström, L.M., Skirstad, B. & Weiss, M.R. (1996). Worldwide trends in youth sport. Champaign, Illinois: Human Kinetics Publishers.

De Knop, P. & Standeven, J. (1999). Sport and tourism: international perspectives. Champaign, Illinois, Human Kinetics Publishers.

Featherstone, M. (1991). Georg Simmel: an introduction. Theory, Culture and Society, 8/3, 1-16.

Giddens, A. (1990). Cit. in M. Waters, Globalisation key ideas (p.50). Great-Britain: Routledge.

Harvey, J. & Houle, F. (1994). Sport, world economy, global culture, and new social movements. Sociology of Sport Journal, 11, 337-355.

Horsman & Marschall. Cit. in P. Donnelly (1996), The local and the global; globalization in the sociology of sport. Journal of Sport and Social Issues, 23, Aug. 1996, 239-252.

Houlihan, B. (1994). Sport and international politics. New York, USA, Harvester Wheatsheaf.

Jong geweld op BK tennis [Young talent at the Belgian champoinchips tennis]. (1997, 23 juli). De Morgen.

Reich (1991) in P. Donnely, The local and the global : globalization in the sociology of sport. Journal of Sport and Social Issues, 23, Aug. 1996, 239-257.

Renson R. (1997). The reinvention of tradition in sports and games. Journal of Comparative Physical Education and Sport, 19(2), 46-52.

Sewart, J. (1995). The commodification of sport. International Review for the Sociology of Sport, 22, 171-191.

Vlaamse Tennis Vereniging vzw. (1997). Jaarverslag 1996 [Annual report 1996]. Brussel.

Walter Goethals beraadt zich over Tenniscup of Flanders [W.G. considers the Tenniscup of Flanders]. (1997, 28 juli). De Morgen.

Whitson, D. & MacIntosh, D. (1993). Becoming a world-class city: hallmark events and sport franchises in the growth strategies of western Canadian cities. Sociology of Sport Journal, 10, 221-240.

Zilberman, V. (1994). The changing face of international sport under new world order. Paper presented at the World Congress Physical Education - Changes and Challenges - AIESEP, Berlin.

Part C

The past explaining the present

Chapter 11

The evolution of physical education in Quebec: the history of two cultural solitude (1875-1965)

Rose-Marie Lèbe
University of Montreal, Canada

To study the evolution of Physical Education in Quebec is quite a challenge. Canadian historians Cosentino and Howell (1971), in their study "A History of Physical Education in Canada" clearly summed up the complexity of the situation when they wrote: "The problems in attempting to trace the development of Physical Education in Quebec are compounded by the duality of culture in that province" [1]. They finally settled the matter by dividing their study of Physical Education in Quebec in two separate parts: Catholic Quebec and Protestant Quebec.

In fact, when consulting the rare reference manuals on Physical Education in Quebec, we realise that each sector wrote about its own Physical Education system and centered on its own universe. Each completely ignored the other's reality. Audet (1971) resumed this characteristic when speaking of two ethnic groups travelling on parallel roads without dialog for almost a century.

French "Quebecois" and English Canadians, living in the same territory, under the same political regime and laws, have succeeded to live side-by-side ignoring one another. It is true to say that everything brought them apart: first of all, language, then origin (France versus Great Britain), social status (the first French settlers were defeated by the English whom they regarded as invaders), occupation (the French majority living off the land, while the English minority owned the industries and the most lucrative businesses).

This situation seemed ideal for a comparative study. Effectively, it is a rare occurrence to observe such dynamic where two cultures stay impervious to one another and undergo different influences in an identical context.

The goal of this study is threefold: (a) trace the evolution of Physical Education in the two sectors of the Quebec education system (English-

Protestant and French-Catholic); (b) bring out the differences in their development; (c) analyse the factors responsible for those differences.

This study examines three distinctive periods chosen because of the importance of events that occurred in the Quebec education system at the time. They are: (a) the last quarter of the 19th century when the education system was divided in two independent sectors: Catholic and Protestant; (b) the beginning of the 20th century during the two World Wars period when the Federal Government imposed militarism; (c) the 60's, during La Révolution tranquille , when French Quebec lived a quiet revolution and started to break away from the Catholic Church.

Figure 1 shows the complexity of the Quebec education system at the end of the 19th Century. Two committees, one Protestant and one Roman Catholic, were responsible to the Superintendant of Education. Each administered the schools falling naturally under its jurisdiction and each enjoyed complete autonomy in improving its own curriculum, implementing its own methodology of teaching and creating its own administration.

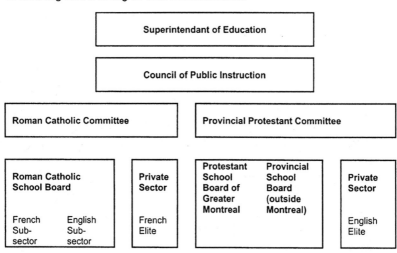

Figure 1 :   The Education System in the Province of Quebec at the end of the 19th Century

Physical Education before 1900

If we believed what Cosentino and Howell said, at the end of the 19th century: "In the French Catholic system, there was little development in the field of Physical Education up to 1900" [2], while in the English sector "... by the turn of the century, gymnastics was firmly established in the Protestant schools of Quebec" [3]. This affirmation is not quite accurate.

It is true that, in the majority of French schools, there seemingly was no need for Physical Education, but rather for horticulture and gardening. The French community favoured this agriculturist approach because it upheld the values and traditions of their culture. Medical doctors and Catholic priests saw only advantages in this form of physical activity: the former because life in the country was healthy [4], the latter because agriculturism kept their parishioners away from city corruption. In cultivating small gardens, the children were involved in a useful and healthy activity.

For different reasons, the same thing happened in the English community outside of Montreal. The rural schools did not teach any physical education but it was due only to lack of equipment, facilities, and trained instructors. In theory, both communities recognised the need for Physical Education but they were far from being able to implement this concept in all the schools. As a result, there was no official program of physical education in either system.

However, it was quite a different story for the children of both the French and English elite who attended private schools. On the Catholic side, there were the Collège Ste-Anne de la Pocatière that owned a royal tennis court and the Collège des Jésuites in Quebec City that was proud to own the first gymnasium in Canada [5]. Similarly, students at the Collège Ste-Marie in Montreal not only had access to a gymnasium but also took swimming, dancing, fencing and riding lessons, their physical education comparing favourably to the best religious schools in France during the same period.

On the Protestant side, there were St. Francis College, which was recognised for its sport curriculum, and the Montreal High School, which was a model for other schools and played an important role in the establishing of physical training in the Protestant school system. [6]

Was then Physical Education a luxury reserved to the elite, be it French or English? It is safe to say that development in this sector was not generalised and that it was dependant on the will of educators who believed in the virtues of Physical Education and took upon themselves to organise its teaching.

However, there was a difference between both communities. In the English sector, Physical Education was taught by laymen who studied outside the province, in such institution as Springfield College in the USA, and became Physical Education specialists. Such was the case of Fred Barjnum who held a position of Director of Physical Training at McGill College at a time when there was little systematic work in the field. He became a real promoter of Physical Education and of the new profession of physical educator. He wrote pamphlets and articles, organised gymnastic demonstrations, spoke at meetings and led people to see the potential of this new field of education. [7] On the other hand, in the French system, education being the prerogative of the Catholic clergy, Physical Education was taught by ecclesiastics who often believed that Physical Education was a recreation and an antidote to intellectual work.

Although the English and French communities did adopt two different names for the physical activity (the English spoke of " physical training" whereas the French preferred the term *gymnastique*), both seemed to share a vision about the effects of physical education. Both thought that physical activity was a mean to achieve discipline, the respect of authority, obedience and the old concept of *men sana in corpore sano*. They used similar methods that were popular in Great Britain at the time [8], the Ling system and military drills.

The French system kept to this approach while the its English counterparts accepted other influences, especially from their American neighbours. In the English schools, one can recognise aspects from the Delsarte system and the Sargent method , the Dio Lewis' callisthenics and, of course, games and sport competitions which were part of the British tradition.

The importance of sport for the development of the character and personality of children was far from certain for the Catholic Church. Neither was the place of sport in the school curriculum. Catholic Physical Education was marked by a dualist approach of the individual, which greatly prioritised the intellectual and spiritual dimensions. Physical Education was only recognised as a mean to discipline and a derivative to studies.

On the other hand, the English sector was starting to think that Physical Education was an integral part of the complete and harmonious development of children. Consequently, the Protestant school system was willing to integrate physical education in its curriculum as early as the beginning of the 20th century, while the Catholics did not think it was necessary to add additional recreational time.

The militarist period (1900-1945)

This is without doubt the most interesting period for a comparative study. It was a time when the English sector greatly differentiated itself from the French. Although, they shared a similar social-economic situation-- two World Wars and the Great Depression of the 1930s – they also found themselves in a similar context: that of the Federal Government which had decided to standardise the teaching of Physical Education across Canada through the implementation of the Strathcona Trust Fund and the imposition of military training in schools. The Protestant sector adhered with reserve, while continuing to put in place its own Physical Education system which had been started at the end of the 19th century. The Catholics gave over Physical Education to the military, thereby abandoning all effort to structure and develop Physical Education, which was left in a precarious state where it foundered for many years.

The Strathcona Plan was not a bad idea in itself. The government offered substantial financial subsidies to help establish the Plan in every province. By introducing the cadet corps and by teaching military exercises and arm drills in the schools, the governmental authorities thought they were taking care of the physical, mental and moral development of the young boys, while, at the same time, giving them abilities which would be useful when they became adults. The government also wanted to foster patriotism "leading them (the boys) to realise that the first duty of a free citizen is to be prepared to defend his country." [9]

Education was of provincial jurisdiction; therefore, each province had to reach an agreement with the Federal Government to receive the advantages of the Strathcona Fund. The provinces had to: (a) encourage the creation of cadet corps in every school; (b) introduce the practice of military exercises and shooting in their programs with the method described in the "Syllabus of Physical Training"; (c) request from every teacher "a certification of proficiency" in teaching this particular method.

In return, the government provided skilled instructors, subsidies, arms, costumes and manuals to teach the method and agreed to conduct the necessary examinations. Lord Strathcona donated $500,000 (quite a fortune at the time) to form a Trust Fund, the interest of which served to finance the plan throughout the provinces.

Quebec joined the Trust in 1909 and had to sign not one, but two agreements: one with the *Commission des écoles catholiques* and the other with the Protestant School Board, thus creating two local committees of the Strathcona Trust operating separately.

The form the Trust took in Protestant Quebec was much the same as in the other provinces: subsidies were divided equally between the cadet corps and physical education in regular classes. We know that the Protestant sector used the money to buy books instead of paying instructors. Instead, they recognised and encouraged monitors by giving them a certificate of proficiency.

There are few details available about the way the subsidies were spent in the Catholic schools. However, what is known is that the adhesion to the program was unanimous. The military movement grew enormously. Membership in the cadet corps went from 5000 in 1911 to 27 000 in 1918, and, by 1933 it had reached more than 62 000. Unfortunately, militarism was the only system of Physical Education in the French school system and was reaching only 15% of the male students. Thus, girls were deprived of any physical activities, and, although it was theoretically compulsory, in reality, physical education did not exist.

During that time, the English sector continued to organise its physical education system and develop its programs, infrastructures and the training of its teachers without taking the federal subsidies, which barely amount to $700 for the 50 Protestant schools.

As early as 1904, many gymnasiums were built, specialists came from England and physical education was introduced in the curriculum of the teachers' training college, such as the Royal Victoria College. The McGill School of Physical Education opened its doors in 1912 and trained specialists into games, callisthenics, gymnastics, rhythmic, and dance; everything but military exercises which were ignored. Miss Cartwright, the pioneer who introduced a physical education program at McGill University as early as 1916, and Dr Lamb, who founded in 1923 the first professional association of physical educators (CAPHER), were opposed to militarism in the Quebec schools. Thus, the profession grew and established itself without any government help and interference.

Teachers of physical education were seen as a lower class of teachers. A promotional campaign was launched to upgrade their status to that of regular class teachers. Physical Education became compulsory in every Protestant schools in 1930 with 60min/week in elementary schools and 40 to 80min in high schools. Intramural sports were introduced. Classes were taught by specialists and a revised program was implemented with a new Syllabus. [10]

During this period, very little happened in the Catholic system. Finally confronted by many deputies and personalities from the French community, the Provincial Government asked expert Jean-Robert Bonnier to conduct an investigation to find out about Physical Education in the province of

Quebec. [11] The result of the enquiry was devastating and showed a huge gap between the two systems.

Even if the Roman Catholic Committee explicitly required daily classes, no administrative decisions were taken to make sure it happened. In fact, physical education was almost absent in elementary French schools and occasional in teachers' training colleges.

Table 1 : Comparative data on the resources and equipment available for physical education in French Catholic and English Protestant schools of the Province of Quebec, 1938 (Source: data from the survey of Bonnier, J.R. (1938))

	Catholic schools	Protestant schools
Number of schools	226	48
Number of students	117 000	32 000
Number of persons responsible for physical education (1)	4	31
Number of gymnasiums	2	30
Number of swimming pools	1	1
Stadium	0	1
Revenues from own sources ($ Can.)	6 000 $	60 000 $
Subsidy from Strathcona Fund ($ Can.)	4 989 $	778 $
Subsidy from Province ($ Can.)	2 612 $	387 $
Revenues from other sources ($ Can.)	0 $	100 000 $

(1) one doctor, two military, one female teacher

Bonnier gave troubling figures that summed up the situation (table 1). Numbers speak for themselves. Bonnier rightly explained that English Protestant superiority stemmed from the skills of their instructors and from their financial and material resources. He blamed Quebec's elite for its attitude towards physical caring and training, and for the choice of military drills over physical education. He criticised the Swedish method and denounced French conservatism with its traditional values that prevented improvement.

Although two World Wars justified the introduction of militarism in the schools, the French sector was wrong to impose this approach for more than half a century, thus preventing the development of regular physical education. It is very difficult to point out the reasons for such a choice . Was the French Catholic Committee not willing to encourage physical education because of it believed in the superiority of mind over matter? Was it the lack of resources and skills, or the willpower of political leaders which left Physical Education of French Quebec in the hands of the Federal Government? Was it a combination of all those factors? It is difficult to establish. It was often said that French Quebec was against anything done in English Canada, was weary of the American system, and did not even adhere to the European ideological movements, preferring to develop in its own way.

One of our historians, Denis Monière, said that Québec was a monolithic, traditional, clerical, and rural society bent on itself. Cosentino and Howell preferred to explain the difference by stressing the cultural enthusiasm of the English community for sports and physical leisure and the belief in the importance of physical training in the development of the individual. This position toward physical activity was actualised when they took up the biggest challenge of all: change people's attitude toward physical educators and physical education.

The French community and its Révolution Tranquille

As of 1950, the English community pursued the development of Physical Education in its entire school system and mixed curricular and extracurricular physical activities. For the French sector this was a time of complete transformation marked by the beginning of a break with the Catholic Church.

This was a period of questioning when certain initiatives were left behind. For example, by 1954, Physical Education became part of the Arts curriculum, but it was suggested to replace its teaching by cinema studies when sports facilities were lacking. However, a serious effort was undertaken to train physical educators. Many universities started programs, such as Laval in 1954, Montreal in 1955, and Sherbrooke in 1969.

Meanwhile, there was a vast inquiry of the educational system to find the reasons of the huge gap between the two physical education programs From then on, governmental studies succeeded one another and voluminous reports were produced, with numerous and complex recommendations, a list of which would be too fastidious to share with you now.

These studies painted an exact portrait of the French system, and of its lacks , thereby fostering a tremendous movement that triggered a change of attitude and the sudden evolution of Physical Education. In a single decade, the French community bridged the gap. A completely new system of education was developed, with new programs and a scientific approach to physical education on the cutting edge of research, comparable to the most advance studies in movement sciences.

Today, the French and English systems cohabit together, yet are still on their own universe. They are truly two solitude living besides one another, two worlds separated by language. Physical Education specialists find it difficult to work together since they have chosen to create two professional associations: CAPHER in the English sector and FEEPQ in the French one.

References

Audet, L.P. (1971). Histoire de l'enseignement au Quebec, 1840-1971. Tome 2. Montreal: Holt, Rinehart et Winston Ltee, 496 p.

Board of Education. (1909). The syllabus of physical exercises for public elementary schools. London, 168 p.

Bonnier, J.R. (1938). Enquête sur l'éducation physique au Québec. Gouvernement du Québec, 35 p.

Commission royale d'enquête sur l'enseignement (1964). Rapport. Troisième partie: les programmes d'études.

Conseil exécutif de la Fondation Strathcona (1911). Manuel de culture physique à l'usage des écoles. Toronto: s.e., 173 p.

Constitution du Fonds Strathcona (1909). Dossier du Département de l'instruction publique de la province de Québec. 1477-09.

Cosentino, F. & Howell, M.L. (1971). A history of physical education in Canada. Toronto: General Publishing Company Limited, 154 p.

Guay, D. (1964). L'éducation physique dans les écoles élémentaires du Québec. Québec: Le Quotidien Ltée, 45 p.

Guay, D. (1969). L'éducation physique dans les écoles normales du Québec 1836-1969. Québec: Collection Sports Loisirs, 96 p.

Guay, D. (1980). L'histoire de l'éducation physique au Québec, conceptions et évènements (1830-1980). Chicoutimi, Canada: Gaëtan Morin et associés Ltée, 151 p.

Gérin-Lajoie, A. (1862). Jean Rivard. Montréal: Les soirées canadiennes

Larouche, R. (1984). L'éducation physique au Québec, professionnalisation et positions des diplômés sur le marché du travail. Unpublished dissertation (PhD), University Laval, Québec.

Neil, G.I. (1963). A history of physical education in the protestant schools of Quebec., Unpublished masters thesis, McGill University.

Notes

[1] Cosentino and Howell, 1971, p.16.
[2] Cosentino and Howell, 1971, p.16.
[3] Cosentino and Howell, 1971, p.19.
[4] Gérin-Lajoie, 1862.
[5] Guay, 1964.
[6] Neil, 1963.
[7] Neil, 1963, p.82.
[8] This method is described in the Syllabus of Physical Exercises for schools.
[9] Constitution du Fonds Strathcona, 1909, p. 1.
[10] This manual was the revised version of the Syllabus of Physical Exercises for Schools from 1933.
[11] Bonnier, 1938.

Chapter 12

Sport in the French Colonies : comparative study. Guadeloupe and Réunion 1925-1950

Evelyne Combeau-Mari and Jacques Dumont
Université la Réunion and Université Antilles-Guyane

Though Guadeloupe is located in the Carribean Sea in the northern hemisphere and Reunion island in the southern hemisphere at the heart of the Indian Ocean and though the two islands could be seen as specific for obvious reasons, they share a lot in common as far as their sport history is concerned

As a matter of fact, both islands being French colonies far from the home country, brings them together, which provides solid grounds for a comparative analysis.

The abolition of slavery has made the inhabitants of these "old colonies" French citizens. Thus, their political status is not the same as the other colonies. Those being governed by the native principle, citizenship, besides the political investment it offers coloured people, is the plinth of a constant claim for social and political assimilation intended to be the proof of true equality with hexagonal citizens. Along with other islands someone described them as « the Empire's confettis », because neither their size nor their population are important enough to create sports investments similar to those observed in the much bigger African [1] or Asian colonies. The setting of sports practices is made possible through militant actions displaying the same virtues as those that characterize sport.

The educational factor is at the core of the role played by sport in these French territories where the Coubertinian definition of sport, imported from the home country, confused by intermingles with aspiration to progress and modern lifestyle symbolized by these practices. There promoters are civil servants and often teachers. Deeply involved with associative life, they try to advocate a conception of man based on progress as well as perfectibility in harmony with the sports ideal. To spread their ideas they create new media which like « resonnance chambers » echo their sports views though emphasizing the social aspects.

The study of this investment will be supported by two local newspapers: *Sporting* in Reunion (1925-1931), *Le Dimanche Sportif* in Guadeloupe (1945-1952). The appearance of sports news paper at a timing point of the colonies history seems significant. The colonies becomes a department [2] in 1946 and it is striking that the time-lag between the two magazines should be so long since numerous similarities in their contents is to be noticed. They are in tight grip with reality, questioning, grobing the impact of "departementalisation" (political change of statute, from colonial to department) on these remote islands. A careful analysis of sports newspapers and of their recurrent themes helps measure and understand the similarity or/and discrepancy in the pedagogical message spread in the colonies.

We thus try to pinpoint : (a) how the newspaper was born in the local context and the way it is distributed (creators, management, situation within the sports, social, cultural and political local movement); (b) the newspaper's objective and the definition of the sport covered. The idea is to go beyond the themes that are dealt with and dig up the promoter's social and political conceptions; (c) the emergence of the concept of autonomy, sport being both an instrument used by assimilation and a lever towards emancipation.

Colonial sport context and appearance of sports magazines

"Turf" and *"bookmaking"* are the first sports activities to emerge. The spirit set within this activity is meaningful :

> *"In any society, you find a group of people who have plenty of time to spare in leisure. It is for these privileged few that England allows the practice of a sport with a kind of religious worship. Arts and sports bear the advantage to introduce in relationships something else than material matters (...). Sports include the noble venery, all forms of huntings, races, high-classed nautical activities, horse-riding, fencing, any work which develop, magnify and idealise the material force of mankind [3]."*

The leading people of the Colony gather mainly within "clubs" [4]. The colonial state of mind reveals a need to "find oneself among people of similar rank". The foremost aim of the club is to establish a membership network. It gives the opportunity to play cards, discuss altogether and also to practice a sport activity. So, "lawn-tennis" is already developed as a leisure activity at La Réunion, at Salazie, at Brûlé and at St Gilles in 1892 and 1894. It is one of the first sports to be introduced at *the Sport-Club Bourbonnais* together with cricket and cycling. Guadeloupe has chosen for its part horse-riding, tennis and yachting.

In fact, the "sport breakthrough", like in France, and despite the conservative opposition due to the colonial political environment, owes a lot to high school students. Although, boys education in high schools maintains military and gymnastic exercises, promoted by the national decree of 1882 setting up military education, sports activities are softly introduced in the educational system. The aim of the teachers is to re-establish game exercises in the educational program, such as the English system, like Jules Simon [5] and Pascal Grousset had set up in the mother country.

The associative sports movement started developing in these islands during or soon after world war one, far more later than in France. Most civil associations were born in schools, founded and run by teachers and ex-students. It is very difficult to keep a full and up-dated record of sports companies because some make an appearance in the press without being officially registered and then disappear. Nevertheless, we should mention as far as La Réunion is concerned suggestive names which have become famous such as : *La Sportive Tamponnaise, La St Pierroise, La Portoise, La France, La Patriote, l'Espérance*, all civil companies to which we should add the military team of St Denis and children in state care organisations : the main high school and the secondary school with two teams : *literature sports and science sports ...*

In Guadeloupe, one society *"la Guadeloupéenne"* organizes tourism, physical education, sport and scoutism from 1915 to 1922. Then clubs appears, at the waning twenties or early thirtees, le *"Good Luck"*, *"la Gauloise"*, le *"Cygne noir"*, and clubs from factories like *"Amical Club Darboussier"*.

Although all of them were general sports clubs, soccer remained their core activity. At this point some discrepancies come to light in the way sports developed in the two islands : the strong British influence in Mauritius, the neighbour island, certainly accounts for the fact that the soaring of physical activities was both more precocious and more dynamic in Reunion than in Guadeloupe. Mauritius was a model which symbolized modern life style.

In Guadeloupe, a social policy is set up during the Front Populaire period under the influence of the Governor Felix Eboué [6] aiming at developing sports education and leisure activities. The first two stadiums are built at the same time.

Despite that stimulating environment, the practice of sport still remained the privilege of a few males in these tropical islands: first came the educated part of the male population: secondary-school pupils, students, a few civil servants, tradesmen, doctors and farmers.
The number of sportsmen was estimated at under a thousand in Reunion as well as in Guadeloupe. Thus around the thirties both colonies started sharing

the same concern: how to develop, organize, structure and transform sport into an educational tool. Although education and army are well ahead of sports in terms of accessibility, the press is also a good weapon for promoting. In this matter, La Réunion is in advance in comparison to Guadeloupe.

Sporting was born at the beginning of may 1925 under the impulse of V. Lasimant, a teacher at Ecole Normale. That magazine was no longer a mere turf paper, like *Sport colonial*[7] at the end of the 19th century. *Sporting* was first and foremost a militant newspaper which, as shown by its title, has been created by educated anglophiles. Its motto: *"a sound mind in a sound body"* reveals its general spirit. Its subtitle: *"soccer, boxing, athletics, cycling, women sports"* clearly expresses its will develop and diversy sports practices. The newspaper was not going to be satisfied with statements of principles, it genuinely wished to change local mentalities and be an active part in the island 's social and political modernization. The pedagogical orientation was absolutely clear from the start. It is a paper made by and for teachers. The change of tune was nonetheless conspicious when E. Dutremblay Agénor,[8] a young militant teacher, became the paper's director and editor. There could be no doubt: the will to use sports as a tool to train Reunion youth was stronger and stronger and Agénor intends to do what it takes to secure the paper's circulation.

> *"(...) Should money be the driving force of the war, it is also the driving force of sports. And it is most unlikely that any sports companies in any country would be able to survive with any membership fee nor financial aid.*
> *It works the same way for a newspaper. Financial supports are absolutely necessary and we like to think that any sportsman, proud to be so will never draw back from the task to achieve, because otherwise it would systematically lead to the death of the sport he loves that glorifies him. (...)"*[9]

Since he needs more money and a wider audience he goes where the money is, to the colony's aristocrats.

Later in Guadeloupe where the context of an anticipated liberation from Vichy's government, makes things more difficult for the 200 000 inhabitants, there are numerous attempts to create sports papers, in both parts of the island. 1943 saw *Match*'s first issue. Grande-Terre sports leaders around Camille Jabbour would freely and twice a month comment in the magazine the sports events that they organize. This magazine has the same motto than *Sporting*, but is very quickly devoted to sport competition, before becoming a traditional newspaper.

Even more important for our analysis, *Le Dimanche Sportif* was published in Basse-Terre in 1945. At first, *Le Dimanche Sportif* was the organ of the "Union sportive Basse-Terrienne" which since 1933 has grouped together all of Basse-Terre's sports clubs and associations. The paper's calling was going to widen quite fast. Sponsored by the Sport federation of Guadeloupe which unities the leagues of Basse-Terre and Grande-Terre, the paper's ambition was to cover the whole Guadeloupe as far as the sport was concerned, and even more as shown by its extended title, from November 1947: *Le Dimanche Sportif et Culturel.*

Sport had opened new avenues in the colonies. It had became a place for investment and recognition, but also a place to express a humanist ideal sustained by the belief in progress and in the affirmation of a superiority.

> *"It is claimed that one can take part in both sports and cultural elite; so as a sum up elite, the true elite cannot be conceived without health and vitality, adding and leading to a long-lasting of the most beautiful existing blooming of the mind* [10]*."*

What was that colonial elite whose message was to carry out the transformation and the evolution of overseas societies through sport ? Where the routes chosen by sport promoters the same or were they different ?

In Guadeloupe, the people who worked for the magazine were deeply involved in associative life. Most members were civil servants. Teachers made up the majority of the editorial staff. Maurice Micaux, football and volley-ball player is the founder and president of the *Racing-club*. Paul Baptistide, is the author of most of the leading articles in the paper "*Propos du Sportif*", under the pen name of Telesphore [11]... Many are members of *Renaissance* association, founded at St Claude in 1944. This association gives a stimulus to the cultural life and radiates its impulse under the influence of the Mayor Remi Nainsouta.

Some members did not actually practice a sport. Bettino Lara whose role was a paramount importance in the organization of sport - he was the president of *Union sportive Basse-Terrienne* and also delegated to the Federation sportive's propaganda-was such a member. He also worked with *"Club des Montagnards"* and various associations, leagues and federations and was the director of *Dimanche Sportif's* editorial staff as well. Lara worked for ten years in *le Nouvelliste* de la Guadeloupe, a widespread daily newspaper of socialist allegiance and directed by A. Lara, his uncle. Bettino's father was a teacher and the young man was the first of ten children. Lara made his debut in journalism as sub-editor. In 1937, Governor Félix Eboué made him head of Guadeloupe's printing office. He held that important position until he retired in 1969. *Dimanche Sportif* was not only printed by the colony's official printing house; but first one then two workers had been detached to work full time to the publishing of the newspaper. They were in charge of the office of sports based in the Conseil General whose speaker was Henri Rinaldo. The magazine thus got the support of three successive governors. *Dimanche Sportif* was one of the elements of propaganda and of education for and through sport of a much larger unit.

Observing sports promoters in Reunion is as revealing. First among them came teachers. Eugène Dutremblay Agénor's personality was to be the perfect model. Dutremblay was also a teacher's son and the first of twelve children. He took up teaching at the top, no less than Saint Denis Ecole Normale. His faith in the positive aspects of education was adamant. Education as he viewed it was the "total" education of man. In this spirit, the republican state school extends its work to a large number of actions among which the association community is the keystone. This peri and post school association movement took birth in the mother country of France thanks to *La Ligue de l'Enseignement* [12]. At La Réunion, everything needed to be done after the first world war.

E. Dutremblay Agénor did everything in his power to spread the values of associative life. In the association he found the republic's social institution that was the most likely to fill the word "socialism" with the utmost intelligible content. Isn't it true that the association movement provides a true force and unity to people gathered for the same cause?

Sport became his first battlefield. His involvement in sport was pregnant with both the Coubertinian humanist ideal and the choices made by the "teaching league" [13].

> *"As a support to "the complete education" of a free man, responsible and jointly liable for a democratic society, based on the principles of the French revolution. Multiple duties must draw out the training action carried out in the republican state school."*

Within the limits of an educational aid, the consequences of the practice of a sport activity are in accordance with the ideology targeted by the Ligue. One of his missions was to keep the movement of physical education and of sports, away from the unhealthy deviations generated by their excessive practise : racing for records, showsports, professionalism and other «moral blemishes». This trailblazer saw in educational sports one of the most efficient means to encourage effort, perseverance, progress and above all solidarity and responsibility when youth is concerned. It is through sport that Reunion youth will take its destiny in its own hands and walk the path of emancipation, he thought. This school teacher's militancy to sports has led him step by step on the road of *Human Rights League*, of trade unionism, of mutualism, and finally as an active political member of the Communist Party of La Réunion.

Some constants emerge from this comparative study: the creation of sports newspapers in the French colonies is not a matter of chance nor does it depend on the local possibilities of the moment. It is the product of an intellectual elite's militant stance, that elite seeing in sports and cultural action a new lever towards commitment and social affirmation. In Guadeloupe they belong to the mulatto middle-class; in Reunion they have a humble background and they want social equality. All of them however, from Guadeloupe or from Reunion are carried by the republican ideal and are the advocates of democratic values. They sincerely believe that associative and educational sport can make their fellow citizens more responsible.

Through their newspapers, they feel they fulfill a universal mission : to renew and change the colonial society.

Sport as a means to carry out assimilation

The interest of the comparative approach is here to underline the similarities between the ideas conveyed in each newspaper though the distance between the two islands is so great. It shows the importance of sport educational value in the context of the assimilation of colonized peoples.
Inside the papers journalists put forward two main thinking lines : the concern to propose a definition of sport and of the sportman in harmony with educational values to be taught at the local level, the necessity to structure and diversify local sport as well as take it to the largest possible public.

Towards a definition of sport

Setting the limits of «good practice forms» also outlines a certain legitimacy. It would be proper to define, set the limits of a territory. Although tautology cannot be excluded : "*Sport is sport*"[14], the line between "*true sport*" practised by "*true sportsmen*" and others can quickly be defined. Five different types are listed :

> "*sportspeople who show an interest in all kinds of sports, but have never practised any of them*"

the public, therefore. Second type of people, those who are members of a club and show off the signs of their membership :

"because of their social rank or their excellent relational network, the group they belong to should be honoured to count them among their members and proud to take advantage of their good services."

Then, the *"active sportspeople"*, with good taste, capabilities, *"but their training is irregular... they go to dance parties and clubs the night before their meetings."*

Fourth category, more serious,

"they are in no way concerned with health and care of their body : sport is a mean for them to achieve fame... We shall bow down before the will power these apprentice champions are delivering, but they should use it in a wiser manner.
Finally, we have the "true sportsmen. They do not think about loud exhibitions, about raising themselves as stars. They play sport for the sake of sport, in order to gain the skill as a source of self-confidence, the lightness and the resistance to strain, gifts which provide to the self a greater assertion." [15]

Sport is conceived as the crowning achievement of a steady and reasoned physical activity. The newspapers echo the notions that prevailed at the time : a sense of moderation, controlled effort... Since the twenties, the classical attitude in the spheres of physical education in France has been to rationalize the practice of basic physical education before even thinking about the negative effects of sport practised to the excess.

"The final aim, we must say is not to win the match; it is the free release of all human abilities developed under a methodical strain. [16]

Do not take for granted these contradictory and second-rated sayings which can be summed up as follows : the practice of a sport activity kills the organism. No! Any excessive practice of any kind may be disastrous and physical overwork could in no way result in positive effects, however the practice of any sports at a reasonable and moderate pace is a powerful weapon against malaria (...)." [17]

However and before everything else, sport is social and moral education.

"(...) This is the reason why, we highly recommend to the young men of this country to pratice a sport : sport is not only a school of patience and physical development, it is also a school of great soul and fraternity." [18]

These papers attached great importance to concerns whose roots were in the home country. Sport should help "regenerate the race".

> "(...) the aim is to spread the good sports message, to democratize sports activities, in order to regenerate mankind diminished in terms of number further to the war, and particularly weakened as a consequence of our present lifestyles so far apart from the normal open space conditions." [19]

We find the same argument in *Sporting* :

> "(...) Because sport, life in open space, are one of the conditions of a revival of the creole breed, a more meaningful revival nowadays." [20]

The excesses of show-sports are also denounced. Those who contribute to the paper would relentlessly criticize the public's lack of education and fair-play. Beyond the stadium, what is really at stake is the training of the citizen :

> "The cornerstone of a democracy is the self-control (...). Is it really necessary to prove that physical activities and sport are without fail the best means to gain a public state of mind ?" [21]

It is therefore necessary to advise, to correct, to stand up, to bring up, as

> "those who are said to be the most advanced - are totally ignorant as far as rules, games and competitions are concerned." [22]

Some excerpts of articles from the very first issues, aimed at calling back the sport spirit, are disappearing for the benefit of aggressive accusations regarding the drifts in sport. The call to "intelligent minds" is constantly repeated.

As important than those who actually practised, than their education, was the credibility of the sport movement's internal organization and structuration.

Structuration and diversification of practicies

The precociousness of sport practising in Reunion as well as the publishing of a specialized paper as early as the waning twenties will be of great help to the structuration of the sport movement. Guadeloupe will be concerned by this much later. Nevertheless one of *Dimanche Sportif*'s functions will be to serve as a real link between Grande-Terre and Basse-Terre. The objective is a "unitarian" sport movement that would be representative of the island's sportmen and that would be acknowledged. *Le Dimanche Sportif* entrust the following mission : *"to promote sports; to encourage its spreading out, to look after the understanding of its message"*.

The aim is *"to favour sport as a pleasure, capable to make spirits and souls feel better."* [23]

In Reunion E. Dutremblay will constantly remind the purpose of a weekly sports magazine : its first function is to systematically, repeatedly and officially proclaim the necessity and acknowledgement of the practice of sport. It must contribute to the organization and structuration of sport.

> *"The organisation of our competitions and officials events have been the subjects of criticisms for too long. An incredible amount of remarks have been said or written regarding the athletic championship held in 1927.*
> *And why the accusations have not found a successful conclusion?*
> *Why the organisation failures, if there were any, could not be forecast nor managed ?*
> *Why has the Cup to the town of St Denis given the opportunity to some people to cry out for injustice ?*
> *Because no sport organism was established ! Because no official newspaper had the courage to open eyes to blind people ! To express to whom it may concern the desiderata of sports companies! To support the fair complaints before the Authorities concerned. (...)"* [24]

One of the real problems *Sporting* proposes to solve is the rational and balanced organization of Reunion's football championship. The paper would "display" the views of those who play, then an organization would be collectively defined and a federation would be created.

> *"Ah ! Should we have had a League ! Things would have been so much easier !... (...)"* [25]

Sporting's hardwork will finally lead to the constitution of Reunion Sport Federation in 1930. It became the federation's official mouthpiece, taking in charge the patronage of sports events.

Though football was the colonies' core sport activity, the newspapers insist on the need for having a wider sports culture. In order to promote diversification they will multiply events : swimming, athletics, boxing, basketball, tennis...

> *"Sport, here is now developing at a fast pace.*
> *Each season gives birth to a new game which unfortunately has no real future. How can we explain this weakness in our will power or this*

*lack of enthousiasm for a sport that we celebrated the night before ?
(...)
Specializing in sports has always been criticized and for justified
reasons. It is therefore wiser to look for a change in games. It is the
reason why the new tennis company formed within the group of
football regulars can be the illustration of a reform in ideas and new
concepts. (...)"* [26]

The specialist is not the may concern here. It is rather the gentleman
presented as a model of balance between body and mind. In *Dimanche
Sportif* that stance can be felt thanks to the paper's references. E Moussat's
works [27], an authentic apology of sport, will keep coming back, like a
leitmotiv [28]. The continuity of the authors and some quotations of a literature
nature: Rousseau, Giraudoux, outline the view of a sport, directly inherited
from the Greek culture.

At La Réunion, the will power to diversify urges to promote new activities.
Agénor undertakes to encourage cycling on the island. Based on the Tour de
France type of competition, he sets up on November 11th 1928 an important
cycling race : the *Challenge Sporting*, sponsored by the newspaper and
financed by townships and shopkeepers. This initiative is the starting point to
a waking up of cycling companies, Eugène Dutremblay Agénor is the initiator
in 1932 of the first club mainly dedicated to cycling at La Réunion : *Le Vélo
Club Réunionnais*. This club serves the purpose of a cycling league at that
time.

A diversification of practices demands a necessary diversification of those
who practise. Both magazines appear as fervent advocate of women sports.
Committing oneself is more innovative in Reunion.

*"(...) Within almost all boys high schools or next to these schools, there
are sports companies. Couldn't we think in the same way for girls ?
Couldn't headmistresses gather their pupils in associations ?
Parents will scream ! one would say to me, everyone will be shocked !
It is true that one has always considered so far, and it is deeper at La
Réunion than everywhere else, woman has a fragile jewellery ready to
break at any uncaring movement; and this state of mind is partly due to
women themselves who have never done anything to prove the
contrary. So, I would not ask young girls to expose themselves in
public as their sense of decency prevents them to do so. But I would
urge them to work within the walls of their schools or within any kind of
closed environment if needed; but they must practice a sport activity,
they must achieve from their earliest stage, this strong beauty which
will improve, when their turn will come, their abilities to be excellent
mothers.*

> *On the other hand, they will have a second advantage: as part of a group, they will have more power to stand up in front of men too self-centered and to make them aware of this new change of facts that they will certainly no longer be able to fight for."* [29]

Agénor E. Dutremblay is a modernist. Fighting moral and social prejudices that keep women away from social and political life, he starts a feminist campaign between the two wars. The number of indepth articles dealing with that issue shows the man's courage.

> *"(...) Come on men, make an effort, be concerned with the house-keeping, give to your sisters, girls, wives the time to practice a sport activity! One is shouting at us. I am ready to admit that if we were willing to behave as such, women would have taken up physical exercises.*
> *But, as it is not an acceptable idea to all men, couldn't we consider the question of women in sport under a different point of view? Of course, yes. (...)* [30]
> *One day will come ?... when women will have a role to play within the Township Council."*

Somewhat visionary Agénor strongly believed in the role women could play in social life. He thinks their involvement in political life may help change mentalities.

> *"(...) But here we are; what a lot of change to bring on to our quiet routine, to our old-fashioned mentality ! The order will have to come from the above authorities in order to get each township to modify their more or less narrow, more or less rocky or grassy school playgrounds into tennis courts, into football fields; that they build swimming pools with lockrooms; that they eventually pay a teacher to train this bulk of children who are meant to lead the nation to morrow !... What a lot of change !... Which township will on its own without any external help dictate to itself these sacrifices to solve this vital problem, which as a final ending is part of their assignments ?"* [31]

There again promoters show their concern to democratize sport practices in order to enhance the principle of "equality between the citizens".

> *"One has spread the inferiority complex in our minds to better take advantage of us. Facts show in all matters that the preconceived judgement is deplorable. Our courage during war is well known and recognised. We have proved in sports that we are as strong and healthy as any other races on earth."* [32]

The democratization of sport is considered as an element of assimilation that will sooner or later lead to the acceptance of equality between populations.

"The French colonial empires outline the power and the expansion of France : they are the sons of its greatness (...). France must keep its influence in its ancient colonies where the French language and culture remains." [33]

It is, no doubt, a claim for *"a total cooperation policy from all the sons of the mother France"* [34].
Even the local communist parties demand "departementalisation". Does not l'*Etincelle* proclaim on March 6th 1946 *"we want total assimilation"* ?

Sport as a factor of emancipation. The emergence of the autonomy concept.

If sport acts as guarantor for national educational values and helps maintain social order, it paradoxically epitomizes colonized populations' claims for identity. Could it not be one of the levers towards emancipation ?

While making possible the widening of the cultural scoop as well as the opening on to the world, sport creates a form of emancipation for the remote populations. As an element that favours responsibility and citizen training, sport incites local populations to be the shapers of their own destiny. Thus, sport soon after departementalization represents a space more liable to help colonized populations in their quest for an identity and as such opens the way to autonomist feelings.

Beneath the issue raised by sport in itself and for itself, these magazines aim at the general training of the colonized populations. The editors try to instill curiosity and the appeal of knowledge in these insular populations. The sports newspaper is an antidote against ignorance and the routine mentality he thinks he has detected in his fellow citizens.
The following excerpt outlines significantly one of the main ideas spread at La Réunion.

"Our colleague" "La victoire sociale" was lately blaming its readers, to not read, and rightly so. (...)
They seem totally unconcerned with what is going on outside their office or sugar cane plantations. The outside world does not seem of any interest to them. Their one and only care is for their own business.

In our point of view, here lies one of the reasons why La Réunion is and remains excluded from any kind of progress, that it gets tied up more and more in this deep rut commonly called routine.

And the difficult times we are going through are the obvious consequences of this regrettable matter of facts. (...)

Why do our dailies look like nothing more than empty papers ?

Because the charges that they engender are hardly covered by the subscription fees or the advertising incomings.

Why ?... and one could write developing this point of view indefinitely. All sectors, agricultural, industrial, literature and social, of our island would be concerned ...

And out about sports ? Well! as far as sports are concerned, it would be the same thing.

Why do not we have a League ? Because we are unable to assess its necessary role, a role which would be more understood should some newspapers be aware of all the services it would offer.

Why do we mainly play football association ?

Because the law regarding advertising for all other sports is unexisting.

Why are most of our sportsmen as far the association rules, the basic techniques of the football game are concerned totally ignorant, that is to say the techniques themselves to offer a decent match ? They are unwilling, because of their natural laziness to learn or to continue to learn with the help of appropriate readings.

(...) To cover up this drawback and in order to give access in some way to a sports cultural information to our illiterate sports readers, we have decided to publish from now on, and whenever the opportunity will rise, summaries of any important matches or international competitions and also "points of view" on the various sports activities from famous and recognized athletes.

Therefore, and shall we repeat it, our state of mind will shape, evolve on the principles of more qualified minds and in the second place, it will allow our readers to be aware of all the major sports events in the whole world.

Should this initiative has for consequences to increase the number of sportsmen and sportswomen at La Réunion and then to encourage the development of sports on the island." [35]

Hence as soon as it comes back out on March 3rd 1928, the weekly newspaper features a supplement: *Sporting littéraire et scientifique* that will deal with arts, sciences and techniques. The same kind of evolution can be felt in Guadeloupe since *Dimanche Sportif* becomes *Dimanche Sportif et Culturel* in 1947 .

The vitality of the local sports movement depends on the capacity to intensify exchanges with the outside world, and neighbour islands. *Sporting* grants a fair amount of space to sports life taking place on the sister islands: Mauritius and Madagascar. Besides the simple data of results of the various competitions, the paper is delivering an evaluation and a comparative analysis of the situation as far as the development of sports on the Indian Ocean islands is concerned. An analysis which shows that La Réunion is far behind its neighbours. A solution emerges : learning how to play against those who are better than you are.

> *"Under an other point of view, one could wish that this match would be the opening match to meetings between local teams, or even outside selected teams, from the sister island for example.*
> *The carrying out of this plan would be with no doubt a fantastic incentive to a few asleep sports companies which are about to sleep; selectors would undertake to form teams, both in the major town and in the suburbs, capable to train with top-ranked teams from Mauritius which talent is recognized. (...)"* [36]

In Guadeloupe, several sport and cultural exchanges are made with the neighbour islands, including the "sister island", la Martinique.

In this program of cultural opening, some people are more aware, better trained than others. A local elite is taking shape which task will be to lead the future of the country.

> *"We would have taken part to this mass education, a group of people unfortunately very often mislead."* [37].

The message is slightly delivered :

> *"It is the duty of the more educated people to set the example. Therefore, one should convince those whose cultural knowledge is more advanced to be the training-masters of their brothers less fortunate."* [38]

To counter the possible risk in the lack of organization of the masses, the local elite grants itself rights and duties towards its countrymen and defines *"the role of the colonial intellectual* [39]*"*. They become the essential intermediary guide.

> *"In-between the European lifestyle that he understands, even adopts for some of them, and a mass of people who is totally willing to undertake the necessary steps to achieve these standards, can't we compare the intellectual colonialist as a guide ? (...) In-between the ones who colonized and those who were colonized, he acts as an interpreter who informs and explains."* [40]

The educative role of sport can be combined with a democratic view of freedom of expression.

The weekly invites all opinions to express *"as long as they are sincere and trustworthy"*. The *"independent"* newspaper, *Sporting* insists on its impartial open-minded nature. Proud of this position, the newspaper publishes as from May 5th 1928 *"a free column"* allowing the free expression of all. The militancy of these weeklies takes all its sense when at La Réunion, Agénor sets the dream to create a political party above all others : "a sports people political party".

> *"Should our readers rest assured. We will, by no means, deviate from our current principles and will never talk about politics. (...) We are and remain sportsmen. And this attitude gives us the opportunity to meet friends and brothers in the corridors of the Commons.*
>
> *Yes, «brothers», because there are sportsmen at the Commons House, and sports militants, should we add.*
>
> *Aside the communists, the socialists, the republicans and the extremists, there is a political party, indeed a small one, but with a promising future, that is the sports political party.*
>
> *And, admire the high pacific value of sports! It gathers under the same flag without any discrimination the elect of all political groups! No matter the political opinion! The sports opinion only matters.*
>
> *What are MM Léonus Bénard, Auguste Brunet and Gasparin waiting for to put their names on the list of the sports group at the parliament? Sport, in general, at La Réunion, would no doubt gain from this situation. (...)"* [41]

Can sport, as the symbol of "human perfectibility" create a new society free of all kinds of prejudices ? A better society with more equality ?

> *"(...) The day when thanks to a triple-based education, that is moral, intellectual and devoted to sport education, most of our sportsmen will be able to assess their acts, will be better aware of their responsibility, and will not be snowed under the events, but on the contrary will have them under control, will make them happen, only then one can hope that our country will enter a new period rich in progress and full of lessons ... for others."* [42]

In *Sporting*, Agénor has expressed his hopes for inner changes within the colonial society. In February 1931, three years after the re-birth of *Sporting*, he must however leave the writing expression. Without any financial aid from the above authorities of the Colony, constantly subject to prudence [43], criticized by rival newspapers, Agénor quits the "sports political party" and *Sporting* to take up the union and political fight.

The political dimension of sports magazines can more directly be applied in Guadeloupe in the somewhat disappointing context of post-departementalisation. The populations had prayed for assimilation to bring about the expected changes. It had not. On the contrary, after departementalization the new departments are totally left to themselves, e prey to malnutrition, paladism, poverty. The idea that local populations should rely upon their own strength starts to emerge.

> *"People from Guadeloupe, active and hard-working people, know they can only rely on themselves to achieve the development of their country."* [44]

This state of mind can be illustrated within the paper *Dimanche Sportif* which planned the construction of a shelter at about 1 000 m altitude in order to ease the climbing of La Soufrière [45], and most of trips with La Soufrière for starting point. The *Renaissance* association is launching the operation and is calling for membership financial aid to various qualified organisms. The magazine is the reliable and accurate translation of this project. Ten lists of contributors are published.

The opening of this "small touristic hotel" on July 6th 1947, is, as Rémy Nainsouta, Mayor of St Claude outlines, "*a show-off and a symbol*" [46]. Indeed, this accomplishment proves "*the team spirit capabilities*" to place in evidence the treasure of Guadeloupe. But it goes further:

> *"'One must fight against the principles of the colonial ideology, the misery it engenders. The key to progress is, indeed included in this simple rule : make the best of each one's abilities (...) a fantastic opening is shaping out to all clear-sighted and patriotic Guadeloupean people anxious to see their beautiful country economically free, an economic freedom necessary to fully ratify the historical work of 1848* [47]*."*

This speech, autonomist orientated, is not denied by the Governor [48] de Nattes, "*this project imagined in a non-profit making aim, and achieved without unceasing financial and material urges.*"
The idea of a necessary autonomy is not the fact of one magazine, but can also be find on the agenda in the magazine *Match*. One can read, written by Léopold Elatre :

> *"One must be aware of this matter of fact, we people from Guadeloupe, who have the tendency - due certainly to our slavery background - to await everything from the central authorities or local administration. Our individual effort and our mass effort must be put together in the achievement of our future."* [49]

Le Dimanche Sportif will put an end to its publication in August 1948 and will start publishing again between 1951-1952 before it completely disappears in July 1952. That demise will coincide with the split in the general sports club federation which manages all sports activities in Guadeloupe. In Reunion, this change will take place in 1956. Since there is no more unity, rivalities between the different leagues and their respective representatives become commonplace. The dream of a complete sport education has gone.

Conclusion

If the originality (should we say specificity ?) of each island cannot be denied, some elements of convergence appear which are more the fact of the French-type colonization than of any human or geographical criteria.
Sport offers thus an excellent place from which one can observe the way the mechanisms of the French colonial society function. Indeed, using an limited but significant corpus of date *Sporting* and *Dimanche Sportif*, we notice surprising similarities in the contents of the two newspapers : themes, references, scale of values... as well as in the promoters of these papers and this despite a real time gap between the two papers. We show that according to contexts and promoters that sport or more exactly what is said about sport can fulfill totally opposed functions.

As the support of emancipation and progress, sport takes part in the tranformation of the colonial society, in its modernization with the advent of departementalization. This new educational tool then makes up on of assimilation's more powerful allies.

However, the new overseas departments soon appear as the casualties of the national policies decided in Paris. The limits of departementalization are being outlined. Sport and the sport argument are renewing themselves. A vector towards the quest for an identity and a new form or emancipation, sport bolsters up the autonomist claim.
Would not the true merit of this comparative approach be to underline, if need be, one more time the fundamentally ideological dimension of sport ?

Notes

[1] Deville-Danthu, B. (1997). Le sport en noir et blanc. Paris: L'harmattan.
[2] Departementalisation act, March 19 th, 1946.
[3] Sport Colonial, 02-28-1879.
[4] Crubelier, M. (1983). Les citadins et leurs cultures. In Duby, G. : Histoire de la France urbaine, tome IV. Paris: Seuil.

[5] Simon, J. (1874). La réforme de l'enseignement secondaire.

[6] Dumont, J. (1997). Félix Eboué, ce grand sportif guadeloupéen. Actes du colloque du 7ème Carrefour du sport. Montpellier: L'Harmattan.

[7] First issue March 1st 1879 disappears in 1900.

[8] Combeau-Mari, E. (1997). Eugene Dutremblay Agénor : le sport et la laïcité à la Réunion (1920-1960). Actes du Colloque 7ème carrefour de l'histoire du sport. Montpellier: L'Harmattan.

[9] Sporting, Editorial, 03-02-1928.

[10] Le Dimanche Sportif et Culturel, N°99, 1948.

[11] The pen name can be used by various authors, or let think several writers are involved, as for Sporting.

[12] Created in 1866 by Jean Macé.

[13] Dubreuil, B. (1986). La naissance de l'UFOLEP. In Arnaud, P. & Camy, J. : La naissance du mouvement sportif associatif en France, sociabilité et formes de pratiques sportives. Lyon: PUL, p. 368.

[14] Le Dimanche Sportif, n°16, 1946.

[15] Le Dimanche Sportif, n°7, 1946.

[16] Le Dimanche Sportif et Culturel, n°106, 1948.

[17] Sporting, 05-19-1928.

[18] Sporting, 03-31-1928.

[19] Radio-Guadeloupe, 12-18 1945, Le Dimanche Sportif, n°2, 1945.

[20] Sporting, 05-19-1928.

[21] Le Dimanche Sportif et Culturel, n°74, 1947.

[22] Le Dimanche Sportif, n°56, 1947.

[23] Le Dimanche Sportif, n°37, 1946.

[24] Sporting, 03-1- 1928.

[25] Sporting, 05-05-1928.

[26] Sporting, 06-30-1928.

[27] Moussat, E. (1936). Etre chic, pour une morale sportive à une morale du sport. Paris: Messein.

[28] This reference is seldom used by Match, the other Guadeloupe Sport Magazine.

[29] Sporting, 03-24-1928.

[30] Sporting, 03-24-1928.

[31] Sporting, 08-18-1928.

[32] Alcande, S. (1945). Europe-colonies. CAOM, SG Guadeloupe, 265/1632.

[33] Le Dimanche Sportif, n°57-58, 1947.

[34] Le Dimanche Sportif et Culturel, n°76, 1947.

[35] Sporting, 07-26-1928.

[36] Sporting, 08-25-1928.

[37] Le Dimanche Sportif, n°56, 1947.

[38] Le Dimanche Sportif, n°19, 1946.

[39] Le Nouvelliste de la Guadeloupe, Feb. 19th 1938.

[40] Le Dimanche Sportif, n°32, 1947.

[41] Sporting, 09-08-1928.
[42] Sporting, 02-02-1929.
[43] A Dutremblay is in fact the only writer. He uses pen names.
[44] Le Dimanche Sportif, n°66, 1947.
[45] La Souffrière is the highest volcano of Guadeloupe.
[46] Le Dimanche Sportif, n°47, 1947.
[47] Ibid.
[48] In 1947, the governor still remains, waiting for the new department Administration.
[49] Match, n°108, 09-16-1949.

Chapter 13

Introduction to a comparative approach to naturism in France and Germany (1800-1939)

Sylvain Villaret and Jean-Michel Delaplace
University of Lyon 1, France

Naturism in France and Germany : common origins

During the 18th century, philosophical writings exalting Nature multiplied in France and Germany. Previously neglected or criticized as opposed to culture and the process of civilization, nature was now vested with all the virtues. For most of the members of the European intellectual élite, it was a case of seeking out nature and submitting to its formative action. Jean-Jacques Rousseau became the champion of this trend.

Such was the prevaling context when the notion of "naturism" arrived in France, through the writings of a doctor [1]. It was a matter of calling attention to a truism which had been circulating among the western medical profession for centuries. Indeed one has to go back to the writings of Hippocrates to find the origin of this notion of medicine. For this illustrious doctor from Cos :

"nature is the doctor to treat illnesses. It is nature which finds the ways and means, not intelligence".

Medical practice may thus be summed up as respectfully following nature. Illness is perceived as a natural curative reaction. The naturist doctor restricts his action to that of accompanying the illness, paying particular attention to diet and thermal parameters. As opposed to medicine-based treatment, the naturist doctor recommends the use of physical and climatic agents (air, water, sun) as well as physical exercise. The Greco-latin origin common to the French and German cultures explains the simultaneous existence of this particular concept in the medicine of both countries, even if the term for naturism, naturismus [2], came into the German language later. It may be noted that German naturism differed little from French naturism up to the beginning of the 19th century.

Origins of the advance of German naturism : an early revival (19th century)

The infatuation with nature became stronger from the beginning of the 19th century with the advent of the Romantic movement in art and literature. Poets and writers in Germany as in France, revered Romanticism and the cult of Antiquity.

Geographical determinism coupled with economic success

However the German naturist revival coincided with the emergence of naturist therapeutic systems created by Swiss and German empiricists.

In 1820 in Gräfenberg (Austrian Silesia) a farmer named Vinzenz Priessnitz proposed a natural cure based on the use of water. Damp compresses, hip baths, showers, prolonged cold baths, a diet of vegetables and dairy products, frictions and physical exercise, these were the principle types of action used to stimulate recovery. His considerable success led to the opening of a health centre, attracting patients from all over Europe. Meanwhile in Lindewiesse [3], another empiricist, Johann Schroth proposed a similar form of treatment, based on damp compresses associated with a special diet (cereals, bread and wine). A few years later, in an isolated village in the high Bavarian plateaux (Wörishofen), a country curate, Sebastian Kneipp, devised a naturist method based on applying water partially and for very short periods. The rapid success of this method transformed Wörishofen into a summer resort.

On the strength of these initiatives, a whole economic sector began to develop in Germany. The phenomenon was aided all the more by the fact that in 1866, from a legal point of view, anyone had the right to give consultations and receive fees.

"Popular" support for naturism

These events found a warm welcome in Germany. The patients took responsibility for publicizing the establishments and spreading the corresponding theories and practices of naturism throughout Germany. The phenomenon took on several forms. For instance, a number of brochures on the Priessnitz cure were published privately [4]. Elsewhere, disciples set themselves up as therapists. A new term was coined to designate Priessnitzian therapy : *Naturheilkund*. It replaced that of *Wasserheilkund* (hydrotherapy), which was considered too restrictive in regard to the doctrine expounded. Under the influence of Rausse, the followers of Priessnitz founded an *"Association for hygiene and therapy without medicine"* [5], in

Dresden, in 1835. Its aim was not only to teach its members how to take care of their health through naturism, but also to popularize non-medicine therapy. Similar associations mushroomed throughout Germany. These *Naturheilvereine*, as they were called, combined to form an extra-medical league: "*The German Union of Societies for Nature-based lifestyle and healthcare* " [6]. They listed over 150 000 members in 1907 and issued a review: *Naturazt* of 145 000 copies. The league had its own lecturers and orators who organized meetings and conferences in all the towns where one or more affiliated societies were to be found.

The birth of modern naturism : Arnold Rikli's atmospheric cure

In 1855, in Veldes, Slovania, Rikli founded an establishment for a natural health treatment of a new kind; his therapeutic method was essentially based on exposure to air, light and sun , in the nude or semi-nude. Rikli's treatment principle can be summed up as : "The water is useful, the air is better, but this light is the best of all" [7]. He set up three parks on the mountain slopes, where his atmospheric baths could be practised. Rikli's ideas were to echo across the Rhine with remarkable force.

Rikli's cure was imported to Germany by a doctor called Lahmann who had discovered it as a patient. In 1888 he founded a sanatorium in Weisser-Hirsch, near Dresden, with the first park designed for atmospheric baths in Germany. In its first year, Lahmann's sanatorium received 385 patients. After 1900, over 3000 people thronged to it each year. This considerable and unprecedented success soon provided a model for new establishments.

The "*Naturheilvereine*" quickly adopted the ideas of Rikli concerning nudity and health hygiene; they installed atmospheric bath parks for their members. Nevertheless there was no question yet of full nudity. Certain towns such as Munich followed the example. In 1906 over 150 areas for "air baths" could be counted throughout Germany. But it was only in 1893 that Dr Heinrich Pudör, expanding on the fertile ideas of Rikli, proclaimed the right to collective nudity, in his work *Nackende Menschen* [8] . In 1906, 83 nudist societies are federated in the league : *Deutsches Bund der Vereine fur naturgemässe Lebens und Heilweise*. They continued to proliferate. In 1905, a famous nudist and vegetarian colony was founded by seven intellectuals with anarchistic leanings in Italian switzerland : *Monté Vérita*.

At the end of the 19th century, German naturism, took on its final form, almost 20 years in advance of French naturism. A little later, the German medical profession adopted these profitable practices by creating the association : *Aerzte Vereine für physikalische-dietetiche Therapie*.

German naturism only begins to affect French naturism at the beginning of the 20th century

The procrastinations of French naturism

Throughout the 19th century, the naturist methods devised by Slavonic and German empiricists remained unknown or derided by virtually all French naturist doctors. It was only in 1890 that awareness was raised, after the publication in France of the works of Kneipp and a brochure by Rikli : *"Die Atmospheriche Kur"*. French naturism at the time was no more than the philosophy of treatment shared by such respectable doctors as Claude Bernard. It was still confined to the medical profession and had no popular following. There are several reasons for this gap in relation to the German movement.

The 19th century in France saw the rise of so-called scientific therapy in medicine. This "phenomenon" strengthened the position of doctors who believed in allopatic medicine. Naturism thus bowed to the scientific method, rejecting any new proposal which did not conform. There was even a fashion for prescribing naturist medicine. Already criticized by the majority of German doctors, the theories and practices of German empiricists were usually associated with charlatanism in France and reduced to mockery. The characteristic chauvinism of the French medical corps accentuated xenophobic reactions. The 1870 war reinforced the hatred for anything coming from the invader from across the Rhine.

The language barrier would also seem to have deeply compromised the spread of naturist methods in France. The work of Rikli : *Médecine naturelle et bains de soleil*, was only published in French in 1905 in Lausanne.

The geographical and climatic conditions specific to France and Germany may also explain the different perceptions of the importance of sun and light on the human body.

As for nudism, Dr. Antoine Monteuuis clearly sums up the position held by naturists in France before the 1914-1918 war :

> *"The German's customary acceptance of nudity in collective bathing will never take hold in France "* [9]

New forms adopted by French naturism on the eve of the "Great War"

Mentalities were nevertheless changing, stimulated by race degeneration and the fight against tuberculosis. Moreover the benefits of heliotherapy as practised by Dr. Malgat in Nice or Dr. Rollier in Leysin confirmed the results obtained by Rikli. The first sanatorium to put Rikli's atmospheric cure into practice was that of Dr. Monteuuis in Nice in 1905.

Breaking the traditional medical monopoly, the whole field of physical education and sports now began to reappropriate naturist theories and practices. Rikli's cure thus became the object of three articles in the review *L'éducation Physique* , in 1912. In 1910 a naturist physical education method appeared: Georges Hébert's *Méthode Naturelle*. In 1912, the promoter was responsible for setting up the first naturist physical culture centre in France : the *Collège d'Athlètes de Reims*.

More and more doctors began to incorporate the concepts and practices of the German naturists. These were nevertheless subjected to certain processes in order to conform to the "French temperament". Rigorous experimentation, reviewed and corrected methodology, an adapted mode of administering, were some of the mechanisms implemented. The naturist doctor Monteuuis thus refers to *"French air baths"* [10]; Differences in climate serve to justify these transformations.

Despite this revival, the development of French naturism remained tentative compared to Germany. The movement was a long way behind the 150 000 members of the German naturist league. At a time when over a hundred nudist societies existed in Germany, in 1914, there was still hesitation in France as to whether to adopt the dress recommended by Hébert for the practise of physical exercises (simple boxer shorts for boys and a sleeveless tunic for girls). There were still no signs of popular following nor of escaping medical surveillance.

The expansion of modern naturism in France and Germany 1919-1939

Similar practices, fostered by contact between the two countries

The traumatism of the 1914-18 war stimulated social change in Europe. At the beginning of the 1920s, nudism was blossoming in Germany and France. Across the Rhine, pro-nudist reviews proliferated, often owing to the support of public powers . *Freikörperkultur und Lebensreform* and *Die Freikörper-kultur*[11] were the official voices of the German nudist federations. On the strength of its success, nudism thus tended to be confused with naturism. In 1930 nudists numbered over 200 000 in Germany.

France, despite its very Puritannical Christian culture, experienced the same phenomenon. This can partly be explained by the thirst for joy and exuberance which characterized a people which had survived the conflict.

The roaring twenties thus witnessed the emergence and rapid rise of nudism largely due to the liberal ideas of certain doctors. Nudist reviews began to be published in 1922. They were often victims of police banning, which was not the case in Germany. Directly inspired by the German movements, the writer Kienne de Mongeot set up nudist centres in each main region and federated them to form the *Association gymnique de France*. This federation also disposed of an official organ : the journal *Vivre intégralement*. Kienne de Mongeot maintained close links with certain members of the German nudist movement, such as Max Kauffmann. Members did not hesitate to go to Germany to study the way in which the naturist movements were organized. According to the estimates of those in charge of the *Association gymnique de France*, there were over 20 000 regularly practising nudists in 1931. Nudism also tended to be assimilated with naturism in the mid 30s which favoured a change in attitudes toward undressing in public.

Between the wars, nudism continued to develop in France and Germany in the same fashion. It was systematically linked with the practice of physical exercise and sport. Kienne de Mongeot spread the movement through gymnastic and sports associations. In Germany, air bath parks were equipped with sports facilities and swimming pools. Adolph Koch was head of one of the biggest gymnastic schools, in Berlin. Men, women and children practised physical exercise together, entirely in the nude[12].

Nudists in France and Germany between the wars belonged to the same class of society i.e. the progressive upper middle class. Nevertheless the movement became increasingly democratic over this period, in both countries. Between the wars, members were also recruited from the middle classes.

A basic difference : the politicization of naturism in Germany after 1920

Beyond naturist practices, such as sunbaths and nudism, naturists in France and Germany embraced the idea of a new life. Whereas these claims remained marginal in France, they led to political expression in Germany. For the majority of German naturists, the will to reform life implied policital commitment. Certain members of the *Monte Vérita* nudist colony were active militants in revolutionary movements. Moreover, the German nudist movement was split into several political parties [13]. According to Kauffmann, three main groups of bourgeois parties and one socialist party can be identified. These groups had subsidiaries in each main city. The centre of the socialist group, the *Verband Volksgesundheit*, was based in Dresden (Saxony). The politicization of naturist movements nevertheless prepared the advent of the IIIrd Reich. The desire to establish a new era, to bring back values which were close to pangermanism, reunited the different movements in a combined philosophical project which supporters of Nazism used to their advantage. From the mid 1930s onwards, naturists were given the task of regenerating the Aryan race and toughening it up in the face of future struggles. Energies had to be combined for the good of the nation. Despite the desperate warnings administered by certain nudist thinkers, naturism was placed in the service of the IIIrd Reich and its racist ideology.

In France, despite the desire of certain instigators of the naturist method to regenerate the race and toughen up the youth, the dominant values were those of hedonism. Political disinterest and the Popular Front's policy of leisure and outdoor pursuits, are partly responsible for this phenomenon. Nevertheless the eyes of many political, military and medical figures were often turned toward Germany, where the naturist physical training of the youth remained a model.

Conclusion : German naturism as a model and guide for the French movement

The 19th century would appear to be a key period in explaining the late development of French naturism in relation to that of Germany. The early popularization of naturism in Germany with its corresponding popularisation, was one of the most dynamic factors in the German movement. This did not occur in France until the beginning of the 1920s. It is patently obvious that German naturism acted as a model for French naturism and conditioned its development. However it was necessary to wait until naturism in France broke the yoke of official medicine for its most modern forms to develop on a large scale. It nevertheless lagged well behind what could be observed in Germany until the end of the 1930s.

References

Monteuuis, A. (1911). L'usage chez soi des bains d'air, de lumière et de soleil. Leur valeur pratique dans le traitment des maladies chroniques et dans l'hygiène journalière. Paris.

Planchon (1778). Le naturisme ou la nature considérée dans les maladies et leur traitement conforme à la doctrine et à la pratique d'Hippocrate et de ses sectateurs. Tournay.

Pudör, H. (1893). Nackende Menschen, Jauchzen der Zukunft. Dresden-Loschwitz.

Rajko, Sugman, Pavlin, Tomaz (to be published). Arnold Rikli and his Heritage. Lyon.

Rausse, der Geist der Gräfenberg Wasserkur, s.d., citated in Sandoz,
   Fernand, Introduction à la thérapeutique naturiste par les agents
   physiques et diététiques, Thesis for a medical Phd, n° 323, Paris,
   Steinheil, 1907.
Ribo, E. (1931). Nudisme. Thesis for a Medical PhD, n° 78. Bordeaux

---

Notes

[1] Planchon, Imprimerie Chez Varle, 1778.
[2] The closest translation of the naturist concept of the 19th century, is the
     term Naturheilkund used to designate Priessnitz' cure.
[3] The number of patients treated in the establishment opened by Schroth in
     Lindwiese increased from 176 in 1850 to 684 in 1882, reaching 1500 in
     1905.
[4] Rausse, der Geist der Gräfenberg Wasserkur, s.d.
[5] "Vereine für Gesundheitspflegue und aszneilose Heilweise".
[6] "Deutsches Bund der Vereine für naturgemässe Lebens und Heilweise"
[7] Rajko Sugman, Tomaz Pavlin, ISHPES 1997.
[8] Pudör, H., 1893.
[9] Monteuuis, A., 1911, p. 62.
[10] Monteuuis, A., 1911, p. 139.
[11] Recorded at the beginning of the 1920s were: Die Schönheit, Die Freude,
     Lachendes Leben, Soma.
[12] The school presented a nude gymnastics demonstration in 1931, involving
     over 500 students, men and women, on the stage of a big theatre in
     Berlin.
[13] "Car chez nous, même pour la nudité, la politique s'en mêle"; (Because
     here, even nudity is bound up with politics) Max Kauffmann, quoted in
     Ribo, Imprimerie Y. Cadoret, Bordeaux, 1931, p. 81.

Chapter 14

A comparative analysis of the training schools for teachers of physical education in Italy and Spain : 1860 - 1910

Teresa Gonzales Aja and Angela Teja
INEF Madrid, Spain and ISEF Rome, Italy

At the end of the nineteenth century, Italy and Spain appeared as nations which both shared common traits such as Catholicism, monarchy, poverty, a lack of a modern social structure and a distinct backwardness in certain sectors, including industry and education. The practice of gymnastics in the two countries shared common characteristics, namely their military origins. In Italy, the gymnastics movement begin to take hold more rapidly, being supported by the new outlook which the Liberal government wished to give to the country in an attempt to modernize it and place it on an equal, footing with the European nations. Gymnastics, at first, and later sports in general, were considered to be means for an effective socio-cultural emancipation, given that they were aimed at maintaining and reinforcing the health of citizens, who would therefore be better prepared to fill the ranks of an army which would be able to compete with the other European armies. The spread of women's gymnastics was symptomatic of the more advanced development of Italian society as compared to that of Spanish society. Indeed, it was the open attitude towards Europe which differentiated the two countries: partly Italy, thanks to its geographic position, maintained close contacts with both France and the Austro-Hungarian Empire, from which it absorbed many traits. The Pyrenees, on the other hand, were not only a stoney wall, but also a cultural barrier, separating Spain from France and the rest of Europe. But let us focus now upon the training schools for teachers of gymnastics in both countries.

Training schools for physical education in Italy

Only four months after Italian unification on 17 March 1861, the Minister of Public Education, Francesco De Sanctis, issued a decree establishing a course of study for gymnastics teachers at the Società Ginnastica Torino. The course lasted for three months, from August to September [1]. This marked the beginning, in Italy, of a school of instruction for teachers of gymnastics. As D'Azeglio had said, once Italy had been created, it was necessary to create the Italians, forging them physically in order to obtain healthy, courageous citizen-soldiers. This was demonstrated by a memorandum issued as early as March 1860 by the Minister of Public Education, Terenzio Mamiani, and addressed to the Royal Boards of Education [2].

The Regulations issued in August of 1860, as part of the school reform of Casati, included references to gymnastics, military exercises and military marches. All of the indications regarded the male students, because, as Mamiani wrote:

> *"The nature of the times and the rebirth of Italy call for an extremely virile approach to education"* [3].

Starting in 1867, women teachers also received their first training courses, organized by the City of Turin, and were attended by five women teachers, some from the City of Milan [4].

Gymnastics appeared in the school curricula as military gymnastics aimed at the training of male pupils. These were the key years of the Italian Risorgimento. Legislative and administrative unification had not yet been obtained, there were considerable economic problems, the roadway and railway systems were entirely inadequate, taxes were on the rise, and the question of Southern Italy called for a solution. Rome for instance was still in the hands of the Church. The Italian Army had shown that it was not up to the important tasks which it had to fulfill. Prussia, on the other hand, had Europe's best prepared army : Sédan (1870) and the rise of the German Reich provided an unequivocal example of how a well trained army could make a nation's fortune. The year 1870 meant also a turning point for Italy : the fall of the French empire of Napoleon III, the establishment of the German Empire, the revival of nationalist sentiments, and, more closely related to Italy, the annexation of Rome to the Italian Kingdom and the end of the wordly power of the Pope.

The need for a strong, well-trained army was deeply felt. Young people were to receive physical education from the earliest age, making it easier to train them once they entered the military. The three-month courses in Turin soon proved insufficient to the task of forming teachers for the hundreds of schools spread throughout the entire territory of the Kingdom.

The result was the creation of the Normal School of Gymnastics of Turin (Royal decree no. 204 of 29 June 1874, signed by Minghetti), whose 'Regulations' stipulated the program to be followed under art. 4. Marksmanship and fencing appear in the first group of subjects to be taught, together with "... tactical exercises, riding and the vocabulary and handling of arms". Swimming and theoretical and practical gymnastics based on the Obermann method were also on the program [5].

The true turning point for educational gymnastics in Italy, and for the training schools for teachers, took place after the rise to power of a left-wing government under De Pretis in 1876. The result was the Coppino Law of 1877, which made elementary school education mandatory. In June of the same year, a memorandum (no. 523) of the Ministry of Public Education to the prefects who presided over the provincial school councils, announced that a course would be created in Turin, for both male and female teachers. It was emphasized that this initiative would have an important impact on the "... future of the country's youth" [6]. The same Minister Coppino also decided that study at the Normal School of Gymnastics was to last for eight months in order to prepare teachers for the regular schools. Coppino wrote that:

> *"The purpose of the Normal School of Gymnastics is to prepare teachers who are capable of instilling within our young people an awareness of their own dignity and energy, in this way developing sturdy arms and generous hearts for our country"* [7].

In the following year 1878, De Sanctis succeeded in passing a law which was to make the teaching of educational gymnastics obligatory in schools of every type and level. The arguments he brought before the Chamber of Deputies were based primarily on the possibility of preparing young men for military service, especially in secondary schools [8]. The metallurgical and mechanical industries embraced the cause of an 'armed nation', enticed by the glamour of Bismarck's militarized Germany. Only a few years later, Italy initiated the colonial policy which was to lead to the establishment of the colony in Eritrea. All of these elements explain the stress placed by the government on the preparation of strong, healthy and courageous young men. Physical education was undoubtedly seen as the most appropriate system for achieving this objective.

The new spirit of the Italian left can be detected in the words written by De Sanctis in a memorandum of August 1878 which established gymnastics courses lasting for a period of twenty days in autumn :

> *"The introduction of gymnastic exercises means that we have adopted a different approach to the administration of the schools, ... that discipline and order must be sought, ... it means that a new spirit is called for in all school institutions"* [9].

De Sanctis further emphasized that "... the purpose of gymnastics is to form citizens capable of defending their country, real soldiers", and that all of a nation's able-bodied men would be required to participate in an eventual war [10].

The same memorandum clearly stated, however, that the courses were not to be designed solely for male teachers, and for military purposes, but that women teachers were also required to familiarize themselves with the new approach to teaching. In female schools the military practices, together with certain exercises "... less appropriate for young ladies", including those involving the chest and the lower limbs, were to be omitted [11].

In the interests of preparing the personnel meant to teach gymnastics in the secondary schools, Minister Coppino established nine gymnastics teachers' schools [12]. The courses consisted of: "1) theoretical-practical gymnastics; 2) elementary teaching concepts and notes on the history of gymnastics; 3) fundamental concepts on the structure of the human body and the physiological and hygienic effect of gymnastics exercises; 4) military exercises accompanied by general concepts on the military establishment of the country; 5) choral singing. Two teaching sessions were held at each school, both running from the first of August to the thirtieth of October, with the first consisting of practical instruction and the second scientific and military subjects [13]. The nine schools were to follow the example of what had already been done for a number of years at the Società Ginnastica Torino, which also trained women teachers [14].

Budget considerations led to the suspension of the autumn courses in 1881, though it was still possible for municipal governments to finance such courses, whenever they could succeed in doing so. The courses were reinstated, for the last time, in 1882, given that the De Sanctis law reached the end of its five-year period in that year. Also in 1882, the gymnastics teachers' courses were held at the teachers' schools of a number of provinces. A Women Gymnastics Teachers' School was established, with a course of study lasting for five months [15]. The year 1882 was also fairly eventful in terms of politics. Italy succeeded in reaching an accord with the German Empire and with the Austro-Hungarian monarchy, creating what was referred to as the Triple Alliance. This put an end to the diplomatic isolation in which the country had languished since the Congress of Berlin(1878). Prussia and Austria thus represented models to emulate in a number of sectors, of which gymnastics was definitely one. In the same year, Italy initiated its colonial policy, with the establishment of the colony in Eritrea mentioned earlier, subsequently reinforced by a full-fledged Italian protectorate covering all of Abissinia. The Italian Army had an increasing need for well-trained young people, in part to compensate for the growing number of draftees rejected for physical reasons. The latter phenomenon was linked to the poor conditions of hygiene in the country, the high level of illness and the high rate of poverty [16]. Gymnastics was supposed to provide a valid remedy to these conditions [17].

The very term 'physical education' appeared for the first time (replacing 'gymnastic education') in the ministerial programs of 1893 (Royal Decree of 26 November 1893). The military debacle at Adua (1896), which led to a sharp reduction in the Italian colonial adventure, had other repercussions as well. The Italian government was unable to address the question of the country's official participation in the first celebration of the modern Olympic Games. Public opinion was focused on much more serious issues, with the result that interest in physical education and sports was reduced.

Nevertheless, the enthusiasm for physical education which marked the end of the century lasted long enough to witness the creation of the Normal School of Gymnastics of Rome (Royal Decree of 27 August 1884, signed by Minister Coppino, and the Law of 23 December 1988). Its course of study lasted for ten months, with a curriculum which still included military exercises, plus marksmanship and fencing, though this last subject was replaced by swimming in the final month [18].

The Rome school for male physical educationists was created in the same year as the Scuola Magistrale Militare di Scherma (or Military School for Fencing Masters), and this was certainly no coincidence. The military personnel practiced gymnastics in the gymnasium of the civilian school directed by Emilio Baumann, in facilities constructed on the octagonal hall of the Baths of Diocletian on the Via Cernaia [19].

In 1890, a Royal Decree signed by Boselli established two normal schools for female gymnastics, one on Naples and one in Turin. Statistics for the year 1900 show that only ten thousand girls were registered in secondary school, while only 251 had entered universities [20]. Nevertheless, there was no lack of students in the two schools. The female program of practical gymnastics consisted of 'special' exercises being limited to running, climbing and jumping, while only two exercises involving apparatus were included: the balance-beam and the horizontal ladder [21]. The number of lesson hours per week was less than the number for the males: thirty instead of thirty-six. The program also included gymnastic games "... excluding, naturally, those not appropriate for the female sex, such as the vaulting horse, rope-climbing, etc.". Dancing, on the other hand, was included in the program. The remaining activities consisted of "... a number of gymnastic applications", such as walking and marches, plus life-saving and swimming exercises [22].

Female gymnastics thus began to run along paths which increasingly converged with those of male gymnastics. A positive value was given to outdoor games - the so-called 'English games' - for females as well as males, while the apparatus exercises for females disappeared from the list. Indeed, it was no longer held necessary to issue instructions for separate programs, but simply to note the adjustments and modifications which should be made in the exercises to accommodate the dress, comportment and "... sexual reserve, as well as the anatomical and physiological conditions of women" [23].

Law no. 805 of 26 December 1909 on the training of teachers of physical education marked a turning point, leading, among other things, to the transformation in October of 1910 of the Gymnastics Teachers' Schools in Rome, Turin and Naples into Educational Institutes for Qualification for the Teaching of Physical Education in Middle Schools, both Male and Female. But, in this paper, we wish to limit ourselves to the training schools in operation at the turn of the century.

A Central School of Gymnastics in Spain

If we turn to Spain, we can say that, at the end of the nineteenth century, this was a nation full of contrasts, to the delight of romantic travelers [24]. Sports activities were the privilege of the very few who belonged to the upper social classes. Horseback riding, shooting and fencing represented the activities most widely practiced by this sector of the population, while the common folk mainly took part in local feasts. Also the bull fights, the national pastime par excellence kept their 'couleur locale' even when, at a later point in time, the development of the railways made it possible to transport both spectators and bulls on a regular basis [25]. The small town and their local feasts characterized Spain while the large cities and the modern sporting events were only of little significance.

As for physical education in the second half of the nineteenth century, it appeared to be tied to three main groups: 1) educators, 2) physicians and experts in hygiene, and 3) politicians and military men.

During this period, steps were taken to modify the courses of study, based on the Law of Public Education of Claudio Morano (1857). Between 1850 and 1870, numerous private gymnasiums were created throughout Spain. According to Fraguas, the teaching in these gymnasiums, "... was offered by empiricists who had originally worked in foreign or domestic circuses" [26].

Not until 1879 was a law proposed declaring gymnastics to be mandatory in secondary schools and in normal schools for teachers. The proposal was presented for the second time in 1881 by Manuel Becerra, 'the Official Father' of Spanish Gymnastics [27]. In his speech, he did not hesitate to state that gymnastics was worthwhile, both from a military point of view, for the defence of the nation, and in terms of moral values, "... because there is no greater wealth for a nation than to have virile, hardworking men" [28]. Becerra called for the Italian model to be followed, saying of it "... the teaching is part of primary-school education ... and it has been extended to even the humblest schools of the most forlorn villages" [29]. Manuel Becerra considered sports to be of fundamental importance for what he referred to as the "... ugly or warrior sex". He also held such activity to be valuable for the "fair sex", in that sport makes it possible to achieve more pleasing and regular forms and proportions, in addition to aiding in the performance of those functions "... to which Nature calls women" [30].

> "What is more, physiology demonstrates the role played by the mother in terms of generating healthy children, meaning that there is no point in hoping to have sturdy men if the women do not present the same characteristics" [31].

In other words, Becerra stated that it was necessary to produce strong citizens who can prove useful in time of war, though this is not possible unless there are women capable of giving birth to sturdy children.

Still, Becerra did not limit himself to considering the physical benefits offered by gymnastics. These benefits also extend to the moral and intellectual spheres. In light of all this, he concluded by asking that gymnastics would become mandatory "... first for one year, and then for three" [32].

The Congress appointed a commission to study the law, which included, in addition to Becerra and others, the important political figure José Canalejas [33]. The findings of the Commission were communicated on 16 May 1882, and it was recommended that the Government would create a central school for male and female teachers of gymnastics. This provided the groundwork for the passage of the law of 9 March 1883, signed by King Alfonso XII. When the Kind died in 1885, the school had still not begun operations, given that it had no by-laws. Another Commission was created to draw up these by-laws [34], which were approved by a Royal Decree issued by the Queen Regent, Maria Cristina, on 22 October 1886. From this moment on, the Central School for Male and Female Teachers of Theoretical and Practical Gymnastics [35] was legally in existence. It was not officially opened though until 1887, as a center operating under the auspices of the University of Madrid. Both men and women were admitted, which was quite remarkable for the time [36]. The school already closed five years later in 1892, seemingly for economic reasons [37].

Both practical and theoretical subjects were taught in the Central School. The theory included anatomy, physiology and hygiene as they pertain to gymnastics, as well as the study of gymnastics equipment and its construction and application. Further, the teaching of gymnastics, the theory of fencing, the study of movement mechanics the main dressings and bandages for wounds and dislocated bones.

The practical teaching included : free and drill exercises without apparatus; reading out loud and declamation; exercises with musical accompaniment or singing; exercises for the eyes and for recognizing distances, measuring heights and judging different gradients; hearing exercises for the purpose of recognizing distances with this sense as well, plus the direction and intensity of the sound, not to mention its rhythm and tone; swimming, horseback riding, fencing, marksmanship and exercises with apparatus.

One article of the legislative proposal which deserves particular attention is the fourth, which reads:

> *"The gymnastics teachers of the Central School and of the other institutes in which the teachings are propagated are to be placed on an equal footing with other State schools".*

By the time the law had been passed, however, it no longer contained this article. All the same, it is worthwhile to note that, in other articles, the law stipulated that whoever is assigned to teach gymnastics to women should be a woman teacher "... with rights and responsibilities similar to those of the Director, though this teacher, as is the case with the other teachers, is to work under the Director" [38]. It shows that a law creating a school, which was to be inaugurated under the regency of a woman, maintained the inequality between the sexes. Apparently women then were entitled to run a country, but not a school !

On the other hand, with the clear intent of preventing this school from monopolizing physical education, a Royal Order stipulated that all those who wished to be examined as 'independent students' of the school could do so, on the condition that they had obtained the official program of the subjects taught, and that they had attempted to pass on this teaching. It was stated that :

> *"... those who wish to officially exercise this type of teaching (gymnastics) have two options: they can either earn a diploma at the Central School of Gymnastics, or they can take the examination of this school as independent students".*

All the same, there would seem to have been a fair amount of consternation over the procedures for managing to take these examinations, a fact which caused a series of protests [39].

To summarize, we can say that the creation of the Central School of Gymnastics can only be understood in the context of the 'new public climate' laid down by the liberal coalitions in power as of February of 1881, with Sagasta as Prime Minister. Their goal was to stimulate the public educational system through initiatives such as the restoration of the freedom of professorships (1881), the creation of the Educational Museum (1882), freedom of the press (1883) and other innovations meant to modernize Spanish society, as well as the introduction into physical education of official curricula, an unmistakable sign of modernity.

The adoption of the gymnastics programs initially, followed by the adoption of games and sports, was first carried out at the secondary school level. The Central School of Gymnastics was meant to prepare male and female teachers for so called middle schools and for normal schools. Unfortunately, the reality of the subsequent history differed significantly from the good intentions which led to the creation of the school. In primary and secondary schools, physical education was practically non-existent, and teachers received scarce and irregular instructions [40].

The creation of the school was the result of the desire to bring Spain in step with the rest of the European countries, which, at that point in time, had already introduced gymnastics into their school programs and had established special institutes for the training of physical education teachers.

Conclusion

Trying to establish a comparison with Italy, it seems that Spain attempted to imitate the liberal form of administration. Indeed, Italy was seen as an extremely modern country at the forefront of European progress, so that the temptation to imitate it, and possibly reproduce a number of its characteristics, was very strong in Spain.

Both in Italy and in Spain, the attempt to organize physical education came from the left, but, while in Italy there was a continuous attempt which led to the development of different laws and different projects. In Spain there was only one initiative, which would soon fail, most probably because of the political tradition of alternating governments.

In both countries, female physical education was aimed at woman's essential function : motherhood. The exercises were therefore intended to develop the bust and the lower body.

In both countries, the educational programs included gymnastics, pedagogy, aspects of physiology and hygiene, military exercises and singing. The fundamental difference was that, while in Italy an innovative educational objective was pursued, in Spain there were no signs of any progressive tendencies in the program.

In Italy the aim was to form *a new man*, while in Spain there was no equivalent interest in the forming of an ideal type of man at that point in time. That would have to wait for a number of years.

We can, therefore, as mentioned earlier, talk about similar propositions, of a similar starting point, but of a different development. The training schools for teachers of physical education in Italy were realized as part of a more global project which was, at the same time, more continuous, with objectives which were part of the global framework of the forming of the Italian man. In Spain, the Central School of Gymnastics was a concrete project, developed at a specific point in time, more practical than ideological in nature, but unfortunately it turned out to be a failure.

Notes

[1]   In the regulations governing these courses (Royal Decree of 13 July 1861), art. 2 specifies the contents of the program of study: "Daily lessons in gymnastics given by the Director of the Society;   concepts regarding the structure of the human body in relation to gymnastics, taught by a Deputy Director of the Society;   daily gymnastics exercises held by an Instructor who is a Deputy to the Director;   trial teaching of young people admitted to the Society's school and selected by the Director.   Gotta, M. (1958). Leggi e ordimamenti dell'educazione fisica nella scuola italiana, vol. I (from 1860 to 1915). Rome, p. 23.

[2]   Mem. no. 69 of 27 March 1860 (in Gotta, M., p. 8).

[3]   Report on the Regulations (in id., p. 18).

[4]   Mem. no. 206 of 22 June 1867. Cfr. Teja, A. (1995). Educazione fisica al femminile.   Dai primi corsi di Torino di Ginnastica educativa per le maestre (1867) alla ginnastica moderna di Andreina Gotta-Sacco. Rome, p. 10.

[5]   Royal Decree no. 2431 of 16 July 1874. The other subjects taught were: "Education, applied to physical exercises and the history of gymnastics; Basic concepts of anatomy, physiology and hygiene applied to physical education; Line drawing applied to the construction of gymnasiums and gymnastics equipment; Choral singing" (in Gotta, M., p. 37).

[6]   Gotta, M., p. 43.

[7]   Memo no. 527 of 10 August 1877 (in Gotta, M., p. 45).

[8]   Cfr. M. di Donato, Francesco De Sanctis, the Minister of Gymnastics, in Alcmeone II, 1, 29-39, 1978. The law also included a brief article (no. 3) devoted to female gymnastics and stating: "In female schools of all types and levels, gymnastics will be strictly educational in nature, and will be governed by a special set of norms".   Apparently, there was no way of avoiding the subject of training girls as well, though it was relegated to a separate set of norms.

[9] Memo. no. 556 of 24 August 1878, signed by De Sanctis. The Ministry of Public Education (1900). L'educazione fisica e la ginnastica educativa in Italia nel sec. XIX. Atti ufficiali - Leggi - Decreti - Regolamenti-Programmi - Circolari. Rome, p. 141

[10] Id. p. 142.

[11] Id. p. 152-153.

[12] The schools in question were created in the cities of Bari, Bologna, Catania, Florence, Naples, Padua, Palermo, Rome and Turin.

[13] Memo. 580 of 1 May 1879 (id. pp. 207-210).

[14] These autumn courses for women lasted for a month (September) and were established with memorandum no. 584 of 27 December 1879, signed by Minister Coppino. The following cities were chosen : Turin, Genoa, Milan, Verona, Padua, Bologna, Florence, Siena, Rome, Bari, Naples, Ancona, Catania, Palermo and Sassari.

[15] The school created in Florence by a decree dated 14 March 1880, was transferred to this new school in Naples.

[16] The trend increased in 1911 with the war in Libya, at which time the position of commander of the Italian troops was assigned to Major General Luigi Capello, who was also a member of the President's Council of the *Federazione Ginnastica*. The result was a virtual "transfer" of the exertion of the gymnasium to the trials of the battlefield. Giuntini, D. (1991). La ginnastica della campagna di Libia. Lancillotto e Nausica, a.VIII, 1-2, 76-83.

[17] On gymnastics-military training in the Italian Army following the Unification of Italy up through the Second World War, see Ulzega, M.P. & Teja, A. (1994). L'addestramento ginnico-militare nell'Esercito italiano (1861-1945). Rome.

[18] The Royal Decree of 30 August 1884, enlarged with the Royal Decree of 13 November 1890. Here is the full list of the subjects taught : educational gymnastics, military exercises, marksmanship, fencing, fire-fighting exercises, drawing regarding the construction of gymnastics equipment and gymnasiums, choral singing, swimming, a concise history of educational theory applied to gymnastics, hygiene, anatomy and physiology related to gymnastics and military exercises. Ministry of Public Instruction, L'educazione fisica e la ginnastica, cit., p. 251.

[19] Teja, A. (currently being printed). Divise e fanfare nelle società sportive romane. In Teja, A. & Tolleneer, J. (1998). Lo sport in uniforme. Cinquant'anni di storia in Europa (1870-1915). Atti del Convegno Internazionale sulla Storia dello sport militare. Rome 7-8 November 1997. Rome, p. 72-87.

[20] Pieroni Bartolotti, F. (1986). Appunti sulle origini del movimento femminile tra '800 e '900. Rome.

[21] Among the 'special' exercises in the male program were the handling of weights, the javelin and wrestling. In terms of equipment, the pieces

with which the men exercised, in addition to those used by the women, were the parallel bars, the horizontal bar, the rings, the inclined board and the vaulting horse. Ministry of Public Education (1891). Regolamenti e Orogrammi per le Scuole Normali di Ginnastica 1890. Rome.

[22] Id. p. 45.

[23] From the general report of the commission assigned to formulate the programs. Ministry of Public Education (1894). Programmi di educazione fisica. Turin, p. 16.

[24] Borrow, G. Bible in Spain. London, p. 116.

[25] Vailletet, P. & Flanet, V. (1986). Le peuple du toro. Paris, p. 29.

[26] Fraguas, J.E.G. (1892). Historia de la Gimnástica Higiénica y Médica, a talk given at the Department of Natural Science of the University of Madrid, Madrid, R. fé, p.27.

[27] Fraguas, J.E.G. (1893). Tratado racional de gimnastica y de los ejercicios y juegos coporales. Madrid, I, p. 159.

[28] Piernavieja, M. (1962). La Educación Física en España, Antecedentes historico-legales. Citius-Altius-Fortius, 4, 46.

[29] Idem.

[30] Idem.

[31] Idem, p. 46-47.

[32] Idem, p. 51.

[33] José Canalejas y Méndez (184-1912) was President of the Cortes in 1906 and Prime Minister in 1910; he was eventually assassinated. In addition to these two figures, the members of the Commission were: Isidro Boixader, José Iranzo, Zoilo Pérez, Eduardo Baselga and Uan montilla, who served as secretary.

[34] The members of the Commission were to be Mariano Marcos Ordaz, Alfredo Serrano Fatigati and José Sánchez y González.

[35] Gaceta de Madrid, 10 March 1883.

[36] Gonzalez Aja, T. (1988). La Educación Fisica en España (1800-1936)". In Francisco Amorós, su obra entre dos culturas. Madrid: INEF.

[37] Regolamento de la Escuela Central de Gimnástica, in the Gaceta de Madrid, 24 October 1886, p. 231 and following.

[38] Piernavieja, M., p. 63.

[39] A wide-ranging set of documentation is found in the doctoral thesis of D. Pedro Zorilla: "L'educazaione fisica nell'insegnamento secondario attraverso i programmi di formazione (1893-1981), unpublished.

[40] Qualification is obtained through examinations given by the Department of Medicine (1896), or by taking the courses of the Army School of Physical Education in Toledo (from 1919).

Chapter 15

The English response to America's national pastime: American baseball tours to England, 1874-1924

Daniel J. Bloyce
University College Chester, U.K.

It is arguably the case that there is an increasing closeness of the ties between English and American people. The success of American sports, and aspects of "American culture" in "crossing the water" is clearly evident. These developments make baseball's failure to catch on in England quite mysterious. This failure becomes all the more interesting in light of the fact that the first tour of professional baseball players to England took place as long ago as 1874. Indeed, over the next half century, professional teams played exhibition matches in this country on three more occasions, in 1889, 1914, and 1924. This paper will examine responses to these attempts to export baseball to England, in order to help account for the failure to export America's "favourite game". In the process, light will be thrown on the cultural and sporting relationships between England and the United States of America (U.S.A.).

In relation to the relative failure to establish baseball in England during the period outlined it will be necessary to investigate issues such as: the lack of media coverage of baseball; expressions of nationalism and national pride in England; the highly commercialised, competitive aspects of baseball; as well as the comparisons made between baseball and other sports, in particular cricket and rounders. Hence, to adequately explain the failure to establish baseball as a major sport in England requires an appreciation of a range of complex and interdependent processes.

In 1874, Harry Wright played a significant part in the decision to exhibit baseball in Britain. He was a leading professional at that time with the *Boston Red Stockings*. Wright enlisted the help of Albert G. Spalding - who at the time was arguably the most prominent baseball player in the USA - to help make arrangements for the tour. As such, Spalding visited England in advance of the proposed tour, early in 1874. Perhaps as a result of the power of the M.C.C. at this time, Spalding agreed to their request, in negotiating venues for the forthcoming tour, that the Americans take part in cricket matches with their hosts as well. However, Spalding had realised that these games would do much to deflect the English public's interest from the baseball.

The tour made an inauspicious start at Liverpool. The *Liverpool Daily Albion* (1874) reported that: "There were not many spectators to witness the introduction of the new game ... because the public do not seem to have been properly informed that the game was coming off" (p.5). However, relatively little coverage was given to either the baseball or cricket games by the English press thereafter. Furthermore, it would seem that many of those watching found baseball "very monotonous" (The Yorkshire Post and Leeds Intelligencer, 17 August, 1874, p.4). The tour was not remotely successful. Nevertheless, Spalding was still sufficiently optimistic about the prospects of exporting baseball. Fourteen years after the first tour he developed plans to play exhibition matches around the world, which eventually culminated in a visit to Britain in the new year of 1889. The two teams of professional baseball players played exhibition matches on eleven occasions in Britain alone. The Chicago White Stockings, the team Spalding managed, and an "All America's" team consisting of numerous professionals from various other teams in the USA, were the two teams involved.

Before this tour commenced Spalding invited a journalist with the then well-known British newspaper, *The Sportsman*, to join him on the British leg of the tour. The journalist travelled with the entourage of American press, ball players and promoters. In doing this, it is likely that Spalding was attempting to respond to certain problems that were faced during the first tour - that the games were not terribly well publicised in advance, and that the nuances of baseball were lost on many British spectators. However, the response of much of the English press was once again not very promising for baseball's proselytisers as the better and more careful planning by Spalding and others had little impact on the amount of press coverage devoted to the tour, although, not surprisingly, *The Sportsman* provided much greater coverage.

The next tour by American professional baseball players to England was made a quarter of a century later. In 1913, financed by the now well established Spalding sports companies, John McGraw and Charles Comiskey led a "World Tour" of exhibition games of baseball. McGraw was then the famous manager and part owner of the New York Giants, and Comiskey was the owner of the Chicago White Sox - and hence, these were the two teams involved in the exhibition matches. The tour ended with games in England, Scotland and Ireland, in the early part of 1914. Even King George V attended a game at Stamford Bridge on the 26th of February. The King threw the first pitch, which one American reporter described as, "a flattering recognition of the American game" (New York Times, 27 February, 1914, p. 1). In general though, "there was the usual polite, bored reception" (Voigt 1970: 49) from the English hosts.

Another tour, involving the same clubs as in 1914, met with a similar lack of success, some ten years later. Charles Comiskey again headed an American League contingent whilst McGraw was in charge of the National League representatives. For the most part, the tour was accorded greater coverage than any of the previous three. This was in all likelihood due partly to the fact that the matches were concentrated in two main cities (Liverpool and London); and partly to the fact that press coverage of sports in general was developing at this time. Moreover, the USA and Britain were becoming increasingly interdependent. However, it would seem that the English public remained rather sceptical of the sport, despite another appearance at a game by King George. Even at this exhibition match, "the generality of the crowd were simply curious; they took but a placid interest in the display" (The Sportsman, 7 November, 1924, p. 23).

In the remainder of the paper the reasons for the lack of success in establishing baseball in England will be examined in more detail. The lack of coverage devoted to baseball in much of the English press was a major contributing factor. In attempting to introduce any cultural innovation, including, of course, sports, those promoting that innovation are heavily - although not completely - reliant on the media, and particularly in the late nineteenth and early twentieth centuries, the print media. Those administrating baseball in the USA were no different. Thus, the relative lack of coverage the baseball tours received in the English press is in direct contrast to the way in which Spalding, and others, had utilised the American press to develop the game there (Furst 1988). These individuals were not in a sufficiently powerful position in England to command the same sort of press coverage there.

The most pertinent question, however, is why, in the press coverage that was devoted to the tours, was much of that coverage so disparaging? In many cases, contemptuous comparisons were drawn between baseball and the game of rounders and baseball was presented in a rather negative light. Several authors dismissed baseball as "glorified rounders" and described it as "nothing but a pitiful fraud" (The Lancashire Evening Post, 23 March, 1914, p. 4). However, perhaps the best illustration of this kind of disparaging coverage is provided in *The Standard* (1914), during the tour of 1914:

> *"They [Americans] are not satisfied, it is not compatible with their new-world pride ... to make use of anything that comes from the Old World. If they do condescend to adopt a thing of foreign origin it must first be Americanised, distorted out of all semblance to its native form. The English language is a case in point! The national game of baseball is a*

shining example of these methods of adaptation. It was once rounders .... It is unlikely that baseball will catch on in England, certainly it will never diminish the popularity of any of our national games." (p. 10)

Over and above the routine comparison with rounders, at least two other pertinent issues are highlighted here. Both may relate to the relative lack of success experienced by those attempting to introduce baseball as a popular sport in this country. Firstly, issues of national identity and expressions of nationalism are raised, and secondly, further comparison is made between baseball and other already established sports played in England - primarily cricket.

National identity, and the nationalism engendered, was of intrinsic importance in the way the English reacted to baseball. Maguire (1994) suggests that "the emergence of intense forms of nationalism" (p. 405) was a characteristic of many people living in relatively developed nations during the period highlighted. This intense nationalism has to be considered in conjunction with the fact that Britain at this time was still an extremely powerful nation. The British empire was vast and "the USA" was once part of it. Thus, it seems reasonable to suggest that many British people, and especially the English, during the latter decades of the 19th century, regarded people from the USA - and many of their activities - as inferior. Consequently, it is no surprise that many Britons considered baseball to be an inferior sport. This was clearly reflected in the patronising tone adopted by many of those reporting on the exhibition matches. This point is illustrated by a commentator writing in *The Liverpool Echo* (25 March, 1889), who offered a "candid opinion" of the Americans and their game:

> *"First and foremost we will suppose that we saw on Saturday afternoon about as complete an exhibition we are likely to get on these shores, saving, of course, that we take it up ourselves. See that sly hint, stranger? ... baseball will never make cricket or football "after pieces" in England. It doesn't fit the bill at all ... Of course, there is national prejudice to be considered. You don't seem to take to our cricket, and we - well, we won't say much about your baseball."* (p. 3)

Many journalists were certainly inclined to believe that the baseball tourists were attempting to threaten "their" national summertime sport, and this seemed to instigate a rear-guard reaction toward baseball. This reaction may have been further compounded by the fact that many English people were still highly active in diffusing their "own" culture and sports at this time. An aspect of "English culture" that was diffused was a strict code of conduct, particularly evident on the sports field - the "gentlemanly-amateur" approach (Mangan 1988, 1992; Perkin 1989). However, by the time of the final two tours, the USA was developing significantly as a nation, and one had the beginnings of the demise of Britain as a "Great" nation. The developing insecurity of the British was reflected in their responses to the American attempt to foist their brash "new" game upon them. As Maguire (1994) has suggested, "this strict regulation of established conduct ... [becomes] ... especially intense when the colonizers feel threatened as the colonized gain power" (p. 403). In other words, as the USA became an increasingly powerful nation, long separate from the British Empire, many British people attempted to distance themselves from the behaviour associated with previous "inferiors".

The timing of the 1914 tour, and response of the English to it, is worthy of comment. Given the potential threat from Germany during this period it might have been expected that the English would be slightly more receptive to their American "cousins" on this occasion, notwithstanding the "cultural threat" from their former colony. One journalist, writing in *The Sportsman* (26 February, 1914), even suggested that "never was the feeling of friendship between Englishmen and Americans stronger than it is today. And their visit, in emphasising the camaraderie among sportsmen, might do much to strengthen that feeling" (p. 6). Under the circumstances one might have expected a less xenophobic reaction from the English to the sport of baseball. However, it would appear from the newspaper coverage of the 1914 tour that attitudes remained very much unchanged. This is emphasised in an article that appeared in *The Daily News and Leader* (27 February, 1914) entitled: "The Invasion of Baseball": "At such time when our political relations are so friendly with America it seems almost an unfriendly act to allege that their great national pastime leaves us cold." (p. 10).

Thus, it would seem that despite the friendly relationship encouraged by the war time threat the English were still unreceptive to baseball. Furthermore, the response of many English people was equally unfavourable in the final tour of the period outlined. Much of the press persisted in attributing this rejection to differences in national character and taste, rather than to the inherent superiority/inferiority of the respective games:

> "So hard it is to imagine any definite reason why the English like cricket and think baseball a mysterious and rather foolish game, while Americans have about the same opinions, reversed, of cricket, that the temptation is strong to doubt the sincerity of these judgements, as judgements, and to explain them as the results of chance-acquired habits strengthened on both sides by national pride." (The New York Times, 27 October, 1924, p. 18).

This leads us on to the second issue and one which is inextricably related to the first. There was a general feeling amongst various journalists and cricket supporters, that the baseball tourists were attempting to threaten the monopoly of cricket as both a spectator and participant, summer team sport.

This was certainly reflected in the almost xenophobic defence of cricket and attack on baseball. However, the balance of power in this relationship lay largely with cricket and with the cricket authorities in England. Cricket, and its organising body, was well established and there was no felt need to introduce a new game.

In 1889, Spalding was careful to avoid making comparisons between baseball and cricket. It is likely that this was to avoid the kind of reaction that the tourists received in 1874. Nevertheless, this did not prevent the press at the time from assuming that the Americans were here to show off their game and its superiority to cricket. A journalist at the time responded:

> *"To compare it with cricket is a piece of audacity of which only an American can be guilty ... In cricket there is vastly more variety, a great deal more science, ever so much more of the picturesque; in short, language fails to describe its superiority."* (Lancashire Evening Post, 14 March, 1889, p. 2)

National pride, and anti-American feeling, lies not far beneath the surface. Throughout the period outlined, cricket was believed to be a far more sophisticated and scientific game than baseball by most of the English observers. Furthermore, criticism was levelled at the inability of the baseballers at bat to even hit the ball and that the odds were apparently so loaded against the batter. Indeed, one reporter made the following, somewhat sarcastic comment: "If the striker can't hit the ball with a club that size he ought to be provided with a bigger to stir the game a little bit" (The Liverpool Echo, 25 March, 1889, p. 3). Nevertheless, in virtually every critique of the game, mention was made of the fine fielding ability of the baseball players.

The unfavourable comparisons drawn between baseball and cricket in the English press, led to subsequent outbursts from various Americans involved in some of the tours. On one such occasion in 1924, McGraw touched upon an important and defining feature of baseball that was clearly not appreciated by the English hosts. Stung by many of the criticisms he defended his sport by stating that,

> *"I am told none of your cricketers can throw like our boys, and as for double 'barracking' it is all good natured, though not an essential part of the game. We Americans could never sit in solemn silence all afternoon watching a game of cricket"* (cited in The New York Times, 3 November, 1924, p. 24)

From this statement, it is apparent that many of the English watching the exhibition games were put off by the style of play exhibited, a style of play, it would seem, which was attributed to the commercialised nature of the game.

Perhaps more specifically, he reveals the apparent English dislike for the unsportsman-like behaviour that this commercialism engendered. By the late nineteenth century, the amateur ethos that many English people adhered to (Dunning 1975; Dunning & Sheard 1979; Dunning 1986; Holt 1989) in various sports, if only on the surface, was of importance in understanding the response toward baseball. Within the English press it was no surprise to encounter general criticism of the way in which baseball was administered and played. A sceptical view of the financial motives of the touring teams was a recurrent theme with certain reporters. Even during the tour of 1924, when professionalism in British sports was much more accepted, a writer for the *New York Times* (27 October, 1924) clearly recognised that the baseball "professionals somewhat too evidently are engaged in a business rather than a sport" (p.18). Several English newspaper articles that were written about the games expressed surprise, and often dismay, at the amount the baseball players were paid. In *The Liverpool Echo* (21 October, 1924) it was noted that, "their salaries run to about 20,000 dollars a year which is about £5,000, or a Prime Minister's salary in England" (p. 12).

Moreover, criticism was not restricted to the administration of the game, but was also directed towards conduct of play. There was a lot of criticism of the barracking of opponents that the touring American teams were party to, which was not well received by many of the sports writers covering the tours. However, this explanation for the lack of success in popularising baseball is again not wholly satisfactory on its own. It is more appropriate to suggest that the rejection of baseball by "the English" was part of a balance and blend of a variety of factors, many of which have been outlined above. Included amongst these inter-related factors are the sense of national pride involved in having a traditional pastime of domestic origin; the existing popularity of cricket; a general lack of understanding of the nuances of baseball; and the feeling of being under threat from a "foreign" cultural invasion. Many English people had been brought up with, and were loyal to, their "own" sports, and felt no desire to adopt the "newer" American game. This was the point made by the author of an article in *The Sportsman* (13 March, 1889) who suggested that, "the fact of the matter is that while baseball has been rendered dear to the heart of Jonathan from long use, and the custom which is second nature, our insular games are deeply rooted from the same cause" (p. 8).

This does not necessarily mean that the English were anti-American, or that the English were just not suited to baseball - although they disapproved of its excessive commercialisation and the "ungentlemanly" behaviour associated with it. But the weight of tradition was especially as strong and, as another reporter suggested, "cricket has obtained a firm hold on sportsmen of the mother country, and it may safely be asserted that neither baseball *nor any other importation* will make an impression on the youth of England" (emphasis added, Lancashire Evening Post, 14 March, 1889, p. 2).

Part of the aim of this paper was to examine some of the factors involved in the successful diffusion of sports. It is clear that the English rejection of baseball, during the period highlighted, involved numerous inter-related developments. The fact that cricket was already well-established in this country was highly significant. Offence was also taken at the suggestions made by some of the Americans involved on the four different tours, that baseball was a superior sport to cricket. After all, they had argued, baseball had superseded cricket as the most popular summer team sport in their own country. This combination of factors, and the belief held by many English newspaper journalists that the American tourists were in England to usurp "their" sport, led to an almost uniform negative response to baseball. It is evident, too, that this response was bound up with changing power balances between the two societies and with growing concern with national identity experienced by both Americans and English. The tension between the two was so strong that the tourists enjoyed little respite when they arrived in England in 1914 and 1924, despite the increasingly friendly political relations between the governments fostered by the First World War. Many English people feared that they were losing ground culturally, politically and economically to the former colony, and this unease was expressed in some very chauvinistic reporting on the upstart baseball game.

Furthermore, the Americans throughout the entire period, were seen to be too brash, too competitive - and the game of baseball too commercialised - for the liking of most English people. It was partly this, and the feeling that baseball was merely a modernised form of rounders, together with the suspicion that the USA was engaging in a form of cultural imperialism, that led many English people to reject baseball and all it stood for, and to accord the professional tours a decidedly lukewarm reception.

References

Daily News and Leader, The (London), (1914, 27 February) p. 10.
Dunning, E. & Sheard, K. (1979). Barbarians, gentlemen and players. Oxford: Martin Robertson.
Dunning, E. (1975). Theoretical perspectives on sport: a developmental critique. In S. Parker et al. (eds.), Sport and leisure in contemporary society. Central London Polytechnic.
Dunning, E. (1992). The dynamics of modern sport: notes on achievement striving and the social significance of sport. In Elias, N. & Dunning, E. (eds.), Quest for excitement, sport and leisure in the civilising process. Oxford: Blackwell.
Furst, R.T. (1988). Conflicting images of organized baseball in the 19th century sport press. Canadian Journal of History of Sport, 19, 1-13.

Holt, R. (1989) Sport and the British. a modern history. Oxford: Clarendon Press.

Lancashire Evening Post, The (1889, 14 March) p. 2.

Lancashire Evening Post, The (1914, 23 March) p. 4

Liverpool Daily Albion, The (1874 31 July) p. 5.

Liverpool Echo, The (1889, 25 March) p. 3.

Liverpool Echo, The (1924, 21 October) p. 12.

Maguire, J. (1994). Sport, identity politics, and globalization: diminishing contrasts and increasing varieties. Sociology of sport journal, 11, 398-427.

Mangan, J.A. (ed.) (1988). Pleasure, profit, proselytism. British culture and sport at home and abroad. 1700-1914. London: Frank Cass.

Mangan, J.A. (ed.) (1992). The cultural bond, sport, empire, society. London: Frank Cass.

New York Times (1914, 27 February) p. 1.

New York Times (1924, 27 October) p. 18.

New York Times (1924, 3 November) p. 24.

Perkin, H. (1989). Teaching the nations how to play: sport and society in the British Empire and Commonwealth. The International Journal of the History of Sport, 6, 145-155.

Sportsman, The (London), (1889, 13 March) p. 8.

Sportsman, The (London), (1914, 26 February) p. 6.

Sportsman, The (London), (1924, 7 November) p. 3.

Standard, The (London), (1914, 28 February) p. 10.

Voigt, D.Q. (1970). American baseball Vol. II. From the commissioners to continental expansion. Oklahoma: University of Oklahoma

Yorkshire Post and Leeds Intelligencer, The (1874, 17 August) p. 4.

Chapter 16

Historical background of undergraduate professional preparation in the United States and Japan. Fragmentation between professional and academic disciplines

Shunichi Takeshita and Kanji Watanabe
National Institute of Fitness and Sports
and Kokusaigakuin Saitama Junior College, Japan

The major change in physical education in U.S. and Japanese higher education over the past few decades has been the reorganization of some programs and domains to reflect the view that physical education is an academic discipline. The research of Takeshita (1991) and Suttei et al. (1994) reported that teacher education has been historically the primary career focus of undergraduate physical education major programs in both the United States and Japan. However, in the late 1980s, there was a significant change in these programs towards a multiple-career track curriculum. Other career tracks than teacher education in the U.S. included fitness specialization, sports management, sports communication and athletic training. In Japanese colleges, tracks included social physical education, life-ling sports, and sports specialization.

Two factors, academic and societal, have produced not only curricular reform but also brought about the establishment of tertiary institutions in both countries. Therefore, it is necessary to view historically the academic and societal factors behind reform of undergraduate physical education major programs. The primary purpose of this paper, which fully incorporates such a view, is that physical education does not necessarily prepare students for specific professional careers. Instead, such programs and academic domains provide a scholarly base of knowledge concerning the human movement sciences or societal context. This paper attempts to focus on the arguments between physical education as professional preparation or as an academic discipline.

Data was gathered about the United States from journals of *Quest, JORPRD* etc., and history books of physical education and sport. The data about Japan was also gathered from Journals of the Japanese Society of Physical Education and printed materials published by the Ministry of Education, Culture and Science. Content analysis of articles of the journals and books was done based on the focus of this study.

Social factors influencing physical education professional preparation in the United States

Decrease of teaching jobs

Zeigler (1988) claims that during the past two decades new tracks have emerged in undergraduate physical education programs in the United States. Clayton and Clayton (1984) agree, stating that many physical education departments in colleges and universities in the U.S. have broadened their programs and are now preparing students for a wider range of careers. The findings of this research supported the statements of both Zeigler and Clayton and Clayton. Many physical education departments in the United States have responded to the need to develop new tracks.
This type of reform is related to declining employment opportunities for teachers. However, other changes in U.S. society over the past several decades have also influenced the development of new professional tracks.

Personal fitness movement

One of these developments has been the personal fitness movement. This movement began flowering in the 1970s and continued into the 1980s (Sage 1987). The interest in personal fitness among Americans covers all age groups. According to Pestolosi and Baker (1984), more than 30 million young people aged six to 21 participate in organized out-of -school programs, and exercise programs for senior citizens are increasing in popularity. At the present time, in the late 1990s, the fitness movement still seems to be strong, and futurists believe that the movement is not just a fad (Sage 1987).

This increased interest in fitness has helped to create new opportunities for physical education graduates. It has led to an expansion of fitness and wellness occupations. More large companies and corporations provide some type of leadership, facilities, and programming for their employees in fitness, recreation, and stress management (Pestolosi & Baker 1984). This in turn has created a demand for trained personnel (Sage 1987).

Sport promotion

Another factor that has helped to create new opportunities for physical education graduates is the growth of sports in the United States. The 1960s and 1970s saw interest in sports among Americans grow tremendously (Lee 1983). That interest remains at a high level. According to Drowatzky and Armstrong (1984), the interest will at least remain at the current level if the standard of living in the United States remains relatively high. This interest in sports has created increased opportunities for jobs in sports management, sports marketing, and sports communication. This research confirmed that a number of U.S. institutions employ education undergraduates for those jobs.

An aging society

Another factor that has influenced some programs is the increase in the number of older people in the United States. Beran (1985a) claims that there is a need for trained personnel to work with the elderly. This need may greatly expand in the future since America's elderly will number over 39 million by the year 2000 (Sage 1987). Because of this increase, it seems likely that physical education departments in the U.S. will develop more programs that are aimed at fitness and wellness for the elderly.

Social factors influencing physical education professional preparation in Japan

Leadership by ministry

One of the most important things to understand about higher education in Japan is the strong control that the Ministry of Education has over education. This is a very different situation from that in the United States. In the United States, individual institutions can consider changing factors in society and research in physical education and then make internal decisions about programs and directions. In doing this, they have more freedom than members of Japanese institutions. In Japanese institutions, the Ministry of Education exerts a strong external influence on many important decisions. In order to make substantial changes to programs or to add programs, institutions often cannot act on their own. If members of an institution believe that changes should be made, first they must frequently attempt to influence Ministry of Education decisions. One way this can be done is by becoming a member of a committee that is set up by the Ministry of Education to investigate the possibility of a change in programs.

Decrease of teaching jobs

Understanding this situation helps to explain some of the recent changes in Japanese physical education and some of the results of this study. Japanese physical education has been affected by some of the same conditions that have affected physical education in the United States. One of these factors is the decrease in employment opportunities for elementary and secondary teachers during the last several decades. This decline in employment opportunities for graduate of colleges of education has continued in recent years. For example, in 1979 a total of 78 percent of students who graduated from colleges of education obtained jobs as teachers, but in 1989 only 60 percent of education graduates acquired such jobs (Ministry of Education, 1989). This decline in opportunities for teachers has also affected physical education teachers.

Fitness and sports promotion

Two other factors that have influenced Japanese physical education are also the same as in the United States. There are the growth in the popularity of both sports and fitness. Following the 1964 Tokyo Olympics, there was an increased interest in personal physical fitness and in sports participation (Kataoka 1978). In addition, the Ministry of Education began promoting sports and fitness as core courses in elementary and secondary schools (Kataoka 1978). Another boost to sport was provided by the Japanese government in 1974 as a result of the quick rise in oil prices. As an economy measure, the government began promoting community sports as a substitute for leisure time activities that required people to drive some distance away from their communities (Kataoka 1978).

An aging society

During the 1980s, community sports included a few events such as Japanese croquet for older people. One of social needs facing an aging society was to offer a variety of sports especially for older people (Tanaka 1985). Some institutions had programs to prepare students to deal specifically with the fitness and wellness of older individuals. The program included several gerontology classes along with other course offerings such as lifelong education and counselling that should fully prepare the student for jobs in that area (Takeshita 1991).

In summary, the social needs affecting physical education programs in Japan led to the development of programs to meet the needs of the Japanese people and to provide jobs for graduates. But the programs developed by Japanese institutions seemed less clearly focused than some U.S. programs.

Balance between professional and academic disciplines in the United States

The start of the balance arguments

All of these social factors, including the decline in opportunities for teachers, have influenced the development of new tracks in physical education. In doing this, they have helped change the nature of physical education in the United States. However, there is another important change that has been occurring in physical education in the United States. This is the move to create an academic discipline of physical education.

There has been a great deal of controversy about the question of whether physical education is an academic discipline, and what its nature should be. Renson (1989) traces this controversy to an address at the 1964 meeting of the National College Physical Education Association for Men (NCPEAM) at which Franklin Henry said that physical education should be considered an academic discipline and that such a discipline is theoretical and scholarly rather than technical and professional.

Balance argument and educational survival

One of the issues arising from this controversy is the problem of balancing professional (career-oriented) and academic discipline program emphasis within physical education departments (Newell 1990). Bressan (1987) believes that the attempt to include both the academic study of human movement and programs of professional education has led to a lack of definition for physical education. She also states that this has resulted in a fragmented group of studies within physical education programs. Park (1989) agrees that there is fragmentation within departments. Park adds that there are hierarchical rankings within departments, with higher ranking being accorded to those faculty members in the so-called "hard sciences." She says that this fragmentation has led to a loss of shared mission. Newell (1990) claims that the lack of uniformity in reacting to the problem of balance has led to a state of chaos for physical education in higher education. Sage (1987) also expresses concerns about the identity of physical education.

Bressan (1987) says that if fragmentation continues, the discipline of physical education will persist only as long as economic and political conditions allow it to continue. Henry (1978) talks about the danger when many courses and research programs in physical education departments could be done in more traditional disciplines. He says that this sends a signal to the administration that physical education can be phased out. He seems to believe that physical education must develop its own clear mission. Sage (1987) points out that some departments, for example the one at the University of Washington, have already been terminated.

The problems of balance and nomenclature

Several physical educators have offered ideas to stop the fragmentation of physical education and unify its different aspects. One of these is Renson (1989). Renson suggests changing the name of "physical education" to "kinanthropology." He describes five divisions of kinanthroplogy. Renson believes that development of his conception of kinanthropology would unify the theoretical and the professional practice aspects of physical education. Such attempts to unify physical education seem to be very worthwhile. Some physical educators believe that problems of fragmentation are a threat to the survival of physical education departments. In addition, at their Sixty-first Annual Meeting, the American Academy of Physical Education took a step for greater unity within the academic discipline of human movement. On April 19, 1989, the members passed the following resolution:

> *"... Finally, in any situation in which an administrative unit feels comfortable in describing the totality of its components by the title of the body of knowledge, the Academy recommends that this descriptor be kinesiology."* (American Academy of Physical Education 1989, p. 104)

Establishment of kinesiology

Although the words "physical education" have long been used, social influences, such as a reduction in the number of physical education teachers in schools, have stimulated reform in major programs and institutions by using the word "kinesiology." Recently kinesiology seems to cover the traditional and vague arguments of balance between the professional and academic disciplines. Through reviewing several journals related to physical education such as *Quest, JORPRD*, etc., the arguments can be somewhat identified but not clearly. Harris (1993) clearly presented essential competencies for professionals of kinesiology : (a) the biophysical sciences focused on exercise and sport; (b) the behavioral / sociocultural sciences focused on sport; (c) the pedagogical sciences focused on school physical education.

Furthermore, she supplements the above fields by the following sub-disciplines: (a) exercise physiology, biomechanics, sport/exercise psychology, anatomy, physiology, psychology, nutrition, health, business, etc., leading to occupations such as athletic trainer, exercise program expert; (b) sport/exercise psychology, sport management, business, the biological, behavioral & social science, etc., leading to occupations such as sport manager, sport psychologist ; (c) pedagogy, motor development, motor learning/control, etc., leading to occupations such as teacher.

In summary, in the United States, professional programs in universities and colleges diversify depending on social needs and produce new job opportunities for graduates . By the same token, development of knowledge based on academic disciplines has given rise to the new concept of "kinesiology" instead of the traditional term "physical education."

Ministry leadership in reform of university standard regulation in Japan

Japanese Regulation Influenced by the United States after World War II

Following the end of World War II, there was a change in American-Japanese relations from wartime hostility to postwar understanding and cooperation. The United States Education Missions that visited Japan in March 1946 and August 1950, at the invitation of the Occupation authorities, evaluated the Japanese educational system. Their reports contributed greatly to postwar educational reform. The first mission was composed of 27 educational specialists headed by G.D. Stoddard and included C.H. McCloy as the representative for physical education (Meshizuka 1956). Under the Occupation authorities, the Japanese Commission on University Standardization in consultation with T.H. McGrail and his colleagues from the Civil Information and Education bureau of General Headquarter set out standard regulations in terms of university and college curricula (Okatsu 1969). Since this time, the curricula and programs have been made based on the standard regulations. The root of these standard regulations was based on American concepts.

Reform in 1980s; Ministry Leadership Era

The basic concepts of the standard regulations had been gradually modified as social needs changed after World War II. The Ministry of Education recognized these changes in 1982 and as a result developed new programs for institutions with colleges of physical education in 1982 (Ministry of Education 1989). At that time the Ministry recommended that colleges of physical education develop non-teaching physical education programs in social physical education, wellness education, and athletic coaching. At the same time, the Ministry presented guidelines that must be followed by any institution that established any of those non-teaching tracks. The guidelines included core courses and electives that must be in the programs (Commission on University Standardization 1982).

The 1982 guidelines did not affect national institutions with colleges of education that had formerly been normal colleges. However, in 1986 the Ministry revised its regulations governing these national institutions and recommended that they also develop non-teaching programs (Umemoto 1986). These regulations went into effect in the following year. In addition, the Ministry set out the same guidelines for program contents that it had set out for the colleges of physical education (Ebashi 1986). Since those days the national institutions have begun developing alternative career tracks.

These efforts of the Ministry of Education and the institutions responses show that one of the main issues in U.S. physical education is also a very important issue for Japanese physical educators. That is the issue of developing programs that answer society's needs and provide careers for graduates.

Reform in the 1990s ; Deregulation Era

Until now, there have been discussions about the balance between professional and academic disciplines in institutions majoring in physical education in Japan as well as in the United States. However the topic of professional and academic disciplines was discussed by the Commission and Council founded by the Japan Ministry of Education, then the Ministry ordered institutions to follow the standard regulations (University Council 1997). The institutions reformed their programs, systems or faculty organizations following the standard regulations.

The standard regulations have been gradually modified since the 1946. In 1991, the standard regulations were drastically changed in response to the University Council's request for advise. The regulations were simplified and an outline based on the institution's programs, systems or faculty organization was suggested. Each institution was authorized to set up its own program, system or faculty organization following its own concept. Therefore, each institution could express its originality. As well as giving institutions decision-making power, the Ministry requested that they submit self-evaluation reports. Broadly speaking, the Ministry gave institutions decision-making power not only in the creation of original programs but also in the running of institutional business such as recruiting students and seeking a new market for graduates (Kusahara 1994; Murata 1995). This is what is called the deregulation of higher education.

Management is now handled at each institution's own discretion. Although big or popular universities have opportunities to run their own affairs at their own discretion, small universities and colleges are facing problems (Tamura, 1993). The up-keep of sports teams is expensive. Few faculty members offer a variety of programs for students because of heavy teaching load. Japanese institutions are now participating in a race for survival, which is the subject of much scholarly debate, Bressan's (1987), Sage's (1987), Park's (1989) Newell's (1990), etc.

Conclusion

In summary, the major issue affecting physical education programs in Japan at the moment is the development of programs that meet the needs of the Japanese people and that provide jobs for graduates. This is also one of the main issues for U.S. programs, but the Japanese way of handling the issue differs partly because of the influence of the Ministry of Education.

In the United States over the past few decades there have been two main kinds of change in physical education programs. Programs have expanded in response to society's needs, and many now provide new opportunities for students. At the same time, efforts to create an academic discipline of physical education have grown. The concurrence of both changes has caused problems in balancing the different aspects of physical education programs. At the present time, the problems of balance and of defining physical education are still not solved. These problems seem to be the main issue for physical educators in the United States today.

The academic discipline issue, which is so important for U.S. physical education, dose not currently seem to be quite as important a concern for Japanese physical education. However, since the 1991 deregulation, the issue has been widely discussed in Japan, and the academic discipline movement seems to have had an effect on many programs. Although the Ministry of Education continues to work very actively to help institutions develop programs that meet the needs of society, it has given institutions opportunities to discuss and create their own academic disciplines and professional programs. In so doing, Japanese physical education programs seem to be in a state of transition.

References

American Academy of Physical Education (1989). <u>The evolving undergraduate major</u>. American Academy of Physical Education Papers no. 23: Sixty-first Annual Meeting, Boston, MA, April 18-19, 1989. Champaign, IL.

Beran, J.A. (1985). Current physical education professional preparation programs in the United States, part 1. <u>International Journal of Physical Education</u>, 22 (1), 35-38.

Bressan, E.S. (1987). The future of scholarship in physical education. In J.D. Massengale (ed.). <u>Trends toward the future in physical education</u> (pp.25-36). Champaign, IL.

Clayton, R.D. & Clayton, J.A. (1984). Careers and professional preparation programs. <u>Journal of Physical Education, Recreation, and Dance</u>, 55 (5), 44-45.

Commission on University Standardization [Daigaku-kijun-kyoukai] (1982). <u>Compilation of laws and regulations of the Commission on University Standardization</u> (Report No.33). Tokyo.

Drowatzky, J.N. & Armstrong, C.W. (1984). Careers and professional preparation programs. <u>Journal of Physical Education, Recreation and Dance</u>, 55 (5), 44-45.

Ebashi, S. (1986). Professional preparation in physical education. <u>Journal of Health, Physical Education and Recreation</u>, 36 (12), 946-949.

Harris, Janet C. (1993) Using kinesiology: a comparison of applied veins in the subdisciplines. <u>Quest</u>, 45, 389-412.

Henry, F.M. The academic discipline of physical education. <u>Quest</u>, 29, 12-19.

Japan Ministry of Education, Science and Culture (1989). <u>White paper</u>. Tokyo.

Kataoka, A. (1978). The development of Japanese physical education and sports after World War II. In <u>Proceedings of the International Seminar on Physical Education and Sports History</u>, Tokyo, 26, September 1978 (p.45-50). Tokyo.

Kusahara, K. (1994). University education in 21 century. <u>Journal of University Physical Education [Daigaku Taiiku]</u>, 21 (2), 7-25.

Lawson, H. A. (1988). Physical education and the reform of undergraduate education. <u>Quest</u>, 40, 12-32.

Lee, M. (1988). <u>A history of physical education and sports in the U.S.A.</u> New York.

Meshizuka, T. (1956). A program of professional training in physical education for colleges and universities in Japan (Doctoral dissertation, State University of Iowa).

Murata, N. (1995). Progress of reform in universities and colleges. <u>Journal of University Physical Education [Daigaku Taiiku]</u>, 22 (2), 8-15.

Newell, K.M. (1990). Physical education in higher education: Chaos out of order. <u>Quest</u>, 42, 227-242.

Park, R.J. (1989). The second 100 years: Or, can physical education become the Renaissance field of the 21st century ? Quest, 41, 1-27.

Pestolesi, R.A. & Baker, C. (1984). Introduction to physical education: A contemporary careers approach. Clenview, IL.

Renson, R. (1989). From physical education to kinanthropology: A quest for academic and professional identity. Quest, 41, 235-256.

Rizzo, T.L., Broadhead, G.D. & Kowalski, E. (1997). Changing kinesiology and physical education by infusing information about individuals with disabilities. Quest, 49, 229-237.

Sage, G.H. (1987). The future and the profession of physical education. In J.D. Massengale (ed.), Trends toward the future in physical education (pp.9-23). Champaign, IL.

Suttie, J.S. & Takeshita, S. (1994). Changing and reform in the Undergraduate physical education major: United States and Japan. Journal of Comparative Physical Education and Sport, 16 (1), 13-18.

Takeshita, S. (1991). Reform in undergraduate physical education major programs in the United States and in Japan (Unpublished doctoral dissertation, Oregon State University, Corvallis).

Tamura, K. (1993). New curriculum of institution majoring in physical education. Journal of Health, Physical Education and Dance, 43 (1), 24-27.

Umemoto, J. (1986). Recent physical education teacher training. Journal of Health, Physical Education and Recreation, 36 (12), 942-945.

University Council [Daigaku-shinngikai] (1997). Report of Reform of universities and colleges 1991, Handbook of University Standardization [Daigaku-secchi-youran]. Bunkyou-kyoukai.

Van Dalen, D.B., Mitchell, E.D. & Bennett, B.L. (1953). A world history of physical education. New York.

Van Dalen, D.B. & Bennett, B.L. (1971). A world history of physical education (2nd ed.). Englewood Cliffs.

Zeigler, E.F. (1988). A comparative analysis of undergraduate professional preparation in physical education in the United States and Canada (1960-1985). In K. Broom et al. (eds.), Comparative physical education and sport vol. 5 (pp.177-169). Champaign, IL.

Chapter 17

The American invasion of the British turf: a study of sporting technological transfer

Wray Vamplew
De Montfort University, U.K.

Sports change: rules are modified, equipment is improved, skills are developed. Yet usually such change is evolutionary. Sometimes, however, as with the Fosbury Flop in high-jumping the change is more dramatic. Such was the case in British horse-racing at the turn of the twentieth century when the impact of a few American jockeys revolutionised riding styles and racing tactics.

The Americans are coming !

In 1895 a solitary American jockey, the Afro-American, Willie Simms, rode in British racing and secured only four wins, insufficient to rank him in the top fifty in the jockeys' championship. These wins, however, were the product of merely nineteen mounts, a winning percentage of 21.5, amongst the highest in the land. Simms's visit was a precursor for an American invasion of the British turf which was to have a significant effect on the practice and performance of horsemanship in the domestic racing industry.

Lester Reiff came over for a spell in 1896 and had 16 winners. Next to arrive was Tod Sloan. On his first short visit in Autumn 1897 he had fifty-three mounts and won on twenty of them. He returned the following Autumn, again as the punter's friend, with 43 winners out of 98 mounts - a phenomenally high percentage of 43.9. He also finished second on twenty-one occasions. At the first October meeting he rode twelve winners out of sixteen mounts on two consecutive afternoons at Newmarket, the headquarters of the English turf. The shocked British experts argued that 'the very great majority of his successes ... would have been gained with any competent jockey in the saddle' and that if Sloan came over for a full season it would be a different story (Watson 1898, p. 588). It was. His strike rate fell to 31.3 per cent but his 345 mounts yielded 108 victories placing him at the head of the jockeys' championship.

By 1900 four of the top ten riders in the British championship were from the United States, including champion jockey, Lester Reiff. Nineteen year old Danny Maher arrived late that season and secured 27 wins from 128 rides, a sign of the talent which was to secure him the jockeys' championship in 1908 and again in 1913. The Derby, perhaps the race jockeys most want to win, fell to the Americans five times in six years; one of the early victories leading to the caustic comment that as American millionaires were buying up other 'English antiquities' 'there is no particular reason why the treasured Derby should not now and again be purchased' (Our Van July 1901, p. 58). The Americans not only won a large number of races, they won a high proportion of the ones in which they took part: in 1900 Maher, Johnny Reiff and John Henry 'Skeets' Martin topped 20 per cent, Lester Reiff won 26 per cent and Sloan almost 27 per cent.

They ventured across the Atlantic for several reasons, though mainly because jockeys go where the work is. As racing came under political threat in some states due to attacks on corruption, betting and turf morality generally, a few American owners decided to try their luck abroad and took their favoured riders with them. Simms was brought over to Britain by Tammany Hall boss Richard Crocker. When he rode Croker's *Eau Gallie* to victory in the Crawfurd Plate at Newmarket he was the first American to win in England aboard an American-owned and American trained horse. Sloan's initial venture was at the behest of American owner James Keene. He then secured a retainer from Pierre Lorillard, the tobacco millionaire, in 1897 and additional ones from Lord William Beresford and the Prince of Wales the following year. Maher came on the advice of American trainer Andrew Jackson Joyner. Johnny Reiff, an outstanding lightweight jockey found that putting on some weight was not so detrimental in Britain where minimum riding weights were higher than at home. It can only be speculated whether some of the American riders also relished the challenge of riding on Britain's courses with their variety of undulation, gradients and curves, most unlike the uniformly flat American dirt tracks.

A technological package

Most of the Americans were outstanding jockeys. Simms had won two Belmonts and had a career winning percentage around twenty-five; Sloan had been principal rider for leading American owner William C. Whitney; and Maher had been a track champion at Providence in America, once winning 60 races in only 30 days. Their ability, however, was not the sole reason for their remarkable success in Britain. They brought with them a new style of racing and riding.

American riders could be distinguished at a glance. English jockeys rode not much different from the style of the hunting field, sitting erect with a comparatively straight knee and a good length of rein; in contrast the Americans pushed the saddle forward, shortened both the stirrups and the reins, and rode with knees bent, crouching along the horse's neck. How the style originated is not clear. One version is that it originated from the bareback riding of native Americans. Another view is that it was devised by black riders in the southern states whose masters put them up without saddles, thus forcing them to grip the mane and lie along the horse's neck for balance. Sloan's claim that he discovered it when larking about in the training yard can probably be discounted (Lambton 1924, p. 241; Richardson 1901, p. 265; Watson 1900, p. 585). Whatever its origin, by cutting wind resistance and giving a better weight distribution on the horse the monkey-on-a-stick style of riding was worth a ten to fourteen pounds advantage (Rowlands 1900, pp. 180-182).

The Americans also brought with them a different style of racing with tactics based on their knowledge of the clock (Rowlands 1900, p. 184). British jockeys had often raced almost half-paced in the earlier stages of a race and then swooped in the final furlong or so. Champions such as Sam Chifney, George Fordham and Fred Archer were all famous for their waiting game in which they came with a late rush to the winning post. In contrast the Americans often raced from the front if they felt their mount could cope with the pace. Here they were sometimes helped by the late introduction of the starting gate to British racing in 1897, an apparatus with which they were already familiar (Purdy 1904, pp. 27-29). Indeed the fact that Sloan was frequently 'out on his own' led to 'on your tod' entering the English language via the nation's propensity to corrupt rhyming slang. Most of the Americans were remarkable judges of pace because American trainers made more use of the stop watch than their British counterparts who generally preferred to try their horses out against each other (Maher, 1905, p. 557). The similarity of many American flat tracks made comparisons of times more meaningful than in Britain where 'horses for courses' was a fair working rule.

The American jockeys also benefited from a concurrent invasion by American trainers. In the three years 1898-1900 the walrus-moustached John Huggins trained the winners of 162 races and was champion trainer in 1899; in 1900 Enoch Wishard headed the list of trainers with 54 winners; and his fellow-American, W. Duke put 31 into the winner's enclosure. Although American training methods contributed to their success with horses having better shoes fitted and being given more fresh air than was common in British establishments, so that 'the general health (of their horses) improves to an extent which is almost unknown in English stables' (Watson 1901, pp. 35-40), trainers such as Wishard, Duke and Eugene Leigh also brought with them skill in the use of drugs. American race meetings lasted for ten days or more and horses raced several times at one meet. This led to the use of dope on tired horses. Wishard and his compatriots were not averse to supplementing their training methods with the application of dope to give their animals a further advantage (Lambton 1924, pp. 253-254). No doubt this explains the querulous comment with reference to one particular trainer that 'the success this trainer has had with all sorts of horses has been surprising' (Our Van August 1899, p. 137). At the time this was not illegal in Britain and it is noticeable that the Americans' success rate dropped sharply after 1904 when the Jockey Club made the doping of horses a turf offence.

Hearts, minds and wallets

The opposition to the American style came from two sources: the jingoists and the conservatives. The former, alleging that 'the swerving horse ... seems to be the necessary concomitant of American jockeyship' (Our Van, October 1900, p. 287), believed that British was best and that in a tight finish (which the Americans tried to avoid by having their races won well before the finishing post) the British would triumph as they had greater control over their mounts (Rowlands 1900, p. 183). The latter could not conceive that 'generation after generation, jockeys have been sitting on the wrong part of a horse's back [and] that the best place for the saddle is not where it has always been' (Watson 1899 p. 27). Yet others, like Alan Haig Brown, had a foot in both camps, claiming that 'of the many abominable American innovations I count the American "seat" the most abominable of all ... it is more hideous than the skyscraper. Even at the risk of being charged with sighing for the good old days, I would point out that we had horsemanship then, not merely jockeyship' (Haig Brown 1903, p. 9). Even when the success of the American seat was obvious, men such as S.E. Clayton, an owner for forty-five years, refused to concede, arguing that 'the introduction of the American seat has entirely destroyed true horsemanship ... it wins races but it is entirely trick riding, and smacks more of the hippodrome and circus than of the racecourse' (Clayton 1904, p.664). Others took refuge in the belief 'that in the higher art of horsemanship as compared with jockeyship [English riders] are certainly superior to the Americans' (Rowlands 1900 X, p. 188). By 1904, however, Clayton and his ilk were in a minority. The market place had already decided the future of the American innovations. Those British owners who wanted to win had employed the American riders.

The visitors vanquished

Yet, despite this acknowledgement of their superiority, by 1902 the American invasion was virtually over. One reason was that home jockeys had decided that the only way to beat the Americans was to join them. In racing success can breed success. When a jockey has a good season the demand for his services rises and if he can judge horseflesh as well as he can judge a race, his choice of rides can reinforce his success. Although not every American had the ability of Sloan, his dominance led to the engagement by British owners of lesser ranked Americans - in 1900 Covington, Jenkins, Lyne, Macintyre, McGuire, Rigby and Cass Sloan all had licences to ride in Britain - so that British jockeys became 'exceedingly doleful with the conviction that they were to be swept practically out of existence' (Watson 1907, p. 429). They were persuaded that their employment prospects would be seriously jeopardised if they did not take up the American style of riding and racing. Kempton Cannon was one of the first to do this and his increased total of winners soon justified the change (Richardson 1901, p. 264). As early as September 1900 it was noted that the *successful* English jockeys 'to a greater or lesser extent all ride more Americano' (Watson 1900, p. 351). Two years later the trainer Tom Cannon, father of Kempton and a highly successful teacher of apprentices, had begun to instruct his young charges to ride more in the American style as he acknowledged that it would be useless to deny the advantage thus obtained (Watson 1902, p. 696).

Initially the pure American style had been adopted but, although it was a decided improvement on the traditional British upright seat, it was not ideal for the British courses which were more undulating than the American flat tracks. Difficulties in rebalancing horses led to a host of accidents and objections for foul riding (Mersey-Thompson 1914, p. 370). Soon, however, modified versions of the American seat appeared: the end result was that stirrups in general remained shorter than formerly, but that the knees of most jockeys did not overlap the withers of their mounts, nor were reins grasped as tightly or held so close behind the ears as in the original American style. Nevertheless the compromise position lay nearer to that of Tod Sloan than of Fred Archer (Mersey-Thompson 1914, pp. 362-363).

The stay of the Americans was brief. Simms never returned after that first season; Lester Reiff came back to ride in 1899 to 1901; his brother Johnny for the same three; and Tod Sloan for only two full seasons. By 1902 only Danny Maher and Skeets Martin were riding regularly in Britain but they were still successful: Maher third in the championship with 106 wins (and the highest winning percentage of 23.50) and Martin fourth with 80 wins. Significantly Maher had changed his style and taken up the Anglo-American seat. Significantly too Maher was regarded as 'a most respectable boy' (Cook 1905, p. 504 quoting Lord Durham) whereas many of the others had a blatant disregard for the rules of racing. 'Our Van', the turf correspondent for *Baily's Magazine*, maintained that 'of the tricks and manners of most American jockeys who have visited England a high opinion has not been held, and there can be little question that they are brought up in a bad school' (Our Van February 1902, p. 154). They paid for their trespasses. Lester Reiff, champion jockey in 1900, was warned off by the Jockey Club in October 1901 for not trying to win at Manchester (Our Van November 1901, pp. 384-385) and Sloan, following an official reprimand for gambling which was against the rules of British racing, had it intimated to him that he need not bother to apply for a renewal of his licence the following season (Sloan 1915, p. 187). It was well known that he had connections with notorious gamblers and that he owned horses, neither of which sat well with Britain's racing authorities. Eventually in 1915 he was deported for running an illegal gaming house. In America he set up an unsuccessful tipping business and died penniless in 1933 in a Los Angeles charity ward; a sad end for a man who had ridden 253 winners from 812 races in Britain and irrevocably changed both British jockeyship and the English vernacular (Dickinson 1950, p. 187).

Simms returned to the States where he went on to win two Kentucky Derbys before turning to training in 1902, possibly a victim of the racism which strengthened in American racing at the turn of the century (Riess 1997). The Reiffs moved to France, though Johnny came back to ride in the occasional big race, winning the Derby in 1907 and 1912 and the Two Thousand Guineas in 1913. Maher took up residence in Britain and continued to ride with success. Even when British riders adopted American techniques Maher continued to win. In 1903 he was never out of the places in the classics and won both the Derby and the St Leger on Rock Sand. In 1906 he was victorious in the Derby again, this time on Spearmint, and in the Oaks on Keystone II. Between 1900 and 1914 Maher rode 1,331 winners in Britain with a winning percentage of 25.3. Eventually he succumbed to tuberculosis, virtually the industrial disease of jockeys exacerbated by their constant efforts to lose weight. On the outbreak of war he returned to America where in died in 1916, aged only thirty-five. Martin too continued to ride in Britain with some success though he never challenged Maher as the leading American rider.

Conclusion

The American riders brought with them an established style of riding which was at first derided in Britain but quickly adopted when its advantages became obvious. The fact that British owners opted for American riders and their winning ways encouraged British riders to adopt American practices in order to secure employment. Pioneers such as Kempton Cannon led the way to be followed at first by other jockeys (though not for a while his brother Mornington) and then by the emerging apprentices as the bandwagon began to roll. This allowed British riders to compete more effectively, especially when they developed a new style, a combination of the old and new, more suited to English racing conditions. They were also aided in combating the invaders by the actions of the Jockey Club which forced out those Americans who refused to conform to other accepted racing behaviour not just the traditional riding style.

Not all the American jockeys came to Britain. Cass Sloan rode mainly in Russia where he became champion jockey. Fred Taral did likewise in Austro-Hungary. Peter Freeman became prominent in France; as did the black rider Jimmy Winkfield, winner of the Kentucky Derby in both 1901 and 1902. Nate Hill and Eddie Ross rode with success in Germany (Reiss 1997). Research is needed to ascertain the impact of the American invaders in those countries. In Britain there is no doubt. Here a handful of extraordinary men, small in stature but large in influence, revolutionised British racing. Few innovations in sport can have had such an immediate and significant impact.

Acknowledgement. I am grateful to the United Kingdom Sports Council and the Research Committee of the Faculty of Humanities and Social Sciences, De Montfort University for financial assistance towards the preparation and presentation of this paper; and to Mrs. Dede Scott Brown, curator of York Racing Museum, for access to the museum library.

References

Cook, T.A. (1905). A history of the English turf. London.
Clayton, S.S. (1904). The state of the turf. Badminton Magazine (19).
Dickinson, A.J. (1950). Jockeys and jockeyship. In E.H. Bland (ed.), Flat-Racing Since 1900. London.
Haig Brown, A.R. (1903). Racehorses or horse-races? Baily's Magazine (80) July.
Lambton, G. (1924). Men and horses I have known. London.
Maher, D. (1905). On race riding. Badminton Magazine (20).
Mersey-Thompson, R.F. (1914). A trial of the monkey seat. Badminton Magazine (28).
Our Van. (1899). The Sandown Eclipse Meeting. Baily's Magazine (72) August.
Our Van. (1900). Yorkshire Summer Meeting. Baily's Magazine (74) October.
Our Van. (1901). Epsom Spring Meeting. Baily's Magazine (76) July.
Our Van. (1901). Lester Reiff. Baily's Magazine (76) November.
Our Van. (1902). Lessons From America. Baily's Magazine (77) February.
Purdy, B. (1904). The passing of the starting gate in American racing. Baily's Magazine (81) July.
Reiss, S. (1997). The American jockey, 1876-1910. NASSH Conference. unpublished paper.
Richardson, C. (1901). The English turf. London.
Rowlands, H.E. (1900). American jockeyship. Badminton Magazine (10).

Sloan, T. (1915). Tod Sloan. London.
Watson, A.E.T. (1898). Notes. Badminton Magazine (7).
Watson, A.E.T. (1900). Notes. Badminton Magazine (11).
Watson, A.E.T. (1901). American training methods. Badminton Magazine (13).
Watson, A.E.T. (1902). Notes. Badminton Magazine (15).
Watson, A.E.T. (1907). The American jockey invasion. Badminton Magazine (24).

Chapter 18

Universiades 1959-1996 :
university games or interolympics ?

Roland Renson and Line Verbeke
K.U.Leuven, Belgium

The International University Sports Federation was founded in 1949 and started a cycle of biennial Universiades from 1959 onwards (FISU 1993; Campana 1994; The history 1999). These Universiades were intended as international sport competitions for 18 to 27 year old university athletes. Universiades share a lot of characteristics with the Olympic Games, after which they were modeled, not only in their organisational structure and political context (Oosterlynck 1960; Ostyn 1980), but also in terms of their participants.

While watching the Edmonton 1983 Universiade as a participant in the joined FISU/CESU and HISPA conferences (Kereliuk 1983), the first author was puzzled -not to say baffled- by the student status of several of the competing athletes. This study will however not focus on individual cases of more than dubious university affiliation or official student age. A comparative analysis will be made of the two-time-successes at Universiades and the Olympic Games between 1959 and 1996. The hypotheses were that the Universiades were as much as the Olympics a symbolic testing ground during the Cold War; that these Universiades gradually became 'Interolympics'; and that their success patterns would change after 1989.

Success rates in Universiades and in Olympic Games

An exploratory comparative study of the medal winners in the Universiades and in the Olympics, revealed that several athletes appeared at the winner's podium of both events. This led to the hypotheses that during the Cold War period not only the Olympics, but also the Universiades served as a symbolic testing ground of prestige and power between East and West Block countries. Moreover, it was hypothesised that in this athletic rivalry, the Universiades gradually lost their original student-like character and became 'Interolympics', where top athletes could meet and test each other in student camouflage. Among the 'student champions' in the Universiade of Sofia 1961, who won gold medals in the Tokyo Olympics of 1964 appeared names such as Valéry Brumel, Igor Ter Ovanesyan, Tatiana Chtelkanova, Eléna Gortchakova, Tamara Press (2x) from the USSR and Yolanda Balas from Rumania. We further assumed that -if these hypotheses were correct- some of the success patterns would change in the 1989-1996 period, after the Iron Curtain had "... come tumbling down".

It was therefore decided to carry out a more systematic comparative analysis of the Universiades and the Olympics between 1959 (Universiade of Turin) and 1996 (Olympic Games of Atlanta) to test these hypotheses (see table 1).

Participation data and success scores of each Summer Universiade were compared with these of the consecutive Summer Olympic Games. The following sport disciplines were programmed at both meets in the 1959-1996 period: track and field (18x); fencing (16x); swimming (16x); gymnastics (14x); fancy diving (14x); wrestling (4x); rowing (3x); judo (3x); rhythmic gymnastics (2x) canoe (1x). The 1959 Universiade of Turin was thus compared with the 1960 Olympics of Rome. However, Universiades are organized at a bi-ennial rhythm, the Olympics only every four years. Consequently, the results of two different Universiades had to be compared with the results of the same Olympic Games, following each of these Universiades. The 1961 and 1963 Universiades of Sofia and Porto Allegre respectively, were thus both compared with the 1964 Olympics of Tokyo.

Universiades seem to have kept pace with the Olympics in terms of increased participation over the 1959-1996 period. Both had a gradual increase in number of participants with a peak period in the seventies, then a relative drop in the early eighties because of the boycott of the Moscow 1980 and Los Angeles 1984 Olympics, which also affected the Universiades of Bucharest 1981, Edmonton 1983 and Kobe 1985. An absolute 'low' were the Rome 1975 Universiade (N: 486) and the Duisburg 1989 Universiade (N: 1785) which had to be improvised to replace two suddenly cancelled other venues.

Universiades always had a higher female participation rate than the Olympic Games until the Atlanta 1996 Olympics. The Universiades in Torino 1959 had 12.2 % female students participating, the Rome 1960 Olympics 11.4 %. The Universiades and the Olympics gradually increased their female participation, but the Universiades already reached an over 20 % rate in the sixties, and a 30 % rate in the eighties. The Olympics reached these female participation rates only a decade after the Universiades. The Sheffield 1991 Universiade peaked with a 36.3 % rate. The Atlanta 1996 Olympics, however, reached a 34.3 % female participation, higher than the Buffalo 1993 (32.8 %) and Fukuoka 1995 (33.2 %) Universiades. This can be seen as a major symptom of the democratisation and emancipation process of female athletes. Female sport participation and competition was earlier accepted in the rather elite university milieu than in other social strata (Renson & Vermeulen 1972).

Table 1 :   Number of 'two-time-winners' in Universiades & Olympic Games: a
comparison of East and West Block countries

YEAR Universiades & Olympic Games	EAST	WEST	
1959-1960 Turin-Rome	7	3	
1961-1964 Sofia-Tokyo	14	1	
1963-1964 Porto Allegre-Tokyo	17	4	
1965-1968 Budapest-Mexico	10	11	
1967-1968 Tokyo-Mexico	0	30	
1970-1972 Turin-Munich	15	9	E>W : 8
			W>E : 5
1973-1976 Moscow-Montreal	20	3	*E=W : 1*
1975-1976 Rome-Montreal	7	2	*Subtotal = 14*
1977-1980 Sofia-Moscow	27	3	
1979-1980 Mexico-Moscow	30	4	
1981-1984 Bucarest-Los Angeles	16	19	
1983-1984 Edmonton-Los Angeles	9	23	
1985-1988 Kobe-Seoul	12	12	
1987-1988 Zagreb-Seoul	22	5	
Subtotal	186 (60%)	124 (40%)	
1989-1992 Duisburg-Barcelona	13	9	E>W : 3
1991-1992 Sheffield-Barcelona	13	9	*W>E : 1*
			Subtotal = 4
1993-1996 Buffalo-Atlanta	13	16	
1995-1996 Fukuoka-Atlanta	16	14	
Subtotal	55 (53%)	48 (47%)	E>W : 11 W>E : 6 *E=W : 1*
Total	241 (58%)	172 (42%)	*Total = 18*

In the present analysis, the names of the student athletes, who were among the five bests in their discipline at the Universiades, were matched against the names of the three medal winners in consecutive Olympics. Countries participating in both the Universiades and the Olympics were divided in (former) East Block (N: 16) and West Block (N: 18) factions [1].

For instance, when the Turin 1959 Universiade was compared with the 1960 Rome Olympics in the track and field events, eight names reappeared: three men and five women. On this basis three different success indices (SI) were calculated. SI.1: number of athletes, who were one out of the five best Universiade athletes, and also won an Olympic medal; SI.2: number of times that two out of the five Universiade winners also won Olympic medals; SI.3: number of times that three out of the five Universiade winners reappeared on the winner's podium of the Olympics. Finally a global success index (GI) consisted of the following combination of the three success indices: SI 1(x1) + Index 2(x2) + Index 3(x3). This global index (GI) remained rather stable over the whole period considered. There were less 'two-time-winners' in the Turin 1959-Rome 1960 (GI=10) and Sofia 1961-Tokyo 1964 (GI=15) comparisons, but there were also less participants in these early Universiades. From then onwards the GI varied between 21 and 30 with the exception of the extremely low result for the Rome 1975-Montreal 1976 comparison (GI=9), due to the fact that only track and field was staged during the 1975 Universiade in Rome. The success rates of the East and West Block countries were compared by contrasting the number of 'two-time-winners' (=GI) in Universiades and Olympic Games (see table 1). These data show that the East Block outdid the West Block in 11 out of the 18 comparisons. Once they ended even, with a 12 - 12 score in the Kobe 1985-Seoul 1988 comparison. In order to explain some of the drastic differences between certain scores, one would have to dig deeper into the specific geographical, political and historical context of these Universiades, which cannot be done within the given time and space limits of this paper. Nevertheless it seems that there might be something like a 'home advantage' or 'geopolitical spill-over' factor. This factor then explains why East or West Block student athletes perform better in the next Olympics when the foregoing Universiade was held in their home country or within their geopolitical territory.

The East Block athletes performed e.g. exceptionally well at the Olympics after the Universiade of Sofia 1961 (14-1 score), Moscow 1973 (20-3 score), Sofia 1977 (27-3 score) and Zagreb 1987 (22-5 score). West block athletes performed also considerably better (... or less bad) after Universiades were held in their geopolitical sphere: after Kobe 1985 (12-12 score), Sheffield 1991 (13-9 negative score), Buffalo 1993 (13-16 positive score) and after Fukuoka 1995 (16-14 negative score). All comparisons linked with the boycotted Moscow 1980 and Los Angeles 1984 Olympics were -for obvious reasons- not taken into consideration. The East Block countries dominated in track en field, gymnastics, fencing and wrestling, whereas the Western countries were more successful in fancy diving, judo and swimming.

Overall the East Block athletes had 241 (58 %) 'two-time-winners' versus 172 (42 %) for the West. When the 1959-1988 period is compared with the post-Cold War period of 1989-1996, some changes seem to appear. In the Cold War period the East beat the West by 186-124 (60 % versus 40 %). After 1988 this contrast became less dramatic: 55-48 (53 % versus 47 %), but still with the East Block countries in the lead. This slow shift (Chi² = 1.33, not significant) is probably due to the overt acceptance of professional athletes since the Seoul 1988 Olympics. This shift also points in the direction of our third hypothesis, which assumed that the post 1989 era would bring some changes in the sport success patterns of the countries which once belonged to one of the two rival Blocks.

Conclusions

A comparative analysis of the Summer Universiades and the Summer Olympic Games between 1959 (Universiade of Turin) and 1996 (Atlanta Olympics), leads to the conclusion that the Universiades have gradually become 'Interolympics', where top athletes can meet and test each other in student camouflage. Both the Universiades and the Olympics have gradually increased their participation numbers, with a flaw however in the 1980-1984 Olympic boycott period. Universiades have always had higher female participation rather than the Olympic Games, but the latter are recently catching up.

In this analysis, the names of the student athletes, who were among the five bests in their discipline at the Universiades, were matched against the names of the three medal winners in consecutive Olympics. For instance, when the 1959 Turin Universiade was compared with the 1960 Olympic Games for track and field events, eight names reappeared: three men and five women. Over the considered 1959 to 1996 period, East block countries outdid the West block countries with a success rate of respectively 241 (58 %) versus 172 (42 %) 'two-time-winners'. The East block countries dominated in track and field, gymnastics, fencing and wrestling, whereas the Western countries were more successful in fancy diving, judo and swimming. From 1989 onwards, the success rate of former East block countries had changed from 60 % before that period to 53 %. This is probably due to the overt acceptance of professional athletes from the 1988 Olympics onwards.

All in all, because of the democratisation of higher education and the increasing internationalisation (globalisation) of sport, more and more 'true and fake' student athletes at the Universiades have not the slightest idea what the Latin medieval song *Gaudeamus igitur*, which replaces the national anthems at the Universiades, might mean.

References

Campana, R. (1994). World university sport: from the beginning to contemporary times. FISU Forum '94 (Catania; 1994), 25-28.

FISU (1993). 1923-1993, the World University Games celebrate their 70th anniversary. FISU Magazine, (25): 17-21.

Kereliuk, S. (ed.) (1983). The university's role in the development of modern sport: past, present and future (Proceedings of the FISU-conference - Universiade '83 in association with the 10th HISPA Congress; Edmonton; 1983). Edmonton: FISU.

Oosterlynck, G. (1960). Geschiedenis van de internationale universitaire sport van 1945 tot 1960. Sport (Brussels), 3(10): 27-32.

Ostyn, M. (1980). 'Politiek versus sport' in de geschiedenis van de internationale universitaire sport. Hermes (Leuven), 14: 115-125; 337-350.

Renson, R. & Vermeulen, A. (1972). Sociale determinanten van de sportpraktijk bij de Belgische volwassenen. Sport (Brussels), 15: 25-39.

The history (1999). The history of FISU. FISU Magazine, (44): 20-48.

Notes

[1] East Block: Bulgaria, China, Cuba, Czechoslovakia, German Democratic Republic (until 1989), Hungary, Poland, Soviet Union (until 1991), Yugoslavia; since 1991: Armenia, Belarussia, Estonia, Georgia, Russia, Ukraine, Uzbekistan
West Block: Australia, Austria, Brazil, Canada, France, German Federal Republic (until 1989) and Germany (since 1989), Great Britain, Italy, Jamaica, Japan, Kenya, Korea, Mexico, New Zealand, South Africa, Sweden, USA, Zambia.

Chapter 19

Old Borders in Olympism.
The Presidency of Baron Henri de Baillet-Latour the Successor of Baron de Coubertin

Karl Lennartz
German Sport University of Cologne, Germany

Of all IOC presidents whose tenure of office endured for at least a full term of eight years, Count Henri de Baillet-Latour has received the least amount of scholarly investigation. The following notations address such a shortcoming, particularly within the context of the Count's trying relationship with neutral Belgium's belligerent neighbour of the 1930s-National Socialist Germany.

Baron de Coubertin's refusal to stand for another term as President of the IOC in 1925, despite the urging of a number of members, left that august organization facing the problem of finding a successor to the man who had been the driving force behind and the representative of the Olympic Movement since the founding of the Committee in 1894. The election, which was featured on the agenda of the 24th IOC Session in Prague, was scheduled for the afternoon of May 28th 1925. Postal votes of absent members were counted in the First round, and given that many of those members had obviously assumed that Coubertin would stand again, they had voted for him. During the first round of balloting, none of the candidates received an adequate majority. Of the 40 votes cast, Baillet-Latour received 17, Coubertin 11, de Blonay 6, Justinien de Clary 4, Melchior de Polignac 1, and one was invalid. In the second round, in which plainly only those present could take part, Baillet-Latour received 19 of the 27 votes cast and was thus elected as the third President of the IOC.

In view of a strong tendency in favour of the Belgian candidate apparent in the first round, it can be assumed that certain agreements had been reached among the IOC members present in Prague, but one can only speculate as to why Baillet-Latour was ultimately chosen. Admittedly, the members of the Executive Committee, which had existed since 1921, were the most obvious candidates, as they already occupied prominent positions within the IOC.

Foremost among them was the Executive Committee's Chairman, the Swiss member Blonay, who had occupied the office of IOC President on an interim basis in 1915 while Coubertin was serving France in World War 1 as a non-combatant. A usually excellent relationship with Coubertin had suffered after the World War, so there may have been a reluctance to elect Blonay for fear of offending the Baron. In contrast, Baillet-Latour had always remained loyal to his predecessor. He had occupied the office of Vice Chairman of the Executive Committee, a Position tantamount to third place in the hierarchy, and had the advantage over the remaining three members of the Committee of having belonged to the IOC for at least ten years longer than any one of them.

Born on March 1st 1876, the son of Count Ferdinand de Baillet-Latour, the former Governor of the Province of Antwerp, and Countess Caroline d'Oultremont de Duras, the young Henri de Baillet-Latour was reared in an environment which included the boy who was to become Albert 1, King of the Belgians (1875-1935). After studying at the University of Louvain, he joined the diplomatic service, carrying out assignments on behalf of the Belgian government. From an early age, he was a passionate and
versatile horseman, becoming President of the Jockey Club de Belgique, an office that meant almost as much to him as that of IOC President and which he held until he died.
In 1903 Henri de Baillet-Latour became the IOC member for Belgium, and Coubertin had this to say about him in the *Revue Olympique:*

> *"Count Henri de Baillet-Latour, the new member for Belgium, is an outstanding sportsman, whose enthusiasm and competence will ensure that Belgium's participation in the Olympic Games is a credit to his country and his sovereign."* [1]

There appeared to be an ulterior motive behind Baillet-Latour's election to the IOC. Coubertin hoped that Baillet-Latour could organize the Olympic Congress in Brussels, which had been postponed from 1903 to 1905 following the departure from the IOC of the previous Belgian member Reytiens. Fulfilling Coubertin's expectations, Baillet-Latour did indeed organize the Brussels Congress of 1905. As a result he came front and center before the attention of all IOC members. Baillet-Latour became a co-founder of the Belgian Olympic Committee, the paramount aim of which was to ensure the regular participation of a Belgian team in the Olympic Games. He served as Chef de Mission of the Belgian team in London in 1908 and Stockholm in 1912.

In 1912 the Belgians proposed their capital, Brussels, as the host city for the 1920 Games, but two years later, Antwerp was proposed instead. The decision, postponed by the IOC until 1915, could not be taken after all because of the war, but Belgian sports leaders, in contact with Coubertin during the German occupation of their homeland, maintained their desire to organize the Games once the war was over. In Lausanne in 1919, at the first IOC Session after the First World War, the 1920 Games were awarded to the Flemish city of Antwerp, a major risk in view of the short time available for the preparations - only one and a half years for a city which had been partially destroyed. The selection of Antwerp was undoubtedly due to the influence of Baillet-Latour. Almost immediately, he assumed the presidency of the Organizing Committee and thus played an important role in the successful staging of the event, an achievement which constituted a great satisfaction for him. [2]

In 1923 Baillet-Latour was elected President of the NOC of Belgium, an office he was to hold until his death. By the time Baillet-Latour ascended to the highest office in the International Olympic Movement, he was able to look back on 22 years of Olympic service, including four years on the Executive Committee, to which he had belonged since its creation. His first term of office was eight years. They were anything but peaceful. The shape of the programme of the Games, the wrangles over the staging of women's events at the Olympics, and, above all, the problem of the definition of an amateur (although the premises which underlay amateur problems in the 1920s tend to raise a smile today) constituted the chief claim on Baillet-Latour's abundant energy. The amateur issue, in particular, gave rise to the most vehement differences between the IOC and the International Sports Federations, particularly those responsible for football, tennis and skiing.

Whereas Coubertin deplored the great importance which had come to be ascribed to technical issues within the IOC, for his successors, these were bound to constitute the very heart of the business. Unlike the Baron, Baillet-Latour was neither a pedagogue nor a philosopher. Nor was he a writer. Coubertin had communicated his thoughts and ideas to the public again and again. This was beyond Baillet-Latour's experience and capability. Only the Belgian's speeches, which he delivered at the opening of each IOC Session, opening remarks at meetings of the IOC Executive Committee, and talks at Sports Federation Congresses, were published. [3] On most of those occasions he had to speak predominantly of the business of the day and, in particular, the amateur problem, which came up time and again. It was on this matter in particular that his intention of preserving faithfully the legacy bequeathed to him was most clearly apparent.

Whereas Coubertin had tried to break new ground in several directions, Baillet-Latour concentrated essentially on defending the Olympic regulations. And, whereas the Baron corresponded with the proponents of workers' sport and took an avid interest, devoid of ideological reservations, in sport in the USSR, his successor flatly rejected anything that smacked of "*Bolshevism*". In his strict adherence to the Olympic status quo, the Belgian IOC President often adopted an inflexible position which cost him a number of defeats, for instance in the cases of the Olympic football tournament in Amsterdam and women's athletics events (track and field), introduced in the teeth of his resistance in 1928. Though he accepted defeat at the ballot-box with a better grace than his predecessor, his obduracy in matters of regulations contrasted markedly with his style of leadership within the IOC, which was more cooperative and tolerant than that of the autocratic Coubertin, and characterized by thorough preparation of all the meetings he was to chair, in terms of both organization and content. [4]

At all events, IOC members appear to have been well satisfied with the way he carried out the duties of his office for his first eight years as President. When the next presidential election occurred at the Session in Vienna in 1933, Baillet-Latour was re-elected by a large majority for a further eight-year term. The ballot had been secret; he himself had insisted on this procedure. One may wonder whether he would have accepted the presidency had he had an inkling that, in the years that followed, the Olympic Movement would be drawn into the maelstrom of interests not germane to sport to an extent which would make the internal wranglings of the preceding years appear, in hindsight, mere child's play in comparison.

The Olympic Games of 1936 had been awarded to Berlin in 1931, and things could have followed their usual course, that is, habitual disputes over amateur status and expansion of the programme, had not the year of Baillet-Latour's re-election seen the seizure of power in Germany by the National Socialists, an event which was to pose the question of political influence on the Games for the first time. It is idle to speculate in this context whether the traditional neutral position supported by the majority of the IOC was really an option, but Baillet-Latour can at least be given credit for having insisted on an assurance that the Olympic Charter be upheld, which, among other things, forbade discrimination against Jews in the forming of national teams. Given the situation of the Jews in Germany, the Reich's assurance on this matter was merely a polite but fictional gesture, something of which the IOC President can be supposed to have been unaware. That Hitter ultimately found a way of turning the Games into a propaganda victory for himself, is part of another story.

Whereas the Nazi regime showed itself relatively well behaved in the days prior to and during the Berlin Games, it sought immediately afterwards to extend systematically its influence over the Olympic Movement, not altogether unsuccessfully, as borne out, for example, by the following: (1) the founding of the International Olympic Institute in Berlin (it was financed by the Ministry of the Interior and placed under the authority of the Reichssportführer), (2) the incorporation of the IOC's official bulletin into Carl Diem's Olympische

Rundschau, (3) the award of the Olympic Cup to the *Kraft durch Freude* association, (4) the presentation of the Olympic Diploma to Leni Riefenstahl for her film on the 1936 Games, and (5) Werner Klingeberg's assumption of the position of IOC Secretary General. The IOC was obliged to look on helplessly as the half-Jewish Theodore Lewald, whose prestige within the Committee had reached its apogee with the splendour of the Berlin Games, was forced to resign on the instructions of the National Socialists in order to make way for a party member, Walter von Reichenau, who, by an irony of fate, became a "resident" of Baillet-Latour's country in May 1940 as Commander of the Germany's VI Army. Lewald's successor on the IOC's Executive Committee was the convinced National Socialist Karl Ritter von Halt.

The fact that in early 1939 the 1940 the Winter Games were withdrawn from St. Moritz owing to disagreements over the skiing competitions and the amateur status of ski instructors and, despite the annexation of Bohemia and Moravia by the German Reich and the events of the so-called Kristallnacht in 1938, the IOC again entrusted Garmisch-Partenkirchen with their organization. During that decision-making process, Baillet-Latour had not mentioned the principle of non-discrimination against Jews which he had raised before Berlin. By all this, one is tempted to conclude that the staging of the Games at any price was seen as a primary objective, while the defence of general humanitarian principles was pursued with lesser zeal. Even after Hitler's attack on Poland and the resulting declarations of war on Germany, there was at first no question of the IOC calling off the 1940 Games.

However, the extension of the war to the whole of Europe soon prompted action concerning the organization of the 1940 Games. On November 22nd 1939 von Halt informed Baillet-Latour that Germany was withdrawing its agreement to organize the Winter Games. Baillet-Latour replied in these terms:

> *"How sad it is to think that the wonderful work you have done to give the V Olympic Winter Games an even more impressive character than was the case in 1936 has now been in vain."* [5]

In view of the fact that the IOC President was fully aware of the plans for the Garmisch-Partenkirchen Games, which included a "Skiing Day" with 10,000 participants, the "high point" of which was to have been a 12-minute speech by Hitler - a flagrant breach of the Olympic regulations - Baillet-Latour's remark must have come as something of a surprise. The records show no protest against the irregular intent.

Indeed, the President, in his reply, added that: "The "Skiing Day" would have been an unforgettable experience for all those fortunate enough to be present." [6]

By 1940 Tokyo had withdrawn as host of the 1940 Summer Games. So, too, had the Finns, who, in spite of the war, had magnanimously agreed to replace Tokyo as host. In July 1940, Diem visited the IOC President in occupied Brussels on the instructions of the Reichssportführer Hans von Tschammer und Osten, who had obtained Hitler's blessing for negotiations with Baillet-Latour on the "reorganization of the International Olympic Committee." Baillet-Latour complained to Diem, in his capacity as President of the Belgian Jockey Club, on the requisitioning of all thoroughbreds by German occupying authorities. The "takeover by the Germans," as Diem noted in his diary, seems to have met with little resistance on Baillet-Latour's part:

> *"On the Olympic issues, he approved my draft, he found it excellent. He only amended the paragraph on the membership. His formulation will be very useful for the subsequent negotiations."* [7]

The National Socialists' objective (the first scenario of which concerned the case of Theodore Lewald relative to the organization of the 1936 Games) was to expand German influence within the IOC. In the centralized system of German sport, which had now come under the aegis of the National Socialist Union for Physical Exercises of the Reich Germany wished to ensure that there was no representative of an international body over who the regime did not itself have control. In mid-November, von Tschammer und Osten, von Halt and Diem travelled to Brussels for further talks with the IOC President. Conclusions as to the contents of the visit may be drawn from two sources. Diem wrote in his diary:

> *"V. Tschammer expressed the hope that Baillet would remain President, he conceded that changes in the membership were a matter for the individual countries and wished to see the IOC rejuvenated something that has been going on for many years. (If he, V. Tsch. were to be elected as a 55-year old, he would declare himself to be a rejuvenation)."* [8]

Upon his return to Berlin, von Tschammer und Osten reported to the German Foreign Minister that Baillet-Latour was in agreement with a reform which stated that:

> *"the wishes of the authoritarian States should be respected; firstly, a radical rejuvenation of the Committee, and secondly, recognition of the principle that, in the authoritarian States, the representatives proposed by them should be appointed members."*

He continued:

> "*I for my part requested that he introduce this reform himself in his capacity as President and assume the leadership until the reorganization.*" [9]

IOC President Baillet-Latour was the most obvious lever for the National Socialists to employ in their quest to assert control of the IOC, but it is nevertheless striking that he should have been invited to act as a puppet of Hitler's Germany in bringing about the desired "reorganization," the obvious upshot of which would have been that the authoritarian States would have delegated their own IOC members who in turn would have decided on the admission of the representatives for the other countries. At first glance, it may seem regrettable that the President did not reject this proposition out of hand, but he was at least far-sighted enough to refuse to convene an IOC Session. This act delayed any possible amendments to the statutes until after the end of the war. Nothing could thus be done until the war was over. Had the National Socialists emerged victorious, they would, in any case, have done as they wished.

Baillet-Latour died during the night of January 6th 1942. Olympic authorities in Berlin were informed of his passing. Hitler, the German Foreign Office and a number of IOC members were sent informatory telegrams from Berlin. Hitler immediately sent a telegram of condolence to Baillet-Latour's widow, who lived with her brother in Schloss Teplitz-Schönau (Bohemia). On her way to her husband's funeral in Brussels, she stopped briefly in Berlin, where she was joined by von Halt and Diem for the trip to Belgium's capital. At the memorial service held in Baillet-Latour's house, only three IOC members were present, each of them from the German sphere of influence. They were: von Halt, the Belgian Edouard-Emile de Lavelaye and the Dutchman Alphert Schimmelpenninck van der Oye, who presented an IOC wreath and spoke a few words of remembrance. Diem, who was officially representing the International Olympic Institute, described in his diary the mood of the members of the Belgian NOC in their discussions with the German delegation concerning the arrangements for and form of the memorial service. Wrote Diem: "*We sensed their concern that we were making ourselves too obvious and seeking to make some kind of propaganda.*" [10]

Since the occupation of his homeland, Baillet-Latour had left the job of keeping up contacts among IOC members to the IOC's vice-president, Sigfrid Edström, in neutral Sweden. This demeanour on the part of Baillet-Latour, in itself, may perhaps be interpreted as an attitude of rejection towards the National Socialists. By the early 1940s, Edström had assumed de jure leadership of the IOC.

Notes

[1] In: Revue Olympique 3(1903), 1, 15.

[2] Cf Mallon, W.B. (1992). The unofficial report of the 1920 Olympics. Durham.

[3] Most were reprinted in the Bulletin Officiel du C.I.O. 1 ff. (1926 ff.)

[4] Reprinted in: Lennartz, K. et al. (1984). Dokumente zum Aufbau des deutschen Sports. Sankt Augustin, p. 191.

[5] Carl Diem, Tage-Bücher, Typescript (Diem-Archiv).

[6] Ibid.

[7] See Tschammer to Ribbentrop, 03.12.1940 (copy Diem-Archiv). Cf. also Teichler, H.J. (1991). Internationale Sportpolitik im Dritten Reich. Schorndorf, p. 291 ff.

[8] Carl Diem, Tage-Bücher, Typescript (Diem-Archiv). Cf. Olympische Rundschau, 5(1942), 17, 1-27.

[9] See Tschammer to Ribbentrop, op. cit.

[10] See Carl Diem, Tage-Bücher, op. cit.

Chapter 20

Coubertin, nationalism and the media: a case study of the Atlanta Games

Catherine O'Brien
University of Sydney, Australia

The world's attention will be on Sydney, Australia, in September 2000 when the Olympic Games begin. In 1998 it seems as if Sydney is one large construction site. Not only are wonderful sport facilities being built at the Olympic site (Homebush Bay), but in downtown Sydney new buildings are being erected and street beautification is taking place. Each week a SOCOG Report is published in the major newspapers and the media is constantly reporting on Olympic-related matters. However, it appears that currently the interest of the general public in the Olympic Games is not high. SOCOG officials argue that this is not unusual, but rather a predictable response two years away from the Games. There was a more enthusiastic and overwhelming response by the general public when Sydney secured the rights to the Games. It is alleged that the same response will be even more evident when the Games begin in 2000 despite the fact that a number of Sydney residents will elect to leave the city for its duration.

From the Opening Ceremony onwards, any prior hassles and disruptions will be set aside and there will no doubt be an outpouring of national pride from the participants, the spectators and their respective home countries. Such national pride has always been a feature of the Olympic Games. In fact, the founder of the Modern Olympics, Baron Pierre de Coubertin, proposed his theory of internationalism as a way of embracing the Olympic spirit. This paper will analyse his concept of nationalism as portrayed in his theory of internationalism. it will then critically examine the role of the media in articulating such ideas. This will be done through a case study example of how the media affected the development of sport heroes in Sydney schoolchildren during the 1996 Olympic Games in Atlanta.

Baron de Coubertin's theory

Baron de Coubertin considered there were two types of nationalism; one "patriotic" based on a love of country and the other "strident" based on a dislike or fear of others. Patriotic love did not exclude the recognition of mistakes and a resolve to correct them. National self improvement was both a process and a goal. There was sympathy for, and joy in, cultural differences and these were used as a basis for friendship with foreign countries. In contrast "strident" nationalism was xenophobic in nature. It demonstrated a cultural arrogance as other nations were considered less worthy.

Coubertin hoped that the Olympic Games would develop not only patriotic nationalism but through it, internationalism. His theory recognized that cultures and peoples are different but are no less than one another. He decried those people who, while visiting other countries, never in fact left their own. They simply transplanted their own country to another, living and acting as if they were still at home. There was at best a skimming of the surface of other cultures with little attempt to understand different beliefs and values. Any basis for friendship or interaction was thus lacking.

In contrast, Coubertin's theory of internationalism transcended such myopic views. He did not believe that any form of nationalism would suffice (Morgan, p. 12). He rejected cosmopolitanism, a longing for a world without borders, as being naive and utopian. Such an idea was also morally fraudulent. Coubertin asserted that genuine internationalism rested on genuine nationalism. As he himself argued, "internationalism should be the state of mind of those who love their country above all, who seek to draw to it the friendship of foreigners by professing for the countries of those foreigners an intelligent and enlightened sympathy" (1898, p. 434). Hence a deep and critical nationalism is a necessary prerequisite for a full understanding of internationalism. His ultimate goal was that through the Olympic Games people should learn to know others so that respect for each other would be implicit in all undertakings, athletic or otherwise.

Coubertin's actual life experiences are lessons in his own development of internationalism. Born into French aristocracy, he received a classical education in the Jesuit tradition which he found repressive. In his later life, he turned away from his royalist conservative connections and, unimpressed with social inequalities, embraced republicanism and more liberal political, educational and social ideals (Loland 1994, p. 28).

His travels to England and to the USA had profound effect on his thinking. In both he visited schools and universities(Rugby, Harrow, Eton, Oxford, Cambridge, Harvard, Cornell, Princeton) and saw the importance of PE in the curriculum. These were significantly absent or minimized in French education, but, more importantly, he saw education as cultivating moral qualities, not merely for the sake of individual amelioration but for the betterment of a democratic society as a whole. Such notions were foreign to contemporary French society. It was other nations, not only England and the USA, who taught him the importance of wholesome national pride and genuine internationalism, both of which were underpinned by moral imperatives.

One such moral imperative was the late 19th Century belief in the possibility of international peace. The great progress of the past several decades seem to provide ample justification for such a view. His ideas of 'enlightened patriotism' were built on positive sentiments which gave no credence to the glorification of war or to the discriminatory treatment of other nations (Loland 1994, p.33). Education as a way of promoting a peaceful ideology was important to Coubertin. So for him the Olympic Games with their roots steeped in Greek history meant the cultivation of the individual through sport and the cultivation of relations between men and society. By this he hoped to promote international understanding and peace as a way of honoring human greatness and possibility (Loland 1994, p. 36-38).

Are these noble concepts of internationalism, conceived before the turn of the last century, still evident and expected in a host Olympic city or country? Can we foresee an outpouring of patriotism by Australians for their own athletes, or is there rather a recognition of the effort and expertise of all athletes, despite their affiliation? Is there evidence of internationalism already inherent in the Australian culture? Such ideas were the foundation of the following case study example.

Survey and results

Views of nationalism in Australian youth were exhibited in their feelings about the Olympics and the heroes it generates. Sydney schoolchildren were polled by the use of a questionnaire immediately following the Atlanta Olympic Games. These participants, aged 11-13 years, were students at ten predominantly middle class public and private schools in Metropolitan Sydney. Two of the schools were situated in a predominantly Asian suburb. There were 594 children in the final group of whom 57% were male and 43% were female. They were a microcosm of Australia's multicultural society, with 72% holding Australian citizenship. The remainder (28%) were foreign-born from 39 other nationalities. In time most of these would be expected to become Australian citizens (O'Brien 1997).

The purpose of the survey was to investigate what the Olympic Games meant to the respondents, particularly in regard to their reasons for watching the Games, who, what and why they watched, and what they saw as the important issues of the Olympics. The amount of time spent watching the Games was also ascertained. There were additional questions which provided choices for the participant to choose from as well as extra space for the participant to fill in his/her own choices.

It was found that 96% of the children surveyed watched the Games coverage on TV for at least one or two hours every day. The most popular reason for watching the Games was to see Australian athletes (50%). Of the five countries respondents could nominate, more than 66% chose Australia as their first choice of countries they were most interested in watching. The United States was the second choice, while the two schools with strong Asian enrollments selected China. The TV Channel Seven coverage perpetuated national fervor by providing extensive coverage of Australian athletes. Special interviews were broadcast with each Australian gold medal winner. Australia's strengths in, for example, swimming, and specific track events resulted in extended viewing in those sports. Thus when the question was asked, "What were the five best performances of the Games?" two Australian medal winners, Kieren Perkins and Cathy Freeman, garnered 22% of the votes. Other strong preferences as best performers included more Aussies: the women's hockey team and Michael Diamond (both gold medal winners), as well as Carl Lewis, Michael Johnson, and the USA Dream Team.

Media

Australia sent its largest team ever to an Olympics. The U.S. athletes, as the largest team in Atlanta, had great presence on TV in practically every sport. There were 300+ hours of broadcast time on non pay TV Channel Seven alone in Australia. This compares with the 125 hours seen in the U.S. on non-pay channels. Additionally there were the highlights on other channels, the complete and uncommercialized radio coverage, several special editions of newspapers, as well as daily sections dedicated to Games coverage. On July 29, over 3.4 million TV sets (in a country of 18+ million) were turned on to watch the great comeback of Kieren Perkins in his gold medal 1500 m. swim. Kieren was the Barcelona gold medal winner, but had struggled to qualify for the Aussie team for Atlanta. A separate newspaper poll taken just after Atlanta's Games of the World's Greatest Athletes (Kogoy 1996, p. 54) showed Perkins tied for second place behind Michael Johnson. Some 11 months later a Channel Nine commentator referred to Perkins' performance and that of cricket captain, Mark Taylor, as two of the greatest Aussie comebacks. Kieren has indeed been one who gained immensely by the media coverage.

Media hype had positive effects on several other performers, but most particularly two mentioned highly by the schoolchildren, the female hockey team and Michael Diamond, a shooter. The Hockeyroos endured much pre-Olympic pressure to perform well. They were touted as gold medal favorites constantly, and were able to read of this favoritism in Sydney newspapers available in the Games Village (Hinds 1996, p. 27). Michael Diamond, on the other hand, was not well known before the Games, but won the first Aussie

Gold of the Games. He is from the small city of Goulburn and was unemployed. Needless to say, the huge amount of publicity he gathered after his win resulted in several job offers. It is fair to say that the publicity engendered for these athletes had a major role to play in the schoolchildren's survey item on preferences for best performances. Would the students have voted differently had they not been influenced by the TV, radio or newspaper coverage? Some commitment on the part of the media was evident toward promoting national pride, and undoubtedly will influence the public in the lead up to the 2000 Games. All of this supports Guttman's theory that nationality is one of the strongest forms of identification. The spectator's "identification is derived from some sociological category, physical aspect, or personality trait that she or he shares (or would like to share) with the athlete." (1996, p. 219). In the Olympic environment, with many nationalities readily displayed via uniforms and flags, it is easy to identify with an athlete from your own country. Guttman's theory was proven in the survey results in terms of attachment to country for Australian schoolchildren, but their choice of US athletes could be attributed to the choice of sport, medal success or personality of the athlete, or extensiveness of media coverage.

Summary and conclusion

The use of athletes as entertainers and the Olympic Games as entertainment has grown way out of proportion to what Coubertin envisioned. Sport is much more commercialized, forcing athletes to spend much more time in their preparation and encouraging National Olympic Committees to contribute more funds to help prepare them. Time and a multiplicity of other factors have become so valuable to some athletes that they do not wish to live in the Olympic Village for more days than their respective competitions. This undermines Coubertin's true purpose of the Village, to bring the Olympic family together and to espouse the ideals emanating from foreign friendships.

Through the ease of travel today, it is possible to say that more athletes are traveling to competitions outside of their countries, and that therefore internationalism is promoted more often than once every four years. The ever-imposing presence of the media results in global sports reporting, escalating the need for billion dollar efforts to broadcast the Olympic Games worldwide. What a contrast Sydney's coverage will be to Melbourne's 1956 Games when black and white telecasts had only just begun in Australia.

It is hoped that by the time of the Sydney Olympics in 2000 that there will be ample demonstration of Coubertin's ideals. However, in common with its predecessors the Sydney Games will no doubt focus on a lesser goal of a tally count of medals for respective countries. Australia's national pride will again be built on the success of the Games themselves as well as the success of its pre-Games favorite athletes. Never having been a 'winner' of the Games, Australia will focus on doing its 'personal best', goals which have been set per sport and aligned with the economic vision for the Games. The national and political struggle, the quest for victory, prestige and money, the pushing of a Western agenda, are often destructive and at variance with Coubertin's ideals of a peaceful internationalism.

Despite these pursuits, or perhaps because of them, the Olympic Games retain their attraction. The survey of Sydney schoolchildren demonstrated that they had appreciation, sympathy, even empathy for athletes of other countries, as well as for Australia's. Every four years nations join together in celebration with rituals and ceremonies defining themselves and others and professing once again the ideals proclaimed by Baron Pierre de Coubertin last century. It is these same ideals, nurtured and developed, that the Sydney Olympics intend to carry forward to the 21st century.

References

Coubertin, P. (1898). Does cosmopolitan life lead to international friendliness? The American Monthly Review of Reviews, (April) 434.

Guttman, A. (1995). The Modern Olympics: a sociopsychological interpretation. In: Barney, R.K. (ed.), Issues in Modern Olympic History and Analogy, University of Western Ontario: Centre of Olympic Studies.

Hinds, R. (1996). Hockeyroos must cope with great expectations. Sydney Morning Herald, Aug. 1: 1.

Loland, S. (1994). Pierre de Coubertin's ideology of Olympism from the perspective of the history of ideas. In: Barney, R.K. & Meier, K.V. (eds.), Critical reflections on Olympic Ideology: Second International Symposium for Olympic Research. University of Western Ontario: Centre of Olympic Studies, 26-45.

Kogoy, P. (1996). World's greatest. The Sun-Herald, Aug. 11: 54-55.

Morgan, W.J. (1994). Coubertin's theory of Olympic internationalism: a critical reinterpretation. Barney, R.K. & Meier, K.V. (eds.), Critical reflections on Olympic Ideology: Second International Symposium for Olympic Research. University of Western Ontario: Centre of Olympic Studies, 10-25.

O'Brien, C. (1997). The 1996 Olympic Games reviewed by Sydney schoolchildren (presentation at the Sporting Traditions XI Conference of the Australian Society for Sports History). Edith Cowan University, Perth, W. A. 30th June-3rd July, 1997.

Phillips, D.R. (1992). Australian women at the Olympic Games. NSW: Kangaroo Press.

Chapter 21

The distinction between the English and American educational concept of amateurism and its influence on the formation of the Olympic Movement

Stephan Wassong
German Sport University Cologne, Germany

The tremendous influence of politics, media and business on the Olympic movement disguises the fact that the re-establishment of the modern Olympic Games was conceived as an educational reform movement. In Coubertin's Olympic thoughts one can find the critique of culture that dealt with the one-sidedness and doubtfulness of educational concepts regarded as inviolable in the 19th century. Coubertin next to other well-known pedagogues criticises the emphasis of a „pure intellectualism" (Hojer 1968, p. 22) in traditional education and calls for one adapted to the new human environment created by technology and industrialization. In modern education more importance should be given to the development of character than to the teaching of purely scientific and humanistic knowledge (Hojer 1ff.). According to this educational maxim, Coubertin regards the traditional dualistic concept of mankind separating mind and body from each other as obsolete and he increases the value of physical education in the educational process. For him physical exercises should not be regarded as antagonists of intellectual education but rather as an useful educational means for the development of characters (Carl-Diem-Institut 1967, 6f.).

By what Coubertin now describes as Olympism his idea is expressed to develop by athleticism a system of moral values preparing human beings for the modern living conditions of a competitive society. As the critique of culture was hotly disputed beyond France Coubertin interprets Olympism as an educational formula for all nations. So, from its very beginning Olympism was conceived as a global enterprise which came into existence by the endeavours of an international network in which American, British and French representatives took the leading role. Additionally, Coubertin tries to use the international dimension of the Olympic movement as a stage for peace education. International athletic events should offer nations a possibility to engage in peaceful competition and, above all, to become acquainted with each other in order to reduce war-creating tendencies such as distrust and prejudices (Quanz 1993, 191ff.).

But Coubertin aims at realizing his concept of an educational athleticism by developing internationally valid amateur rules which should protect the educational aims of amateur athleticism against the constantly growing danger of professionalism. Coubertin claims that professionalism lacks educational potential of any kind because commercialization in athleticism is often closely connected with the manipulation of competitions and leads to a motivation which is strictly based on extrinsic factors of financial kind (Carl-Diem-Institut 1971, 2f.).

On his study trips in England and America Coubertin gained important experiences with an educational concept of amateur athletics. In both countries he orientated himself on the endeavours to use amateur athletics as an effective educational means by protecting it against professionalism. In this process of orientation - which was, of course, decisive for the later formulated concept of Olympism - Coubertin was confronted with two concepts of amateurism which were both educational but which differed from each other in their social exclusiveness.

The educational class - orientated amateur idea

In Olympic historical research it is maintained that Coubertin was stimulated for his study trips to the English elitist educational institutions by Taine's *Notes sur Angleterre* and by the Hughes's famous novel *Tom Brown 's* Schooldays. Based on a mixture of fiction and reality Coubertin reports enthusiastically in articles and books on the public schools` and universities` educational programmes which has been extended by different kinds of athletic sports.

Concerning this topic it is relevant to point out that the noble educational institutions visited by Coubertin produced an amateur idea by which the educational values of athleticism, as well as the social exclusiveness of athleticism, were secured. Apart from the teaching of humanistic ideals the British public schools and universities aimed at forming their pupils and students to gentlemen. In athletic sports British educators saw a useful means for the education of gentlemen. Cricket, hockey, soccer, rowing, track and field competitions were said to teach the basic traits of a prospective gentleman such as tolerance, self-confidence, self-control, self-determination, honesty and ambition.

But the educational concept of amateurism remained a privilege of the noble educational institutions. Whereas the education of a social elite was the first and foremost educational aim of the public schools and universities, the disciplination of the masses was the educational task of the state schools. So the athletic games of the Etonians were said to be inappropriate activities for the masses. Instead of them pupils at the state schools were taught in the kind of physical activity which promote work, health, obedience, discipline and military efficiency. To this end the pupils were forced to engage in various systems of drill and gymnastic exercises (Ingham & Beamish 1993, p. 181). To be more critical one can claim that it was exactly those activities which were of little value in the character training of gentlemen.

Implicitly the gentleman education of the noble educational institutions even led to the maintaining of the class differences in athleticism in a non-educative environment. Born out of the desire to play athletic sports among one's equals even after the education at the public schools and universities, the amateur thought functioned as a means of social distinction by using "gentleman", "sportsman" and "amateur" as synonyms. The social status of a gentleman was used to regulate both the membership in a club and the eligibility at amateur athletic competitions. The Amateur Athletic Club founded by students in 1868 drew up the following rule for an amateur:

> *"An amateur is any gentleman who has never competed in an open competition, or for public money, or for admission money, and who has never at any period of his life taught or assisted in the pursuit of athletic exercises as a means of livelihood or is a mechanic, artisan or labourer"* (Lovesy 1979, p. 22).

The exclusion of workers from amateur athletic competitions was not only justified by the lack of the workers` gentleman - education but also by the shallow argument that workers would train their muscles in their daily manual work and would, therefore, have an illegal advantage in competitions with gentlemen. Additionally, it was claimed that workers do not respect the rules of the fair-play concept because their motivation for taking part in an athletic competition was supposedly directed by profiteering. It becomes obvious that by this class-orientated concept of amateurism which, of course, aimed more at preserving the social exclusiveness of athleticism than at guaranteeing equal opportunities in competitions not only gentleman and amateur were synonyms but also working-class and professional.

Although the English concept of amateurism was still marked by a strict class-consciousness (Ingham & Beamish 1993, p. 181) tendencies of democratization were recognizable in the fading 19th century because many associations, apart from the Amateur Rowing Association, dropped the gentleman-paragraph and some private and religious organizations tried to extend the educational value of athleticism to a much wider social spectrum. Informally an interpretation of amateurism remained closely connected with a gentleman - and he was educated at the noble public schools and universities.

The educational democratic amateur idea

A scholarly interpretation of Coubertin's sojourns in America is a neglected field of research in Olympic history and pedagogy up till now. Unlike the research on Coubertin's trips to England, even the more topical essays on the formative years of the Olympic movement lack some kind of an interpretative approach to Coubertin's visits in America in 1889 and 1892/93. By traditionally remaining on a purely descriptive level it has been neglected to ask in which way American educators or politicians had influenced Coubertin's Olympic thoughts, and to what extent the American system of an educational athleticism itself served as a model for Coubertin's Olympic enterprise.

A first approach to this new topic is that Coubertin was confronted with the initial impulses of the progressive movement during his America sojourns. It is central for our topic that in this progressive movement thoughts were always active in using the educational value of athletic amateurism as an effective educational means for socio-political purposes. But the representatives of the progressive movement did not regard amateur athleticism as an educational means that could only be used in the education of prospective gentlemen but rather as a class-transcending educational means for the alleviation of social misstandings, social upheavals and state-threatening cultural diversity caused by industrialization and the masses of immigrants which had been pouring into the USA at the end of the 19th century. By a more democratic formula of amateurism designed to teach respect for law and constitutionalism, discipline, tolerance, democratic attitudes and, above all, designed to assimilate immigrants into the American culture progressives aimed at adapting Americans to a modern environment (Dyreson 1995, p. 205). According to the progressive historian F. Paxon athleticism functioned as a social technology by which the USA developed into a unified, modern and democratic society (Paxon 1917, 143 ff.).

Now, it becomes interesting to elaborate that Coubertin had to be confronted by his studies of American athleticism, by his interest in the American educational system and by his contacts with American progressive - minded professors and politicians with the initial endeavours of realizing the educational spirit of a democratic athleticism.
Particularly, by his close relationship to W.M. Sloane, professor at Princeton, one of the founders of the American college sports and organiser of the US - Olympic team for Athens 1896, and by his acquaintance with Th. Roosevelt, president of the USA from 1901 to 1908 and founder of the strenuous - life

movement, Coubertin knew two Americans (MacAloon 1984, p. 124) who sympathized with the educational aims of the progressives and who, therefore, worshipped the American democratic conception of amateurism as an important educational means for national purposes (Dyreson 1995, pp. 136-193). In his essay *Professionalism in sports*, which was originally published in 1890 in the magazine *North American Review*, Roosevelt describes this democratic orientated amateur thought:

> "*In England the average professional is a man who works for his living, and the average amateur is one who does not; whereas with us the amateur usually is, and always ought to be, a man who, like other American citizens, works hard at some regular calling - it matters not what; so long as it is respectable - while the professional is very apt to be a gentleman of more or less elegant leisure, aside from his special pursuit*" (Roosevelt 1926, p. 587).

As one can see the terms worker and professional were not used as synonyms in the USA and, therefore, the concept of amateurism failed at serving as a means of social distinction. Additionally, one can interpret that ROOSEVELT places the "gentleman" in close proximity to the "professional". The educational aim of amateurism is not the prospective gentleman but rather the "useful citizen" (Roosevelt 1926, p. 586). This can also be proved by the following quotation:

> "*Our object is to get as many of our people as possible to take part in manly, healthy, vigorous pasttimes, which will benefit the whole nation*" (Roosevelt 1926, p. 587).

An outcome of the progressives' endeavours was the spread of athleticism in the nation's high schools, a nation-wide interest in the YMCA movement, the emergence of the Playground- and Park-Movement, and the founding of working class athletic clubs. This popularisation was and is interpreted by many historians as an essential democratizing force in American society (Baker 1983, 6).

But the democratic orientation of the amateur concept also led to harsh criticism. The most famous critic was the anglophil American sports journalist Caspar Whitney. He was so impressed by the class-restrictive amateur definition of the Royal Henley Regatta that he constantly demanded the introduction of this concept of amateurism in the USA. The following quotation taken from his book *A Sporting Pilgrimage* is evidence of his affinity for the English amateur concept:

"There is no reason why we should not have a Henley in America; but we cannot under present rulings. Why there should be such a constant strife to bring together in sport the two divergent elements of society that never by any chance meet elsewhere" (Whitney 1894, p. 163).

Coubertin´s growing affinity for the USA

A detailed analysis of primary and secondary sources of Coubertin's America sojourns can lead to further interpretations of the following thesis formulated by MacAloon:

"He [Coubertin] returned to France a passionate publicist for the American way, the United states having to no small degree replaced England in his heart" (MacAloon 1984, p. 124).

Coubertin himself mentions his interest in the American system of athleticism in his article *The re-establishment of the Olympic Games* that was published in the American magazine *The Chautauquan* in 1894. In this article Coubertin is so emotionally touched by the atmosphere at the yearly football festivals held on Thanksgiving Day that he describes it as an Olympic flair (Coubertin 1894, p. 698).

Coubertin's knowledge of the educational instrumentalization of amateur athleticism which, of course, had been built up by his experiences with the English formula of an educational athleticism, was deepened on his study trips in America. In America Coubertin found a prospering state whose strength and sensitivity he traced back to the power of athleticism (MacAloon 1984, p. 125) and, above all, in which education was adapted to a new human environment. In the ideology of American reformers Coubertin's vision of democracy as the cornerstone of athleticism (Carl-Diem-Institut 1967, 7 ff.) as he mentioned it in various essays approached some kind of reality.

For Coubertin himself amateurism should not function as a means of social distinction. In his article for the *Chautauquan*_magazine he criticises the English class-orientated way of thinking that does not fit into the rising age of democracy:

"It is surely a mistake to refuse to a workingman the right to become an amateur, and to connect with manual labor the thought of professionalism. The discord between this decayed legislation and our democratic age is sharp" (Coubertin 1894, p. 699).

The democratic understanding of amateurism served as a model for Coubertin's pedagogical thoughts and was favoured over the class restrictive English concept of amateurism at the Congress for the Re-Establishment of the Olympic Games. It is no accident that Sloane, who in his essays does not tire of stressing the importance of amateurism and democracy as cornerstones of a truthful Olympism (Sloane 1912, 408 ff.), held at the congress the office of the vice-president in the commission dealing with the amateur question.

Concluding remarks

Concluding we can say that a more profound analysis of Coubertin's America sojourns can and should lead to a more serious consideration of the American influence on the Olympic Movement. The current results of research allow to make statements about Coubertin's growing interest in the political, educational and social situation of America and about his contacts to a circle of progressives who influenced his thoughts on the pedagogical orientation of the Olympic enterprise, and above all, who gave support to the organisation of both the Congress of the Re-Establishment of the Olympic Games 1894 and the first Olympic Games in Athens 1896. The concluding quotation shows that in view of the successful formation and development of the Olympic Movement Coubertin owes his gratitude not only to the English side, mostly represented by the legend of Th. Arnold, but even to the American one:

> "In doing so I evoke the memory of Theodore Roosevelt, of William Sloane ....and so many of my American friends who have worked willingly with me, understood me and sustained me throughout that long period in which I have had to struggle throughout the world .agianst the lack of understanding of public opinion ill-prepared to appreciate the value of the Olympic revival" (Coubertin 1937, p. 17).

References

Baker, W.J. (1983). The rise of organized sports. In: Baker, W.J. & Carrol, J.M. (eds.): Sports in modern America. St. Louis, pp. 3-15.

Coubertin, P. de (1894). The re-establishment of the Olympic Games. The Chautauquan, 19, 696-700.

Coubertin, P. de (1937). Olympic Leader. The New York Times September, 17.

Carl-Diem-Institut (Ed.) (1967). Pierre de Coubertin. Der olympische Gedanke. Reden und Aufsätze. Schorndorf.

Carl-Diem-Institut (Ed.) (1971). Die Olympischen Spiele 1896. Köln.

Dyreson, M. (1989). America's athletic missionaries: the Olympic Games and the creation of a national culture, 1896 - 1936. Dissertation , Arizona.

Hojer, E. (1968). Olympia - oder: der Sport zwischen Pädagogik und Ideologie. Veröffentlichung der Deutschen Sporthochschule Köln Heft.5. Köln 1968.

Ingham, A. & Beamish, R. (1993). The industrialisation of the United States and the „Bourgeoisification" of American sport. In: Dunning, E., Maguire, J. & Pearton, R. (eds.): The sports process. A comparative and developmental approach. Champaign, II., 115-148.

Lovesey, P. (1979): The official centenary history of the Amateur Athletic Association. Enfield.

MacAloon, J. (1984). This great symbol. Pierre de Coubertin and the origins of the modern Olympic Games. Chicago / London.

Paxon, F. L. (1917). The rise of sport. Mississippi Valley Historical Review 4, 143-168.

Quanz, D. R. (1993). Die Gründung des IOC im Horizont von bürgerlichem Pazifismus und sportlichem Internationalismus. In: Gebauer, G. (ed.): Die Aktualität der Sportpädagogik. St. Augustin, 191-216.

Roosevelt, Th. (1926). Professionalism in sports. In: Roosevelt, Th:, American ideals. the strenuous life. 13. New York, 583-588.

Sloane, W.M. (1912). The Olympic Idea - its origin, foundation, and progress. The Century Magazine 84, 2, 408 - 414.

Whitney, C. (1894). A sporting pilgrimage. New York, N.Y.

Part D

Sports challenging the world

Chapter 22

Sport for All ! ?
Variations of inclusion in Germany,
France and Great Britain

Ilse Hartmann-Tews
German Sport University Cologne, Germany

Many papers within the field of the sociology of sport and leisure have identified general cross-cultural trends in sports. Amongst others, these general
trends include increasing participation in sport and physical exercise up to the
1980s, growing demographic variety of participation, i.e. processes of
democratisation in participation, engagement in a broader and diversified
range of sports and a pluralisation of organisational settings. The focus of this
paper is to gain a better understanding of the social processes that lie behind
these general trends - and probably cause some international variations. To
gain a better understanding of international variations we are going to analyse
in more detail the development of Sport for All in three countries: Germany,
France and Great Britain. Unlike modernisation theories which analyse
changes in demand and supply as a part of social change, continuous and
unfolding naturally through time, we take a closer look to the role and
strategies of organisational agents and their impact on inclusion and structural
change of social systems.

Sport for All - a sociological perspective

Sport for All is a rather young idea in modern society. The sixties can be
considered as the pioneering period of Sport for All in Europe, and the
seventies can be considered as a period of reflection and incubation of Sport
for All. The European Sport for All Charter was ratified in 1975 and relates to a
comprehensive sports policy which attempts to extend to all sections of the
community the beneficial effects of sport on health, social, educational and
cultural development. With this document the European Council expresses
the belief that all its member countries should foster inclusion of people into
the sports system (Marchand 1990, p. 12).
To understand the challenge the European Charter created for the sport
systems it is crucial to realise that the concept of „sport for all" is strongly in

variance with the traditional sport concept. Sport in this context „is to be understood in the modern sense of free, spontaneous physical activity engaged in during leisure time; its functions ... being recreation, amusement and relaxation. Sport in this sense includes sports proper and various other physical activities provided they demand some effort" (Marchand 1990, p. 3). It does not only include sport as such - competitive games and sport -, but also and especially multifarious forms of recreational physical activities.

To illuminate this challenge for the sports policy and the identity of the sport system it is helpful to recur to some basic elements of differentiation theory. According to theories of differentiation there are three cornerstones of any social system (cp. Hartmann-Tews 1996, 31 ff.) : (a) a central idea to frame orientation of action taken in this social context; (b) a socio-structural foundation, i.e. an institutional framework and specialised roles that support and perpetuate this central frame of action, and (c) the inclusion and potential access of all sections of the population to the social system.

The central idea and reference point of any action within the sports system has been the communication of physical ability and increase in performance. Looking back to the end of the 18th and beginning of the 19th century when sporting activities began to take clear shape of a social system we see - especially in Great Britain - competition, performance and improvement as the nucleus and reference point of all sporting activities. Looking back it seems that „communication of physical ability and competitive physical performance" is the spearhead of differentiation (Stichweh 1990). This general orientation of action can be seen as the driving force to carry out regional and national meetings, to codify plays, to establish rules of competition and gambling, to create clubs for gentlemen-amateurs, to compete nation-wide, to integrate clubs and associations into federations, and to establish national Olympic Committees as well as an international Olympic Committee. In this context voluntary organisations are the trailblazer of a complex sociostructural foundation of the sports systems throughout Europe. The accomplishment of a self-contained social system requires the inclusion of all people. Translated to the full establishment of sport as a social system of society this implies that all sections of the community should have access to sport and physical recreation.

These three processes of social differentiation are the central cornerstones to secure the accomplishment of a self-contained social system. From a theoretical point of view inclusion of people into the social system is a crucial factor for any social system to get recognition and to secure autonomy of action. Against this background it is assumed that sports systems are trying to integrate people into their structure - thus being the central idea of the European policy Sport for All.

Inclusion into the sports systems

In order to identify the degree and feature of inclusion into the sports systems of Germany, France and Great Britain we can look at two indications for the measurement of inclusion in sport: the most often used indication is self-reported participation rates as they are documented in survey data; the other one is membership in voluntary sport associations.

Self-reported participation in sport

There are several well-known methodological reservations concerning the reliability and validity of survey data. Nevertheless, most recent comparative analyses on single country studies of participation in sport allow for some empirically based assumptions (see Hartmann-Tews 1996; Andreff et al. 1994).

In Germany, Great Britain and France: (a) participation in recreational physical activities and sport has been rising throughout the past 25 years; (b) the number of people who formerly had been underrepresented in sport - elderly people, women, socially deprived - is growing steadily; (c) the global participation rate in recreational physical activities and sport in these countries seems to be about 60% of the population aged 16 and over; (d) if differences are discernible it seems that participation in France is slightly lower than in Germany or Great Britain

Membership in sports clubs

Range and preciseness of official statistics of membership in clubs vary enormously in these countries. Although Great Britain can be said to be the trailblazer of the development of voluntary organisations in sport, there are only few systematically collected data on voluntary sector sport in Britain today.

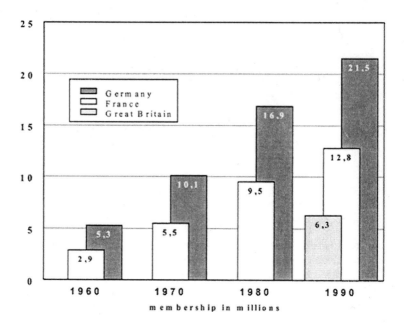

Figure 1 : Membership in Sports Clubs in Germany, Great Britain and France
1960-1990

With reference to 1990 there are at least two notable differences [1]. First, it is
evident that the voluntary associations in Germany include many more people
than those in France and Great Britain. In order to derive a comparative rate
of inclusion in the voluntary sector of sport, multiple memberships have to be
considered and the ratio of net members of sports clubs to the population of
the respective country has to be calculated. The results then show that in
Germany about 30% of the population is a member of at least one sports club
compared with about 17% of the population in France and about 12% in Great
Britain (Ministère de la Jeunesse et des Sports 1988, 1992; Sports Council
1991; Deutscher Sportbund 1990). Second, the social structure of the clubs is
different: comparing France and Germany on the basis of detailed statistics
there is some evidence that French clubs include less women (28% vs. 37%
in 1990) and the increase of female membership from 1960 to 1990 is only
small. In addition French clubs include far less elderly people than German
clubs. Whereas in Germany the percentage of adult membership has been
continuously increasing over the past thirty years (from about 50% in the 60s
up to 65% 1990) the respective percentage in France is constantly low at
about 25% (Hartmann-Tews 1996).

Together these findings on self-reported participation rates in physical exercise and membership in sports clubs show similarities in the development of Sport for All as well as marking differences. Overall there are increasing participation rates as well as a growing variety of people who take part in physical activities and sport. At the same time there are different rates of inclusion into the sports clubs in general and especially in respect to social aspects such as gender and age. The inclusion of people into the traditional structure of the sports systems is highest in Germany and lowest in Great Britain and the intention of Sport for All seems to be far more adequately realised in German sports clubs than in French.

How and why have these national features developed against the background of a) the theoretically derived assumption of a uniform interest in inclusion of people and b) a uniform and common European Sport for All Charter?

There is a traditional assumption in the study of voluntary associations that Germany is a 'nation of joiners'. This is a comparative statement, yet, surprisingly there has been little comparative research and none I know about sport association membership. Looking at a most recent comparative study of voluntary association membership in 15 countries, it turns out that membership levels in Germany and Great Britain are almost the same and range in the middle of the countries analysed - this ranking is even true when excluding membership in churches or religious organisations and in trade unions (Curtis et al. 1992, p. 143). Trying to explain differences two general effects may play a role: First, effects of a demand pull, and second, effects of a supply push.

Effects of a *demand pull,* i.e. a growing demand of people in physical recreation and sport result from the concurrence of a series of factors. These include an increase in leisure time, a higher standard of living, the acceptance of sport as a factor of health and well-being, growing interest via media-coverage etc. These factors are prerequisites and driving force for a growing demand in physical recreation and fitness activities and may well explain the general growth in the number and in the variety of participants in sport. Although, these effects do not explain differences of inclusion into the sports clubs.

This may be explained by variations in *supply push*, i.e. the organisation of sport and physical activities and provision of respective facilities. Participation in sport is an optional interest, it is a leisure time activity chosen from a diverse range of alternatives on a voluntary basis and against an individual background. Thus, people have to be attracted. They have to be convinced that sport and physical recreation is just what they need, what they want and which can be best organised within the voluntary sector.

To explain differences of inclusion via variations in supply push the following sections take a closer look at three organisational agents, their interest and their strategies. These three 'variables' are firstly sports clubs and associations as the structural grass and root basis of the sports systems, secondly sports confederations that integrate clubs at the national level, and thirdly governmental agencies as intervening agencies into the sports systems. [2]

Interest of the voluntary sector at grass root level

Looking at the interest of the sports clubs and associations two general features can be identified. Following the theoretical perspective of recent work on differentiation theories it is supposed that voluntary sports associations are interested in keeping and broadening the autonomy of their action. The process of including a growing number of people seems to be a very rational strategy for them to put into effect these interests. Increase of membership can be looked at as a driving force for expanding the structural fabric of voluntary associations which in turn helps to meet the demands of their membership more adequately. Thus inclusion is likely to enhance the significance of organisations and to broaden the latitude and autonomy of their action. Against this theoretical background one can assume clubs and associations to become active agencies in the realisation of Sport for All.

On the other hand we know that competition, performance and improvement are the central reference points of action of the sport systems and the traditional values and orientations of the clubs. As this concept is in variance with Sport for All, we expect that voluntary associations have an ambivalent attitude towards Sport for All, take muted action and pursue the effort to 'play a waiting game'. Indeed there is overwhelming empirical evidence, that in all three countries most of the clubs and federations did not actively foster Sport for All (Hartmann-Tews 1996, 278ff). In this context the size of clubs plays an eminent role. Clubs and associations that are small in size are based on social networks, mutual support via voluntary work and confidence in social benefits out of it. For them inclusion of many more people implies the integration not only of a wide spectrum of performance ability but also of social heterogeneity. These effects of inclusion may well be able to spoil social integrity and community of clubs. Although there has been empirical evidence that in all three countries most of the clubs did not actively foster Sport for All we can assume that the size of clubs is an intervening factor in the extent of resistance to inclusion. A closer look at the data of sports clubs in 1970, at the beginning of Sport for All, reveals that, contrary to the findings of membership figures, the number of sports clubs in Germany was lower than in France and Great Britain. On average there were 250 members in German sports clubs in 1970 - and about 90 in French clubs. The size of British clubs is assumed to be even smaller, ranging at about 40. These findings are likely to support the data about variations of inclusion into the voluntary sector sport.

Action taken by the sport confederations

Germany: Sport for All - the elaboration of values and differentiation of functions

The historical setting for the development of sport in Germany after World War II was such that the structural and moral fundamentals of the organisations were broken down. Organised sport in Germany had to regain recognition and acceptance not only in view of the Allies but in view of the people in Germany in general. Thus from the beginning on the German confederation of voluntary sector sport (Deutsche Sportbund - DSB) was in favour of Sport for All and developed manifold activities to foster inclusion of people into the sports system, amongst them: (a) elaboration of central positive effects of participation as there are educational values, health-related positive effects (prevention and rehabilitation) and social integrative effects; (b) public campaigns to attract people who had not (regularly) taken part in sport (adults, women, older people); (c) professionalization of internal structures by establishing specialised committees and working units for Sport for All at all administrative levels; (d) lobbying at governmental level and convincing central agents of the political system about the relevance and positive effects of physical recreation and sport for the social system as a whole.

With this manifold strategy the DSB not only attracted millions of people, but the DSB successfully gained state support and secured a range of tax reliefs of its member-organisations. Of course, these positive effects helped the DSB to convince the clubs to foster Sport for All and to implement leisure sport activities and physical recreation right beside its traditional structures of performance and elite sport.

France: The legacy of Coubertin and strategies of social closure

In France the structure of the sport systems strongly reflects the support of the Olympic idea. In 1972 the sport confederation of the voluntary sport sector amalgamated with the National Olympic Committee to form one macro-organisation: The "Comité National Olympique Sportif Français" (CNOSF). The central ideas of Pierre de Coubertin - the strive for excellence in sport - remained unanimously the central reference point of action for sports clubs. Within this context most of the federations implemented strategies of social closure that excluded all sorts of leisure sport activities or physical recreation.

Against this background it is symptomatic that France had some difficulties to find a label for the "Sport for All" initiative of the European Council. A representative of the CNOSF commented in 1973: "There is too much included in the term "for all" (Grunewald 1973)".

Turning to the development of Great Britain we expect that the British sport confederation did not foster the idea of Sport for All either.

Great Britain: The legacy of particularism

The Central Council of Physical Recreation (CCPR) is the sport confederation of voluntary sport sector in Great Britain (CCPR 1991). Even before the general European Sport for All initiative the CCPR launched its initiative called „opportunities for all" and in the 60s Prince Philip - long-standing president of the CCPR - characterised its work as follows: „The CCPR does two things - it introduces all forms of physical recreation to people and it introduces people to all forms of physical recreation" (Evans 1974, p. 86). This characterisation is surprising as we see from the data that British sports clubs include a lower percentage of people in sports clubs than French clubs, although the CNOSF and its federations showed a long-standing persistence against Sport for All.

A closer look at the interior structure of the British sport system reveals a constellation of NGOs that does not seem to be very supportive to foster and organise Sport for All. The structure of the British sport system is characterised by fragmentation and, - as insiders put it - „confused roles and responsibilities" (Sports Council 1991). Although the United Kingdom is a unitary and not a federal state, most sports set up individual governing bodies for each of the Home Countries England, Wales, Scotland and Northern Ireland. In addition there are various sports that are organised along gender lines, separating males from females. Moreover various sports organise their sub-disciplines separately in specialised federations (Sports Council 1991).

This fragmentation has had its impact on the implementation of politics of the CCPR. Looking back to the 70s and 80s it is obvious that the CCPR was unsuccessful in bringing together the heterogeneous and particularistic interests of its member organisations. None of them really wanted to delegate power to the CCPR and empower it to act as an authority or a pressure agency for the benefit of the voluntary organisations. Quite different from the DSB the CCPR never established working units that reflect the goals to be set and the action to be taken to reach these objectives. The inability of the CCPR to put into effect its initiative of 'opportunities for all' and to mobilise the federations and clubs is closely linked to the role of government and its intervention. To explain the unexpected differences in inclusion of France and Great Britain a closer view at the role of government is quite helpful.

Action taken by the governments

Great Britain: the development of a social service

Concern about male juvenile delinquency and the identified gap of recreational and sporting facilities led to the establishment of an Advisory Sports Council in 1965 that was given executive powers in 1972. The Sports Council is an institutional body that is attempting to mediate between the requirements of social investment strategies and the plurality of demands from various recreational communities and lobbies (Coalter et al. 1986, p. 22). As such it is neither a governmental organisation (GO) nor a non-governmental-organisation (NGO) it is a QUANGO - a quasi-non-governmental-organisation. In 1975 the Sports Council adopted the 'Sport for All' Charter and sought not only to modernise the elite sector but to promote and market sport as a good merit available for all. At the outset, the CCPR was effectively incorporated into the new state-appointed organisation. From the mid-1970s onwards a growing number of tasks made professionalization necessary and inevitably led to the replacement of the personnel. More and more emphasis was placed on managerial efficiency and accountability with the attendant shift from providing a framework for voluntarism to a more interventionist approach. Thus - quite different from Germany - British clubs were never incorporated into the Sport for All campaigns of the Sports Council. These instead mobilised public funding for the expansion of public sector facilities as part of social service.

France: From excellence for all to a welfare service

In the 60s and 70s French policy was characterised by General de Gaulles project of restoring the nation's grandeur (its greatness). As a part of this project he also wanted to improve the international image of French sport, supported voluntary sport sector in their strive for excellence and made physical education in school a significant part in the idea of "excellence for all". Central strategies to put these ideas into effect were the establishment of clubs and federation at all levels of the education system in order to include as many young people as possible to allow for an efficient search for new talents and strong financial support of federations of Olympic sports.

Changing social conditions and governments led to new policies in the 80s with the expectation that sports federations should promote general welfare and foster Sport For All. This was quite new for the federations which had been striving solely for excellence and supporting the model of Coubertin. So to say, they were not willing and not prepared for sport for all activities - to them there was no reason to include the lesser talented or those who wanted to take part in physical activities for other reasons than high-level-competition e.g. for reasons of health, fitness and fun. Given the huge potential of state intervention into voluntary sport sector federations were manoeuvred into a difficult position and had to give up their traditional policy sooner or later. They did it later than expected by government, which as a consequence, led to the establishment of public sport centres. Nowadays, they are part of the cultural program of many regions and have become a central part of Sport for All programs.

Concluding remarks

The central intention of this paper was to convey a better understanding of international variations of inclusion into the sports systems by incorporating socio-structural configurations, agency and political factors into the analysis. Although it is impossible to examine the influence of three variables by comparing only three cases, i.e. three countries, this extract of a far more complex piece of research provides a glimpse of the social processes that produce different paths and paces of inclusion and structural changes of the sports systems.

References

Andreff, W., Bourg, J.-F., Halba, B. & Nys, J.-F. (1994). The economic importance of sport in Europe: financing and economic impact. Brussels: CDDS.

Central Council of Physical Recreation (1991). The organisation of sport and recreation in Britain. London: CCPR.

Coalter, F., Long, J. & Duffield, B. (1986). Rationale for public sector investment in leisure. London: Sports Council, ESRA.

Curtis, J. E., Grabb, E. G. & Baer, D. E. (1992). Voluntary association membership in fifteen countries: a comparative analysis. American Sociological Review, 57, 139-152.

Deutscher Sportbund (ed.) (1990). Deutscher Sportbund 1986-1990. Bericht des Präsidiums. Frankfurt am Main: DSB.

Evans, J. (1974). Service to sport: the story of the CCPR, 1935-1972. London: Pelham Books.

Grunewald, M. (1973). Sport für Alle in Frankreich. In: Deutscher Sportbund (Hrsg.): Trim and Fitness International. Report of Expert Conference in Frankfurt/M. 1973. Frankfurt a.M.: DSB, 42-43.

Hartmann-Tews, I. (1996). Sport für alle !? - Strukturwandel europäischer Systeme im Vergleich: Bundesrepublik Deutschland, Frankreich, Großbritannien. Schorndorf: Hoffmann.

Hartmann-Tews, I. (1998). Development of leisure sport and structural changes of the sports systems in Germany and Great Britain. In:

Hardmann, K. & Standeven, J. (eds.), Cultural diversity and congruence in physical education and sport. Aachen: Meyer & Meyer Sport, 205-221.

Kamphorst, T. & Roberts, K. (eds.) (1989). Trends in sports - a multi-national perspective. Enschede: Giordano Bruno.

Marchand, J. (1990). Sport for All in Europe. London: HMSO.

Ministère de la Jeunesse et des Sports (Hrsg.) (1988). Evolution des licences sportives 1975-1985. Paris: SEJS.

Ministère de la Jeunesse et des Sports (Hrsg.) (1992). Licences sportives et sections de clubs 1990. Tome I: Documentation de synthèse. Paris: SEJS.

Sports Council (1991). A digest of sports statistics for the UK. 3rd Edition. London, The Sports Council.

Stichweh, R. (1990). Sport - Ausdifferenzierung, Funktion, Code. Sportwissenschaft, 20, 4, 373-389.

Notes

[1] Data presented here do not refer to the development after 1990 because the unification of Germany implies the unification of two different sports systems, thus adding to the sample of three countries an additional „case".

[2] There are some important structural variations in the features of the three sports systems - for more details see Hartmann-Tews 1996, 1998.

Chapter 23

The evolution of sport participation in Flanders : a comparison between cities and municipalities

Lies Van Heddegem, Kristine De Martelaer and Paul De Knop
University of Brussels, Belgium

In this contribution it is our intention to sketch the evolution of the sport participation in Flanders, particularly taking into consideration the degree of urbanization.

For many years sport participation has been subject of many studies, including many social variables such as gender, age, profession,.... However the relationship between sport participation and the degree of urbanization appears to be a less frequently studied aspect. It is however obvious that the social environment in which someone is growing up and/or is living in, contains a number of stimuli or barriers that partly determine someone's sport participation. The social environment in itself is part of a network of many social characteristics which are constantly influencing eachother. This has to be taken into account while studying the social environment as a fragmented piece.

Research regarding the influence of the degree of urbanization on sport participation

We are presenting a chronological overview of the research over the years in Flanders regarding sport participation and the degree of urbanization.

Therefore we will point out a trend (by means of numbers), that could be derived from the results of the consulted research.

In 1964 (Van Mechelen) the relation between sport participation and social environment was mentioned for the first time. This study revealed a more varied sport participation in the urban environment in comparison with a more rural environment.

In 1969 Renson and Vermeulen (1969) found that the percentage of sport participants gradually increases as the degree of urbanization increases. People living in the city participate more in sport than those living in rural or semi-urban environments. Moreover these urban-rural differences were more explicit for women than men.

Ten years later, in 1979 three studies were conducted respectively in a rural municipality (Van Poyer & Lamon 1981), a medium-sized city (Vanreusel 1981) and a major city (Laporte et al. 1981). After comparing these three studies the highest degree of sport participation was noted in a medium-sized city (76%) and a major city (75%). The rural municipality came a little behind with a sport participation of 61%. One year later, the research of Bollen et al. (1980) showed similar results. Also in this research the sport participation in the rural municipalities was still represented insufficiently.   However the existing gap between the rural and the urban population in those days had become smaller than ten years earlier.   There was thus an obvious trend towards a geographically more equally spread sport participation in Flanders.

Ten years later, the research of Taks et al. (1991) clearly confirmed this trend. The sport participation in rural municipalities was almost similar to the sport participation in large agglomerations, respectively with 59,0% and 60,5% participants.

On the one hand this trend can be explained by the "Sport for All" policy which started in the seventies. The many campaigns promoted the idea that sport is good and healthy for everyone. The population clearly followed this policy and the threshold to sport participation was crossed by many. On the other hand we notice that sport infrastructure also influences these urban-rural differences.   Research into the situation and the need for sport accommodation, conducted in 1983 (Claeys et al. 1983), shows that there was more sport infrastructure in the more urbanized areas at that time. These sport infrastructure was also larger in average than those in the rural areas. This study also pointed out that 'more infrastructure' in a municipality stimulates people to participate in sport. This influence only had an effect from the level of 15 to 20 m^2 per 100 inhabitants, the standard postulated at that time by "Commissariaat-generaal voor de Bevordering van de Lichamelijke Ontwikkeling, de Sport en de Openluchtrecreatie" (Bloso) in order to stimulate people to participate in sport.

Next to the mentioned policy options which influenced sport participation, we have also taken into account the fluctuating, difficult to measure, social trends that influence our pattern of sport participation. Think of the increasing leisure time, the influence of top-class sport, sport advertising, new sports, ... We have to consider these social processes, despite the fact that the variables are difficult to measure.

From all this we can conclude that the differences in sport participation between the city and the rural areas by which existed in the sixties and seventies have faded in the eighties.

Our research

Today we notice that the gap in sport participation between cities and rural municipalities, that existed in the seventies and to a lesser extent in the eighties, no longer exists. Recent research (De Martelaer et al. 1998) again revealed urban-rural differences, this time however with a negative turn for the cities. It is shown that children living in urban areas participate less in sport than children living in rural municipalities. In this research youngsters between 9 and 12 years of age (N = 564) were asked about their sport participation in organized agencies. It regarded the extra-curricular school sport, the sport club and the municipal sport initiatives. For the data collection inquiries were used, in which youngsters in first instance were asked to indicate whether or not they participated in sport in the given sport organising agencies, after which they were asked to write about their experiences. These inquiries were conducted through an aselect clustersample in twelve schools in Flanders, six of which in a city and six of which in a municipality. These inquiries were conducted in class and in the presence of the poll-taker for further explanation in case of problems.

The results of this research showed that 44% (p<.05) of the children in urban schools was actively involved in at least one of the previously mentioned organisations, compared to 57% of the children from the more rural areas. If we consider the three organizing sport agencies - schoolsport, sport club and municipal sport - we notice that in all three organizations children from municipalities participate more in sport than children living in cities.

Although the sample in previous studies always included adults and youngsters, in this research we have only questionned children from 9 till 12 years of age. It has however been proven repeatedly that parents act as role model and in this way play a significant role in the sport socialization of their child (Sage, 1980 ; Yang et al., 1996). More specific, physically active parents will pass on their pattern of behaviour to their child, which will result in a higher sport participation of these children (Coley et al. 1992; Yang et al. 1996). That is why we can assume that the results of this study of children are a reflection of the sport participation of the population in general.

Discussion

We are thus noticing a shift in sport participation from the city to the rural areas. In the sixties and seventies the people living in the city clearly participated more often in sport, whereas today the inhabitants of more rural municipalities contemplate a higher sport participation.

As indicated above, the "Sport for All"-campaigns played an important role in this. Before the starting of these promotional activities sport had a strong urban cachet, and after that the whole population was sensitized to participate in sport. The "Sport for All"-policy also had its consequences on the local level, through the foundation of local sports departments. Every city, but also every municipality was granted subsidies for the foundation of their own sports department that was and still is charged with the local sport promotion and organization of promotional activities. These local initiatives stimulated and are still stimulating the local population, in large cities as well as in more rural municipalities, to participate in sport. Next to these increasing promotional efforts for sport, it seems founded to look into the city life and its inhabitants more closely, with regard to the decreasing sport participation in the cities. In comparison with the past due to its increasing administrative and commercial functions the city has increasingly dispelled its housing function (De Dijn 1991). The original citizens are now living in degenerated neighbourhoods, together with the large migrant families (Kesteloot 1996). The enormous increase in the number of allochtones has given some city neighbourhoods the style of a ghetto. These people in particular constitute a section of the population, which has difficulties engaging socially, and in particular in sport. Research shows for example that migrant youngsters participate much less in sport in an organized setting (De Knop et al. 1993). Especially migrant girls seems to have a low sport participation because they are obstructed by their religion.

The shift of the city population participating more in sport in the past to a more sporty rural population today, could be due to the ever more elaborated sports policy, the increasing number of migrants in the cities, ... and many other social processes - such as the increase in leisure time, the influence of parents,... - which have led to such a shift.

In this presentation we have cited a number of possible explanations. However this is such a complex phenomenon which could probably also be influenced (directly or indirectly) by many other variables. Therefore it is advisable in further research to investigate more profoundly, taking into account all possible influences.

References

Bollen, K., Claeys, U. & Hertogen, J. (1982). Sportbeoefening in Vlaanderen opnieuw bekeken. Leuven: Sociologisch Onderzoeksinstituut, Katholieke Universiteit Leuven, vol.4.

Claeys, U., Hertogen, J. & Mercy, M. (1983). Sporthallen in Vlaanderen : situatie en behoefte. Leuven: Sociologisch onderzoeksinstituut, Katholieke Universiteit Leuven.

Colley, A., Eglinton, E. & Elliott, E. (1992). Sport participation in middle childhood : association with styles of play and parental participation. International Journal of Sport Psychology, 23, 193-206.

De Dijn, H. (1991). Postmodernismen : de vlag en de lading. Een poging tot diagnose. Kultuurleven, 6, 18-25.

De Knop, P., Bollaert, L., De Martelaer, K., Theeboom, M., Van Engeland, E., Van Puymbroeck, L. & Verlinden, T. (1993). Onderzoek naar de integratie-mogelijkheden van de georganiseerde sport voor migrantenjongeren. Koninklijk Commissariaat voor het Migrantenbeleid.

De Martelaer, K., Van Heddegem, L. & De Knop, P. (1998). Kindgerichtheid van de sport, georganiseerd door gemeenten, sportclubs en scholen : de visie van kinderen. Tussentijdsrapport, OZR-project, Brussel : VUB.

Kesteloot, C. (1996). De verwaarlozing voorbij? Achtergestelde buurten en hun ontwikkelingskansen. In Hubeau B. & De Decker P. (eds.): In de ban van de stad. Berchem: EPO, 23-60.

Laporte, W., Claessens, B. & Benoit, E. (1981). Sportparticipatie in de grootstad Gent. Gent: Hoger Instituut voor Lichamelijke Opvoeding, R.U.Gent.

Renson, R. & Vermeulen, A. (1969). Sociale determinanten van de sportpraktijk bij Belgische volwassenen. Sport, 15, 25-39.

Sage, G.H. (1980). Parental influence and socialization into sport for male and female intercollegiate athletes. Journal of Sport and Social Issues, 4, 1-13.

Taks, M., Renson, R. & Vanreusel, B. (1991). Hoe sportief is de Vlaming ?, Een terugblik op 20 jaar sportbeoefening 1969-1989. Leuven: Instituut voor Lichamelijke Opleiding, K.U.leuven.

Van Mechelen, F. (1964). Vrijetijdsbesteding in Vlaanderen deel 1 : Een sociologisch onderzoek bij de aktieve Nederlandstalige bevolking van België. Antwerpen : Ontwikkeling.

Van Poyer, S. & Lamon, A. (1981). Sport in een landelijke gemeente. Brussel: Centrum voor navorsing van de vrijetijdsproblematiek.

Vanreusel, B., Devroye, W., De Meulder, B. & Renson, R. (1981). Sportparticipatie in een middelgrote stad. Leuven: Instituut voor Lichamelijke Opleiding, K.U.Leuven.

Yang, X., Telama, R. & Laakso, L. (1996). Parents' physical activity, socio-economic status and education as predictors of physical activity and sport among children and youths. International Review for the Sociology of Sport, 31, 273-289.

Chapter 24

The Canadian experience: federal government sport policy on the eve of the new millennium

Darwin M. Semotiuk
University of Western Ontario, Canada

For several decades, Canada has been held in high regard by the international sport community for the important contributions it has made in providing sport, fitness and recreation. This paper will examine the role that federal government sport policy has played in shaping Canada's amateur sport system. Since the publication of *Sport: The Way Ahead* (1992), the Canadian sports system has undergone a stimulating introspective assessment of its structure, function and future. Two important policy initiatives, the *Sport Funding Accountability Framework* (1995) and a *Business Plan for Sport* (1996) provide the foundation for current government policy in sport. More recently, three distinct themes have emerged. Firstly, Canada remains firmly committed to assigning a high priority for successful participation in international sport. Secondly, it is abundantly clear that the Canadian sport system is being strongly encouraged to become more self-sufficient and less reliant on government funding support. Thirdly, new resources have been identified to financially support athletes, coaches and expenses associated with international competition.

Motives underlying national government involvement in sport

In trying to develop a more complete understanding of the relationships that exist between the National Government and the system of sport, several penetrating questions arise concerning the nature of this connection. Why are National Governments involved in sponsoring sports program? For what purposes? Why are some national systems more involved than others? Is their degree of involvement dictated by a philosophical orientation of individualism or collectivism? The fact that there are not easy responses to these queries suggests the need for a scheme to determine reasons for involvement. An attempt is made to isolate the numerous motives for governmental participation with the realization that some of the reasons are openly proclaimed and obvious, whereas, some are more subtle, and consequently more difficult to detect.

A perusal of the literature providing a historical perspective on the role of National Government involvement, and the scrutiny of contemporary documents obtained from different countries results in the identification of several motives underlying the commitment of a National Government to support sport (Semotiuk 1981).

National Governments are motivated to participate in programs of sport for specific reasons. The motives that are outlined here are those which explain or justify a permanent intervention by the government into the domain of sport. Meynaud isolates three major reasons for government involvement. They are concern for the maintenance of public order; concern for physical condition, and affirmation of national prestige (Meynaud 1966). Using an expanded version of Meynaud's classification scheme, the motives underlying government involvement in sport can be further divided. It should be emphasized that each of these functions is not exclusive of the others, but rather they are often closely aligned and interrelated. In all, nine motives/functions can be identified; individualizing, socializing/nationalizing, international goodwill, national prestige, military, labour productivity, economic, political indoctrination and legislative (Semotiuk 1981).

In Canada, an analysis of the budgetary expenditures over the last three decades leads one to conclude that success in international sport remains as the most important motive and priority for government sports officials, politicians and decision makers.

Sport Canada: part of the Department of Canadian Heritage

The Department of Canadian Heritage was created about five years ago on June 25th, 1993 to be exact. In her first few weeks as Prime Minister of Canada, Kim Campbell, put her personal stamp on the structure of the Government of Canada by reducing the size of government by eliminating some departments and combining others. Canadian Heritage became a new Department made up of all or parts of previous Departments. For example, multiculturalism, official languages, human rights and national symbols came from Department of Communications; and national parks and national historic sites came from the Department of Environment. Sport came from the Department of Fitness and Amateur Sport, with the responsibility for fitness going to the Department of Health and Welfare. The creation of the Department of Canadian Heritage brought together, under one department, the various federal programs and policies which help define us as Canadians i.e., our shared values, our culture, our history, our peoples and our land.

The present Minister, the Honorable Sheila Copps, describes the Department of Canadian Heritage as the "soul of the Government of Canada" and talks about its central role in building a better Canada. This change has meant that sport has lost a dedicated minister solely responsible for sport. On the other hand, there is a perceived benefit to be realized in linking sport to other key elements of Canadian culture and identity, along with opportunity to position sport within the federal agenda.

It can be both argued and demonstrated that sport fits well within this construct and that sport is an integral component of Canadian culture and identity: (a) sport contributes to social cohesion and the development of communications - it is estimated that 1.9M Canadian aged 15 and over are volunteers in amateur sport; (b) sport helps define and reflect societal values; (c) sport provides opportunities to celebrate achievements of Canadian athletes at home and abroad.

Federal government involvement through Sport Canada contributes directly to three major objectives for the Department of Canadian Heritage: (a) enhancing pride in Canada; (b) encouraging participation in society; (c) contributing to economic growth i.e., a 1994-95 study estimated the direct and indirect impact of the sport and recreation sector reached 7.7B or 1.2% of GDP.

It is important to note that, from 1994 to 1997, all federal programs were subjected to a comprehensive assessment as part of a Federal Program Review. The following questions were posed: Is it still necessary and relevant ? Could it be done effectively by someone else? Is it an appropriate role for the Federal Government to play?

Sport Canada programs were not immune to this process and were also subjected to the review exercise. This resulted in an affirmation or continued federal commitment to sport, as an end in itself and for its many benefits to individuals and Canadian society. The predominant focus still remains on high performance sport.

Funding support for Canadian amateur sport

Since 1961, the Government of Canada has directly contributed in excess of one billion dollars (Canadian) in support of Fitness and Amateur Sport. It would be relatively safe to claim that approximately 80% of that amount has been directed towards high performance sport objectives. On an annual basis, the Federal Government spends approximately ninety million dollars on fitness and amateur sport programs. With the Government of Canada's global budget for 1998-99 set at $151.0 billion, this represents .060 of one percent of that total. Of particular concern to the Government and all Canadians is the matter of a 583.2 billion public debt for 1998-99 (*Budget Information* 1998, June 25, 1998).   On a more encouraging note, the federal government has proposed a balanced budget for 1998-99 and two years beyond. Expenditure control and expense reduction strategies are beginning to have immediate impact on the funding levels for amateur sport. Everyone in sport is being affected, and all organizations, without exception, have embarked on courses leading to greater fiscal self-sufficiency. Those sports organizations which have established strong ties with the corporate sector will be well positioned to deal with the anticipated reductions in Federal Government funding support.

What is sport Canada ?

Sport Canada is a branch of the Citizenship and Canadian Identity Sector within the federal Department of Canadian Heritage.   The Department is dedicated to strengthening and celebrating Canada - its' people and its' land. Sport Canada has two divisions: Sport Program and Sport Policy. Through Sport Canada, the Government of Canada supports and promotes high performance sporting excellence by Canadian athletes who compete internationally, nationally and interprovincially while demonstrating strong ethics and fairness.

Currently, Sport Canada has an annual Contributions budget of approximately 48 million. The key Sport Canada programs include support of $19.5 million to the high performance programming of 38 National Sport Organizations; $7.1 million to 14 Multi-Sport/Service Organizations; $1 million to a network of National Sport Centres in Calgary, Montreal, Winnipeg, and Victoria; $7 million to Canada's top high performance athletes in approximately 45 sports to assist with their training and living costs; $4 million to the Canada Games; and $7 million for the hosting of world championships, major games and international sport events.

Sport Canada funds 38 National Sport Organizations via the Sport Funding and Accountability Framework (SFAF); four additional Sport Organizations via the Domestic Sport Pilot; and nine additional National Sport Organizations for athletes with a disability via the Funding and Accountability Framework for Athletes with a Disability.

There are currently 837 athletes funded through the Athlete Assistance Program, consisting of 173 A cards, 96 B cards, 503 C cards and 65 developmental cards. With the new funding announced January 22, the number of carded athletes will increase to approximately 1,150. (*Canadian Heritage News Release*, January 22, 1998, Ottawa).

Sport Canada Mission:
- *to strengthen the unique contribution that sport makes to Canadian society, identity and culture.*
- *to support the achievement of high performance athletic excellence through fair and ethical means.*
- *to work with key partners to sustain the development of the Canadian sport system.*

Sport Canada Policy Priorities
- *Canada's high performance athletes and programs supporting them.*
- *coaches and coaching development.*
- *delivery of services to athletes and coaches by national sport organization and other means.*
- *increased access for women, athletes with disabilities and aboriginal persons.*
- *initiatives that help advance broader federal social and economic policy objectives.*

Sport Canada: Programs and Policies
- *National Sport Centres: Calgary, Montreal, Winnipeg, Victoria (PSI), Toronto,*
- *NSO/Multi-Sport/Multi-Service Program Support*
- *Athlete Assistance Program (AAP)*
- *Hosting Support Programs Single/Multi-Sport*

Sport Canada Policies
- *Federal Policy for Hosting International Sports Events*
- *Women in Sport Policy*
- *Official Languages Policy (Treasury Board)*
- *Tobacco Sponsorship Policy of NSO's*
- *Policy on Penalties for Doping (1993)*

The Canadian government and sport - new directions

Recent reports on sport policy expressed the generally unanimous view that fundamental adjustments had to be made to the sport funding system in Canada. No fundamental changes to the funding system had been made since the federal government first began directly supporting amateur sport development more than thirty years ago. As a result, the Department of Canadian Heritage (Sport Canada), in consultation with the sport community, developed the Sport Funding and Accountability Framework (SFAF). It was piloted and refined in 1995, for full implementation beginning April 1, 1996.

The SFAF is a comprehensive objective tool to ensure that federal funds are allocated to NSOs that contribute to federal sport objectives and priorities.

The notion of accountability is fundamental to the framework and its application.   It encompasses three main components: eligibility, funding determination and accountability (table 1).

Table 1 : The sport funding and accountability framework (SFAF) criteria

Category	Area	Sub-area		
			Eligibility	Funding
High Performance (60 %)	Athlete Results	Olympic Games	19 %	18 %
		World Championships	19 %	18 %
	High Performance Systems	National Team Program	16 %	16 %
		High Performance Athletes in Decision Making	2 %	2 %
		High Performance Coaching	2 %	2 %
		International Officiating	N/A	2 %
		International Representation	1 %	1 %
		Hosting of Competitions	1 %	1 %
Sport Development (30 %)	Athlete Development	Membership	7 %	7 %
		Provincial Championships	2 %	2 %
		National Championships	8 %	7 %
		Canada Games	2 %	2%
		Technical Resources	2 %	2 %
		Athletes with a Disability	1 %	N/A
	Coaching	Coaching Development	2 %	2 %
		Coaching Certification	6 %	6 %
	Officiating	Officials Development	N/A	2 %
Management (10 %)	Management	Finance	4 %	4 %
		Official Languages	3 %	3 %
		Women in Sport	3 %	3 %
100 %	100 %		100 %	100 %

Specifically, the objectives of the SFAF are to: (a) align the new funding system with government priorities in sport; (b) rationalize Sport Canada's funding contributions to NSOs; (c) provide a more objective system of allocating funding to NSOs based on merit; (d) ensure accountability as part of the federal government and NSO relationship (SFAF, March 1996).

In the high performance category (60%), an organization's score is based on athlete results and the NSO's high performance system. The score for athlete results is arrived at by weighting World Championships and Olympic results by factors that reflect the competitive profile for each sport. An NSO's score for its high performance system takes into account how an NSO operates its national team and support programs.   For example, factors relating to coaching, training, athlete monitoring, and athlete involvement in decision-making are used to determine this part of an NSO's score.

Sport development (30%) considers athlete development, coach development and officiating. These in turn are scored according to the NSO's membership, participation in national and provincial championships and the Canada Games, technical resources, and the certification of coaches and officials. Technical resources in this case refers to the extent of leadership provided by the NSO in the development of resource materials and programs for athletes, coaches and officials.

The management category (10%) assesses an NSO'S financial operations, service capacity in both official languages and the opportunities provided for women in sport.

In January 1996, the development of a *Business Plan for Sport in Canada* was launched. At that time the federal government distributed the *Business Plan Think Piece* (December, 1995) and draft *Work Plan* (December, 1995) to stakeholders in the sport community. Factors in the current environment, such as declining resources for sport from traditional sources, have motivated the federal government to provide leadership to the development of a *Business Plan for Sport*. This is a consultative, cooperative public policy exercise undertaken in conjunction with partners in sport to enhance the self-sufficiency of the sport system and sustain the development of sport in Canada (Ostry May 1996).

The results of the Business Plan project will focus on recommendations and strategies leading to new sources of funding for sport, increased self-sufficiency and effectiveness of sport organizations and delivery mechanisms, the financing of high performance sport, and the closer linking of sport with other government priorities.

Participating with Sport Canada in the certain aspects of the Business Plan are the provincial and territorial governments, NSOs, MSOs, the corporate sector, other units within the Department of Canadian Heritage, and other federal departments (Finance/Revenue).

It is significant to note that the re-focused federal directions and actions have highlighted the presence of policy fragmentation between the federal and provincial/territorial governments. Since the federal government is focusing its' funding on high performance sport, there is now a potential for gaps in the system. As well, the issue of how to ensure the development of athletes for the future has been raised.

In order to address these important policy issues, the Business Plan is collaborating with and soliciting input from the following stakeholder groups: provincial/territorial governments, a Corporate Advisory Committee, the national sport community, the Minister's Athletes' Advisory Committee, the

Canadian Olympic Association, and other federal government departments. Data collection/research, including international comparative data, in areas such as the economic impact of sport and the value of sport will provide supporting rationale for the recommendations arising from the business plan. A business case will be presented to all partners, including the public sector, as a central justification for continued public support, as well as enhanced private support, to the sport system.

Reform in the public service

The Government of Canada and its public service have undergone significant change over the past five years. Indeed Sport Canada (structure and operation) is being impacted by the following themes and directives: (a) fiscal pressures and deficit reduction strategies will result in affordable government; (b) better accounting will lead to greater accountability and will serve the public interest; (c) effective program delivery will create better policy development; (d) there is increased recognition of the importance of partnerships and strategic alliances; (e) there is a need to build on the strength of others, including voluntary and not for profit sectors as well as the private sector.

In a recent speech, Jocelyne Bourgon, Clerk of the Privy Council and Secretary to the Cabinet, made some important observations about Canada's approach to redefining the role of government and reforming public sector institutions. Here, she summarizes the underlying principles of the "Canadian model" of public service reforms. These include: (a) the Canadian model of public sector reform recognizes the importance of affordable government, but rejects the philosophy that less government is synonymous with better government; (b) the Canadian model of public sector reform recognizes the importance of partnership and strategic alliances; (c) the Canadian model reaffirms the importance of citizens well beyond their role as customers and clients; (d) Canadian public sector reform has given equal weight to strengthening policy capacity and modernizing service delivery; (e) the Canadian model requires strong leadership from both elected and appointed officials.

Bourgon provided an interesting comment on the role of public sector agencies and the business world

> *"We are as committed as the private sector to quality of service and to efficiency gains, but for reasons of public interest. Quality out of respect for those we serve, efficiency, because each dollar saved can be applied either to providing more service to Canadians or to reducing their tax burden."* (Bourgon, May 27 1998).

Where to now ? Towards the next millennium

The Government of Canada, through the programs and services provided by Sport Canada, supports the achievement of high performance sport excellence and the development of the Canadian sport system to strengthen the unique contribution that sport makes to Canadian identity, culture and society. Currently, Sport Canada is in the final stages of development of a Strategic Plan for 1998-2001. The document is to be distributed to the sport community and the public in the summer of 1998. Four major strategic directions are expected to be a part of the plan: (1) high performance athletes and coaches-enhancing the ability of Canada's athletes/coaches to excel at the international level; (2) Canadian sport system development - working with key partners to enhance the coordination and integration of Canada's sport system; (3) strategic positioning - advancing broader federal objectives through sport, position sport and promote the contribution of sport to Canadian society; (4) access and equity - increase access and equity to sport for targeted under represented groups (Smith June 16 1998).

The challenges are there for Sport Canada to build effective partnerships with the corporate community, the private sector and the sport community and to establish a better alignment of federal, provincial and territorial policies and programs in the domain of sport. As well, the challenge exists for Sport Canada to be more progressive in enhancing the availability and quality of sport opportunities for under represented groups.

The Government of Canada has already made a positive start in realizing the objectives associated with its' strategic directions with the January 1998 announcement of a funding infusion of $10 million a year for five years for sport in Canada.

The new funding will be directed to three areas: training and competition opportunities for athletes; coaching support; and direct assistance to athletes. The funding will be provided in partnership with National Sport Organizations, National Sport Centres, and National Multi-Sport Organizations. In all these programming areas, the Government of Canada will continue to underline the importance of equity and access for women, athletes with disability, and Aboriginal people. This additional funding will enable the federal government to deliver on a promise made to Canadians in the Red Book.

Nearly half of the new funds will be used to provide more opportunities for athletes to train and compete, particularly in international events.

About one-third will be used to develop and employ the finest Canadian coaches. The intention is to double the number of federally funded, full-time high-performance coaches and help create numerous part-time coaching positions. Particular emphasis will be placed on increasing the number of female coaches and coaches of athletes with a disability. Support will also be provided for the development of Aboriginal coaches.

The rest of the funds will be allocated to Sport Canada's Athlete Assistance Program to provide direct support to an additional 300 developing high performance athletes to help offset their living and training expenses. One hundred of these will be athletes with a disability. Approximately 850 athletes now receive direct support from the Government of Canada (*Canadian Heritage News Release*, January 22, 1998)

Another significant development occurred with the May 1998 announcement by Minister of Canadian Heritage Sheila Copps that Canada would be hosting a world conference on women and sport in 2002. Canada was chosen as the next conference site at the Second World Conference on Women and Sport which was held in Windhoek, Namibia. Some 400 delegates from 74 countries participated in the 1998 Conference designed to advance sport as a strategy for addressing global issues affecting women, to exchange good practices, to strengthen international, national, and regional networks, and to build action plans for effecting change. The Windhoek Call for Action outlined priorities for the women and sport movement from now until 2002 (*Canada to Host Conference on Women and Sport in 2002* May 1998, Ottawa). The strategic direction of access and equity will be realized through this important international initiative (Canadian Heritage News Release, May 26, 1998).

It would appear that conditions are somewhat favorable for the Government of Canada to strategically re-position itself internationally as a leader in the world of sport. Certainly the vision and the will are present - it remains to be seen whether or not the necessary human and fiscal resources will be made available to allow for this to happen.

References

Best, J.C., Blackhurst, M. & Makosky, L. (1992). Minister's task force on federal sport policy. Sport: the way ahead. Ottawa, Ontario, Ministry of State, Fitness and Amateur Sport.

Best, J.C. (1994). Report of the core sports commissioner. Ottawa, Ontario, Department of Canadian Heritage.

Bright, D. (1992). The Canadian national sport system: current changes and future directions, 1988-1992. London, Ontario: Unpublished Masters degree thesis.

Budget Information 1998 (1998) Ottawa, Ontario: Department of Finance

Cadieux, P. (1993). Federal directions in sport. Response to the Minister's task force on federal sport policy. Ottawa, Ontario, Ministry of State, Fitness and Amateur Sport.

Canadian Heritage news release (January 22, 1998). Athletes and coaches to get additional federal support. Ottawa, Ontario, Department of Canadian Heritage.

Canadian Heritage news release (May 26, 1998). Canada to host conference on women and sport in 2002. Ottawa, Ontario, Department of Canadian Heritage.

Meynaud, J. (1966). Sport et politique. Paris, Payot Publishers.

Neil, S. (1996). Sport Canada business plan for sport in Canada. Edmonton, Alberta, University of Alberta.

Notes from an address by Jocelyne Bourgon, Clerk of the Privy Council and Secretary to the Cabinet (May 28, 1998). Association of Professional Executives of the Public Service of Canada Symposium: Ottawa, Ontario.

Semotiuk, D. (1981). Motives for national government involvement in sport. International Journal of Physical Education, 18(1), 23-28, and Comparative Physical Education and Sport, 7(2), 13-23.

Semotiuk, D. (1989). Canada's efforts in international sport: A critique of the government of Canada's high performance initiatives. Comparative Physical Education and Sport, 6.

Semotiuk, D. (1992). Restructuring Canada's national sports system: the legacy of the Dubin inquiry. Paper presented at the 8th biennial conference of the International Society for Comparative Physical Education and Sport. Houston, Texas.

Semotiuk, D. (1994). Federal government sport policy in transition: new directions for Canadian amateur sport. Paper presented at the 9th biennial conference of the International Society for Comparative Physical Education and Sport. Prague, Czech Republic.

Semotiuk, D. (1994). High performance sport in Canada. Paper presented to the Kuwait Olympic Committee, Kuwait City, Kuwait.

Semotiuk, D. (1996). Public accountability: federal government initiatives in Canadian Amateur Sport. Paper presented at the 10th biennial conference of the International Society for Comparative Physical Education and Sport. Hachi-ohji, Japan.

Smith, D. (June 16, 1998). Federal government sport policy. National forum on Canadian interuniversity sport. Collingwood, Ontario.

Sport Canada (1996). Assessment rating guide. Sport funding and accountability framework. Ottawa, Ontario, Sport Canada, Department of Canadian Heritage.

Sport Canada (1996). Business plan for sport in Canada - strategies for continued growth and self-sufficiency. A Sport Canada Think piece. Ottawa, Ontario, Sport Canada, Department of Canadian Heritage.

Sport Canada (1996). Business plan for sport in Canada - in update. Ottawa, Ontario, Sport Canada, Department of Canadian Heritage.

Sport Canada (1996). Sport funding and accountability framework (SFAF) - overview. Ottawa, Ontario, Sport Canada, Department of Canadian Heritage.

Sport Canada (1996). Sport funding and accountability framework for national single sport organizations. Ottawa, Ontario, Sport Canada, Department of Canadian Heritage.

Wilcox, R. (ed.) (1994). Sport in the global village. Morgantown, West Virginia, Fitness Information Technology, Inc.

Websites

Department of Canadian Heritage - Government of Canada
   http://www.pch.gc.ca

Sport Canada - Government of Canada
   http://www.pch.gc.ca/sportcanada/Sc_e/E_Cont.htm

Department of Finance - Government of Canada
   http://www.fin.gc.ca

Chapter 25

Regional divisions, pyramids and twin towers: a comparison of national football league structures in Europe

Vic Duke
Football Research Unit, University of Liverpool, U.K.

In July 1998 football is reconfirming its position as *the* world game during the climax of the World Cup Finals in France. Europe has played a key role in the development of football and continues to be the dominant continent in international competition. Six of the eight quarter finalists in France 98 are from Europe.

The aim of this paper is to undertake a comparative analysis of the development of football in Europe. The level of analysis is the nation state (with occasional exceptions such as the four football associations in the United Kingdom). Particular emphasis is placed on the development of a national football league structure in each state. A variety of structures are evident currently ranging through regional divisions, pyramids and towers. Examples of each type will be described later.

In the next section an ideal typical model of football development will be presented concentrating on the founding of the national football association, the establishment of a national championship (knock out principle) and the achievement of a national football league. The second section will examine the empirical evidence for European countries in relation to the proposed model. Differences in football league structure are revealed only when analysis delves below the national first division to the second and third levels of competition. The third section will document the current disposition of second divisions (level 2) throughout Europe. The remainder of the paper will be taken up with examples of the different national football league structures evident towards the end of the twentieth century.

The development of football in Europe: an ideal typical model

One of the most useful ways of conceptualising the growth of a sport is in terms of innovation diffusion (Bale 1989). An initial pattern of uneven spatial development gradually disperses into a more even national and international spread. Bale has stressed the importance of a national transport network to inter-regional movement, and the switch from local sporting consciousness to national sporting consciousness.

The institutionalisation of football in a nation state usually begins with the formation of a national football association, and may be deemed to have reached maturity with the establishment of a national football league (comprising initially a single first division). A more advanced stage of development then involves the refinement of the national football league structure at levels 2 and 3 beneath the top division.

In a given nation state the introduction of football is likely to occur in a specific city or region, more often than not either the capital city (the most cosmopolitan with the most foreign nationals) or a major port (the locus of imports of various kinds and foreign traders/seamen). From this starting point in a specific location the game will spread around the country, the pace of which will be determined by several factors; for instance the degree of geographical and social mobility, the extent of the national transport network, and the receptivity of regional subcultures to imported ideas.

When the number of functioning football clubs attains a critical mass and there are at least two rival centres/regions vying for competitive dominance, pressure will mount for the formation of a national football association. This organisation will ensure compliance with the same set of rules throughout the country and also provide a link with the international football community.

One of the main benefits of setting up a national football association is the possibility of introducing an official national championship. This is likely to occur shortly after (or indeed contemporaneously with) the founding of the football association, and the championship will usually take the form of a knockout tournament between regional champions, or alternatively a knockout cup competition open to all affiliated clubs.

Historically (i.e. late nineteenth and early twentieth centuries) it was unlikely that progression directly to a national league with a single division would occur, because of organisational, financial and transport constraints. More recently constituted nation states (i.e. the post-communist 1990s) are likely to skip the knockout national championship stage and proceed immediately to a national football league.

Eventually every nation state will overcome the various constraints and establish a national league initially with a single first division (the principle is that each club plays every other club in the league home and away during the football season). Regional structures will be formed at levels 2 and 3, which are linked to the national first division. In time level 2 may also comprise a single national division with regional structures beneath it.

The nature of the national football league structure will alter along with the maturation of the country s administration, transportation and economic systems. Earlier structures are more likely to comprise regional divisions, which may change over time into towers or pyramids. The most advanced structure is a pyramid with the number of sections increasing gradually at each level as one descends from the top division. Each level in the pyramid is linked to those above and below it, thereby enabling clubs to find their own level in the national football league structure.

The development of football in Europe: the empirical evidence

Consideration of the empirical evidence must begin with the birthplace of football, namely England. The origin of organised football can be traced to the founding of the first football association in 1863, which is still called the Football Association to this day instead of the English F.A. All of the eleven founder members were from the London region. Growth was slow to begin with such that there were only 50 member clubs by 1871, the year that the F.A. Cup competition was launched. Great public interest was stimulated by the national knockout tournament both in England and elsewhere in Britain. By the formation of the Football League in 1888 (again note the rather than English), F.A. membership exceeded 1,000 clubs. (Currently there are over 42,000 affiliated clubs in England).

The instant success of the Football League enshrined the league concept in football organisation and led to a proliferation of leagues - national, regional and local. Now the league concept is such an accepted part of the sporting universe that it is difficult to imagine the need to justify it s inception in 1888.

Mason (1980) suggested that the league idea probably came from American baseball. However, the Football League s official centenary history confirms that the league s founding father, William McGregor, took his inspiration from the English County Cricket Championship (Inglis 1988). Furthermore, McGregor's initial proposal was for an Association Football Union rather than the term league. Others considered the name too similar to the Rugby Football Union and on their decision Europe is now full of football leagues instead of football unions.

One of the key arguments in favour of a league system was the need for a fixity of fixtures - a guaranteed match against guaranteed opponents on a guaranteed date (Inglis 1988). Previously the cancellation or postponement of friendly matches at short notice was a regular occurrence, much to the infuriation of officials, players and spectators. The only other matches were knockout cup matches, which by definition had no continuity for the losers.

Table 1 summarises the development of football in Europe in terms of the years in which each football association was founded, the setting up of a national knockout championship (or cup tournament), and the start of a national league (with a single top division). The countries are divided into groups chronologically ranging from the British founders through to the post-communist period in the 1990s.

Table 1: Development of football in Europe

	Football Association Founded	National Championship	National League
(i) British founders			
England	1863	1871	1888
Scotland	1873	1873	1890
N. Ireland	1880	1880	1890
Wales	1876	1877	1992
(ii) First converts - late 19th century			
Denmark	1889	1912	1929
Holland	1889	1897	1956
Belgium	1895	-	1895
Switzerland	1895	1897	1933
Italy	1898	1898	1929
(iii) Early 20th century - pre first world war			
Germany	1900	1902	1963
Malta	1900	-	1909
Hungary	1901	-	1901
Norway	1902	1902	1937
Austria	1904	1897 (Vienna)	1911
Sweden	1904	1896 (Gothenburg)	1924
Finland	1907	1908	1930
Luxembourg	1908	-	1909
Romania	1908	1909	1934
Russia	1912	-	1936
Spain	1913	1902	1928
Portugal	1914	1921	1934

(iv) Inter war period			
France	1918	1917	1933
Poland	1919	1921	1927
Yugoslavia	1919	1923	1927
Estonia	1921	1921	1929
Rep. Ireland	1921	-	1921
Bulgaria	1923	1924	1937
Latvia	1923	1922 (Riga)	1927
Lithuania	1923	-	1922
Turkey	1923	1922	1959
Greece	1926	1927	1959
Albania	1930	-	1930
Cyprus	1934	-	1934
(v) Post-communist period			
Moldova	1990	-	1991
Azerbaijan	1991	-	1991
Croatia	1991	-	1992
Georgia	1991	-	1990
Ukraine	1991	-	1991
Armenia	1992	-	1992
Belarus	1992	-	1992
Macedonia	1992	-	1992
Slovenia	1992	-	1991
Czech Rep.	1993	-	1993
Slovakia	1993	-	1993

What emerges is generalised support for the main features of the model proposed earlier. Other than in the post-communist period the progression for most countries is from football association to national knockout to national league. In the discussion below particular attention is devoted to the outliers or exceptions to the general pattern, and where possible an explanation will be offered.

In the path-breaking English case it took 8 years to establish a national knockout competition and 25 years to achieve a national league. It is to be expected that others following on would make the transitions more quickly unless other factors intervene. Scotland and Northern Ireland (at the time the Irish F.A. represented the whole of Ireland) match this expectation with instant national cup competitions and a shorter time period to the formation of national leagues. Wales is the exception here, not in terms of the cup but in that a Welsh national league was not achieved until 116 years later in 1992. The explanation for this is partly geographical (mountainous terrain and poor transportation links between the north and the south) and partly political. As part of the United Kingdom the leading clubs in Wales (such as Cardiff City and Swansea City) have long played in the (English) Football League (for more detail on this see Duke and Crolley 1996).

Among the first converts most of them proceeded immediately to a knockout championship but experienced a longer delay to a national league than in the English case. The latter reflects the need for a sound transport network and economic infrastructure. Belgium provides the outlier among this group with the formation of a national league in the same year as the F.A. This was possible because Belgium was a small compact country with a relatively developed transport network. By contrast Holland had separate western and eastern leagues from 1897 but no single national first division until 1956 - two years after the advent of professional football there.

Most of the early twentieth century group moved within a couple of years to a national knockout competition (in Vienna, Gothenburg and Spain a tournament preceded the official F.A.). In only two of the twelve countries was there a national league within a year. The Hungarian case is partly explained by the presence of only Budapest clubs in the league until 1926. Luxembourg is one of Europe s smallest countries in area, equivalent to a region elsewhere.

The time gap between the football association and a national league among the early twentieth century group is mostly less than in the English case. There are two main exceptions. Norway took 35 years mainly for geographical reasons (a large elongated mountainous country with communications problems) and it was fully 63 years before Germany created the Bundesliga. Germany has remained large in area throughout the period but has been subject to several political boundary changes. It is often claimed that Germany was the last European country to attain a single national first division but this ignores the case of Wales.

Eight of the twelve countries in the inter war group either set up knockout championships quickly or already had them. The other four immediately started a national league. Albania, Cyprus and Lithuania are small in area, and the Republic of Ireland was a breakaway from the (Northern) Irish F.A. founded in 1880. By the inter war period the delay in forming a national league was far less than in the English case. The only exceptions are France, Turkey and Greece. The first two are large in area and Greece is geographically diverse.

Finally the eleven countries in the post-communist group all proceeded instantly to the formation of a national league. By the end of the twentieth century all European countries have the requisite administrative, transport and economic infrastructures to do this.

Current national leagues in Europe: first and second divisions

A summary of the data is provided in table 2. All countries now have a single first division at the apex of the structure and more than three quarters also have a single second division. Eight countries have two second divisions, which are usually split along geographical lines; for instance north and south sections in Finland and Sweden, with west and east sections in Hungary and Georgia. Turkey s structure of five regional second divisions is due to a large surface area and a relatively underdeveloped infrastructure.

Table 2 : National first and second divisions in Europe: number of clubs in each division 1996-97 (source : *European Football Yearbook 1997/98*)

	Division 1	Division 2
Albania	18	-
Austria	10	16
Belarus	16	15
Belgium	18	18
Bulgaria	16	18
Croatia	16	16
Cyprus	14	14
Czech Republic	16	16
Denmark	12	16
England	20	24
Estonia	8	8
Faroe Islands	10	10
Finland	12	10 x 2
France	20	22
Georgia	16	20 and 17
Germany	18	18
Greece	18	18
Holland	18	18
Hungary	18	16 x 2
Iceland	10	10
Italy	18	20
Latvia	10	13
Lithuania	8	8
Luxembourg	12	14
Malta	10	10
Moldova	16	14
Northern Ireland	8	8
Norway	14	12 x 2
Poland	18	18 x 2

Portugal	18	18
Republic of Ireland	12	10
Romania	18	18 x 2
Russia	18	22
Scotland	10	10
Slovakia	16	18
Slovenia	10	16
Spain	22	20
Sweden	14	14 x 2
Switzerland	12	12
Turkey	18	10 x 5
Ukraine	16	24
Wales	21	18 x 2
Yugoslavia	12	12

Considerable variation persists in the number of clubs in the national divisions. Football s European governing body (UEFA) has decreed that national first divisions should have a maximum of 18 clubs. This is in order to leave sufficient room in the fixture list for the three UEFA club cup competitions and also international matches for the national teams. Seven countries comply with the UEFA standard perfectly in having 18 clubs in both first and second divisions. Germany sticks to the directive most rigorously with four sections of 18 clubs at level 3.

Four countries have top divisions larger than recommended by UEFA. France and Spain are large countries in both area and population with many rival metropoli to be included (Spain switched in the 1997-98 season to 20 in the first division and 22 in the second). England had 22 clubs in the top division until 1995, which reflected a long tradition of large divisions at all levels in an attempt to accommodate the largest number of professional football clubs in the world. The Welsh league is relatively new and still making room for additional transfers from the English semi-professional leagues (see Duke & Crolley 1996).

Smaller first divisions of 12 or less clubs are predominantly found in countries with relatively small populations, which are attempting to achieve a higher quality elite division in order to compete internationally. The remainder of the paper will be taken up with case studies of the different types of national football league structure evident currently.

Regional divisions

Many countries introduced competitive football via regional leagues with a national championship decided on a knockout basis between the respective regional champions. Although all European countries now have a single national first division, some still retain a regional divisions structure beneath the top two levels.

A regional divisions structure can be defined as an abrupt increase in the number of sections as one descends to a lower level in the league structure. In the two examples presented in table 3 the league structure broadens from a single second division to four regional sections at level 3. This contrasts with the more gradual increase (say from one to two, or from 2 to 4) associated with a pyramid structure.

Table 3: Examples of a Regional Divisions Structure

(i) Germany 1997-98
level 1   Bundesliga - 18 clubs
level 2   2.Bundesliga - 18 clubs
level 3   Regionalliga - 4 x 18 clubs
Nordost, Nord, Sud, West-Sudwest
level 4   Oberliga - 10 sections
Niedersachsen/Bremen, Hamburg/Schleswig-Holstein,
Nordost Nord, Nordost Sud, Nordrhein, Westfalen,
Sudwest, Bayern, Baden-Wurttemberg, Hessen
(ii) Spain 1997-98
level 1   Primera - 20 clubs
level 2   Segunda - 22 clubs
level 3   Segunda B - 4 x 20 clubs

Germany and Spain are relatively large in both area and population, which accounts for their retention of a regional divisions structure. In Germany four Regionalliga at level 3 are linked to ten Oberliga at level 4. Three Oberliga feed into the Sud and West-Sudwest Regionalliga, whereas two Oberliga feed into the Nord and Nordost. Spain exhibits a similar progression of 1:1:4 from levels 1 to 3. Level 3 is known as Segunda B and the four sections are geographically based (North west/west, north/Basque, Catalonia/east, south).

Pyramids

It was argued earlier that a pyramid is the most advanced form of football league structure. As one descends from the apex of the structure the pyramid should broaden only gradually, ideally in a 1:2:4:8 pattern. Countries which are relatively small in area are more likely to achieve a pyramid league structure. Two examples are provided in table 4.

Table 4: Examples of a pyramid structure

(i) Belgium 1997-98
level 1   Eerste - 18 clubs
level 2   Tweede - 18 clubs
level 3   Derde A and B - 16 clubs x 2
level 4   Vierde A, B, C and D - 16 clubs x 4
level 5   9 provinces all with a first division - 16 clubs x 9
(ii) Czech Republic 1997-98
level 1   I.LIGA - 16 clubs
level 2   II.LIGA - 16 clubs
level 3   Czech (18 clubs) and Moravian (16 clubs) sections
level 4   9 sections - 5 in Czech lands and 4 in Moravia

Belgium has an almost perfect pyramid structure with a 1:1:2:4:9 pattern. This format of two sections at level 3 and four at level 4 was introduced in 1952. Belgium may have been the first country to attain this advanced national league structure.

The Czech Republic has moved towards a pyramid structure with a pattern of 1:1:2 for levels 1 to 3. The third division is split into Bohemian and Moravian sections. Level 4 has nine sections, which is an abrupt increase from 2 at level 3, and therefore more in keeping with a regional divisions structure. Five sections feed into the Bohemian half of level 3, and four into the Moravian.

The idea of a gradual progression from regional divisions to a pyramid structure is supported by recent changes in two countries. Italy currently has a single Serie A, a single Serie B, two Serie C1's, three Serie C2's and beneath this the Campionato Interregionale with nine sections. The 1:1:2:3:9 pattern is closer to a pyramid structure than was the 1:1:2:4:12 pattern of the 1980s.

A similar progression has occurred in France, which currently has a perfect pyramid; a single division 1, a single division 2, two national 1's, four national 2's and eight national 3's. In the 1980s France possessed a 1:2:6:8 national football league structure, which can be categorised as regional divisions.

Towers

Particularly distinctive are the national football league structures of England and Scotland (see table 5). These two countries were home to the world s two oldest football associations and also the first to legalise professional football in the nineteenth century (not until the 1920s did three Central European countries follow this lead). The tower structure extends the principle of a single division at each level down to level 3 and beyond.

Table 5: Examples of a tower structure

(i) England 1997-98

level 1 Premier League - 20 clubs
level 2 Division 1 - 24 clubs
level 3 Division 2 - 24 clubs
level 4 Division 3 - 24 clubs
level 5 Conference (semi-professional) - 22 clubs
level 6 3 sections - 22 clubs x 3

(ii) Scotland 1997-98

level 1 Premier Division - 10 clubs
level 2 Division 1 - 10 clubs
level 3 Division 2 - 10 clubs
level 4 Division 3 - 10 clubs

England had regionalised third divisions (north and south) until 1958, when the league was restructured into single third and fourth divisions. The four level tower structure is probably best explained by the existence of 92 professional football clubs in England (including three from Wales), which is more than anywhere else in the world. In 1979 the 20 leading semi-professional clubs even formed a single national division at level 5, which for the last decade has provided the possibility of promotion into the professional level 4.

Throughout this century the Scottish league has comprised a tower structure of some kind, mostly two or three divisions until the adjustment to four divisions of ten in 1994. The presence of only 10 clubs at the top level (Premier division) is intended to achieve higher quality competition among the elite.

The twin towers of Cyprus

Finally, a unique case of twin towers can be found on the island of Cyprus (see table 6). Following the Turkish invasion of 1974 the island has effectively been partitioned into the Turkish north and the Greek south. Either side of the boundary the football league displays a tower structure with three levels in the unrecognised north and four levels in the south. Interestingly both leagues possess refugee football clubs, which continue to exist and play at new locations across the partition from their home towns (see Duke & Crolley 1996).

Table 6: The Twin Towers of Cyprus

(i) Turkish North 1997-98 (unrecognised by FIFA)
level 1   Division 1 - 12 clubs
level 2   Division 2 - 12 clubs
level 3   Division 3 - 12 clubs
(ii) Greek South 1997-98
level 1   Division 1 - 14 clubs
level 2   Division 2 - 14 clubs
level 3   Division 3 - 14 clubs
level 4   Division 4 - 15 clubs

Conclusion

Any conclusions from the comparative analysis must be regarded as provisional at this stage in that detailed historical study of more individual cases than presented here must be undertaken. Nonetheless there was considerable evidence in support of the model of football development outlined in the paper. A single national first division now exists in all European countries, although both the time and route taken to achieve it has varied.

Comparative analysis has the advantage of identifying exceptional cases, which must then be investigated in greater depth in order to explain the anomaly. There remain wide variations in national football league structure, exemplars of which have been presented in the paper. The future is likely to see a continuation of the trend towards more pyramids and less regional divisions structures. It is also debatable whether the English and Scottish towers can survive long into the twenty first century. Other issues for further research include differences in promotion/relegation procedures between the levels and the nature of regional disparities in national football league structures.

References

Bale, J. (1989). Sports geography. London: E&FN Spon.

Duke, V. & Crolley, L. (1996). Football, nationality and the state. Harlow: Longman.

Hammond, M. (ed.) (1997). European Football Yearbook 1997/98. Warley: Sports Projects Ltd.

Inglis, S. (1988). League football and the men who made it. London: Collins.

Mason, T. (1980). Association football and English society 1803-1915. Brighton: Harvester Press.

Chapter 26

Major issues of design for comparative research in sport sciences

Herbert Haag
University of Kiel, Germany

The special logic of comparative research in sport sciences has been dealt with in specific contributions especially at the two-year conferences of ISCPES (Simri 1979; Pooley & Pooley 1982; Krotee & Jaeger 1986; Haag, Bennett & Kayser 1986; Broom, Clumpner, Pendleton & Pooley 1988; Standeven, Hardman & Fisher 1991; Wilcox 1994).

The five major issues of design for comparative research in sport sciences presented in this analysis have to be seen in the context of a holistic research methodology. This can be described in three approaches in order to prove what holistic means and why this is very important for comparative research in sport sciences (Haag 1991; Haag 1994b).

First of all, holistic research methodology can be described with the dual approach of Guba and Lincoln (1998, 81-85), who distinguish a rationalistic and naturalistic research approach.

Secondly is the Kiel Model for Research Methodology (KMRM) is an understandable model for a holistic approach in research methodology. It contains six steps or dimensions (Strauß & Haag 1994): (1) philosophy of sport sciences; (2) research methods; (3) research designs; (4) techniques of data collection; (6) techniques of data analysis; (7) knowledge transfer. The KMRM is designed for usage in any kind of research with a wide application from natural to social-behavioral – up to cultural sciences (Strauß & Haag 1994; Haag 1994b).

Following this line of holistic conceptualization of research methodology Strauß and Haag are using the paradigm "data coded in words and/or numbers", especially in order to overcome the often used, but misleading distinction of qualitative and quantitative research. A classification of semantic models according to Gigerenzer (1981, p. 19) was used as a theoretical framework and can *thirdly* give a good justification for the holistic approach defined on the basis of data coded in words an/or numbers (figure 1).

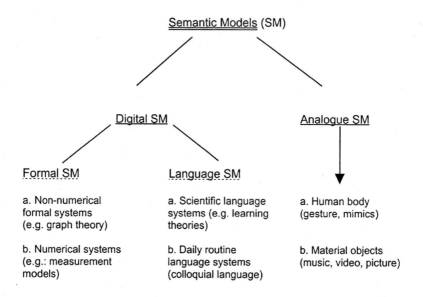

Figure 1: Semantic models (Gigerenzer 1981, p. 19)

In this model it is clear that words or/and numbers are basic modes for communication and therefore also fundamental for any research process, especially also for complex research situations like in comparative research, where hermeneutical and empirical research approaches are necessary.

The five major issues of designs for comparative research in sport sciences concern: (1) basic assumption and/or hypothesis; (2) variety of data base; (3) sampling of data; (4) variables; (5) categories. These issues have to be seen in this holistic context, since they are valid for any kind of research, this means descriptive, correlational or experimental.

Basic assumption and/or hypothesis

Starting from the research topic the design of a research process is a continuous process of differentiation from general to specific. In this process the formulation of basic assumptions and/or hypotheses is an important step, which can be seen in its position in the logic of the research sequence in figure 2.

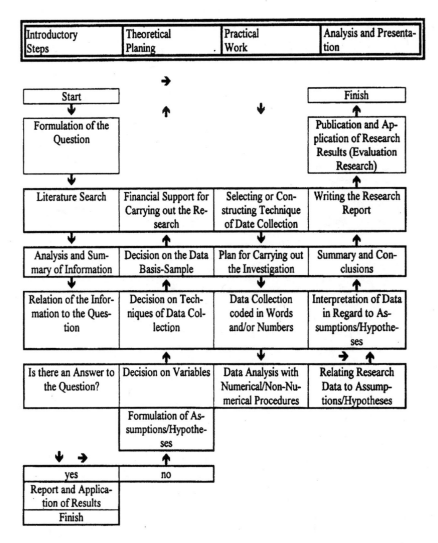

Introductory Steps	Theoretical Planing	Practical Work	Analysis and Presentation
Start			Finish
Formulation of the Question			Publication and Application of Research Results (Evaluation Research)
Literature Search	Financial Support for Carrying out the Research	Selecting or Constructing Technique of Date Collection	Writing the Research Report
Analysis and Summary of Information	Decision on the Data Basis-Sample	Plan for Carrying out the Investigation	Summary and Conclusions
Relation of the Information to the Question	Decision on Techniques of Data Collection	Data Collection coded in Words and/or Numbers	Interpretation of Data in Regard to Assumptions/Hypotheses
Is there an Answer to the Question?	Decision on Variables	Data Analysis with Numerical/Non-Numerical Procedures	Relating Research Data to Assumptions/Hypotheses
	Formulation of Assumptions/Hypotheses		
yes	no		
Report and Application of Results			
Finish			

Figure 2 : Logic Research Sequence (Haag)

Thus it is obvious from figure 2 that this building of basic assumptions and/or hypotheses is an important procedure.

Basic assumptions are considered to describe the word-based data situation where evaluation of data is carried out with hermeneutical strategies.

Hypotheses are considered to describe the number-based data situation where evaluation of data is carried out with statistical strategies.

Research topics are more often due to their complexity characterized by words and numbers as a data base which is another reason, why an holistic research approach is necessary especially also for comparative research (Haag 1994a).

Variety of data base

In order to define this variety of the data base the three ways within hermeneutic strategies can be of some help. Hermeneutics can be related to texts, objects (other than texts) and acting human beings.

All three situations are possible within sport science. The following figure is an intent to summarize this possible variety of data base.

Level one:	Texts as document
	a. Accidental documents (primary character)
	a.1 Personal documents (e.g. letters)
	a.2 Non-personal documents (e.g. protocols, participant observation results)
	b. Systematic documents (e.g. sport science literature in form of books, journals, research reports)
	c. Various documents (e.g. statistical data, address lists)
Level two:	Objects as document
	a. Audio-visual media
	b. Cultural objects (e.g. art)
	b. Technical objects (e.g. sports shoes)
Level three:	Persons as document
	a. Sport for all
	b. Top Level athletics

Figure 3 : Variety of data base for sport sciences (Haag)

Sampling of data

The finding of a sample, if the research situation is not the extreme form of case study, is an important step in research design, especially if the whole population cannot be included in the study, no matter if the data are coded in words and/or numbers.

For the number situation sophisticated strategies have been developed with accidental sampling, cluster sampling, making parallel group or panel and trend designs in longitudinal studies. The issue of deterministic versus probabilistic evaluation concepts also has to be seen in this context.

For the word situation sampling also can be performed by choosing a justified selection of documents (texts). Five procedures can be recommended in this regard as explained in figure 4:

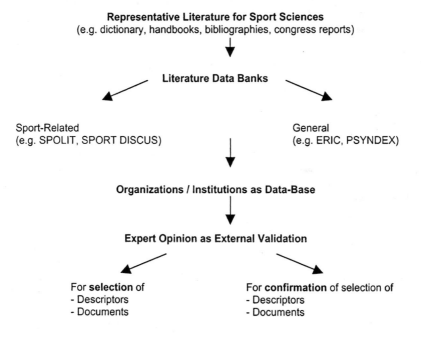

Representative Literature for Sport Sciences
(e.g. dictionary, handbooks, bibliographies, congress reports)

Literature Data Banks

Sport-Related
(e.g. SPOLIT, SPORT DISCUS)

General
(e.g. ERIC, PSYNDEX)

Organizations / Institutions as Data-Base

Expert Opinion as External Validation

For **selection** of
- Descriptors
- Documents

For **confirmation** of selection of
- Descriptors
- Documents

Figure 4: Sampling of data base for words (Haag)

Variables

Even if this term is so far mostly used in empirical research it is used in this context as a term for the design of any research process, also in the hermeneutic orientation of sport sciences.

As usual it can be distinguished between mono-, bi- or multivariate designs. Furthermore, the distinction of independent, dependant, and intervening variables has to be observed.

Variables can be defined on four different levels: personal, group, institution, and society. Furthermore, the large variety of variables can be distinguished in four different dimensions, according to their characteristics: absolute, analytical-comparative, structurally-relational, and contextual. These two times four (2 x 4) aspects are combined in figure 5 in a matrix, which indicates the large range of variables within a holistic concept of research methodology.

Within figure 5 the concrete examples can prove that the variables, relevant for a certain research topic, can be manifold and that they have to be selected with great diligence.

Categories

Categories are important in the context of basic assumptions and/or hypotheses as well as variables of an investigation. They serve as indicators in order to collect data related to variables in a detailed and systematic way. They are the key points of the respective technique of data collection no matter if this is observation, questioning, or content collection.

The following requirements can be formulated in order to be valid as a category: (a) being in accordance with the purpose of the investigation and thus also with the basic assumptions and/or hypotheses; (b) relation to the relevant information; (c) possibility to match content with categories; (d) formulation of categories on a similar level of abstraction; (e) semantic correctness.

In the following example (figure 6) a distinction is made between external and internal categories as keys to analyze for example study curricula for school physical education in comparison of different countries.

Unit	Characteristics based on			
	Signs (absolute)	Distributions (analytical-comparative)	Structures (structural-relational)	Contexts (contextual)
Individuum: Topic: C. Diem and his importance for the development of sport, sport education and sport science after 1945 in Germany.	Biographical data	Position in: - Sports Univ. of Cologne - German Sport Self-Administration - German Public Sport Administration	Relation to other leading representatives for sport, sport education, and sport science	Membership in international organizations
Group: Topic: Comparative analysis of the fitness level of beginning p.e. students in Canada, Germany, and USA	Personal signs of the group like age, BMI , sport club-membership	Status of fitness in regard to basic aspect like sensory abilities, condition, coordination, body experience	Relation of fitness to the acceptance of the students in the relevant peer groups	Context (e.g. society, education, religion, economy, climate, politics).
Institution: Topic: Comparative analysis of physical education in the school setting in USA and Germany	Aspects characteristic for schools and school physical education in USA and Germany like years of schooling, type of school, size, hours, etc.	Criteria like aims, content, methods, evaluation	Teacher-student relationship; relation of p.e. as subject to other school subjects, relation of school sport to sport clubs	Context (e.g. society, education, religion, economy, climate, politics)
Society: Topic: The appreciation of school physical education in different societies like USA, Brazil, Nigeria, Australia, Indonesia, and Germany	Facts about the participating countries	Keys for understanding appreciation like motor, cognitive, and affective aims and objectives	Position of school p.e. in relation to other school subjects	Context (e.g. society, education, religion, economy, climate, politics)

Figure 5 : Overview of variables (Haag)

External categories (examples)

Country	Name of curriculum	Year of publication	Format	No. of pages	Pictures	etc.
Germany						
USA						

Internal categories (examples)

Country	Aims	Content				
	Health	Recreation	Socialization	Individ. sport	Dual sport	Team sport
Germany						
USA						

Figure 6 : Examples for external and internal categories

This example is taken from written documents (content collection); however the necessity of building categories is valid for any type of technique of data collection.

Concluding comments

Since comparative research in sport sciences is very complex and difficult, it is advisable to consider the major issues of design in detail. Due to this complexity it is also valuable to use the Kiel Model of Research Methodology in order to be able to deal with different research situations (hermeneutical-empirical or word and/or hypothesis). The following major issues of design for comparative research in sport sciences have been discussed: (1) basic assumption and/or hypothesis; (2) variety of data base; (3) sampling of data; (4) variables; (5) categories.

All of them are important to be considered in the context of research methodology, especially related to comparative research in sport science.

References

Broom, E., Clumpner, R., Pendleton, B. & Pooley, C.A. (eds.) (1988). Comparative physical education and sport. Volume 5. Champaign, Ill., Human Kinetics.

Gigerenzer, G. (1981). Messung und Modellbildung in der Psychologie. Basel, Huber.

Guba, E.G. & Lincoln, Y.S. (1988). Naturalistic and rationalistic enquiry. In Keeves, J.P. (Ed.). Educational research, methodology, and measurement. An international handbook (pp. 81-85). Oxford, Pergamon.

Haag, H. (1991). Qualitativ und quantitativ. – Ein falscher Gegensatz in der forschungsmethodologischen Diskussion der Sportwissenschaft. In Singer R. (Hrsg.), Sportpsychologische Forschungsmethoden. Grundlagen. Probleme. Ansätze. (pp. 69-76). Köln, bps.

Haag, H. (1994a). Triangulation: a strategy for upgrading comparative research methodology in sport science (pp. 501-507). Morgantown, FIT.

Haag, H. (1994b). Theoretical Foundation of Sport Science as a Scientific Discipline. Contribution to a Philosophy (Meta-Theory) of Sport Science. Schorndorf: Hofmann.

Haag, H. (n.y.). Forschungsmethodologie in der Sportwissenschaft. Grundlagen des vergleichenden Forschungsansatzes. In Kapustin; P. (Hrsg.), Beiträge zu Grundfragen des Sports und der Sportwissenschaft. (pp. 28-40). Schorndorf, Hofmann.

Haag, H., Bennett, B. & Kayser, D. (eds.) (1986). Comparative physical education and sport. Volume 4. Champaign, Ill., Human Kinetics.

Krotee, M. & Jaeger, E.M. (eds.) (1986). Comparative physical education and sport. Volume 3. Champaign, Ill., Human Kinetics.

Pooley, J. & Pooley, C.A. (eds.) (1982). Proceedings of the Second International Seminar on Comparative Physical Education and Sport. Halifax 1980. Halifax, University of Halifax.

Simri, U. (ed.) (1979). Proceedings of the First International Seminar on Comparative Physical Education and Sport. Wingate, Israel, Wingate Institute.

Standeven, J., Hardman, K. & Fisher, D. (eds.). Sport for All: into the 90s. Comparative physical education and sport. Aachen, Meyer & Meyer.

Strauß, B. & Haag, H. (1994). Forschungsmethoden- Untersuchungspläne – Techniken der Datenerhebung in der Sportwissenschaft. Forschungs-methodologische Grundlagen. Schorndorf, Hofmann.

Wilcox, C.R. (ed.) (1994). Sport in the Global Village. Morgantown, FIT.

Chapter 27

Attitude towards fouls in German and Japanese rugby players

Dieter Teipel and Akihiko Kondo
Friedrich-Schiller-University Jena, Germany
and Keio University, Japan

Various aspects of the attitude of players towards fouls in soccer players have been investigated in several studies (see Gabler 1987; Pilz 1982; Pilz et al. 1982; Teipel et al. 1983). In contrast to soccer, there exist hardly any systematic studies on specific aspects of fouls in rugby players.

Mellor and Murphy (1988) investigated the attitudes towards violence and fouls in rugby in groups of English players on high amateur level. They applied a semi-standardised questionnaire with 10 specific questions concerning aspects of attitudes towards fouls. 42 male rugby players on high amateur level answered this questionnaire. 60% of the rugby players admitted that they had already been sent off the field during their careers. 64% of the rugby players confirmed the notion that an opponent who was in an obvious scoring position had to be brought down by a foul tackle, when there was no other way to stop him. Besides, 64% of the rugby players responded positively to the item that they would decide to 'knock' a dangerous opponent out of the game. 58% of the rugby players confirmed the idea to start a fight with the opposition when they thought it would help them to win the game. In the case of being the victim of the foul or dangerous play, which went undetected by the referee, 64% of the rugby players admitted that they would wait for the next opportunity to 'get even'. Furthermore, 79% of the rugby players considered the possibility of outbreaks of violence during the game to be an acceptable and inevitable part of the game. Mellor and Murphy (1988) resumed that these attitudes which manifested a tendency of legitimation of fouls was due to the high importance of success and winning even on high amateur rugby level.

In the present study the attitude of German and Japanese rugby players towards various specific characteristics of fouls in rugby is analysed.

Method

For the analysis of specific attitudes towards fouls in rugby players a special questionnaire was developed and applied. This questionnaire included attitudes towards general and rule-specific actions in respect of aggressive play, evaluation of group influences on fouls, assessment of foul frequency in several conditions of game standings and appraisal of several foul conditions. The questionnaire included parts of the official rugby rules, Thus the rule-specific actions were taken in respect of various kinds of fouls (rule 25), the penalty kick (rule 26) and the free kick (rule 27) (see Bach 1992).

On the whole, 94 male German and Japanese rugby players answered the questionnaire. The 44 German rugby players played in various teams in the two highest German leagues. The 50 Japanese rugby players were members of a university team on high performance level. The German rugby players were, on an average, 26.68 years old, whereas the Japanese rugby players were with an average of 20.10 years more than 6 years younger. The average experience of rugby players was in the German players with 12.18 years more than 5 years higher than in the Japanese rugby players.

The statistical analysis of the attitudes towards specific aspects of aggressive play was conducted by means of descriptive and inferential procedures. The emphasis was laid on the analysis of attitudes towards fouls in the whole group and in comparison between German and Japanese rugby players.

Results

The description of the results refers to the analysis of attitudes towards fouls in the whole group of the 94 German and Japanese rugby players and in the comparison of attitudes towards general and rule-specific actions in relation to aggressive play, to the group influence on fouls, to foul frequency in several game standings and foul conditions in different game situations between 44 German and 50 Japanese rugby players.

Concerning the attitude towards *general actions,* the whole group of the German and Japanese rugby players considered the attempts to get in control of the ball by hard fighting, hard defensive actions, early attacks against the player being in possession of the ball as well as the attempt to give no ball lost and to fight hard against the opponent as being characteristic of an aggressive play.

In respect of the attitude towards general actions, 5 of 12 aspects were found to be at least tendentially different between German and Japanese players.

The German rugby players evaluated the aspects of high physical efforts, early attacks against the ball-carrying opponent and the attempt to overpower the opponent in a higher extent as characteristic for aggressive play than the Japanese players. In contrast the Japanese players regarded the actions of hidden fouls and the attempt to threaten the opponent verbally or by gestures as by far more characteristic of an aggressive play than the German rugby players.

In respect of the *rule-specific actions* the whole group of the German and the Japanese players associated with aggressive play when a player attacked an opponent physically early or late, when a player pulled an opponent away from the ball, when a player intentionally charged or hindered an opponent who had just kicked the ball away and when a player beat an opponent.

In 6 of the 23 rule-specific actions significantly different assessments were found between German and Japanese rugby players. The German rugby players regarded the conditions as more characteristic of aggressive play than the Japanese rugby players when a player beat an opponent, when a player kicked an opponent intentionally against the leg, when a player attacked an opponent physically early or late and when a player conducted a hard arm-grip. In contrast, the German players regarded the condition as less characteristic of aggressive play when a player intentionally cheated time.

Concerning the *group influences* on fouls, the whole group of the German and Japanese rugby players evaluated the rank order of the group influences of the opponents, the referee, the teammates, the own coaches and the opponents' coaches. This meant that, according to their opinions, the attitudes towards fouls were mostly influenced by the behavior of the opponents, secondly by the behavior of the referee, thirdly by the actions of their teammates, fourthly by the behavior of their own coaches and finally by the actions of the opponents' coaches. Only one of 8 aspects was found to be different between German and Japanese rugby players. The Japanese rugby players regarded the influence on fouls by reports of the journalists to be by far higher than the German rugby players did.

In respect of the *foul frequency in various game standings* the whole group of the German and Japanese rugby players assessed that most fouls occurred in the game standing being close behind. Hereafter the game standings of being in low lead and being in a tie situation followed. The German rugby players were in a higher degree of the opinion than the Japanese players that many fouls occurred in the condition of being close behind. In contrast, the Japanese players confirmed the aspect in a higher extent than the German players that many fouls were found in the situation of high lead.

Concerning *specific situational components* of fouls the whole group of the German and Japanese rugby players admitted that they got angry when their teammates did not fight enough. Besides they were of the opinion that fouls were more likely in important games than in unimportant games. Furthermore they confirmed the item that they wanted to win, even if they had to apply fouls. They affirmed the aspect that defensive players committed more fouls than offensive players.

In 6 of 8 aspects significantly different attitudes became obvious between German and Japanese players. The German players were in an essentially higher degree of the opinion than the Japanese players that fouls were more probable in important games than in unimportant games. In contrast, the Japanese players confirmed the item in significantly higher extent than the German players that they would apply fouls in order to win, that fouls were sometimes practised during training and that successful teams manifested fouls more often than unsuccessful teams. Besides, the Japanese players affirmed the condition in a markedly higher degree than the German players that there were more fouls after the start of the game than in later periods and that defensive players committed more fouls than offensive players.

The attitudes towards fouls of the whole group of German and Japanese rugby players manifested a similar tendency in terms of legitimation like the English rugby players in the study of Mellor and Murphy (1988).

Conclusion

In the present study specific aspects of the attitude towards fouls were investigated in 44 German and 50 Japanese rugby players on high league levels by means of a questionnaire.

The German rugby players showed in many aspects similar attitudes like the Japanese rugby players. But the German rugby players evaluated the general actions of high physical efforts and early attacks against the opponent as characteristic for aggressive play in a higher extent than the Japanese rugby players. Furthermore the German players regarded the rule-oriented actions of beating an opponent and of intentional kicking at the leg as more characteristic for aggressive play than the Japanese players. The Japanese players confirmed the aspects in a higher degree than the German players that they applied fouls in order to be successful and that they sometimes practised fouls in training. All in all, the German rugby players showed a stronger tendency of the avoidance of fouls than the Japanese rugby players. The attitude of the Japanese rugby players was directed in a higher extent to competitiveness and the legitimation of fouls.

It can be assumed that the differences in attitudes towards fouls can be due to experience and age differences between the groups of players. The more experienced and older German players obviously displayed more confrontations with fouls and their negative consequences than the less experienced and younger Japanese players. Besides, the relevance of rugby for the players and in public was evaluated by far higher in Japanese university players than in German high level players.

References

Bach, K.P. (1992). Rugby. Die offiziellen Regeln. Wissenswertes von A bis Z. Niedernhausen.

Gabler, H. (1987). Aggressive Handlungen im Sport. Schorndorf.

Mellor, S. & Murphy, W.J. (1988). Players' attitudes towards violence and foul play in amateur rugby league. In T. Reilly, A. Lees, K. Davids & W.J. Murphy (eds.), Science and fooball (pp. 583-588). London.

Pilz, G.A. (Hrsg.) (1982). Sport und körperliche Gewalt. Reinbek.

Pilz, G.A., Albrecht, D., Gabler, H., Hahn, E., Peper, D., Sprenger, J., Voigt, H.F., Volkamer, M. & Weis, K. (Hrsg.) (1982). Sport und Gewalt. Schorndorf.

Teipel, D., Gerisch, G. & Busse, M. (1983). Evaluation of aggressive behavior in football. International Journal of Sport Psychology, 4, 228-242.

Chapter 28

Youth culture in New Zealand: the changing face of sport

Rex W. Thomson
University of Otago, New Zealand

In the contemporary world, sport is regarded as a 'universal language', and since Coleman's classic (1961) study, sport has been seen to hold a privileged position at the centre of male adolescent culture, at least in American schools. However, youth sport participation and the meaning that sport holds for adolescents may well be influenced by wider cultural differences. This current study is an attempt to examine the importance of sport within the wider context of youth culture with a particular focus on the influence of globalization versus historical national differences.

Sport as a national characteristic

Rees and Brettschneider (1994) have suggested that while sport for adolescents was probably encouraged for the same reasons in many different countries, i.e. 'to build character', sport also helped to build something else. This tradition in sport then became seen as a national characteristic. In Britain, or perhaps more specifically England, team sports emphasised 'fairness', and in America 'winning'. For Australia and New Zealand perhaps the emphasis is, or was, on masculinity. In Australia, this can be seen in Daly's (1971) 'noble bushman' ethos (mateship, egalitarianism, courage, tough masculinity). As McKay et al. (1993) have suggested, Australian sport has been viewed as "irredeemably masculine" (p. 24), and "constitutes and reproduces heterosexual men's power" (p. 25).

In New Zealand, Phillips' (1987) traces the transition from the 'pioneer man', (a community of manly frontier bachelors, a powerful male culture in which a fiercely heterosexual 'mateship' was crucial), to the modern 'kiwi bloke' (rugged, practical, and loyal to his mates).

Sport is a key ingredient for Phillips in the forging of this national character. The male stereotype came about through "the interaction of two powerful traditions: the desire to keep alive the muscular virtues of the pioneer heritage, and the concern to contain that masculine spirit within respectable boundaries" (Phillips, 1987, p. 86). The best expression of this stereotype was to be found in New Zealand's national game, rugby football.

In cross-cultural analyses of sport, there are many similarities to be found. As Brandl-Bredenbeck and Brettschneider (1997) suggest, "increasing globalization is a major feature in the development of sport culture(s) among adolescents in western industrial societies" (p. 357). However, there are a number of significant national differences that are also of considerable interest, and these presumably can be traced to differing historical and cultural patterns.

The present study investigates the place of sport within youth culture in New Zealand, and attempts to identify both the effects of globalization and historical national differences within the adolescent sporting context. While the concept of globalization is clearly significant in modern sport, specific local development patterns and cultural traditions must also be taken into account. It is the interplay of personal, social and cultural factors that is perhaps most helpful in explaining adolescent interest and involvement in sport.

The current study

Part of a larger investigation of German and American adolescents conducted by Wolf-Dietrich Brettschneider, formerly of Free University, Berlin, and C. Roger Rees, Adelphi University, New York, the current New Zealand study surveyed just under 1,100 students in twelve secondary schools in the Auckland, Wellington and Christchurch regions.

The 1,095 subjects ranged in age from twelve to eighteen years, and there were 592 males and 503 females in the sample. With regard to ethnicity there were three major groupings, with 700 subjects classified as Caucasian/European or pakeha, 255 as Polynesian (Maori or Pacific Island), and 120 as Asian.

The importance and meaning of sport

Participating in informal and organised sport ranks highly as a leisure activity in adolescent culture in this present survey, ranking ahead of spending time with friends, listening to music, and watching television. With regard to the importance of sport, subjects rated this at 74.64 on a scale of 1-100. The time spent on sporting activities is also significant, with subjects averaging 4.5

hours per week on school sporting activities and a further 5.8 hours per week on sporting activities outside the school context.

As far as the meanings attached to sport are concerned, 'fun and enjoyment' rated highest as the preferred meaning, followed by 'team sports', with 'health and fitness' also being an important component. Favoured sports included rugby, basketball, cricket, soccer, swimming, volleyball, touch rugby, rugby league, and netball. Subjects rated their ability in sport, with the majority having a positive evaluation of their physical abilities. Subjects saw themselves as average (33.5%), good at different sports (47.1%), or really good at one sport (9.3%), and most (40.8%) were regular participants for school sports teams, with 17% being in the top school teams.

In terms of social status in secondary schools, and despite the popularity of sport, subjects rated 'being an individual', 'being popular', 'being a good student', 'getting by without making waves', and 'being a student leader', as the most important factors ahead of 'being a good athlete', a ranking similar to that found by Rees (1994) for American adolescents, although 'being physically attractive' was ranked two places higher by the latter group.

Gender differences

While both males (77.45) and females (71.38) rate sport highly, the gender difference is still obvious. Sport was clearly a favoured leisure activity for males, and while this was also true for females, for the latter spending time with friends was also very important. With regard to the meanings attached to sport, males were far more likely to think of 'team sports', followed by 'enjoyment', while for females, 'enjoyment' is clearly the most salient meaning, with 'health and fitness' rating next highest ahead of 'team sports' (see table 1).

Table 1: Meaning of sport: gender differences

	Total %	Male %	Female %
Enjoyment	21.3	19.0	24.2
Team sports	17.8	23.4	11.3
Health and fitness	10.0	6.9	13.9
Physical demands	7.8	7.5	8.3
Individual sports	6.0	4.6	6.5

Differences are also apparent in the time spent on sporting activities, with males averaging 5.4 hours per week in school sports activities compared with 3.36 hours for females, and averaging two additional hours per week in sporting activities outside the school. There remain clear gender differences with regard to favoured sporting activities. Males list rugby, basketball, cricket and soccer as their favoured activities, while for females, the traditional women's sport of netball is a clear number one choice, followed by basketball, swimming, volleyball, and touch rugby (see table 2).

Table 2: Favoured sporting activities: gender differences

	Total %	Male %	Female %
Rugby football	32.3	47.1	11.2
Basketball	30.3	32.3	27.7
Cricket	18.5	26.3	4.2
Soccer	15.8	20.0	4.2
Swimming	15.2	-	23.3
Volleyball	15.2	-	22.6
Touch rugby	14.7	13.0	21.9
Rugby league	9.9	14.3	-
Netball	9.8	-	36.5

While both groups had similar leisure interests, males were significantly more likely to play computer or video games, while females were more likely to read books or play a musical instrument, take part in arts and crafts, be involved in volunteer work, go shopping, and do extra school work. All these differences may be seen to support stereotyped gendered activities. Male students ranked 'being popular' as the most significant aspect of gaining social status in schools, but for both genders the importance of 'being an individual' rated highly.

Both genders rated the performance of males in sport ahead of females, but there was strong support from both males and females for the involvement of women in sport and a clear indication that the notion of 'gendered sports' is losing its hold on the national psyche, at least as far as adolescents are concerned. Despite expressed differences in sporting preferences, both males and females felt that girls could participate in any sport, although the males were more ambivalent in suggesting that boys could similarly take part in all sports.

Ethnic differences

Although members of different ethnic groups may adopt mainstream sporting activities, Allison (1988) suggests that these groups often use these sports as clear expressions of their own ethnic identity. In addition, the meaning that sport has for different adolescent ethnic groups in New Zealand is worthy of further consideration. In rating the importance of sport, Polynesian youth rate sport highest (77.69), followed by pakeha (74.62), but it clearly diminishes in importance for Asian youth (67.82). There are also clear ethnic differences with regard to the meanings attached to sport, with pakeha adolescents rating 'enjoyment' ahead of 'team sports' and 'health and fitness'. Polynesian youth attach similar meanings to sport but rate both 'enjoyment' and 'team sports' significantly higher. Asian adolescents, however, rated 'team sports' highest, followed by 'enjoyment', and gave a significantly higher ranking for 'individual sports' than any other group (see table 3). In addition, Polynesian students devote the highest hours per week for sport, with Asian students devoting the least amount of time, particularly with regard to sporting activities outside school time.

Table 3: Meaning of sport: ethnic differences

	Total %	Pakeha %	Polynesian %	Asian %
Enjoyment	21.3	17.1	24.1	18.2
Team sports	17.8	16.3	21.4	22.6
Health and fitness	10.0	10.9	9.4	6.4
Individual sports	7.8	5.9	-	14.0
Physical demands	6.0	7.7	8.8	7.2

There are also salient differences in sporting preferences. While pakeha list the two traditional sports of rugby and cricket at the top of the list followed by basketball and soccer, Polynesians give basketball a very high rating, followed by rugby, touch rugby, volleyball and rugby league. Asians also rate basketball very highly, followed by badminton (a sport that has clear historical and cultural roots in many Asian countries), and individual sports such as swimming and tennis (see table 4).

Table 4 : Favoured sporting activities: ethnic differences

	Total %	Pakeha %	Polynesian %	Asian %
Rugby football	32.3	35.3	36.5	-
Basketball	30.3	19.9	51.4	49.1
Cricket	18.5	22.9	4.3	10.0
Soccer	15.8	18.0	4.0	14.1
Swimming	15.2	16.7	-	25.0
Volleyball	15.2	4.0	33.0	5.0
Touch rugby	14.7	11.9	34.9	-
Rugby league	9.9	8.5	24.3	-
Netball	9.8	10.7	18.5	-
Tennis	8.6	4.9	4.3	19.2
Badminton	-	-	-	39.2

More Asian and Polynesian youth were concerned that studying left them with insufficient time for sport and leisure activities (this despite the fact that Polynesian youth spend more time on sporting activities than any other ethnic group), but perhaps the most striking ethnic difference relates to attitudes towards sport as a career. For Polynesian youth, in common with a number of minority groups in other cultures, there was a very significant increase in the number who participated in sport because they hoped to make a career out of their participation.

Cross-cultural differences

The role of culture in explaining variability in sport behaviour is highly significant, and it seems that the 'universal language' of sport still has some clearly defined 'accents'. With regard to the importance of sport, the New Zealand adolescents' rating of 74.64 is higher (but not markedly so) than the scores of 72.87 for New York adolescents and 69.32 for Berlin adolescents reported by Brandl-Bredenbeck en Rees (1996). The number of hours per week spent on sporting activities is much greater than that found by Waser and Passavant (1997) in France for both boys and girls, but as those authors point out "the French school day is the longest in Europe... and the school population has relatively little free time during the school term" (p. 10).

Perhaps the most striking cross-cultural differences, however, are to be found in the meanings that adolescents attach to sport in different cultures. American adolescents typically think of 'team sports', ahead of 'victory' and 'physical demands'. German adolescents choose 'team sports' and 'individual sports' ahead of 'physical demands' and 'health and fitness'(Rees & Brettschneider 1994). Neither of these groups sees 'enjoyment' as having any particular significance with regard to the meaning of sport. In marked contrast to this, New Zealand youth think of 'enjoyment' ahead of 'team sports', and both New Zealand and German adolescents give a much higher ranking to 'health and fitness' than their American counterparts (see table 5).

Table 5: Meaning of sport: cross-cultural differences

	New Zealand %	Germany* %	USA* %
Enjoyment	21	-	-
Team sports	18	15	35
Health and fitness	10	8	4
Individual sports	8	15	5
Victory	-	1	8

*Figures taken from Rees and Brettschneider (1994).

The differing cultural and historical roots are clearly evidenced in some of the sport preferences. Rugby, historically the most significant sport for New Zealand males, remains the number one preference of New Zealand adolescents, but not surprisingly does not feature in the preferences of American and German adolescents (Brandl-Bredenbeck 1994).

Significantly, however, basketball is popular in all three cultures, although this is not necessarily reflected in the number of subjects actually participating in the game. Evidence in New Zealand suggests that while just over 30% of adolescents list basketball as one of their three most favoured sports, participation rates are probably at least 10% lower than this figure would indicate (Wilson, Hopkins and Russell, 1993). With the advent of globalization this clearly illustrates the impact of global figures like Michael Jordan. In fact, in a study of hero-worship among primary school boys in Invercargill, the southernmost of New Zealand's towns, as much as seven years ago, Jordan ranked just behind the All Black (New Zealand national rugby team) captain on the list of sports heroes (Donne & McDonald 1991), providing early evidence of his emergence as a global popular cultural icon (Andrews et al. 1996).

While New Zealand adolescents clearly support the increasing involvement of women in sports that have previously been regarded as specific 'male preserves' (such as rugby football), this appears to differ significantly from the attitudes of youth in some other cultures (see e.g. Soos & Thomson 1997).

The changing face of sport

Perhaps the most obvious change that has occurred in recent years with regard to adolescent attitudes towards sport in New Zealand has been this highly significant growth in the popularity of basketball. This interest has not necessarily been translated into participation, and hence supports the notion of global cultural consumption. There is also the growth in popularity of activities that are less organised and regulated and have less emphasis on traditional sporting values. Informal sport and leisure activities such as mountain biking, beach volleyball, informal basketball, rollerblading, touch rugby, and skateboarding tend to emphasise values such as excitement, spontaneity, rebellion, non-conformity, sociability and creativity, and these are assuming considerable importance both in New Zealand and worldwide within the context of youth culture (Brandl-Bredenbeck 1994; Eckerstorfer 1995; Loret 1995; Waser & Passavant 1997).

There are other aspects of the adolescent culture, however, that provide evidence of the significance of specific local conditions. There is a striking acceptance of the notion that sport should not be seen as a gendered activity. Both boys (64.4%) and girls (81.1%) felt that all sports were suitable for male participation, and the figures were even higher for female sport participation (69.7% of boys and 81.9% of girls felt that all sports were suitable for girls). This represents a significant change over the past decade or two. For example, in Handcock's (1981) study, adult males felt quite strongly that while swimming, netball and gymnastics were appropriate sports for women, soccer and particularly rugby were deemed quite unsuitable. Crooks and Palmer (1983), in a study of secondary schoolgirls, found that rugby was seen as the most desirable sport for males and the least desirable for females, and that the reverse applied to netball. The present acceptance by a majority of adolescents of the idea that participation in all sports is acceptable for either gender represents success for the work of the Hillary Commission (the organisation set up by the New Zealand government in 1987 to oversee sport, fitness and leisure) in mounting a challenge against gendered attitudes in sport (Thomson 1996).

References

Andrews, D.L., Carrington, B., Jackson, S. & Mazur, Z. (1996). Jordanscapes: a preliminary analysis of the global popular. Sociology of Sport Journal,3 (4), 428-457.

Allison, M.T. (1988). Breaking boundaries and barriers: Future directions in cross-cultural research. Leisure Sciences, 10, 247-259.

Brandl-Bredenbeck, H.P. (1994). A cross-cultural comparison of selected aspects of adolescent sport culture - USA/Germany. Paper, AIESEP World Congress of Physical Education and Sport, Berlin, Germany, 24-28 June.

Brandl-Bredenbeck, H.P. & Rees, C.R. (1996). Physical self-concept in German and American adolescents. In G. Doll-Tepper & W.D. Brettschneider (eds.), Physical education and sport. changes and challenges (pp. 443-460). Aachen.

Coleman, J.S. (1961). The adolescent society. New York.

Crooks, M.C. & Palmer, S.A. (1983). Schoolgirls' attitudes towards female participation in sports. Research Reports in Sport and Leisure, 1 (May), 1-40.

Daly, J.A. (1971). The role of sport and games in the social development of early Australia. Canadian Journal of History of Sport and Physical Education, 11 (2), 50-60.

Eckerstorfer, K. (1995). Alternative forms of movement as an expression of a new youth culture. In L. Komadel (ed.), Physical education and sports of children and youth (pp. 25-26). Bratislava.

Donne, A.M. & McDonald, K.A. (1991). Sports hero worship in New Zealand. Special Topic, School of Physical Education, University of Otago, Dunedin, New Zealand.

Handcock, G.A. (1981). Male attitudes toward female sports participation. Research Papers in Physical Education, 3 (2), 1-44.

Loret, A. (1995). Generation glisse. Dans l'eau, l'air, la neige...la revolution du sport des 'annees fun'. Paris.

McKay, J., Lawrence, G., Miller, T. & Rowe, D. (1993). Globalization and Australian sport. Sport Science Review, 2 (1), 10-28.

Phillips, J. (1987). A man's country? The image of the pakeha male - a history. Auckland.

Rees, C.R. (1994). Sport in the lives of American adolescents: The effect of age and gender. Paper, NASSS Conference, Savannah, Georgia, USA, 9-12 November.

Rees, C. R. & Brettschneider, W. (1994). The meaning of sport for German and American adolescents. Paper, ISCPES Conference, Prague, Czech Republic, 4 July.

Soos, I. & Thomson, R.W. (1997). Sport and youth culture - a cross-cultural research project. Open lecture, School of Physical Education, University of Otago, Dunedin, New Zealand, 5 December.

Thomson, R.W. (1996). Youth sport involvement in New Zealand: Issues, images and initiatives. Journal of the Federation Internationale d'Education Physique, 66 (1), 22-27.

Waser, A.-M. & Passavant, E. (1997). Sport as a leisure time pursuit among the youth of Caen, France. International Review for the Sociology of Sport, 32 (1), 7-17.

Wilson, N.C., Hopkins, W.G. & Russell, D.G. (1993). Physical activity of New Zealand teenagers. Journal of Physical Education New Zealand, 26 (2), 16-21.

Chapter 29

The difficult path of the women in the Olympic Movement

Edeltraud Odenkirchen
German Sport University, Cologne

On June 23rd 1894 as the participants of the first Olympic congress at the Sorbonne in Paris decided to restart the Olympic Games it was obvious that in the first Games no women would be participating. This level of competitive sports were still purely for men. Competitive sports for women existed only seldom and within strict limits. The initiator of the Olympic movement, Pierre de Coubertin, was an avid opponent of competitive sports for women. As a result of the discussion whether or not women should take part in track and field at the Olympic games in 1928 in Amsterdam, Coubertin decided to resign from his position as the IOC president. In his welcome speech as honoury president 1928 he even warned the men of the damaging effect of women's participation in the Olympic Games. It was reported that he said that the only role for women in the Olympic Games was to carry the cushion on which the medals are presented to the athletes.

In spite of this several women played a distinct role in the 1896 Olympic Games in Athens. Shortly before the Games a young lady, Melpomene, probably a pseudonym, ran the most part of the marathon route from Marathon to Athens in a time of 4 ½ hours. One day after the magnificent victory of the famous marathon winner Spiridon Louis, the 35 year old peasant woman, Stamatia Rovithi, inspired by the people also ran the marathon route. She needed 5 ½ hours and through her performance she wanted to draw attention and obtain an apprentice for her son.

Even more important for the success of the 1896 Athens Games were the influence of 2 women. Crown Princess Sophia, wife of Prince Konstantine who was at this time president of the organizing committee, asked her brother, the German Emperor Wilhelm II, and her mother, Empress widow Viktoria, for support. They agreed to send a German gymnastic team to Greece in spite of the political resistance of the German gymnasts, which stemmed from the fact that Coubertin was a Frenchman. Viktoria and Wilhelm II bought out the tickets for a sport festival and the proceeds were given to financing the trip to Athens. It should also be mentioned, that the wife of the German photographer Albert Meyer, Elisabeth, also a photographer, helped her husband with his work in Athens. Mrs. Gerrett, the mother of athlete Robert Garrett, assisted as a chaperone for the Americans.

At the sport competition of the international world exhibition in Paris 1900, considered today as the Games of the II Olympiad, Coubertin played only a secondary role as referee. Those responsible for the event handed over the organization of the sport competition to the local sport clubs and federations who then had a free hand in decisions regarding the sport program. It was then logical that the women would be included in the tennis and golf programs as it was normal at this time for women to compete in both sports.

Recently it has come to light that a woman was involved in the Olympic sailing competition. Helen Pourtalés, wife of Bernhard Count de Pourtalés, was in her husband boat, the „Lerina", and took part in at least one but probably two sailing competitions. This makes her the first female Olympic participant as well as the first known female to have won a gold medal, as her boat took first place.

Hot air balloon racing was also included in the world exhibition and was therefore in the Olympic program. It has also been discovered that women took part in this competition. In the „competition over the greatest distance", Madame Maison and her husband flew to Silesian which earned them 2nd place. In the competition „photography from a hot air balloon" Mademoiselle Vallot won 2nd place.

At the Games of the III Olympiade in 1904 in St. Louis, which was also held in conjunction with a world exhibition, Coubertin had just as little influence as he had in Paris, but the women were only included in the archery competition. The archery program was for both women and men. The women archers were for the most part wives of the men club members. For the women there were 3 archery competitions.

Two years later at the 1906 Olympic Games in Athens, for which Coubertin had no interest, the women were once again included in the tennis competition. Even more important for the development of women's sports was the participation of a Danish gymnastic squad. For decades the Olympic Games offered the representatives of the various gymnastic systems the opportunity for discussion and comparison. The various systems were German gymnastics, Swedish gymnastics and competitive gymnastics. The comparison of which system was better took place in advertised competitions, but even more through demonstrations. In Athens 16 Danish gymnasts demonstrated their gymnastic system and received resounding approval. Two years later in London there were two teams present, the Danish again and the British. The Olympic Games in 1912 in Stockholm: Denmark, Norway, Sweden and Finland all sent large women's teams to the Games. This was continued on until the 1948 Olympic Games in London. These displays had a larger influence on the development of women's gymnastics than the introduction of women's teams into the competition program in 1928 and also 1936.

The 1908 Olympic Games in London allowed more participation by women but didn't really offer much new competitions. Women's tennis was offered indoors as well as on grass. Archery was offered. One woman accompanied her husband by motorboat racing. In the sailing competition Frances Clytie Rivett-Carnac sailed in her husband boat and with him won first place, which by today's standards is a gold medal.

A new sport introduced to the Games was figure skating. Women had participated in figure skating for some time but it wasn't until the turn of the century that the men's and women's groups competed separately. Until that point the men and women competed against one another. In 1902 the worlds best female figure skater, "Madge" Syers, placed 2nd to Ulrich Salchow at the World Championships. The International Skating Union changed the rules to allow for separate women's and men's competitions that starting in 1906. Syers, who won the English championship more than once when it was still mixed, won the first women's competition in the Olympic Games in London 1908 and skated in the mixed doubles competition with her husband. There they won third place.

Another point from the London Games which deserves mentioning is that women from Finland and Sweden participated in the springboard diving demonstration which took place shortly before the English Queen Alexandra presented the medals at the award ceremony. In addition the women's British Floret fencer Millicent Hall fenced against the former British champion Jenkinson in the floret fencing demonstration.

Until this point women were just slowly edging their way into the Olympic program. The first big step occurred 2 years later at the 12th IOC session in July 1910 in Luxembourg when the British and the Swedish IOC members convinced their colleagues, in spite of Coubertins resistance, to allow women's swimming in the 1912 Stockholm Olympics. This was the first large step towards legalization. Looking back at the perception of properness at the time it was quite a brave move to allow women in bathing suits to compete in public. The well known Photo of the British 4x100-m-freestyle relay team with their chaperon is probably the best example. One of the problems can be documented in the case of Fanny Durack, who was at that time the worlds best woman freestyle swimmer. Her swimming club, the New South Whales swimming association in Australia, was strictly against women participation in swimming competitions where men were present, even if the men were only spectators. So that she could travel to London for the games her club had to change their rules and the president, "naturally a man", stepped down. To finance the trip to England the newspaper Sun took up a collection. Accompanied by her sister and another swimmer Wilhelmine Wylie the three ladies set off on the long boat ride over to England and then to Stockholm. It was quite an adventure for three ladies to set off for an 8 week journey to the other side of the world without being accompanied by men. The two swimmers then won both the gold and silver medal in the women 100 m crawl. The first post-war Games in Antwerp in 1920 didn't offer for the women much that was new. The women participated in both singles and doubles tennis, figure skating, swimming, and gymnastics as a demonstration. The next progress occurred at the 1921 Olympic Congress in Lausanne. There the international fencing association achieved in having Floret fencing included in the 1924 Games in Paris.

The conflict of the second important step, namely allowing the women into the stadium (track and field), had already been in discussion. At the anniversary congress in Paris, at which the program for the planned 1916 Games in Berlin were to be discussed. A plan to allow women to participate in track and field was easily thrown out. After the war the situation had changed considerably. The women were more self confident. During the war the women from most countries had taken on positions and careers that were traditionally for men. In many countries both the active and passive women's right to vote had been introduced. As the IOC moved further to ban women from track and field the women started to organize their own sport events. In France there were already sport clubs which primarily supported track and field. In several countries the track and field associations had already take responsibility for the women's jumping, running and throwing events. In Germany for example there was already a women's track and field championship. In Paris on October 1921, one day after an international track and field competition between England and France, a world women's sport association, the Fédération Sportive Feminine International was formed under the leadership of Alice Milliat. One year later they successfully organized the Women's Olympic Games (Jeux Olympique Féminins) in Paris. This put the international track and field association and even more so the IOC under pressure. Because there were also a Student Olympic Games and a Chess Olympiad. The IOCs monopoly on the term Olympics was in danger. The three associations had to talk and reach some sort of compromise. The FSFI (Fédération Sportive Feminine International) gave up the term Women's Olympic Games and changed it to the Women's World Games (Jeux Féminins Mondiaux). The IAAF (International Amateur Athletic Association) recognized women's track and field and worked to bring rules development and record lists in agreement with those of the FSFI. The IOC was willing to include 5 of the 12 women's track and field events in the 1928 Olympic program in Amsterdam. With this the 2nd important step was completed. The women competed in the public eye in running, jumping and throwing events. During the IOC sessions and congresses the IOC repeatedly tried to discontinue or set aside women's participation but failed each time. Several times they came very close but they failed.

The main point of the critics was an instance when after the women's 800 m run in Amsterdam in 1928 two Canadian runners, distraught that they didn't win, fell onto the grass after the race. In the eyes of the public a lady on the ground was unfemale. The race itself was unusually fast that day. The winner, the German Lina Radke, improved the world record by almost 7 seconds. One of the Canadians was so "exhausted" that the next day she ran a leg for the 4x100 relay team which set a world record. In the finals the same 4x100 team set yet another world record. This and the fact that after the various running events a total of 18 men fell to the ground exhausted was not taken note of.

The third step, the total integration of women in the Olympic program, is nearly complete. From Olympic Games to Olympic Games more and more sports and events for women are being included. With the inclusion of soccer in Atlanta 1996 the last major men's stronghold had fallen. At the Sydney Games in 2000 well over 40% of the participants will be women. In spite of this all of the problems have yet to be taken care of. Namely the following: The IOC has for years set a good example through the hiring of women (12 female IOC members), but there is still a deficit in the amount of women working in the various sport federations. In regards to human rights a more important note is the continuing policies of many Islamic countries which discriminate against and ban women from taking part in the Games. These borders also have to be crossed.

Chapter 30

Women's careers in sport and leisure sciences studies.
A German-English comparison

Karen Petry
German Sport University Cologne, Germany

Although in Germany the demand for equal rights for women did not stop at the door of universities and many lobbyists in the scientific community support the principle of equality there still has been no noticeable change in the past ten years: in Germany women in Sport and Leisure Studies play a rather marginal role - as is shown in figure 1.

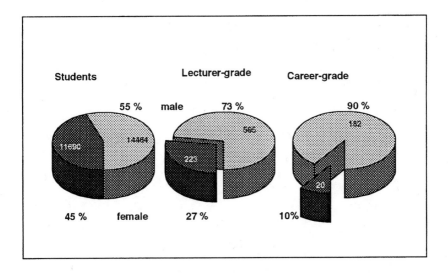

Figure 1: Women in sport and leisure science or studies in Germany
(Source: Statistisches Bundesamt 1996)

Meanwhile numerous national studies and publications concerning the barriers against women in universities now exist, dealing with hierarchical discrimination and the self-image. Within that institutional perspective very often a national point of view is taken – even if the under-representation of women in higher education institutes is a problem, which exists nearly all over the world. Concerning the situation of women in academic fields there are a few international comparative surveys (cf. Onnen-Isemann & Oßwald 1991). Concerning the phenomenon of under-representation of women in sport and leisure science or studies in comparative perspective further regard is necessary for two reasons: (a) there is hardly a study which explicitly mentions sport and leisure science or studies. It is only mentioned within broader collective categories and the specific situation in our field is not convinced; (b) international comparative research about female issues hardly exists so far.

To fill this gap we conducted a survey about the professional careers of female academics working in sport and leisure science or studies at universities in England and Germany. This comparative perspective is based on the fact that the specific structural conditions differ regarding the social system and the university system (e.g. age at the beginning of studying and the so called "habilitation").

Before talking about the research project, I would like to make some remarks about the main differences concerning sport and leisure studies in higher education in Germany and England.

The origin of the German "Sportwissenschaft" is the theory of physical education; however, there has been a terminological change in Germany: the beginning of the seventies a process started which regards sport activities more and more scientifically. The result of this process is a huge differentiation in the fields of research. A variety of universities offer sport science degrees in different types of studies): Diploma, Certificate of Teacher Education and the so called "Magister".

In England the terminological differentiation between Physical Education and Sport Science also exists, however, the term 'Physical Education' has been accepted until now for sport at school. The term 'sport science' is still used to describe more or less the natural science subjects. The replacement of the term physical education – as it took place in Germany is not found in England, as here we find terminological pluralism: Sport Science, Sports Studies Courses, Recreation/ Leisure Management Courses etc. – a variety of studies for specific job areas. This model is aided by the university system: 3-year studies leading to a Bachelor degree lend themselves to be followed by job-specific follow-up studies.

Some selected results of the study

The research project is based on a questionnaire which was sent to women working at Universities and Institutes of Higher Education in Sport and Leisure studies in Germany and England. The collected data of the empirical evaluation comprises a sample of 187 interviewees from Germany and a sample of 102 interviewees from England. The English version of the questionnaire was designed in cooperation with Celia Brackenridge, Professor of Sport and Leisure, Cheltenham and Gloucester College of Higher Education. In the second part of the study narrative interviews were conducted with English experts. The experts were selected according to (a) their own careers and the experience in the field; (b) their knowledge about this particular issue; (c) and their own scientific expertise.

The institutional structure of the universities in England and Germany and the individual orientation of the women in Germany and England vary in some areas. I would like to emphasize these differences in three ways: (a) steps in their academic career; (b) combination of professional and family life; (c) advantages and disadvantages of the profession as sport scientist at university.

Stages in biography concerning education and job

Because of the different systems of higher education in Germany and England the English women studied more subjects and obtained more degrees. Looking more closely at the subjects the women studied, it is obvious that the English women have a education oriented towards teaching: within the "undergraduate studies" the most frequent studies being "Bachelor of Education" (BEd.) - what is a 4 year teacher education. The "Bachelor of Science" (BSc.) – the sport scientific qualification for non-school job areas – is far less frequently chosen. Within the "postgraduate studies" the "Master of Arts" (MA.) is most frequently chosen. Among the German interviewees the "Diploma" and the "State examination" are equally popular. Only a minority obtained the German "Magister".

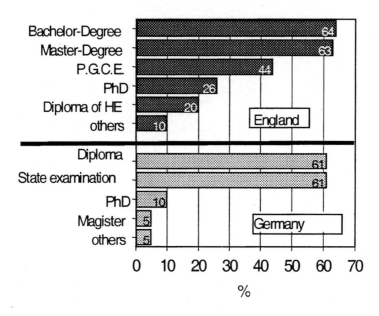

Figure 2 : Level of award/ degrees

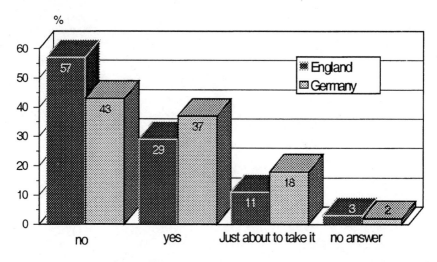

Figure 3 : Do you have a PhD ?

As the diagram illustrated the number of PhDs is slightly higher in Germany. It is significant that one in three English academics obtained the PhD or the MA as they considered it a prerequisite for the academic post they were aimed at. One expert is quoted confirming the increasing necessity of the PhD:

> *"... A lot of people who had to do the PhD really need to make progress in academic life (part-time working, school teaching or lecturing). But it is difficult to get into higher education without a doctorate now. Or if you are appointed then you do a doctorate. There are a lot of people who have done it later. If you want to stay in academic life it's necessary."*

Looking at the age at which the degree was completed at every step the German women are slightly older than their English colleagues. This age difference decreases gradually to only 6 months with the PhD.

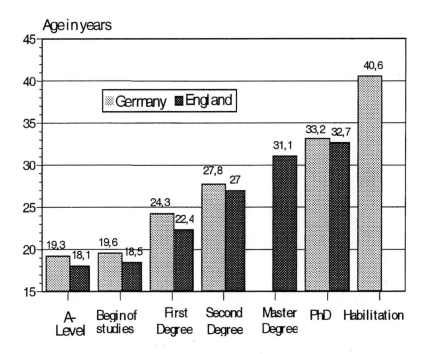

Figure 4 : Age at which the degree was completed

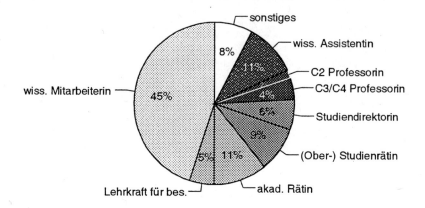

Figure 5 : Current job position in Germany

The study confirms the view that most German women have positions at lecturer grade. This includes, however, the new generation of scientists who may be at a transitional stage, possibly aiming at more senior positions. As many as 11% of the German women interviewed hold a post as "Assistant Professor". Assuming that these women want to qualify for a professorship, they can be seen as progressing towards it; Only 4% of the German women hold a professorship.

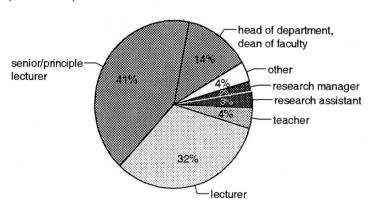

Figure 6 : Current job position in England

It is obvious that more English women work in higher positions (career grade) than their German colleagues: 41% are working in the position as 'Senior Lecturer', 'Principal Lecturer' and/or 'Professor' and 14% have a position as 'Head of Department' or 'Dean of Faculty'.

Relevance of the combination of profession and family life

The study shows that the combination of profession and family life is more important for German women than for their English counterparts. All in all children and family are not as important a focus as they are in Germany. English women are more frequently bread-winners in their family and employing mothers with children is more accepted than it is in Germany.

Germany   **England**

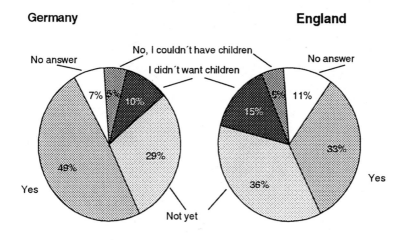

Figure 7 : Do you have children ?

Advantages and disadvantages of the profession as sport scientist at university

German academics value highest in their job self-determination, their English counterparts see teamwork and student support as a clearer advantage.

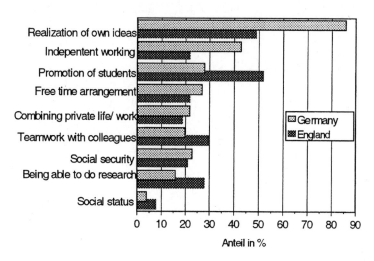

Figure 8 : Advantages of the current job (3 answers possible)

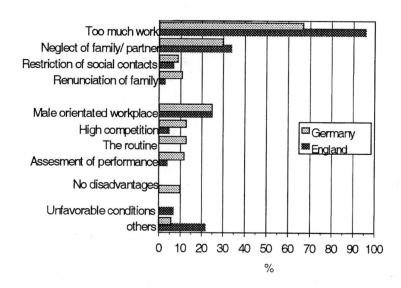

Figure 9 : Disadvantages of the current job (3 answers possible)

As the diagram illustrated the biggest draw-up disadvantage for the English and for the German women is the temporal demands of the job. Another disadvantage is the university felt to be a male orientated workplace. The German-English comparison shows that because of the present changes in higher education in Britain the English women are more dissatisfied with their situation – however this dissatisfaction must be the same for the male. One expert explains the chances as followed:

> *"... The disadvantages are very real ones, and I think that they have envolved along with the changes that the government has done. The university sector now is very hard pressed, I think there is no question about it. We have increasing numbers all the time, decreasing amounts of money; we don't have a lot of money for research, for example, that's why I have to compete with other people. There is a lot of pressure to produce publications, there is no extratime given for us to do that. So it is very difficult and I think it is effectively a result of the government´s attitude towards Higher Education."*

Some implications for sport science in higher education in Germany

As my study showed, the attitudes and behaviour vary between the English and German female academics working in sports science in higher education: the German are more orientated towards family than their English counterparts. The career-orientation of the German is less marked, they are more interested in getting satisfaction from their job than furthering their career. The cause of this difference is to be seen in social conditions: Great Britain has the second highest percentage of working women in the countries of the European Union. The fact that women are working is in general more socially acceptable in Britain. The following quotation illustrates the differences:

> *"... When I came to work in Germany I was shocked at the difference - it seems that in Germany the whole social system is organized around the family ...Schools are organized to start early and finish early. There are structural features in German society which built up this ideology. In Britain these features are much less significant now ... a very low proportion of people live in traditional families and women have to work to survive."*

This aspect could be discussed further but I want to use the remaining place to consider two issues concerning improved perspective for women in sport faculties in German universities: the introduction of more degrees on the one hand and the lose in importance of the German "Habilitation" on the other hand.

The introduction of more degrees

In Germany at the moment the idea of introducing Bachelor and Master-Degrees in Sport and Leisure is under discussion. From my research I can only support this trend in so far that this will improve chances for women. Two or three years of studies offer more possibilities for women to integrate a phase of motherhood and childcare. The mover and the drop-out rates which are very high during a career in universities can be decreased. Not only the international compatibility of university degrees in the field of sport should make German universities more attractive but also better equal opportunities for both, women and men could be achieved through the introduction of a system with Bachelor and Master-Degrees.

The lose in importance of the German "Habilitation"

In Germany there is after the PhD another qualification: the so called "Habilitation" which as you know is a condition for getting a professorship. That this is a further hurdle for women in the academic field of sport is proved by my study: only 5% of the interviewees have this qualification. Politically active women in universities demand the abolition of this anti-women ritual, because it is oriented towards a male career pattern: you have to devote many years of your life writing the "habilitation" – mostly at the age of 30 to 40. For women who want to combine a university career with family life this is a challenge which can not be solved. I am assuming that in the next ten years a lot of professorships in our sport faculties at universities will become vacant because many professors will be coming up to retirement. Because of this there is a need of a new generation of academics and a great chance for women to get to the top. As I mentioned, in England - a country without this qualification - more women are in higher positions in sport faculties in universities. From my point of view it is absolutely necessary to create other criteria of qualification which take into consideration the particular situation of women.

References

Bultmann, T. (1995). Die absurde Personalstruktur des deutschen Hochschulsystems. Werkauftrag der Bundestagsgruppe PDS/ Linke Liste an den BdWi Bonn e.V. .
Onnen-Isemann, C. & Oßwald, U. (1991). Aufstiegsbarrieren für Frauen im Hochschulbereich. In: Studien zu Bildung und Wissenschaft, Bd. 99, Hrsg.: Bundesministerium für Bildung und Wissenschaft, Bonn.

Part E

The world confronting physical education

Chapter 31

Border guards in and of physical education

Dawn Penney
De Montfort University, U.K.

Particularly in the United Kingdom, but also elsewhere, the 1990s have been times of much publicised 'reform' of education, often in response to a claimed crisis, with falling standards and inadequate accountability in schools (see for example Apple 1993; Day 1997). Physical education has not escaped being labelled as in a state of crisis, nor being a target for reform (see Evans 1990). In a number of countries the scale of the political attention directed towards education and physical education specifically has seemed unprecedented. In England and Wales we have seen the development and revision of the National Curriculum for Physical Education and in Australia, the issuing of national texts for newly established Key Learning Areas (KLAs), including Health and Physical Education (HPE). However, as previously I emphasise that amidst (and to some extent because of) these reforms, we have seen important potential for critical review and development in and of physical education go unrealised (see Evans, Penney & Bryant 1993; Penney 1994). Thus, "despite radical changes in the organisational structure of the educational system, the underlying fabric of curriculum has remained surprisingly constant" (Goodson 1993, p. 22); we have seen a curriculum model from the 19th Century deemed appropriate as a basis for teaching and learning in the 21st (Tomlinson 1994, cited in Hargreaves & Evans 1997) and for many teachers it seems, "the past 20 years have been years of survival rather than development" (Day 1997, p. 44).

Picking up on the themes of this conference, in my view there has been maintenance and reinforcement, rather than dissolution, of long-standing boundaries that serve to define physical education, and shape its actual and potential development. In this paper I pursue the nature and origins of boundaries that I believe we must address if we are to see any distinctly new developments in the subject. With reference to recent events in England and Wales and Australia, I discuss both the potential and willingness to challenge established boundaries that following Goodson (1993), I emphasise are both ideological and structural in nature.

Conceptual borders

The development of a National Curriculum for Physical Education (NCPE) in England and Wales presented an apparent opportunity for a redefinition, reorientation and restructuring of the subject. As has been documented, the process of development of this curriculum was destined to be contentious, given the many different and firmly established interest groups within 'physical education' in these countries (see Evans & Penney 1995a). A key characteristic of the development, however, was its failure to challenge the bases of these groups, or their relative status within the 'physical education profession' and subject. Instead, under the auspices of 'reform', existing foci, biases and boundaries in thinking were reinforced and in many schools the curriculum provided as the NCPE seems all too familiar rather than notably 'new' (see Evans, Penney & Bryant 1993). Neither the traditional and established structure of the curriculum, nor the distinctions between the identified constituent parts have been seriously questioned. We should surely ask why the development of the NCPE featured such *distinct* interests ? Who has been retaining and/or reinforcing the boundaries between them ? Who are the 'border guards' within, but also 'of' physical education, since in retention and reinforcement of these boundaries serves to retain a particular identity for the subject.

In raising these issues I direct attention to the work of Basil Bernstein (1990, 1996). For Bernstein it is the maintenance of the "insulation" between different categories that is at the heart of the maintenance of a particular "voice" or "principle of classification" in curricula. Bernstein thus provides powerful tools to employ in investigating the ways in which subjects are "...articulated discursively within certain regimes of truth and evaluative categories that function as gatekeepers" (McLaren 1993, p. x) and "disciplinary discourses may be seen to posses the power to admit certain knowledges ... into select archives of the disciplinary traditions" (ibid, p. x). In the development of the NCPE some groups actively reinforced such insulation. Although it is important to acknowledge that within any interest group a range of different views were expressed, we can nevertheless associate particular responses with specific groups. For example, 'dance' was a group that sought to distance itself from 'physical education', emphasising the *distinct* characteristics of dance, and questioning the appropriateness of it being a component of physical education (see Penney 1994; Talbot 1993). This served to increase the strength of classification inherent in the NCPE and ultimately, the interests of dance have not been furthered by these actions, as it continues to struggle for a place and recognition in the curricula of many schools.

'Health' has been another interest group clearly pursuing a stronger representation in the curriculum, but definitely within rather than outside of physical education. Initially, this 'lobby group' pushed for equal recognition and status to the identified areas of activity (such as games and gymnastic activities) in the NCPE (see Penney 1994; Penney & Evans, forthcoming). Effectively therefore, the pressure was for further boundaries within the subject framework. Subsequently (and when it was clear that health was never likely to achieve such a position in the curriculum), there have been moves towards the dissolution of boundaries between the various areas of activity, with health actively promoted as a potentially unifying force in the physical education curriculum (see for example Harris & Elbourn 1992a,b).

However, these and other divisions of interests have not arisen solely from the groups themselves. It is not only individuals within the various groups who need to be seen as retaining or reinforcing borders within and around the subject. In presenting a particular framework and rationale for the curriculum, the NCPE texts themselves provided particular discursive frames for the development. Both the writers of these texts and the politicians and government agencies to which they have been answerable, need to be acknowledged as key figures in the 'defining of the subject' (see Evans & Penney 1995a; Penney & Evans, forthcoming). Again, though, we need to delve deeper, and recognise that the matters of 'who had what say', "...where when and with what authority " (Ball 1990, p. 17) and who therefore, was accorded the opportunity to determine or shift boundaries in thinking, arose from particular (and notably inequitable) processes of policy development. The *context* of the policy development, as well as the texts themselves, was critical in shaping (and directing) developments, in ensuring that particular interests were dominant and that the NCPE expressed and promoted a particular conception of physical education. If we pursue the source of these influences, we return once again to the politicians establishing the arrangements for the policy development, and determining the key matters of who was in a position to 'speak', and whose voices would be listened to. In recent years in England and Wales we have therefore seen the borders of and for physical education strictly policed by politicians (Evans & Penney 1995a; Penney & Evans, forthcoming).

In attempting to understand contemporary directions in physical education we must also look beyond single initiatives, and indeed, beyond education. Politicians do not exist or make decisions in a vacuum, but rather in complex and particular social, historical, cultural and economic contexts. Policies, curricula and the decisions and actions of politicians, teachers and teacher trainers need to be set 'in context'. All are inevitably influenced by 'surrounding discourses' and society's privileging of some discourses over others. All subjects are players that are "...part of a larger web of differentially empowered publics" (McLaren 1993, p. x; see also Apple 1993). In the development of the NCPE we have seen very clearly that physical education is set within communities and societies that are largely unfamiliar with many educational interests, but that are highly attuned with (and frequently subjected to by the media and politicians) interests of elite sport. For many parents and politicians, performance in elite sport is what they can relate to and see value in children pursuing. It is also what many children probably expect physical education to focus upon. In relation to these matters there has been both a dissolution and simultaneous reinforcement of particular conceptual borders in relation to physical education. On the one hand, the distinction between physical education and sport has been all but dissolved, as politicians and policies equate physical education with sport, and progressively seem to be subsuming the interests of physical education within those of sport. On the other, it is *particular* discourses of sport that have been privileged. The boundaries have been very clear with respect to what is regarded as acceptable content for sport and in turn physical education (see Evans & Penney 1995b; Penney & Evans 1997). With elite performance in a few selected sports remaining a prominent feature of both policy and much practice in physical education in England and Wales, we have struggled to see any real shifting of established borders.

One of the apparent ironies of this situation is that there seems a strong rationale for embracing and giving recognition to an increasing range of physical activities within physical education. There are claims from many quarters (both within and outside of the profession) that physical education has a key role to play in encouraging the development of patterns of behaviour and attitudes towards physical activity that are critical to lifelong health. However, in physical education teaching and teacher training the conception of sport that seems dominant centres upon elite performance, not matters of participation for health and many PE teachers may well be more concerned with pursuing fitness for sport, than fitness for life. 'Sport' and 'health' have largely remained quite distinct voices within but also outside of physical education. While at various times physical education has given voice to, and aligned itself with each of these interests, as yet it seems to have failed to promote a conceptualisation of sport in physical education that firmly embraces and is compatible with interests of lifelong health. Physical education may make claims to be serving both sets of interests (see for example, BAALPE 1998), but whether teachers or teacher trainers are clear about the implications of these claims for the physical education curriculum and the pedagogies that they should employ, is doubtful.

If we turn attention to Australia, we come across some interesting contrasts in terms of the relations between physical education, sport and health, but equally, further evidence of familiar boundaries in developments. The identification of 'Health and Physical Education' (HPE) as one of eight Key Learning Areas (KLAs) in the curriculum, signalled a clear association between health and physical education, but also an underlying and historical divide between health education and physical education (see AEC 1994a,b). In this development there was also strong lobbying from sport organisations for the change of name of the KLA from merely 'health' to 'health and physical education' (see Penney & Glover 1998). Clearly, there was discomfort and a perceived threat associated with the loss of the *explicit* identity of the subject of physical education, and elsewhere I have drawn attention to the tendency, certainly in some parts of Australia, for traditional rather than new identities to be privileged in the implementation of the KLA. I have argued that in Bernstein's terms, we have witnessed the "message" redefining and/or 'resisting' the "voice" provided by the KLA based national framework (see Penney 1998). Some teachers have seemed anxious to retain and protect boundaries that define the subject and their own professional identity. Boundaries between subjects have become "faultlines of conflict" and we have seen that "school subjects are protectively encoded clusters of discourses negotiated in conflictual arenas of political manoeuvring" (McLaren 1993, p. ix). In pursuing the factors underpinning these responses I have emphasised the importance of organisational structures within schools in producing this outcome, but have also drawn attention to the key role of teacher educators in facilitating or equally inhibiting changes in thinking and practice (Penney 1998). Reports that student teachers have struggled to see the relevance of and to grasp some aspects of the KLA, have indicated that training is perhaps not fostering new thinking in physical education, but rather, may all too often be actively reproducing the status quo, with its inherent borders and boundaries (see Glover & Macdonald 1997).

Structural borders.

There are a number of levels or sites of policy and curriculum development at which divisions within and boundaries to curriculum subjects are actively created and maintained by virtue of structural features of systems, organisations and institutions, as well as ideological influences. If we return to developments in England and Wales, it is not insignificant that the identified interests of physical education, sport and health are respectively addressed by three different government departments; the Department for Education and Employment (DfEE), the Department for Culture, Media and Sport (DfCMS) and the Department of Health (DoH). The degree of communication between these departments and the coherency and compatibility of their respective agendas has certainly been questionable, and at times a matter of clear tension. In the development of the NCPE the Minister for Sport voiced a commitment to securing 2 hours per week of physical education in schools; a commitment that the Minister for Education could not consider in the light of an overcrowded curriculum and at a time when the government did not have the authority to prescribe the time that schools should devote to particular subjects (see Evans & Penney 1995b; Penney & Evans, forthcoming). More recently, and this time under a Labour rather than Conservative central government, there have been parallel announcements that greater rates of participation in physical activity is to be a focus within the 'health of the nation' strategy (DoH 1998), while physical education is to become a non-statutory aspect of the national curriculum in primary schools (Blunkett 1998). The government thus seems to be sending somewhat contradictory messages about the importance of physical education.

Meanwhile programmes developed by the Youth Sport Trust (YST) and English Sports Council (ESC) have been introduced in primary schools in England. Currently, at a 'policy level' these initiatives stand parallel to the statutory physical education curriculum, rather being an integral aspect of it. Integration has been encouraged (YST, 1996) and it remains to be seen whether or not the boundaries and borders are formally dissolved in any future revision of the NCPE. Structural issues are critical here. 'Sport' has actively invested in resources and training for physical education, and boundaries between teaching and coaching are being crossed. Inherent in concerns expressed about this development are matters of conceptual coherency and compatibility of the different arenas (sport and education) with which teaching and coaching initiatives are respectively aligned, and from which they emerge (see for example, Talbot 1997; Penney & Evans, forthcoming). We therefore see very clearly the important inter-relationship between the two dimensions of the divisions with which we are concerned.

Events in Australia have also pointed to the significance of structures in curriculum development and particularly those in tertiary institutions and in schools. In addition, they have drawn attention to the importance of relationships between these two sites in considering the potential for any shifting or dissolution of conceptual borders. The maintenance of both subject based departments in schools, and training programmes that develop expertise in only a part of the KLA of HPE (for example, human movement studies as distinct from health and physical education), have seemed key barriers to the development of more integrated curricula in schools. Tertiary institutions in particular appear to be arenas with a clear ability to influence the strength and the scope of boundaries within the physical education profession, and between it and others who have interests in it. Are tertiary educators acting as border guards in and of physical education, and if so, in what and whose interests ? Like teachers, we have professional interests, identities and status at stake. Are we equally guilty therefore, of 'border guard' mentality ? The reactions of some within physical education towards new initiatives (such as sport education or health promoting schools) have clearly indicated a desire to retain rather than shift boundaries (see for example Tinning 1995, 1996; Talbot 1997).

Conclusion

Caution in building bridges and partnerships is justified. There are practical difficulties to consider in contemplating the dissolution of established boundaries to subject matter, such as a lack of adequate expertise to cover an extension in the breadth of curriculum content. In addition, there is a need to ensure that the terms and basis upon which any dissolution or extension of boundaries occurs is such that the subject will provide for the needs and interests of all rather than only some children. However, whether our responses are of caution, resistance, or support, we should be sure of the directions and interests that will be expressed in either new or old agendas. I therefore emphasise the need for all involved in physical education to perhaps start be looking inwards, and to question and clarify what it is that they seek in the future for physical education, before initiating moves towards new or no borders for the subject and profession. In conclusion I return to structural concerns and specifically conditions in England and Wales. Changes in recent years have meant that the potential influence of tertiary institutions and educators to shape the future of physical education, to define, shift or retain its borders, appears to have been fundamentally undermined (see also Evans, Penney & Davies 1996). Like teachers and schools, initial teacher training institutions now have to develop programmes with reference to government requirements and directions, and politicians openly hold a degree of control over critical borders in and of physical education.

References

Australian Education Council (1994a). A statement on health and physical education for Australian schools. Carlton.

Australian Education Council (1994b). Health and physical education - a curriculum profile for Australian schools. Carlton.

Apple, M.W. (1993). Official knowledge. London.

BAAPLE (British Association of Advisers and Lecturers in Physical Education) (1998). Press Release. Primary Physical Education in the New Millennium. The Bulletin of Physical Education, 34 (1), 76-78.

Ball, S.J. (1990). Politics and policy making in education. Explorations in policy sociology. London.

Bernstein, B. (1990). The structuring of pedagogic discourse. Volume IV: Class, codes and control. London.

Bernstein, B. (1996). Pedagogy, symbolic control and identity. Theory, research, critique. London.

Blunkett (1998). Blunkett strengthens curriculum focus on the basics. Press Release, 13/1/98. London.

Day, C. (1997). Teachers in the twenty-first Century : Time to renew the vision. In A. Hargreaves & R. Evans (Eds.). Beyond educational reform. bringing teachers back in. Buckingham.

Department of Health (1998). Our healthier nation. London.

Evans, J. (1990). Defining a Subject : the rise and rise of the new PE ? British Journal of Sociology of Education, 11 (2),155-169.

Evans, J., Penney, D. & Bryant, A. (1993). Improving the quality of $pPhysical education ? The education reform act, 1988 and physical education in England and Wales. Quest, 45, 321-338.

Evans, J. & Penney, D. (1995a). The politics of pedagogy : making a national curriculum physical education. Journal of Education Policy, 10 (1), 27-44.

Evans, J. & Penney, D. (1995b). Physical education, restoration and the politics of sport. Curriculum Studies, 3 (2),.183-196.

Evans, J., Penney, D. & Davies, B.(1996). Back to the future ? Education policy and PE. In N. Armstrong (Ed). New directions in physical education. change and innovation. London.

Glover, S. & Macdonald, D. (1997). Working with the health and physical education statement and profile in physical education teacher education : case studies and omplications. The ACHPER Healthy Lifestyles Journal, 44 (3),.21-25.

Goodson, I.(1993). School subjects and curriculum change. studies in curriculum history. (3rd ed.). London.

Hargreaves, A & Evans, R. (1997). Teachers and educational reform. In A. Hargreaves & R. Evans (eds.). Beyond educational reform. Bringing teachers back in. Buckingham.

Harris, J. & Elbourn, J. (1992). Highlighting health related exercise within the National Curriculum - Part 1. British Journal of Physical Education, 23 (1), 18-22.

Harris, J. & Elbourn, J . (1992). Highlighting health related exercise within the National Curriculum - Part 2. British Journal of Physical Education, 23 (2),.5-9.

McLaren, P. (1993). forward to Goodson, I. (1993). School subjects and curriculum change. Studies in curriculum history. (3rd ed.). London.

Penney, D. (1994). "NO CHANGE IN A NEW ERA ?" The impact of the education reform act (1988) on the provision of PE and sport in state schools. PhD Thesis, University of Southampton.

Penney, D. (1998). School subjects and structures : reinforcing traditional voices in contemporary 'reforms' of education. Discourse : Studies in the Cultural Politics of Education, 19 (1),.5-18.

Penney, D. & Evans, J. (1997). Naming the game. Discourse and domination in physical education and sport in England and Wales. European Physical Education Review, 3 (1), 21-32.

Penney, D. & Evans, J. (forthcoming). Politics, policy and practice in physical education. London.

Penney, D. & Glover, S. (1998). Contested identities : A comparative analysis of the position and definitions of physical education in national curriculum developments in England and Wales and Australia. European Journal of Physical Education, 3 (1), 5-21

Talbot, M. (1993). Physical education and the National Curriculum : some political issues. In G. Mcfee & A. Tomlinson (eds.). Education, sport and leisure : connections and controversies. University of Brighton.

Talbot, M. (1997). Values and aspirations for the profession. The Bulletin of Physical Education, 33 (3), 6-23.

Tinning, R. (1995). The sport education movement : a Phoenix, Bandwagon or Hearse for physical education ? The ACHPER Healthy Lifestyles Journal, 42 (4), 19-20.

Tinning, R. (1996). Physical education and the Health Promoting School : opportunities, issues and challenges. The ACHPER Healthy Lifestyles Journal, 43 (2), 8-11.

Youth Sport Trust (1996). TOP Opportunities for Primary Schools. Primary PE Focus, Spring 1996, 11-14.

Chapter 32

Health education as a part of the P.E. curricula in Sweden and Germany (State of Northrhine-Westphalia) within the last ten years

Annette Fouqué
University of Essen, Germany

Not only because of the phenomenon Ling-gymnastics, Sweden is known to be avid for reform in the field of gymnastics. And these strivings for reform had a considerable and long-lasting impact on Swedish school P.E. as well as on the P.E. systems in various other countries. Having this historical background in mind, together with the fact, that sport activities are extremely popular in Sweden (Engström 1996, p. 231), one can hardly believe, that in 1990 the Ministry of Education came up with the proposal to do away with compulsory P.E. in the upper secondary school (Annerstedt 1991, p. 114). Around the country, this proposal aroused a massive storm of protest, forcing the National Curriculum Revision Committee to devote some more of its attention to the subject P.E. As a result P.E. changed its name to "Idrott och Hälsa" ("Sport and Health") in 1994 and was kept compulsory in comprehensives as well as upper secondary schools, but had to face a heavy reduction in time-allotment.

P.E. in Sweden after the School Reform in 1994

These changes to Swedish P.E. have to be seen within the frame of general development at school and in society. I am not able nor willing to explain the social background responsible for this change in P.E. from Sport to Sport and Health. I will compare the Swedish and the Northrhine-Westphalian concept for health education by means of P.E. as fixed in syllabi and similar material. But it's obvious that Sport and Health mirrors a development in (Swedish) society, a healthy nation is becoming more and more an issue of importance for an ideal society (and therefore pupils have to be taught a healthy lifestyle at school).

Concerning the Swedish school system, already in the 1970s the deficiencies of a central state control over school matters were realised (above all not taking the very different regional conditions and needs into account). At the end of the

1980s the Swedish school system finally became decentralised by law. Since then, education aims are formulated in national curricula, leaving decisions about the way to reach these aims above all to communities and teachers (Skolverket 1994, p. 28). This development can already be traced in the P.E. curricula of the 1980s: binding state instructions about content and structure of P.E. lessons were continuously reduced, while aims became broader all the time and many new contents found their way into P.E. syllabi. In consequence P.E. teachers increasingly lacked a clear orientation, when in the beginning of the 1990s the state felt obliged to reduce it's expenses on a broad scale, not sparing the education sector. A National Curriculum Revision Committee was set up to reflect recent social changes (like globalisation, individualisation, environmental conservation, the growing importance of a healthy lifestyle, and of cause economy measures) in a school reform. As a result in 1994 new curricula were passed for both, the comprehensive and the reorganised upper secondary school, showing clearly the marks of decentralisation (distribution of responsibility) as well as goals and product orientation (generally stated objectives).

Together with the new curricula came a syllabus ("Kursplan") for every subject – also valid nationwide. While the curricula explain the moral concept, basic guidelines and goals of schooling in general, the syllabi specify the goals of education in individual subjects, containing information about the purpose, content and aims of the respective subject (Utbildningsdepartement 1996, p. 5-7). The syllabi for the comprehensive and the upper secondary school are structured according to the following pattern:

Grundskola
(Comprehensive school)

Specification of general education goals (cf. curriculum) for the respective subject.
Idrott och Hälsa: Sport, outdoor-living and various forms of movement and recreation are of high importance for people's health. For this reason it is important to get children and youth to know how their body works and how one can improve physical as well as mental well-being with the help of good food, regular physical activity and outdoor-living...

Goals, that the education in the respective subject shall *strive for* (specify the qualitative development desired in school).
Idrott och Hälsa: The school shall, by means of P.E. teaching, see to it that the pupils...
(e.g.) ... get to understand and be interested in the longer term in regular physical activity as well as basically good habits, that can lead to health and well-being.
... get to know various forms of play, games, dance, sport activities and outdoor-living and can deepen their knowledge in some of these.

Gymnasieskola
(Upper Secondary School)

Specification of general education goals (cf. curriculum) for the respective subject.
Idrott och Hälsa: Sport and Health has a broad health-perspective. The pupils are to get an advanced knowledge about how their body works and how one can improve physical and mental well-being with the help of good food, regular physical activity and outdoor-living...

Structure and character of the subject *Idrott och Hälsa*:	Structure and character of the subject *Idrott och Hälsa*:
- Movement, Rhythm and Dance	Health includes physical, mental and social
- Nature and Outdoor-living	well-being and can lead to a higher degree in
- Lifestyle, Surroundings, and Health	quality of life...

Goals that everybody shall be given the opportunity of achieving (minimum level; basis for evaluation and follow-up of daily work). Stated explicitly in the goals to be achieved:
a) by the end of grade 5
b) by the end of grade 9
Idrott och Hälsa:
a) (e.g.) experience in current sport activities; ability to swim and manage difficult situations in the water;
b) (e.g.) understanding of the connection between food, movement and well-being; skills and knowledge of the currently most popular sports, together with the ability to organise and lead a sporting activity.

Goals that everybody shall be given the opportunity of achieving (minimum level; basis for evaluation and follow-up of daily work). Stated explicitly in the goals to be achieved:
a) by the end of course A (80 hours)
b) by the end of course B (60 hours)
Idrott och Hälsa:
a) (e.g.) knowledge of different factors influencing man's health as well as the connection between health, lifestyle and surroundings – seen out of an individual and a social perspective;
ability to analyse different physical activities regarding their meaning for health and well-being;
ability to arrange, carry out and analyse a personal programme for physical training;

The word "sport" has vanished completely out of the headlines structuring the subject Sport and Health and is featured only in "Movement, Rhythm and Dance". Taking the concrete goals for grade 5 and 9 into consideration, it becomes clear, that P.E. not only changed its name, but has really undergone a change in the sport paradigm. P.E. has become a health subject with sports playing a different role: sports now serve as a means to achieve general aims of schooling, with the central focus on health (Skolverket 1993, p. 3; Skolverket 1994, p. 29). But, according to the decentralisation and product orientation, these goals lack detail about content and methods by which healthy pupils have to be physically educated.

P.E. in Northrhine-Westphalia according to the current Curriculum and the Health Campaign started in 1987

In the beginning of the 1970s all relevant Northrhine-Westphalian schools got a new P.E. curriculum. But after having provided primary school and the different types of secondary schooling with new guidelines and syllabi, one recognised, that they didn't fit together properly (secondary school curricula e.g. presupposing qualifications that primary school curricula didn't contain, use of inconsistent terminology etc.) (Naul & Großbröhmer 1996, p. 31-34). So in 1974 a curriculum commission was set up to revise and unite all the single curricula to one big harmonised oeuvre. At the end of 1980 the "Richtlinien und Lehrpläne für den Sport in den Schulen im Lande NRW" ("Guidelines and syllabi for P.E. in the schools of the State Northrhine-Westphalia") were passed.

The goals for P.E. were presented in the form of 9 tasks for school sports (Kultusminister 1980, p. 9-13): (1) preventive training and healthy lifestyle; (2) material and physical experiences by means of movement; (3) sporting performance and self-confidence; (5) self-organisation of sports situations; (6) variation of sport; (7)compensation and leisure at school; (8) reference to peer group sport; (9) reference to adult sport.

Originally all these 9 tasks were given more or less equal importance. But in 1987 the Minister of Education in Northrhine-Westphalia started a campaign on "Health Education in School by means of P.E.", focusing on the first task "preventive training and healthy lifestyle". This campaign was based on "The Action Programme for the Promotion of Health Education in Schools by means of P.E.", published in 1987. A mass of articles and books, all dealing with health education in school P.E., was and still is being published. I will concentrate on the "Handreichungen" ("Recommendations") prepared by a health insurance company, politicians, P.E. teachers and scientists. These recommendations inform P.E. teachers about the pedagogical concept and give practical advice for the realisation of health education by means of P.E. (Kultusminister 1990; 1993).

Comparison of Health Education by means of P.E. according to Swedish Syllabi and Northrhine-Westphalian Recommendations

The goals for health education by means of P.E. in Northrhine-Westphalia are centred around the idea of "health education" that has a much broader objective than health promotion. Health promotion is limited to physical factors, aiming to prevent diseases and physical defects by making and keeping pupils fit. This notion of health promotion formed the basis for Swedish school P.E. for one and a half centuries.

A comparison of the Swedish syllabus for upper secondary Sport and Health with the Northrhine-Westphalian recommendations for upper secondary health education shows that it is possible to correlate individual suggestions by the Northrhine-Westphalian recommendation with matching goals for upper secondary sport and health as written down in the Swedish syllabus:

Sweden: upper secondary Sport and Health (Syllabus from 1994)	Northrhine-Westphalia: upper secondary Health Education by means of P.E. (Recommendations from the end of the 1980's)
Ability to arrange, carry out and analyse a personal programme for physical training (goal no. 4)	Learn how to train and pursue selfset goals (theme no. 3)
Ability to apply ergonomic knowledge to different working situations (goal no. 9)	To integrate movement into everyday life and know how to handle stress (theme no. 9)

These are not the only stunning similarities to be observed between the Swedish and the Northrhine-Westphalian concept of health education by means of P.E.:

1. The purpose of health education according to P.E. recommendations/ syllabi: Both countries are aiming at a health education that contains physical, mental and social aspects of well-being. In the long term, health education has to improve pupils health by making them feel better (subjectively and objectively). This is valid for Sweden as well as Northrhine-Westphalia, especially the later one talking of „wellness" that is to be achieved on a physical, mental, social and ecological level by suitable experiences and insights on the pupils' side. For Sweden this means that P.E. took a turn from health promotion to health education. *P.E. = Tool to get healthy pupils conducting a healthy lifestyle throughout their lives.*

2. The content of health education by means of P.E. as fixed in the syllabi/recommendations: in general the Swedish syllabi lack details about the content of Sport and Health, naming: (a) ergonomics; (b) food and nutrition; (c) health, lifestyle and environment; (d) hygiene; (e) outdoor-living; (f) relaxation; (g) eating disorders, doping, cheating and spectator violence besides the common contents: sports, dance etc.. It can be stated that ergonomics and outdoor-living have featured as an important part in Swedish P.E. at least since the mid-war-period and as such were also taken into consideration by the curriculum commission when dealing with the concept Sport and Health. In Northrhine-Westphalia however, ergonomics and outdoor-living were not really discovered for school P.E. until 1987, when they were implemented for health education reasons. *The content of P.E. in Northrhine-Westphalia resembles to a high degree the Swedish subject matter.*

3. The principles for teaching arrangements: both the Swedish and the Northrhine-Westphalian papers stress the importance of: (a) ore theoretical instruction; (b) extension of pupil influence and responsibility.

Besides the stunning conformity between the Swedish and the Northrhine-Westphalian understanding of health education by means of P.E., one should not forget that in Sweden health education forms an essential part of the binding syllabi for Sport and Health since 1994, while in Northrhine-Westphalia no P.E. teacher is compelled to teach along the recommendations reflecting the action programme from 1987.

The Northrhine-Westphalian P.E. Curriculum 2000 in relation to the Swedish Model "Sport and Health"

On the other side, this important difference between compulsory health education in Swedish P.E. and recommended health education in Northrhine-Westphalian P.E. might be gone in 2 or 3 years time. In 1995, 20 years after the last curriculum commission was set up, the Northrhine-Westphalian ministry of education engaged a group of P.E. researchers and teachers to prepare a revision of the current P.E. curriculum.

In the meantime, the first proposals for the curriculum revision were presented (Landesinstitut für Schule und Weiterbildung 1997), dealing with: (1) the future pedagogical basis for school P.E. in Northrhine-Westphalia; (2) the schooling tasks that are to be solved by inter-disciplinary P.E. teaching; (3) the future contents of P.E.

Concerning the pedagogical basis, the 9 tasks for P.E. were replaced by 6 pedagogical perspectives, covering more or less the "old" tasks. With respect to health education, one perspective is worth mentioning: "improving fitness and developing health perception", substituting for "preventive training and healthy lifestyle". The fact that fitness is mentioned explicitly indicates that in the future P.E. teachers are not only supposed to strive for their pupils wellness (which is difficult to measure), but also have to improve their fitness in terms of muscular power, flexibility and endurance. This means that while Sweden tried to overcome it's old concept of health promotion that was limited to physical training, aiming now at a broader health education, Northrhine-Westphalia wants to implement measurable physical training into the existing wellness concept.

The current Swedish curricula stress the importance of inter-disciplinary teaching especially when it comes to health education. The Northrhine-Westphalian proposals name the contribution of P.E. to health education first, listing the inter-disciplinary tasks for P.E., and thus follows the Swedish model also in this respect.

The curriculum revision group is no longer talking of sports when concerned with P.E. content, but uses the expression "areas of movement and sport". According to the committee's suggestion, P.E. in the future is to contain 9 such areas of movement and sport (Landesinstitut für Schule und Weiterbildung 1997, p. 46): (1) body awareness and movement foundations; (2) play (knowing how to play and how to arrange playing); (3) running, jumping, throwing - track and field; (4) movements in the water - swimming; (5) swinging, rolling, climbing, balancing - gymnastics and acrobatics; (6) design, dance, show - dance and arts of movement; (7) Regulations (acceptance and variation) - games; (8) roller-skating, skateboarding, rowing, sailing, winter sports; (9) wrestling and fighting - single combat sports.

The first two areas are meant to form the heart of future P.E. in Northrhine-Westphalia, promoting the development of human movement in general and thus see to the preconditions necessary for participation in sports culture. Health education gets distinguished as an important subject of the first area, containing fitness training, relaxation methods, functional gymnastics, ergonomics etc. In addition, the 4th area is to be taught along the pedagogic perspective "fitness and health perception".

The 9 areas are supplemented by a 10th issue, stressing the importance of

knowledge and reflection in P.E., which is especially true for health education by means of P.E..
Altogether, the proposals for the curriculum revision in Northrhine-Westphalian P.E. are pointing in the same direction that P.E. in Sweden already took in the beginning of the 1990s. This development for P.E. shared by Sweden and Northrhine-Westphalia is characterised by: (a) sports no longer determine the goals and content of P.E.; (b) the learning of motor skills is not kept in the forefront any longer; (c) a more and more concurring health perspective being of central importance; (d) the aim to get all children interested and involved in physical activities is highly weighted; (e) lifestyle, environment and ecology are looked upon in relation to health and physical activities; (f) integration of theory and practice; (g) inter-disciplinary working; (h) pupils' influence and responsibility.

Conclusions

Though there are even some more general developments to be observed in Northrhine-Westphalia that are similar to the Swedish P.E. policy in the recent past, like the strive for decentralisation, enabling each school to decide more on it's own about teaching methods and content as well as on what to spent money, there's no evidence for greater links between Swedish and Northrhine-Westphalian P.E. authorities. As modern Europeans we should learn from our ancestors who travelled to Stockholm in order to get familiarized with Ling-gymnastics, and look out for foreign experience when occupied with P.E. (curriculum) matters. Especially when there's a country at hand that, a few years ago, already implemented a concept of health education by means of P.E. very like our own one!

In order to be able to profit from Swedish experience with health education by means of P.E., an international commission is to be set up. At the University of Gothenburg a comprehensive study has been carried out, evaluating the implementation of the new upper secondary curriculum and P.E. syllabi from 1994 among others in terms of (Annerstedt & Patriksson 1996, p. 2): (a) pupils' physical fitness; (b) pupils' exercise and leisure-time activities; (c) teachers' opinion.

There's one part of the Gothenburg research project that should be studied intensively by the Northrhine-Westphalian curriculum committee: dealing with pupils' health habits when they start upper secondary school in comparison with their health habits when leaving upper secondary school (Berggren 1998). In combination with an empirical study evaluating the current health education by means of P.E. following the Northrhine-Westphalian recommendations, an expressive empirical basis could be created for further considerations and decision-making in connection with the Northrhine-Westphalian P.E. curriculum 2000.

References

Annerstedt, C. (1991). Idrottslärarna och Idrottsämnet. Göteborg, Vasastadens Bokbinderi.

Annerstedt, C. & Patriksson, G. (1996). The New Swedish Curriculum in Physical Education – is the outcome as expected? Poster presented at the AISEP International Seminar in Lisbon, Portugal 21-24 November 1996.

Berggren, C. (1998). Ungdomars Hälsovanor. Tidskrift i Gymnastik & Idrott, 3, p. 14-17.

Engström, L.-M. (1996). Sweden, in De Knop, P., Engström, L.-M., Skirstad, B. & Weiss, M.R. (eds.), Worldwide trends in youth sport. Champaign IL, Human Kinetics, p. 231-243.

Kultusminister des Landes Nordrhein-Westfalen (ed.), (1980). Richtlinien und Lehrpläne für den Sport in den Schulen im Lande Nordrhein-Westphalen, vol. 1. Köln, Greven Verlag.

Kultusminister des Landes Nordrhein-Westfalen & AOK in Nordrhein-Westfalen (eds.), (1990). Gesundheitserziehung in der Schule durch Sport – Handreichung für die Sekundarstufe I. 2nd edition. Bonn, AOK Verlag.

Kultusminister des Landes Nordrhein-Westfalen & AOK in Nordrhein-Westfalen (eds.), (1993). Gesundheitserziehung in der Schule durch Sport – Handreichung für die Sekundarstufe II. Remagen, AOK Verlag.

Landesinstitut für Schule und Weiterbildung (ed.), (1997). Vorschläge zur Curriculumrevision im Schulsport in Nordrhein-Westfalen, Heft 3. Soest.

Naul, R. & Großbröhmer, R. (1996). 40 Jahre Schulsport in Nordrhein-Westfalen. Düsseldorf, Concept Verlag.

Skolverket (ed.), (1993). Idrott – Huvudrapport. Stockholm, Katarina Tryck.

Skolverket (ed.), (1994). Idrott på Landsbygd och i Storstad. Stockholm, Katarina Tryck.

Utbildningsdepartement (ed.), (1996). The School lays the foundation for the future. Stockholm.

Chapter 33

The role of physical education and sport in nation building

March L. Krotee and David J. Waters
University of Minnesota, USA and Institute of Education,
Singapore

> *"When speaking of the play-element in culture we do not mean that ... an important place is reserved for play nor ... that civilization has a risen out of play by some evolutionary process, in the sense that something which was originally play passed into something which was no longer play and could henceforth be called culture. The view we take ... is that culture arises in the form of play, that is played from the very beginning ... It is through this playing that society expresses its interpretation of life and the world."* (Huizinga 1955 : p. 46).

In today's modern society it is clear that the survival of humankind will require cooperative solutions to the myriad of challenging problems that face an ever more complex and interdependent world. Our educational institutions and professions, specifically the profession of physical education, health, recreation, dance, and sport [1], whose operational philosophies, processes, and practices were conceived and nurtured in a pre global era, now face perhaps the greatest challenge in their short history: the challenge of educating the diverse populations of the globe about the world — about other nations' and cultures' beliefs, feelings, aspirations, attitudes, and actions. The profession faces the challenge of educating the youth to the inter-relatedness and interaction of humankind (intercultural development) rather than simply identifying pluralistic uniqueness or difference in a artificial, isolated, self-contained, and self-serving fashion. They face the ultimate challenge of showing both our communities at home as well as the global neighborhood abroad the importance of physical education and sport to nation building and constructing a better place to live.

The concept of global education or education for world understanding, including "global fairness," intercultural development, and nation building, sets a significant conceptual stage that affects the profession. This manuscript delves into the vital role that physical education and sport can play in the nation building process. The authors share a model National Sport Development Index (NSDI) as well as the International Sport Management Questionnaire (Waters & Krotee 1995) (ISMQ) rooted in such global research initiatives as the Human Development and Physical Quality of Life studies (Morris 1979; ODC 1991; UNDP 1994) and explore the NSDI's potential contributions to the profession.

The concept of a shrinking earth and the inter relatedness of humankind are not new, having been prominently integrated in the United Nations Educational, Scientific, and Cultural Organization's (UNESCO) International Charter of Physical Education and Sport developed in Paris, France, November 21, 1978. The Charter supports the notion that geographical or geopolitical regions or peoples are no longer, nor can they be envisaged as, isolated from the rest of the world (UNESCO 1993). Likewise, the intimate relationship between sport and nation building is not new. Sport as it was practiced and recounted in past societies became a foundational cornerstone of cultures and countries that often linked sport and nation building through its role of building strong bodies for national defense and its embodiment of civil commitment and national character (Carr 1977; Crawford 1987; Riordan 1986). Thus, when one nation builds it is bound to effect and influence those in the global neighborhood. At this writing it is crucial that the profession through its councils, commissions, and research and development arms take leadership in the shaping of a positive nation building process that fully integrates all domains and players of sport in its contextual mix.

In order to accomplish this task we must face this educational reality responsibly, and begin to cultivate a sensitivity to the need to gain greater knowledge and understanding regarding all phases of this dynamic inter relatedness and process (Hoogvelt 1988; Morgenthau 1991). Rapidly dispersing beliefs, attitudes, values, and social thoughts, delicately intertwined with distributive demographic factors (i.e., population, health, wealth, and life expectancy), the birth of new nations, and the world's capability of advanced technology and accessing the cyber fiber-optic highway point to the urgency for greater global understanding, cooperation and coalition building rather than differentiated containment and competition. At no time in the brief history of humankind has this urgency been intensified to the level that now exists.

> *"Many great civilizations in history have collapsed at the very height of their achievement because they were unable to analyze their basic problems, to change direction and to adjust to the new situations which faced them by concerting their wisdom and strength. Today the civilization which is facing such a challenge is not just one small part of mankind — it is mankind as a whole."* (Kurt Waldheim)

Our profession, through organizations such as the American Alliance for Health, Physical Education, Recreation and Dance (AAHPERD), the International Society for Comparative Physical Education and Sport (ISCPES), and the International Council for Health, Physical Education, Recreation, Sport and Dance (ICHPER.SD) among others must lead the way to develop sound and meaningful conceptual frameworks from which to launch the message that we intend to meet the teaching (including curricular reform), research, and service challenge of the 21st century! We intend to deal with the challenge of attacking and impacting on global issues that transcend national boundaries, such problems and issues as peace, hunger, disease, energy, human rights, economy, environmental and ecological harmony that are integral to developing a healthy and productive quality of life. These problems and issues can be influenced by our profession which by nature is transnational in scope and dimension and woven into the fabric of nationhood. Thus, physical education and sport provides an unmatched educational vehicle to develop not only the full potential of the individual, but enhance the quality of life for all.

Nation building: current status, challenge, and path toward the 21st century

There is little doubt that those of us concerned and actively involved in the profession have a difficult path ahead. Research by UNESCO (1993), Fagerlind and Saha (1989); Guttman (1988); Howell and Howell (1988); Krotee and Elnashar (1996) confirm that myriad forms of physical education and sport have evolved over time. These sport forms are pervasive in most societies and may serve as a crucial vehicle for socialization; to preserve and pass on culture, serve as a agent of change, and as a salient form of cultural expression and empowerment. Coakley (1998) further characterized sport's role and relationship to national development and nation building as follows: (a) to safeguard the public order; (b) to maintain and develop fitness and physical abilities among citizens; (c) to promote the prestige of a community or nation; (d) to promote a sense of identity, belonging, and unity among citizens; (e) to emphasize values and orientations consistent with dominant political ideology in a community or society; (f) to increase citizen support of individual political leaders and the government itself.

Mallison's (1975) model of building identity and national character, an endeavor with which physical education and sport has long been associated, further defines the role that the profession should be undertaking to build a better society. Yet, something is missing from the equation. Something that researchers ranging from Anthony (1980) to Ziegler (Krotee & Jaeger 1986) have called for — the development of a systematic approach, plan or strategy for the world–wide assessment and analysis of our area of concern which is the role of physical education and sport in nation building. An instrument or index whose aims would focus on the following: (a) to establish reliable data on each country and system; (b) to reach for and describe similarities and differences between systems and infrastructures that deliver sport; to interpret why these exist; (c) to estimate the relative effect and relationship of the variables or factor components that serve to be influential in the conduct of sport in its various domains (mass, educational, elite); (d) to determine the need for systematic reform and lay the groundwork for strategic planning, policy formation, program development and coalition building.

With this challenge in focus and keeping in mind that development is a widely participatory process of social change and material advancement including greater fairness, equality, and freedom for the majority of people through their gaining greater control over the environment, the authors set about to construct and refine the ISMQ that would lead to the development of a conceptual framework of a National Sport Development Index (see figures 1 and 2).

The NSDI model represents the various sport delivery systems and infrastructures that a nation needs if it is to be "developed." The framework has its roots in modernization theory (Inkeles 1969). The theory postulates that when individuals, institutions, and even traditional societies view the NSDI model that they will change. Change that according to the model will be thoroughly planned, systematic, phased, progressive and irreversible, allowing for sport to develop. In time, as the sport institutions and systems develop, they impart modern values and programs which enable individuals to enact modern behavior which in aggregate define a modern society. A cycle that will continue to form, grow, and become more refined as each nation invests in the health and welfare of its human resources or capitol.

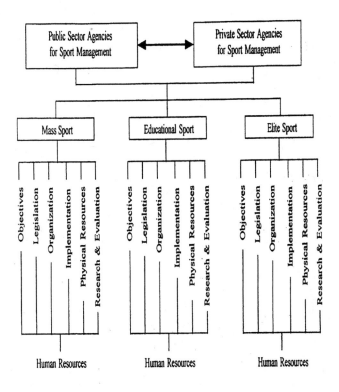

Figure 1 : Conceptual framework of sport delivery and infrastructure of the
National Sport Development Index (NSDI) (Waters & Krotee 1995)

Nation: ....   Region: ....   Sub-region: ....   NSDI Total : ....

Name of Domain and Factor Components	% of Total	Actual Score
1. Mass Sport Domain		
A. Objectives	5	_____
B. Legislation	5	_____
C. Organization	5	_____
D. Implementation	5	_____
E. Physical resources	5	_____
F. Research and evaluation	5	_____
G. Human Resources	3	_____
	Possible Total = 33	_____
2. Educational Sport Domain		
A. Objectives	5	_____
B. Legislation	5	_____
C. Organization	5	_____
D. Implementation	5	_____
E. Physical resources	5	_____
F. Research and evaluation	5	_____
G. Human Resources	3	_____
	Possible Total = 33	_____
3. Elite Sport Domain		
A. Objectives	5	_____
B. Legislation	5	_____
C. Organization	5	_____
D. Implementation	5	_____
E. Physical resources	5	_____
F. Research and evaluation	5	_____
G. Human Resources	3	_____
	Possible Total = 33	
4. Contribution to Nation Building*	Possible Total = 1	_____
	Possible Total = 100	_____

*Contribution to Nation Building: this factor component was a summary of *Yes* or *No* responses and rating results on the IMSQ for each of the three sport domains (mass, educational and elite).

Figure 2 : National Sport Development Index (NSDI) (Waters & Krotee, 1995)

The ISMQ consists of 138 questions divided among three physical activity and sport domains (mass, educational, elite). The instrument was developed and pilot tested over a period of two years and eventually sent to 197 nations' representatives — primarily sport administrators and educational leaders. The results provided a National Sport Development Index whose purpose is to comprehensively and empirically explore and evaluate nations' sports delivery systems and infrastructures. The NSDI may be employed in a global fashion (Waters & Krotee 1997) where participating nations' mass, educational, and elite rankings can be examined (table 1) or regionally, (Krotee & Waters 1998) where, for example, African nations' status is addressed both comparatively (table 2) and developmentally (table 3). Regardless, the NSDI was found to significantly correlate to other indices (Human Development Index, Physical Quality of Life Index), thus opening the door for physical education and sport to be included as part of each nation's overall development strategy and policy–making process — a process that as professionals we can and should contribute to by taking an active part and reaching out, networking, and coalition building with our counterparts in the shrinking global community so that all may develop to their fullest potential. This is the challenge that we as professionals must vigorously undertake if indeed physical education and sport is to continue to play an integral role in building a better society for greater understanding and peace.

Table 1: Educational sport: global ranking of 30 respondent nations on the NSDI

Rank	Nation	Educ. sport	Rank	Nation	Educ. sport
1	Japan	30.9	16	Libia Arab. Rep.	21.9
2	U.S.	29.2	17	Iran, Islamic Rep.	21.5
3	Finland	26.5	18.5	Canada	21.3
4	Egypt	26.2	18.5	China, Peo. Rep.	21.3
5	Poland	26.0	20	Trinidad & Tobago	21.2
6	Czech Rep.	25.9	21	Hong Kong	21.0
7	Singapore	25.2	22.5	Kenya	20.6
8.5	Israel	24.5	22.5	Tunisia	20.6
8.5	Russian Fed.	24.5	24	Netherlands	20.4
10	Liechtenstein	24.0	25	Rwanda	20.2
11	Korea, Rep. of	23.4	26	Ghana	20.0
12	Mexico	23.1	27	Hungary	19.1
13	Belarus	23.0	28	Brunei Darussal.	18.9
14	Australia	22.5	29	Uruguay	18.5
15	U.K.	22.0	30	Belgium	18.4

Table 2 : Comparative NSDI data for African respondent nations with contributions of domains of sport and nation building factor

Nation	Mass sport	Educ. sport	Elite sport	Nation building	NSDI total
Botswana	1.1	15.2	13.4	1.0	30.7
Egypt	26.1	26.2	26.3	1.0	79.6
Ghana	16.7	20.0	16.9	1.0	54.6
Kenya	12.0	20.6	15.1	1.0	48.7
Libia	26.9	21.9	22.6	1.0	72.4
Namibia	8.6	12.3	12.7	1.0	34.6
Nigeria	11.9	17.3	4.1	1.0	34.3
Rwanda	15.5	20.2	19.1	1.0	55.8
Somalia	21.4	17.1	5.5	1.0	45.0
South Africa	14.0	14.7	22.5	1.0	52.2
Tanzania	0.5	11.8	1.9	1.0	15.2
Tunisia	18.4	20.6	25.1	1.0	65.1
Zambia	0.2	1.6	3.9	1.0	6.7
Zimbabwe	8.1	11.9	3.4	1.0	24.4
Means	*13.0*	*16.5*	*13.8*	*1.0*	*44.2*
Stand. dev.	*8.7*	*6.0*	*8.7*		*21.2*

Table 3 : Factor components for mass sport, educational sport, and elite sport: Africa versus developed nations

Factor component	African nations (n=14) mean	Developed nations (n= 20) mean
1. Mass sport domain		
Objectives (5 pts.)	2.4	3.1
Legislation (5 pts.)	1.4	2.3
Organization (5 pts.)	3.6	3.2
Implementation (5 pts.)	1.6	2.1
Physical resources (5 pts.)	1.7	2.9
Research and evaluation (5 pts.)	1.1	2.4
Human resources (3 pts.)	1.2	1.4
Mass sport total (33 pts.)	*13.0*	*17.2*
2. Educational sport domain		
Objectives (5 pts.)	3.4	4.0
Legislation (5 pts.)	3.2	4.2
Organization (5 pts.)	4.2	3.7
Implementation (5 pts.)	1.7	2.9
Physical resources (5 pts.)	1.2	2.9
Research and evaluation (5 pts.)	1.0	2.1
Human resources (3 pts.)	1.8	1.8
Mass sport total (33 pts.)	*16.5*	*21.4*
3. Elite sport domain		
Objectives (5 pts.)	2.8	2.3
Legislation (5 pts.)	1.9	2.6
Organization (5 pts.)	3.1	3.7
Implementation (5 pts.)	1.9	2.9
Physical resources (5 pts.)	1.6	3.1
Research and evaluation (5 pts.)	1.0	2.0
Human resources (3 pts.)	1.5	2.0
Mass sport total (33 pts.)	*13.8*	*18.5*

References

Anthony, D. (1980). A strategy for British sport. London.

Carr, G. (1974). The use of sport in the German Democratic Republic for the promotion of national consciousness and international prestige. Journal of Sport and History, 1(2),123–136.

Coakley, J.J. (1998). Sport in society. Issues and controversies (6h Ed). New York, NY.

Crawford, S. (1987). Some comments on the nineteenth century pattern of British sporting and recreational life. Physical Education Review, 10(1) 21–29.

Fagerlind, I. & Saha, L.J. (1989). Education and national development. Oxford.

Guttmann, A. (1978). From ritual to record: The nature of modern sports. New York.

Glasser, W. (1972). The identity society. New York.

Hoogvelt, A.M. (1988). Sociology of developing societies. Hong Kong.

Howell, M.L. & Howell, R. (1988). Physical activities and sport in early societies. In E.F. Zeigler (ed.), History of physical education and sport (pp. 156). Champaign, IL.

Huizinga, J. (1955). Homo ludens: A study of the play element in culture. Boston.

Inkeles, A. (1969). Making men modern: On the causes and consequences of individual change in six developing countries. American Journal of Sociology, 75(2), 208–225.

Krotee, M.L. (1979). The dimensions of sport sociology. West Point, NY.

Krotee, M.L. (1979). The rise and demise of sport: A reflection of Uruguayan society. The Annals of the American Academy of Political and Social Science, 445, 141-154.

Krotee, M.L. (1981). The saliency of the study of international and comparative physical education and sport. Comparative Physical Education and Sport, 8, 23-27.

Krotee, M.L. & Bucher, C.A. (1998). Management of physical education and sport. New York, NY.

Krotee, M.L., Chien, I.-H. & Alexander, J.F. (1980). The role of the psychosocial study of physical activity and sport. Asian Journal of Physical Education, 3, 8389.

Krotee, M.L. & Elnashar, A. (1996). Physical Education and sport: Middle East perspective. Paper presented at the annual convention of the American Alliance for Health, Physical Education, Recreation, and Dance, Atlanta, GA.

Krotee, M.L. & Jaeger, E. M. (Eds.) (1986). Comparative physical education and sport: Volume 3. Champaign, IL.

Krotee, M.L. & Waters, D.J. (In Press).   The status of African sport development: A fourteen nation perspective. African Journal of Health, Recreation, and Physical Education.

Mallinson, V. (1975). An introduction to the study of comparative education. London.

Moore, W.E. (Ed.) (1967). Global sociology: The world as a singular system. Order and change: Essays in comparative sociology. New York.

Morgenthau, H.J. (1991). Politics: among nations. New York, NY.

Morris, D.M. (1979). Measuring the condition of the world's poor. The Physical Quality of Life Index. New York.

Overseas Development Council. (1991). Figure 15. Economic and social indicators of development (pp. 37–43). In J. Edlund–Braun (ed.), U.S. foreign policy and developing countries. Discourse and data 1991. Washington.

Riding, A. (1989). Distant neighbors. New York, NY.

Riordan, J. (1986) State and sport in developing societies. International Review for the Sociology of Sport, 21(4), 287–303.

United Nations Development Program (UNPD). (1994). Human development report 1994. New York.

United Nations Educational, Scientific and Cultural Organization (UNESCO). (1993). International charter of physical education and sport. Paris.

Ward, B. (1966). Spaceship earth. New York.

Ward, B. (1962). The rich nations and the poor nations. London.

Waters, D.J., & Krotee, M.L. (1997). Educational sport: An international and comparative study. In Proceedings of the AIESEP World Congress on Teaching, Coaching, and Fitness Needs in Physical Education, and the Sport Sciences, pp. 498-503.

Note

[1] For the purpose of this manuscript the term *sport* will be used to denote the comprehensive spectrum of human movement based on the *Physical Activity and Sport Continuum* (PASC) developed by Krotee in 1980 (Krotee, Chein & Alexander 1980). The PASC ranges from play and physical education to professional and performing sport and dance (Krotee & Bucher, 1998).

Chapter 34

A comparative analysis of physical education programs in Puerto Rico, the United States and Europe

Ilia N. Morales-Figueroa, March L. Krotee
and Laurence E. Myeres
University of Minnesota, USA

The need for cross-national and multicultural research in education has been identified by a number of prominent researchers (Krotee & Hanafy 1986; Paige 1986; UNESCO 1993) as paramount to a vibrant professional future. The comparative and cross-national research that has been conducted within the profession of physical education has been varied in nature. Research ranging from Anthony's (1966) guiding purposes and principles to Ziegler's (1987) appeal to cooperatively communicate and conduct comparative research as part of a new world order strategy have served to lay the conceptual framework for not only the need to conduct comparative studies in physical education and sport, but also the inherent values of cross-cultural and trans-national cooperative collaboration.

Although there has been some systematic comparative research concerning physical education and sport structures and systems (Broom 1989; Portela-Suarez 1974), academic programs (Krotee, Larson & Ratigan 1991; Haag 1987), educational opportunities (Gee 1987; Haag 1987), and nation building (Waters & Krotee 1997; Tye 1990; Fagerlind & Saha 1983), there seems to be a dearth of investigation concerning Hispanic secondary schools (Portela-Suarez 1974; Olivella-Benjamino 1981) and international schools and their structures, programs, and resources. With this in mind, it seemed appropriate to explore the nature of delivery of physical education and sport in these two specific environs and compare them with their United States secondary school counterpart in order to gain a greater understanding of not only the systems of secondary school physical education and sport, but their significant differences and common needs in order to meet the challenges of the 21st century.

Purpose of the study

The purpose of this study was to explore and compare the institutional structure and delivery systems, the status of the physical education academic programs, physical resources, intramural and recreational sports, and interscholastic sports in secondary schools in Puerto Rico, the State of Minnesota, USA, and selected European International Schools. It was postulated that in comparing the three settings a more complete understanding of the similarities and differences in academic programs, physical resources and facilities, interscholastic sports, and intramural and recreational opportunities can be developed. Also, a greater appreciation for, and understanding of, the differences in the structures and delivery services of our international neighbours would be acquired. In our changing and shrinking global community, it is imperative that we gain a greater understanding of both the role of physical education and sport in society, and the status of its myriad delivery systems so that we can meet the challenges of the new millennium.

Methods of the study

Development of the questionnaire

The Physical Education and Sport Program Inventory (PESPI) was developed for the conduct of the study. The PESPI is intended for use in secondary school settings. Specifically, the PESPI incorporates elements of the Educational Sport section of the International Sport Management Questionnaire (Waters & Krotee 1995), as well as educational segments contained in the CIC study of graduate programs questionnaire (Feltz 1995). In its final form, the PESPI contains 33 questions divided into five sub-areas. It allows the attainment of information concerning the physical education and sport programs, systems, and resources of secondary schools.

A Spanish version of the PESPI was developed after the English version was pilot-tested. The English version of the PESPI was tested as to its clarity and usability through a pilot study at the University of Minnesota with physical education teachers and professionals from Finland, Greece, Kenya, Spain, and the United States. The Spanish version was also tested using the same procedure with professionals in Puerto Rico. The PESPI was appropriately back translated to insure the integrity of the instrument. Once finalized, the PESPI was distributed to athletic directors or heads of physical education departments at member schools of the European Council of International Schools (n=112) and randomly selected secondary schools in Puerto Rico (n=150) and the state of Minnesota (n=150).

Table 1: Response rate

School Location	Sent	% of All Schools	Returned	% Returned
Puerto Rico	150	42%	38	25.33%
Minnesota	132	30%	26	19.70%
Europe	112	100%	31	27.70%
Total	394	42.73%	95	24.11%

All the International Schools that were identified as meeting our criteria received a questionnaire. Originally, there were 150 questionnaires sent to schools in Minnesota. They represented 34% of all the schools identified as meeting our criteria. Of those, only 132 (30%) received the questionnaire because of a change in address.

Selection of schools

Secondary Schools were deemed as those schools which comprise the final stage of pre-university study. Many schools differ in regard to their secondary status, and may vary from the equivalent of 9th year in school to 13th year (excluding kindergarten or pre-school education), with several options in between.

International Schools are those schools whose primary language is not that of the host country, or that have a curriculum that is fundamentally different from that of the host country. For reasons of practicality, it was decided that the schools involved in the study would be those with English as their primary language of instruction and that were members of the European Council of International Schools (ECIS). They were identified through the 1996 ECIS Directory of International Schools. Upon examining the listed institutions, 112 were identified as secondary schools with English as the language of instruction (or at least one of the languages of instruction).

Puerto Rican secondary schools were identified through the Directory of secondary schools of the Department of Education in Puerto Rico. United States' secondary school listings were obtained from the 1996 Directory of the Minnesota State High School League (MSHSL) and the 1996 Directory of the Minnesota Department of Children, Family, and Learning.

Data analysis

One-Way Analyses of Variance were conducted on 22 variables, categorized under each of the following four sub-areas: Academic physical education program, facilities, interscholastic sports, and intramural and recreational sports.   Using an alpha level of .05, results indicated that there were significant differences on 20 of the 22 variables tested.

Results of the study

Descriptive statistics

The initial part of the PESPI explored the area of institutional demographics and organizational structure. Variables included in this section of the study were: high school enrollment, school grade levels, gender make-up of physical education classes, administrative departments for physical education and interscholastic sport, physical education teachers educational level, interscholastic coaches educational level, staff most often teaching physical education, staff most often teaching adapted physical education, and staff most often coaching interscholastic sport. The following tables illustrate the results for the first three variables:

Table 2: High school enrollment

Setting	Less than 201	201-400	401-600	601-800	Over 800
Puerto Rico	0 (0%)	5 (13.16%)	7 (18.42%)	3 (7.89%)	22 (57.89%)
United States	6 (23.08%)	8 (30.77%)	6 (23.08%)	0 (0%)	6 (23.08%)
Europe	14 (45.16%)	11 (35.48%)	5 (16.13%)	0 (0%)	1 (3.23%)
Total	20 (21.05%)	24 (25.26%)	18 (18.95%)	3 (3.16%)	29 (30.53%)

Table 3: School grade levels

Setting	9th-12th	9th-13th	10th-12th	10th-13th	Other
Puerto Rico	7 (18.42%)	0 (0%)	31 (81.58%)	0 (0%)	0 (0%)
United States	23 (88.46%)	0 (0%)	1 (3.85%)	0 (0%)	2 (7.69%)
Europe	12 (38.70%)	6 (19.35%)	1 (3.23%)	1 (3.23%)	11 (35.48%)
Total	42 (44.21%)	6 (6.32%)	33 (34.73%)	1 (1.05%)	13 (13.68%)

Table 4: Gender make-up of classes

Setting	Co-Educational	Single-Gender	Both
Puerto Rico	35 (92.11%)	2 (5.263%)	0 (0%)
United States	22 (84.62%)	0 (0%)	4 (15.38%)
Europe	23 (74.19%)	1 (3.23%)	7 (22.58%)
Total	80 (84.21%)	3 (3.15%)	11 (11.59%)

The majority of schools (76.84%) have a department solely responsible for physical education while 46.32% of the schools have a department solely responsible for the coaching of interscholastic sports. Also, the majority of teachers in the schools (58.95%) held a bachelor's degree with teaching certification. Very few teachers held higher degrees (25.26%). There were as many coaches holding a bachelor's degree as there were coaches holding a bachelor's degree with teaching certification (31.58%) with only 11.58% holding higher degrees.

The majority of the schools (96.84%) had a physical education teacher teaching physical education classes while 7.37% of schools indicated that other staff members filled this role as well. Only one international school and two schools in the United States did not have a physical education teacher conducting their physical education classes.

Most of the schools (71.58%) did not have an adapted physical education program. Those that did either had an adapted physical education teacher or the regular physical education teacher in charge of this program.

Only 24.21% of the schools had a coach coaching interscholastic sports. The rest had the physical education teacher performing these duties. Interestingly, 48.38% of the international schools had other certified teachers and staff members coaching.

One-way analyses of variance results

The variables were divided into four categories as follows:

Academic program. This category was composed of the variables class size, minutes of class time per week, years of physical education required for graduation, individual sport classes offered, team sport classes offered, theory (i.e., non-activity) classes offered, and total number of physical education classes offered.

Results indicated that, except for theory classes offered, the variables were significantly different (table 5). The means for theory classes offered ranged from 1.09 for international schools to 1.81 for schools in the U.S. International schools revealed the lowest mean class size (19 students per class). They also possessed the highest requirement for graduation (a mean of three years of physical education required), but required less minutes of class time per week (mean of 134) than the U.S. schools (mean=209 minutes) and Puerto Rican schools (mean=218 minutes). On the other hand, Puerto Rican schools offered the least variety of both individual and team sport classes (a mean of about three options offered for each) and the least variety of physical education classes in general (mean of 7.4). International Schools and schools in the United States were similar in these categories with a mean of total physical education classes offered of 14.6 and 14.9 respectively.

Table 5 : Results for academic program

Variable	Pto. Rico (mean)	USA (mean)	Europe (mean)	Sig. (F prob.)
Individual	3.08	7.81	7.45	.0000*
Team	3.21	5.27	6.06	.0000*
Theory	1.13	1.81	1.10	.1188
Total PE	7.42	14.88	14.61	.0000*
Class size	29.27	26.04	18.97	.0000*
Minutes	218.38	209.23	134.07	.0000*
Years requ	1.00	1.61	3.04	.0000*

Availability and quality of physical resources. Variables in this category included indoor facilities, outdoor facilities, total number of facilities, and quality of facilities.
Results indicated that all the variables were significantly different (table 6). Puerto Rican schools had the least total number of facilities (which included both indoor and outdoor facilities), with a mean of 5.5 facilities per school, whereas international schools revealed a mean of 11.8 facilities per school, and the U.S. obtained a mean of 18.0 facilities. In terms of quality of facilities, the mean ratings of Puerto Rican school teachers placed their facilities in the low-medium category, whereas means obtained for the ratings of teachers in schools in the U.S. and Europe placed their quality in the medium category.

Table 6 : Results for physical education

Variable	Pto. Rico (mean)	USA (mean)	Europe (mean)	Sig. (F prob.)
Ind. facility	1.32	4.96	4.50	.0000*
Out facility	4.16	13.11	7.69	.0000*
Total facillity	5.47	18.08	11.83	.0000*
Fac. quality	1.68	2.35	2.27	.0000*

Intramural and recreational sports. Variables in this category included intramural opportunities for: disabled students, for boys, for girls, coeducational opportunities, and total number of opportunities available (table 7).
The only variable not significantly different was intramural offerings for disabled students. The means were lower than one offering per school for

each of the three school settings sampled. In this case, each environ was lacking in program offerings. On the other hand, Puerto Rican schools offered more activities for both boys and girls (means of 4.1 and 3.8, respectively), whereas international schools offered more coeducational activities (mean of 2.8). Both Puerto Rican and international schools obtained a mean of 8.7 activities per school, whereas schools in the U.S. obtained a mean of 3.1 intramural activities per school.

Table 7 : Results for intramural and recreational sport

Variable	Pto. Rico (mean)	USA (mean)	Europe (mean)	Sig. (F prob.)
IM adapted	.0263	.1538	.1290	.4583
IM boys	4.158	.9231	3.000	.0000*
IM girls	3.790	.9615	2.807	.0002*
IM coed.	.8158	1.077	2.774	.0010*
IM total	8.790	3.115	8.710	.0012*

Interscholastic sports and activities. This category included the variables of junior varsity teams for boys and for girls, varsity teams for boys and for girls, teams for disabled students, and total number of teams available.
Results indicated that all the variables were significantly different (table 8). Schools in the United States offered the highest number of interscholastic opportunities for their students in all categories. The mean number of offerings for disabled students was about one sport team per school, but neither Puerto Rican, nor international schools offered opportunities for this student population. The means for total number of interscholastic sport opportunities or teams (which includes all the variables mentioned above) were 35.3 teams for the U.S. schools, 18.7 for international schools, and 9.8 for Puerto Rican schools.

Table 8 : Results for interscholastic sports

Variable	Pto. Rico (mean)	USA (mean)	Europe (mean)	Sig. (F prob.)
JV boys	1.00	8.32	4.61	.0000*
JV girls	.842	8.48	4.25	.0000*
Var. boys	4.18	8.92	5.32	.0000*
Var. girls	3.76	9.20	4.55	.0000*
Adapted	.000	.385	.000	.0170*
Total sport	9.76	35.32	18.74	.0000*

Discussion

Academic program. It is apparent that in these three types of school environs, emphasis is placed on physical activity classes when compared to theory classes. This is an area that should be more well balanced because knowledge and understanding of anatomy, health, nutrition, biomechanics, and history and sociology of sport, among other topics should be considered as crucial as the acquisition and development of motor skills or "playing the game."

Availability and quality of physical resources or facilities. International and United States schools had far more indoor and outdoor facilities available for use when compared to their Puerto Rican counterparts. The majority of teachers in schools in Puerto Rico indicated that they share the facilities of the community in which they are located, whereas the majority of schools sampled in the U.S. and Europe indicated that they own the majority of their facilities. The quality of the facilities was also poorer in Puerto Rico, which may be attributed to dependence on the government for facility care and maintenance. Clearly, Puerto Rican teachers are more challenged to develop an efficient program when it comes to scarce physical resources.

Intramural and recreational sports. Disabled students do not get as many opportunities to develop their motor skills as their "able-bodied" counterparts do in each of the three samples. Even with a Federal Law (i.e., IDEA) concerning equal opportunity and access for this student population in both the United States and Puerto Rico, the availability of opportunities was reported as minimal. It is apparent that Puerto Rican schools have placed as much emphasis on the intramural and recreational sport component of their program as on the interscholastic component, whereas their European and U.S. counterparts seem to place more effort and resources into interscholastic opportunities. This is certainly a challenge that must be addressed so that the majority of the students can be served.

Interscholastic sports and activities. There were no opportunities offered for disabled students in Puerto Rico or in international schools. Some United States schools have just begun to move in this direction. Also, U.S. schools offered two to three times the amount of opportunities than both Puerto Rican and International schools offered for interscholastic participation.
Even though the mean numbers of opportunities offered were slightly higher for boys, some improvement has been achieved in treating girls fairly and as equal to boys concerning their opportunity to participate in interscholastic sport. Lack of adequate equipment, facilities, resources, and a limited budget could be the causes of the marked differences found in this area.
Without question, more systematic research is needed to add to the literature concerning the delivery and conduct of pre school through high school

physical education and sport programs. Research into philosophies, laws, leadership, mission, and public and private policy is requisite so that we may better enhance the roles that physical education and sport can and should play, not only in nation and community building, but constructing and maintaining a peaceful and respectful global village.

References

Anthony, D.W. (1966). Physical education as an aspect of comparative education. Gymnasium, 3(2), 3-6.

Broom, E. (1989). An international perspective of the changing role of the school in the provision for competitive sport. In F.H. Fu, M.L. Ng & M. Speak (eds.), Comparative physical education and sport (Vol. 6, pp.175-181). Champaign, IL.

Fagerlind, I. & Saha, L.J. (1983). Education and national development: a comparative perspective. New York.

Feltz, D.L. (1995). Report of departments of kinesiology in CIC institutions. Unpublished document. Michigan State University.

Gee, M. (1987). School physical education: Cross-national issues to be researched. In H. Haag, D. Kayser & B. Bennett (eds.), Comparative physical education and sport. (Vol. 4, pp. 139-147). Champaign, IL.

Haag, H. (1986). Comparative sport pedagogy--Comparative education: A basic interrelationship within educational sciences. In M.L. Krotee & E.M. Jaeger (eds.), Comparative physical education and sport. (Vol. 3, pp. 33-48). Champaign, IL.

Krotee, M.L. & Hanafy (1986). The role of comparative and international physical education and sport in modern society. In M.L. Krotee & E.M. Jaeger (eds.), Comparative physical education and sport. (Vol. 3, pp. 7-12). Champaign, IL.

Krotee, M.L., Larson, J.E. & Rattigan, P. (1987). An east-west comparative study of physical education and sport. In H. Haag, D. Kayser & B. Bennett (eds.), Comparative physical education and sport. (Vol. 4, pp. 175-191). Champaign, IL.

Olivella-Benjamino, C. (1981). Practitioners' evaluation of the physical education programs in Puerto Rico public schools. Unpublished doctoral dissertation, Florida State University, Tallahassee.

Paige, R.M. (1986). Conceptualizing physical education across cultures: International development education and intercultural education perspectives. In M.L. Krotee & E.M. Jaeger (eds.), Comparative physical education and sport. (Vol. 3, pp. 13-18). Champaign, IL.

Portela-Suarez, J.M. (1974). An evaluation of the physical education programs in the public secondary high schools of Puerto Rico. Unpublished doctoral dissertation, Florida State University, Tallahassee.

Tye, A.K. (1990). Global education school based strategies. Orange, CA.

UNESCO (1993).   International Charter of Physical Education and Sport. Paris.

Waters, D.J. & Krotee, M.L. (1997). Educational Sport: A comparative study of fifty-three nations. Proceedings of the AIESEP World Conference (pp. 498-503). Singapore.

Waters, D.J., & Krotee, M.L. (1995). The International Sport Management Questionnaire.   Instrument developed at the University of Minnesota, Minneapolis.

Ziegler, E.F. (1987). Comparative physical education and sport needs bifocal eyeglasses. In H. Haag, D. Kayser & B. Bennett (eds.), Comparative physical education and sport. (Vol. 4, pp. 25-39). Champaign, IL.

Chapter 35

To move with a different view

Winston A. Kloppers
University of Western Cape, South Africa

In the present transitional phase between two political orders in South Africa, there is a struggle for increased control and self-determination by a wide range of movements and institutions in order to define the nature of the new order in South Africa (SA), not only within the domain of the government of national unity, but across all dominant power constellations including national sporting codes, private enterprise, foreign agencies etc.

Nowhere is this dynamism of defining the new order more apparent than in the world of sport and recreation, for it is played and supported by all sectors of the population and has tremendous potential for nation building as witnessed in the nation's support for its national teams since independence.

However, because of the State's retrenchment of teachers, a general lack of resources and a host of socio-economic constraints, physical education (PE) is not offered at many Black schools in South Africa. Only a small percentage of students at these schools are involved in extra-mural sport and recreation. The opposite is true of many of the former White schools, which have the means to employ PE teachers and sport coaches despite the State's rationalization policy. Participation in sport is also compulsory for all students at these schools (Dharsey, Hendricks, Najaar and Bongo). This does not auger well for most of our national sport teams; one only needs to examine the demographics of these teams (soccer being the notable exception), to realize that they do not relate to the demographics of the country. If we do not provide Black schools with physical and human resources for the teaching of relevant physical activities, then not only are we perpetuating poor health, but we may also end up like Zimbabwe, who after 16yrs of independence, could only field one Black cricketer in their national team. Despite the praiseworthy remarks of our State President, Mr Mandella, and the Minister of Sport Mr Steve Tswete, sport is not contributing sufficiently and in a meaningful way to nation building. They are however not alone in acknowledging sport as a social phenomenon. Francine Fournier of UNESCO commented that sport today is one of the major individual and social expressions of our time and that it is a factor of social integration and cohesion; of group building and nation building (Fournier 1998, p. 20).

However, the solution to the problem is not a simple one. During this transitional phase, one cannot simply simulate Western approaches to curriculum planning, because none of these approaches or western philosophies of PE took cognisance of the political struggles and social constraints which prevented the development of sport, PE and recreational activities in developing countries. Neither did any of these philosophies take into consideration the rapid social changes in many of these countries which were either in the throes of national liberation struggles or who had recently obtained independence from their oppressors or colonial powers.

This paper therefore sets forth an argument for restructuring PE, especially within the informal settlements, so that all South Africans, and possibly other developing nations on the African continent, may have access to primary health care, leisure activities and an opportunity to play competitive sport if they so desire. It is instructive however, to first have a brief look at the socio-economic and political constraints which may limit the teaching of physical activities at schools.

The constraints limiting sport and PE at schools in South Africa

The Department of Water Affairs and Forestry's annual report 1994\5 stated that approximately one third of the population had no access to adequate water supply & half had no access to adequate sanitation.

According to the Minister of Public Enterprises, Ms Stella Sigcau, 3.3m rural and 1.1m urban households were without electricity (*South Africa Survey 7* 1996, p. 732).

In 1996 there were about 2,5m formal and 5.3m informal home owners in South Africa (*Business Day* 16, 5 June 1996).

About 8m people did not have formal road access to their homes or any storm water drainage (*South Africa Survey* 1996\7, p. 733).

36 888 rapes were reported to the SAPS in 1995 (SAPS, *Report on the incidence of serious crimes during 95*, April 1996).

On average, 52 people were murdered daily (*South African Survey* 1996\7, p. 58).

The Minister of Law and Order, Mr Mufamadi said in March 1996 that 28 432 cases of child abuse were investigated in 1995 (Hansard (S:Q) 2 col.99, 14 March 1996).

Between January and August 1996, police in Gauteng arrested 1 405 suspects for crimes against children: 842 for rape, 242 assault, 168 indecent assault, 86 kidnapping, 41 sodomy, 14 incest and 12 for attempted murder (*The Citizen* 16 August 96).

60 000 classrooms were needed nation wide (*South African Survey 7* 1996, p. 185).

Prof. Bengu, Minister of Education, said that significant numbers of teachers were chronically absent, reported late for duty, knocked off early or were drunk (*Sowetan*, 12 June 1996).

In many black schools as few as 100 actual teaching days out of a possible 195 were realised (*Frontiers of Freedom* 10, 96).

About 46% of African teachers were under or unqualified in 1994 (*South Africa Survey 7* 1996, p. 150).

A survey of malnutrition among school children in South Africa in 1994 found that more than one million children between 5 and 9 years of age were malnourished (SAIRR, *Annual Report*, 1995\6, p. 194).

1 in 5 children was anaemic and 1 in 10 was iron depleted (*South Africa Survey 7* 1996, p. 464).

By August 1995 there were officially 8 405 cases of AIDS in South Africa (*South Africa Survey* 1996, p. 449).

The incidence of notifiable diseases in South Africa in 1995: Malaria: 5996; Measles: 6777; TB: 84402; Typhoid: 753; V. hepatitis: 1507; Tetanus: 40; Mening. Inf.: 393 (*South Africa Survey 7* 1996 p. 452).

The incidence of sexually transmitted diseases in teenagers 13-19 years of age in 1995: Syphilis: 206; Gonorrhoea: 1387; Other: 454; Total: 2047 (SAIRR, *Annual Report*, Vol.2 (6), 1995 p. 32).

Toward the restructuring of physical activities at schools

It is instructive to revisit UNESCO's 1961 conference on education in Africa where it was observed that:

> "*The content of education in Africa is not in line with either existing African conditions or the postulates of political independence ... but is based on a non-African background*" (UNESCO, 1961).

With the transition to African political independence underway, the conference then recommended that:

> "*African educational authorities should revise and reform the content of education in the area of curricula, textbooks and methods, so as to take account of the African environment, child development, cultural heritage and the demands of technological progress and economic development*" (Ibid).

UNESCO'S formulations reflect both current discontent and considerations which inform curriculum restructuring in South Africa. With this as background, we shall therefore need to contextualize physical activities at school within the specific socio-economic conditions of South Africa.

Given, therefore, the institutional and political problems of physical education and sport as a school subject, what are the implications of this study for those concerned with an emancipatory practice in the subject at the school level? The main arguments are shown below.

Students and teachers need to be centrally involved in the planning of health promoting physical activities during this period of transformation. This assumes that schools will have some degree of autonomy in curriculum decisions and, by extension, that subject teachers within a school will play a prominent role in curriculum/syllabus planning. There is no reason why students could not contribute to the curriculum process by drawing on their after school physical activities as one knowledge source for the formal school curriculum content.

If physical education teachers are to be involved with curriculum planning, they should also be thoroughly initiated in a relevant theory of physical education and curriculum studies, enabling them to engage in a thorough explication of the nature, point and purpose of the enterprise. This would mean that teacher education curricula should develop critical theories of physical education that will move us beyond the hegemonic influence of a conservative, top-down, state educational "theory" of what should obtain. Within this model, teachers are viewed less as creative and imaginative thinkers.

The curriculum could also be planned around modules relating to physical activities (sport, games-traditional or otherwise, dancing, recreation, work related sport etc.). The number of modules or the duration of each module will depend entirely on the nature of the activity and the number of modules they wish to include within a year. Schools within a given area could together deliberate on their modules, if they so wish, so that they may team teach in their area.

These PE modules should also be characterized by fun, popular uninhibited and unregimented activities. Encouraging students to express themselves in a relatively unconstrained environment could help to rekindle lost values and also propagate positive values such as compromise, consensus or respect for minority opinions which may contribute to the abating of violence among some of our youth.

We will also need to contextualize curricular activities within the specific socio-economic conditions of South Africa. For example, an integrative model of curriculum will draw on knowledge domains from the different disciplines; thus, school communities affected by malnutrition, could use the collective knowledge of geography, agriculture, biology, science, mathematics and physical education to harvest their own crops. The planting, harvesting and tilling of the soil could afford students physical and recreational activity, while simultaneously bridging the school-community gap by using parents at school to prepare school meals from the harvested crops. Each class could work for a few weeks in the garden during their physical education period, as yet another module to add to their play, dance and recreation modules for the year. Such an integrative curriculum model is not necessarily advocating that students should be "hewers of wood or drawers of water", nor is it promoting streaming or tracking, it is merely proposing options which would benefit youth who have been left desolate by the injustices of the past.

In a similar vein, schools lacking classrooms could engage in the construction of extra rooms. The collective knowledge of maths, science, woodwork, etc., could contribute to the success of the project. The work could be continued by the community after school hours.

Collective school projects could also address the whole ecological problem. The objective here is to strengthen the capacity of everyone concerned to create an environment that would encourage better knowledge, attitudes and health promotion practices at schools. Presently, economic greed is destroying our environment through over-production and reckless industrialization projects without concern for the future. There is also gross neglect of our natural habitat. Students as future custodians of the environment, could be involved in conservation activities as yet another health promoting PE module: (a) combatting soil erosion by the planting of ground covers etc.; (b) embarking on a paper jog, collecting waste paper; (c) cleaning of rivers; (d) planting of trees; (e) weed control; (f) hedge cutting; (g) nature hikes; (h) building of ponds, etc.

Production programmes

These work related modules could aptly be referred to as physical education with production programmes. The central aim of physical education, therefore, should be the provision of suitable physical activities to each and every student in the class, sufficiently intensive, so that it becomes worthwhile to each. The natural spin-offs of such activities could be cardiovascular development, fitness development, neuromuscular development, the acquisition of sport skills, learning something useful, and the acquisition of positive values.

The new PE curriculum could also shift the emphasis from individual competitive sport in favour of group participation in physical activities. There is no reason why the school could not open up some space for a sports counter-culture which distributes the rewards for success on a group basis and which also recognizes the attempt to succeed, irrespective of the final result, as a worthy goal. Competitive sport should not however be banished from schools, but it has to be watched because if left unattended, it could degenerate into the moral equivalent of war and become destructive to democracy and positive values.

The effective power of physical education and sport in the solution of social problems depends greatly upon the decision as to how our schools are used. In some townships, schools are the only communal places; in others, they can go a long way in supporting what is available. Therefore, schools will have to undergo a transformation and become community schools in the sense that they will become open door centres for youth activities, after school hours and during the vacations.

Curricular organization and activities, irrespective of their nature, should be integrated not only by race but also by gender. This eliminates the argument that girls are "inherently" disposed towards certain types of physical activity and begins to chip away at the powerful socializing influences on gender-differentiated physical education.

Clearly there are several other issues around the restructuring of physical education and sport in developing countries, which should be opened up for public debate and policy deliberation. These proposals simply suggest a starting point for such action, one which links physical education and sport to progressive politics or, to put it somewhat differently, which allows our students "to move with a different view".

Conclusion

In emphasising the restructuring of PE and sport at school, the International Charter of PE and Sport stipulates that PE and Sport are essential elements of permanent education and that every educational system must allot the necessary space and importance to sport and PE in order to establish a balance and reinforce the links between the physical activities and the other elements of education (Fournier 1998, p. 21).

But rethinking PE and sport as a social project will require movement beyond the pessimism that claims an "incompatibility of sports with liberation" (Hendricks 1989, p. 109). The success of such a venture will to a large extent be determined by political support and that support can't be assumed, it must be struggled for.

References

Bongo, N. (1998). Principal of Chumisa primary school in Khayalitsha. Conducted an interview with Mr Bongo on the current state of PE and sport at township schools.

Dharsey, A. (1998). Chairperson for the southern regions of the United Schools Sports Association of South Africa (USSASA). Conducted an interview with Mr Dharsey on the current state of PE and sport at primary and high schools within his region.

Fournier, F. (1998). Assistant director general for the social and human sciences, UNESCO. Promoting physical activity around the world. ICSSPE Bulletin, 24, Paris.

Hendricks, D.J. (1989). Preliminary perspectives on the strains within the sports-ideology/liberation ideology nexus in South Africa. Context, 2.

Hendricks, P. (1998). Principal of Cornflower primary school in Mitchell's Plain. Conducted an interview with Mr Hendricks on the current state of PE and sport at schools in the Western Cape.

Najaar, R. (1998). Principal of spine road senior secondary schools Mitchell's Plain. Conducted an interview on the current state of PE and sport at high schools in the Western Cape.

SAIRR (South African Institute of Race Relations) 1995. Race Relations Survey 6.

SAIRR (1996). South Africa Survey 7. Johannesburg.

UNESCO (1961). Final report of the Conference of African States on the Development of Education in Africa, Addis Ababa, 15-25 May, 1961. Paris: UNESCO.

Chapter 36

Sport education at the University of Ljubljana

S. Burnik, M. Doupona and M. Bon
University of Ljubljana, Slovenia

The University of Ljubljana was established in 1919. In the beginning we had five faculties: arts, law, theology, engineering and medicine. Today there are fourteen faculties and three university academies.

When the University of Ljubljana was established there was no organised sport in the programme of studies. It was not before 1958 that a commission for physical culture and premilitary education was set up. This commission prepared the guidelines for the development of sports at the university. Two years later there was founded a section of physical culture employing two sports teachers who prepared short-term and long-term proposals for the development of sports at the university and organised sports recreation for the students attending the University of Ljubljana. In 1963, the University Council proposed at the suggestion of the Commission of Physical Culture to all faculties to introduce sport education as a compulsory subject in the first year of the studies, and provide a possibility of regular sports exercising for students in the higher years as well. This recommendation was first implemented at the Faculty of Mechanical Engineering and at the Faculty of Natural Sciences and Technology. There followed the Faculty of Arts and Faculty of Medicine. Other faculties had an organised optional sports exercising which gradually became compulsory.

Until 1969, all the members of the University of Ljubljana had in their study programmes, and students in their matriculation books, regular sport education. The largest problem was a lack of space, therefore in 1973 the University built, with the help of the state, a university sports hall which was already at its opening too small to meet all the needs of the students' sports involvement. The number of regularly enrolled students increased from 1963 to 1969 from 7,000 to 10,000, while the number of those who engaged in compulsory sport education increased from 1,000 to 3,300. The both figures have increased up to now to 40,000 students from which number 20.000 have sport education as a regular subject. The number of sports teachers has increased as well. In the beginning there were two sports teachers for every 1,000 students; in 1969 even 18 for 3,400 students, while today there are approximately 28 for 20,000 students.

However, to the first sports hall there has been added only one sports hall and a 25-m pool which will be opened in autumn this year.

Organisation of sports at the University of Ljubljana

The University of Ljubljana is relatively young, and in addition, its development has been affected by very heterogeneous socio-political conditions in which it has emerged and evolved. The same applies also to the university sport education and sports. The facts and professional arguments convinced the then government that it financially supported the programmes and curricula of the university sport education. In our educational system we begin with systematic sport education already in kindergartens and it is appropriate that we conclude sport education at the university. The university sport education must also be accessible to all students, irrespective of their motor and financial abilities. Its main goal is to develop and reinforce permanent sports recreational habits in students by means of which they will enrich their life and at the same time preserve their psychomotor and work abilities. Everybody has agreed that sport education at the university is also "a moral, life-expressive, behavioural, work and social education" (Pedi ek 1970).

In addition to professional programmes in which all objectives and goals of the university sport education were presented, we also had enough professionals for their implementation. These professionals worked and still work today at individual faculties. They have formed a professional association; however, they are, as regards the programme and finances, independent within the framework of their respective faculties.
On the other hand we have never had material conditions - especially sports halls - for optimal implementation of the envisaged sports programmes. The solution to this problem was mainly left to the faculties and their sports teachers who each in his or her own way tried to solve the lack of space and the associated problems. Thus, there have emerged almost so many models as there are faculties and sports teachers. At smaller faculties there is employed one, at larger faculties three sports teachers. At some faculties they have sport education only in the second year, at others again in all four years.
During the time of real socialism this did not represent a problem as, despite everything, the state in this or another way also controlled the sports at the university. However, after gaining independence and the changing of the socio-political system, sport at the faculty has been to a large extent left to the resourcefulness of individual sports teachers. An analysis of the existing situation has shown a rather sad picture: (1) only one half of regular students have regular sport education; (2) the faculties with a large number of enrolled students do not have sport education in the first year: in this way they solve the space problem and save some money; (3) the number of students not having regular sport education increases every year due to increased

enrolment in the university; (4) the number of sports teachers has remained the same for a number of years; (5) the average age of sports teachers is 54 years; (6) regular sport education takes place only two hours a week, and even this two hours take place in the so-called "block-hours" (90 minutes); (7) the sports facilities are not placed at or near the faculties; (8) the hours of sport education are outside the faculty curricula at often very unsuitable times; (9) approximately one half of the students at the University of Ljubljana are females, while among the sports teachers there are less than 10 % women.

Owing to the above, it is not surprising that every year an inexplicably large number of students brings various kinds of medical certificates for exemption from sport education.

Modern needs and a terrible pace of life face the university, especially university sports, with completely new and different requirements. The changed socio-political system also calls for changes and adjustments in the organisation, financing and management of university sports and sport education. For many it were the most easy to give up the present model of organisation. This, however, is out of the question as only the present "obligation" ensures that regular financial support is provided for university sports by the state, i.e. by the Ministry of Education and Sports. That sport has positive effects on the development of the young people also at the university level has been proved by many authors in their expert and research reports (Petkovšek, Koprivnjak, Stani , Mihel i , Burnik); hence, the question now is not anymore whether there should be sport education at the university or not, but the main problem is the offer of suitable contents and forms of sports at the university and its organisation. Here we can paraphrase the thought by Karlheinz Giesele: Let's return to the proper meaning of the sport: let's not seek people for the sport, rather find the sport for man.

On the basis of experiences gained by some sports teachers abroad (Germany, Austria, USA and Canada) we have prepared the guidelines for the development of the university sport. Of course, we have taken into account the specific nature of our country and university as blind acceptance of the programmes and systems of other environments can cause more damage than benefit.

In these guidelines we have suggested that the university sport should become in all its segments the content-related, vital part of the renewed Slovenian university. It should mean an open possibility for free expression through sports for all its members, students, teachers and alumni.
The university sport should find its suitable place in the National Programme and Law on the University Education as this is the case in the modern developed world.

The foundation of the renewed university sport should be the old programme, enriched with contents-related and organisational changes. The university sport should consists of: (1) regular sport education included in the curriculum and (2) other sports activities organised and led by the sports teachers of the University of Ljubljana: (a) educational and training programmes and courses; (b) sports recreational programmes during the year, between exams and during holidays; (c) sports training for recreation purposes; (d) championships of the University and other competitions.

At the university there should be set up a permanent professional and management body for the programming, co-ordination and monitoring of the university sport. Together with the engagement of professionals for co-ordination of the common issues of the university sport, the work of sports teachers at the university should also be arranged and organised in a more up-to-date manner as well, i.e. according to the models of the universities in the Central Europe. New organisation of sports teachers at the University would centralise and simplify many important matters, while on the other hand it should not have an adverse effect on or even destroy the present positive forms and results of the work of sports teachers at individual faculties. Our model has been the organisation of sports at the University of Waterloo and University of Toronto in Canada, the University in Buffalo in USA, and the universities in the neighbouring European cities: Vienna, Munich, Erlangen and Nuerenberg. Everywhere they have a centre for sports which takes care of and organises sports life at the university. As the financial conditions at the said universities are incomparably better than in our country, we cannot fully imitate their systems. However, we can adopt and use their central organisation which in our environment would result in better utilisation of the facilities and teachers and offer the students a wider and better selection of sports activities.
Regular sport education within the scope of the study programme and the fields that are in the closest relation with it must be financed by the Ministry of Education and Sports directly over the university or over the faculties.
The guidelines have been accepted and supported both at the Ministry of Education and Sports and at the University and individual faculties. Regrettably, the proposed changes have not been implemented so far.

Methods

Into the sample of measured subjects, 5520 parents have been included: from this number 2760 persons were females and 2760 persons were males - parents of children of school-age living in the Republic of Slovenia, (Doupona 1996). The sample was stratified according to the regions (10 places), and selected at random inside the regions.

Five variables have been dealt with (see table 1) : (1) age (SOCLR); (2) education (IZOB); (3) sport education in the primary school during the schooling of the parents (MSV-O); (4) sport education in the secondary school during the schooling of the parents (MSV-S); (5) sport education at University during the schooling of the parents (MSV-F).

Table 1 : Variables and measurement scales

Variable	Label	Scale
SOCLR	Age	RATIO
IZOB	Degree of Education (1=not finished primary school, 8=master degree, Phd) (1= none .. 5=two or more	ORDINAL
MSV-O	Attitudes toward PE in Primary School (1=strongly disagree to 5= strongly agree	ORDINAL
MSV-S	Attitudes toward PE in Secondary School (1=strongly disagree to 5= strongly agree	ORDINAL
MSV-F	Attitudes toward PE at University (1=strongly disagree to 5= strongly agree	ORDINAL

The data have been processed on a personal computer in the Windows and DOS environments. Used have been the statistical program SPSS for windows. With standard procedures we calculated basic descriptive statistical indicators and thus obtained the data on the distribution of the applied variables.

Results and discussion

The problem of the university sport in Slovenia is serious which fact is also evident from the results of the study (Doupona 1996), which was conducted by means of polling, i.e. by a survey using a questionnaire, which covered 5520 parents of the Slovenian primary school children. For the sake of a better insight into the situation of sport education in the entire Slovenian education system, and especially at the University of Ljubljana, we shall focus hereinafter on that part of the study which analyses the opinions of people as regards sport education at all levels of education and the associated attitude of individuals towards sports.

The parents of primary schoolchildren (average age 37 years) have a relatively positive opinion about sport education which was offered to them within the scope of primary, secondary and university education.

The parents expressed their opinion by means of a five-grade ordinal scale (from very bad up to very good opinion). Characteristic of the fathers is that they evaluate sport education during the time they were at school within the highest rank of the employed scale. This means that mainly men think that sport education was very good during their education. Women decide on a lower value more often and think that they had good sport education, although not very good as expressed by men. The average values show that a positive opinion which is the most obvious for sport education at primary schools (A.S.=3.6) falls with each subsequent education level. However, all agree that their education at the university was not good as their opinions show a downward tendency (A.S.=2.8).

Several interpretations of the obtained results are possible. The diverse opinions of the parents on sport education which depend on the level of attained education (primary school, secondary school, university) are the consequence of the various factors. It is necessary to point out that the quality of sport education at individual levels of education changed from period to period. In the sixties and in the first half of the seventies, sport education was the best at grammar schools. In the eighties, the school system underwent changes in the contents (the so-called guided education). The number of secondary school pupils increased, which led to poorer conditions for the implementation of sport education at secondary schools. In the period when the conditions for sport education at secondary schools deteriorated, there came to a positive shift at primary schools. The largest progress in the quality of the execution of sport education lessons was achieved on the basis of the new regulation which limited the number of pupils in a group (to 20).

The number of lessons, material possibilities (gym, sports equipment) and training of professional staff for teaching sport education also changed from one period to another. Today, the largest number of hours of sport education is at primary schools and the smallest at the university. A rule, each primary school has today a separate room (gym) for the execution of sports education. This is not anymore true of secondary schools - although recently the conditions have been improving - and even to a lesser extent in the case of faculties. Poor conditions are above all at the University of Ljubljana, better at the faculties within the University of Maribor. Due to the fact that all larger qualitative and quantitative changes in the university sport began only in the last few years, it is logical that the opinions of the parents show a negative tendency.

The differences in the evaluation of the quality of sport education by parents occurred due to the varying age of the parents and the associated conditions of sport education in a given social situation.

The second possible explanation of the varying opinions of the individuals is seen in connection between the education level they have attained and their evaluation of the quality of sport education. The best opinion about sport education at primary schools can with certainty also be attributed to the fact that a large number of parents have lower education than secondary education. In all probability many of them were never included into sport education at secondary schools, and even less of them have experiences with sport education at the university. All parents, however, could not express their opinion about the quality of sport education as they did not have any. This fact involves also a series of other concerns. If we depart from the fact, which is also shown in our research, that parents with a lower education level mainly do not engage in sports, we can summarise that the only sports experience of less educated parents is connected with the lessons of sport education at primary schools. This is also why they are less critical in the evaluation of the quality of sport education. On the other hand, the parents having university education have acquired in the process of education certain sports experiences both within the scope of curricular and extracurricular sports activities. On the basis of their experiences these parents have formed their opinion, therefore we assume that education which lasts longer also has a positive effect on the formation of permanent sports habits and on the consciousness of people. As already mentioned, higher educated parents are more active in sports. This means that their evaluation criteria are also higher owing to the fact that their demands and expectations are certainly higher, or we could even say that their opinion about sport education is more realistic.

From the basic statistics it is evident that 60 % of the parents have a positive opinion about sport education in the time when they were at primary schools. Positive responses of the parents as to sport education at primary schools point to the quality of the teaching of sport education.

The quality of sport education at primary schools was in Slovenia better than in many more developed countries; however, in the way of thinking of many people there still prevails a negative association when physical activity of girls is concerned. Not only older people think that sport is not "suitable" for women, but also children (even the girls themselves) (Doupona 1995). Many also have a stereotyped opinion about which sports activities are suitable for women and which for men. This fact was also evident from the statistical data of the research by J. Strel and collaborators (Strel et al. 1993) which covered Slovenian primary school children.

It is possible that the parents who have a bad opinion about sport education, and such are even 40 %, had a negative experience as regards sport education at school. For mothers and fathers (and mothers are probably especially subjected to bad experiences) sports activity usually ends with the conclusion of their education.

Sport education should deal with the personality of a schoolchild in a complex manner, and it should, in addition to completely professional tasks, include in the curriculum the introduction of schoolgirls and schoolboys into some moral categories and value judgements which arise from the relations between people, especially between the sexes. An important task of sport education is still the elimination of prejudices and the introduction of thorough changes into the environments with a hundred-year long tradition...

In our system we are still not sufficiently aware of the importance of sports. There is often seen the legacy of the past with too conservative and underestimating views of the sports activity.

Conclusion

We have reached the following conclusions : (1) only one half of regular students have regular sport education; (2) the faculties with a large number of enrolled students do not have sport education in the first year: in this way they solve the space problem and save some money; (3) the number of students not having regular sport education increases every year due to increased enrolment in the university; (4) the number of sports teachers has remained the same for a number of years; (5) the average age of sports teachers is 54 years; (6) regular sport education takes place only two hours a week, and even this two hours take place in the so-called "block-hours" (90 minutes); (7) the sports facilities are not placed at or near the faculties; (8) the hours of sport education are outside the faculty curricula at often very unsuitable times: (a) approximately one half of the students at the University of Ljubljana are females, while among the sports teachers there are less than 10 % women; (b) the average values show that a positive opinion which is the most obvious for sport education at primary schools (A.S.=3.6) falls with each subsequent education level. However, all agree that their education at the university was not good as their opinions show a downward tendency (A.S.=2.8); (c) today, the largest number of hours of sport education is at primary schools and the smallest at the university; (d) the differences in the evaluation of the quality of sport education by parents occurred due to the varying age of the parents and the associated conditions of sport education in a given social situation; (e) education which lasts longer also has a positive effect on the formation of permanent sports habits and on the consciousness of people.

References

Burnik, S. & Strel, J. (1991). Analysis of motor status of the students at the University of Ljubljana and their motives and interests in sport education courses. In: Bilten FISU-CESU Conference, Sheffield, 390-399.

Burnik, S. & Kurner, D. (1995). Academic achievement related to motor abilities and personal traits of students of the Faculty of Mechanical Engineering. In: Proceedings FISU-CESU Conference, Fukuoka, 398-399.

Doupona, M. (1995). The construction of gender differences in sport. V: Kinesiologija Slovenica, Faculty of sport, Institute of Kinesiology, Ljubljana, 11-16.

Doupona, M. (1996). Socio-demographic structure of others and fathers of children of school age and their attitude towards sports. Doctoral thesis, Faculty of Sport, University of Ljubljana.

Pedi ek, F. (1970). Pogledi na telesno vzgojo, šport in rekreacijo. Ljubljana, Mladinska knjiga.

Strel, J. et al. (1993). An analysis of the developmental trends of motor abilities and morphologic characteristics and an analysis of their relations with psychological and sociological dimensions of the Slovene children and the youth between the age of 7 and 18 in the period of 1970 - 1983 - 1993. Ljubljana.

Chapter 37

Harmonization of the Physical Education Teacher Education (PETE) in Europe: a challenge for comparative studies

Willy Laporte
University of Ghent, Belgium

My first contact with comparative physical education was at the occasion of the ICHPER World Congress in Kiel 1979, where I attended a meeting of the Committee for Comparative Physical Education with Lynn Vendien, Uri Simri, Herbert Haag and others. From the discussion I could tell that a comparative discipline was a necessity for better communication understanding and evolution of both theory and practice in physical education and physical education teacher education (PETE).

Since then the European Unification has been providing a lot of impulses for action in which PETE was involved from the beginning: examples are: Erasmus' student and staff exchange, intensive courses, curriculum development. My contribution aims at providing some ideas for research in this field by comparative researchers. This contribution does not aim at the improvement of research methods. It only tries to open a field for study that could be beneficial for the harmonization process in PETE in Europe.

I propose to discuss the following topics: (a) harmonization in a European context; (b) what makes PETE in Europe so different that it has to be harmonized?; (c) some comparative studies related to European PETE; (d) opportunities for comparative research in a harmonization perspective.

Harmonization in a European context

Harmony is a term used in musicology. Its meaning has changed frequently: two sounds heard at the same time, two or more sounds one after the other, succession of tones in an octave, etc. ... Just as in music, different meanings can be given to harmony in a broader context: (a) co-operation or connection of a number of elements into a well organised and pleasant whole or entity; (b) adaptation of elements to each other and to the environment. I refer as an example to the harmony in nature where many elements, birds, plants, etc. ... reflect a pleasant whole notwithstanding the variety.

In European Union context we could interpret harmonization as the co-ordination of a multitude of differences issued from cultural and political traditions in the fifteen countries until now. Harmonization consequently does not mean to bring all elements in a uniform system. It is rather an adaptation of existing different systems in a common European framework in order that it would function, not only for one's own institution or country but that it would also be accepted by others as an equivalent with its specific characteristics.

"Be European, be different" is a slogan typical for the European policy. Respect for the cultural identities, acceptance of regional differences, acceptance of different languages, etc... but still some supra-national laws and a common currency to facilitate communication and the free moving of persons and goods. This respect for differences and identities does not make it easy to coordinate or to harmonize. In educational matters one not only has to take into account the fifteen member-states but also the forty regions which have cultural and educational autonomy (e.g. sixteen Länder in Germany, three communities in Belgium, four in the UK, seventeen in Spain, etc. ...), which encompasses about fifty units to be involved in the harmonization process. Moreover, there are about four hundred physical education institutions, which all want to have and to keep their autonomy in order to build their own identity and image.

What makes PETE in Europe so divergent that it needs to be harmonized ?

From our personal contacts and from our research results, the following striking facts appeared: (a) concepts on physical education and PETE differ widely; (b) there are different levels of education between university and pedagogical institutions, but there are even major differences among universities; (c) qualification varies from one to more subjects. In Portugal e.g. a student has to study only physical education for five years whereas in Northern Ireland students study three years and have to select three subjects, one being physical education.

Table 1 : Number of semesters and contact hours needed for a graduation in physical education in EU countries (Laporte 1997, p. 26).

	Semesters	Contact hours
Austria (T.T. College)	6	1200-1333
Austria (Univ.)	9	1800-2000
Belgium (T.T. College)	6	2250
Belgium (Univ.)	8 (min.)	2000-2400 (+ 300 for supplementary teacher education)
Denmark 1	5	1200 (20 hours/week)
Denmark 2	9	2160 (20 hours/week)
Finland	10	2500-3000
France 1	10	2350 (1750 academic training + 600 supplementary training)
France 2	12	2900
Germany	12	3000 (1700 academic training + 1300 for supplem. training)
Greece	8	2700 (1300 academic training + 1400 practice)
Ireland	8	2200 + 18 weeks teaching practice
Italy	6	1750
Luxembourg	14 (8+6 supl.)	8 semesters of scientific study in a foreign country + 6 pedagog. studies in Luxembourg
Netherlands	8	2880
Portugal	12	4084 (3484 academic training + 600 supplementary training)
Spain	10	3000 à 3200
Sweden	6	1440 (20 hours/week)
UK: England and Wales	8	1344 (=12-16 hours/week, 50% on professional study and 50% on subject)

This leads to divergences in: (a) duration of the study and the study load devoted to physical education (table 1); (b) the programmes which differ depending on the concept and on the time spent on PETE; (c) the structure of the teacher education which can be integrated or consecutive; (d) the qualification of the staff which can differ considerably. In some institutions nobody has a Ph.D., in others about 50%.

Comparative studies related to PETE in Europe

Physical education concepts in European Teacher Education programmes

Concepts about physical education often have their origin in history. However, it would be impossible, to trace here all the historical facts that influenced physical education and PETE concepts. One of the most 'striking' conflicts is the position of PETE towards sports. Since the German physical education leaders made a declaration of love to the sport movement in the late seventies, sport has invaded into the school curriculum as its unique content. At this moment three EU countries use the term 'sport' instead of physical education. France was making a deal and adopted Education Physique et Sport as the name of the school subject. All the others remain with the traditional term of physical education. The use of a different name does not necessarily mean that there is a totally different concept.

Crum (1998) asked colleagues from 28 different European universities for the leading physical education concept in their university and in their country. The results of this pilot study show quite divergent concepts in movement education, sport and PETE. Moreover some faculties pretend not to have one single concept but refer to the freedom of each teacher. In a European harmonization context this issue should at least be addressed, because the concept refers to guidelines for the whole teacher education: the curriculum, the assessment, the recruitment of staff, etc. ...

Aims for physical education

In the frame of the physical education-committee in the ENSSHE [1] Ken Hardman (Laporte 1997b) compared the official curricular aims and objectives for school physical education of twelve countries. The analysis revealed some differences in meaning attached to some concepts. However, there were close similarities with some variations, which can be regarded conceptually and/or linguistically as equivalences. The physical education committee could agree on a European rationale for physical education and on European aims and objectives for physical education in schools.

Aims for PETE

In the same context of the physical education committee, common European aims for PETE were distilled out of the aims from twelve participating universities. Besides the general and specific aims, the professional competences and tasks of the beginning teacher were formulated at three levels: (a) at the micro level: the teacher in the class with the students; (b) at the meso level: tasks within the school environment, planning, implementing and evaluating; (c) at the macro level: related to professional development e.g. curriculum development, involvement in regional and national structures, undertaking (action) research.

Concerning the curriculum

In the same curriculum development project, PETE programmes of the now fifteen participating universities were compared. This seemed to be a very difficult issue, especially because of the many divergences in curriculum structures and concepts. Moreover the language barrier doesn't make it easy to compare. First we had to manage to construct a frame or tool for clustering modules and courses.

Starting from the fields of study mentioned in the *European Physical Education Review* (Ursprung, Freitag & Schilling 1995), we conceived a model with seven fields of study in which we could bring all modules/courses of the different programmes, differentiating general and applied courses, theoretical and practical modules, dissertations, etc. ...
For the quantitative approach we used the ECTS [2] as an instrument containing theory contact hours, practice contact hours practice, personal work, study load and ECTS-credits (example in table 2).

This work hasn't been finished yet because some partners in the project need more time to adapt their programmes to the ECTS rules. This clustering of fields of study shows the convergences and divergences in the programmes. These are mostly related to conceptual specificities concerning the PE-teacher, biological or humanistic approaches, the importance of theory and practice, teaching period in schools, dissertations, etc. ... (table 3).

Table 2:   Curriculum of the Physical Education Teacher Education (PETE) at the University in Ghent (Belgium) following the European Credit Transfer System (ECTS)

NAME OF THE INSTITUTION	UNIVERSITY OF GHENT					
FIELDS of STUDY	A Contact Hours Theory	B Contact Hours Practicals	C* Personal Work	D Study Load	E ECTS- Credits	%
1. Physical and Sport acti-vity	150	930	150	1665	66	25%
1.a. Theory & practice	110	700	110	1250	50	19%
1.b. Learning + training methods	40	230	40	415	16	6%
2. Educational and Teaching Sciences	210	220	200	1590	53	20%
2.a. Gen. Pedag. + Did.	45	55	20	360	12	4.5%
2.b. Did. appl. to P.E. (TH + PR)	165	45	30	600	20	7.5%
2.c. Teaching practice in schools	-	120	150	630	21	8%
3. Natural and Biological Sciences	727.5	135	-	2475	83	31.5%
3.a. General courses	375	90	-	1350	45	17%
3.b. Applied to Mov. and Sport	352.5	45	-	1125	38	14.5%
4. Social and Humanistic Sciences	375	1155	15	1170	39	15%
4.a. General courses	195	-	-	630	21	8%
4.b. Appl. to Mov. and Sport	180	-	15	540	18	7%
5. Scientific Work. (dissertation-research projects)	-	-	450	450	15	6%
6. Others - Compulsory options	60	60	-	180	6	2.5%
7. Teaching period in schools to obtain a teaching licence for P.E.	-	-	-	-	-	-
TOTAL P.E.	1522.5	2500	815	7530	262	100%
8. Second (or third) subject (in a bi of trivalent system)	-	-	-	-	-	-

Situation March 1997

C* = Personal work not related to A or B : Ex. dissertation, teaching practice in schools
     = all hours spent to activities except the study related to A or B

Table 3:   Importance of different fields of study in seven universities
            (expressed in ECTS- study points)

	Uni 1	Uni 2	Uni 3	Uni 4	Uni 5	Uni 6	Uni 7
1. Physical & Sport Activities	66	63	50	24	48	78	57
2. Education & Teaching	53	38	52	52	84	20	21
3. Natural & Biol. Sciences	83	69	27	58	54	29	39
4. Social & Hum. Sciences	39	40	18	33	54	23	39
5. Scien. Work	15	18	-	-	-	14	24
6. Others	6	24	3	2	-	23	-
7. Teaching period in school	-	-	-	-	-	78	60
TOTAL PETE	262	252	150	169	240	265	240
8. Second Subject	-	-	90	71	-	-	-
TOTAL	262	252	240	240	240	265	240

Structural issues

The ENSSHE conducted a large project concerning the sport occupations in the EU: the observatory of sport occupations in the EU. Part of the study concerns the physical education teacher (Laporte 1997a). In the study an important part was dedicated to structural and organisational issues. An extensive inquiry was addressed to key witnesses from the fifteen member-states. They were chosen for their competence in this field and as national representatives.

This doesn't mean that it was an easy task. The regional educational autonomy generates differences and difficulties, which are often more related to politics than to science or education. Nevertheless we received a lot of information and we were able to compare several topics such as: (1) levels and regional differences; (2) one or more academic qualifications; (3) integrated or consecutive teacher education (4) duration of the study and study load; (5) access conditions; (6) number of graduates in the last years; (7) qualification and certificates; (8) official regulations.

External assessment of institutions

In order to improve their quality of education, institutions or governments organise assessments through external experts. An assessment instrument for university education has been developed by Vroeyenstijn (1994). This instrument was already used for PETE-assessment in the Netherlands, in Belgium and at this moment in Portugal (table 4).

The same instrument has been adapted for an investigation of eleven university partners in the *European Review of P.E.-Institutes* (Ursprung, Freitag & Schilling 1995). In fact this instrument may inspire the construction of a model for comparative research as it concerns the whole education, encompassing: student, staff, curriculum, management and policy.

Table 4:   Components of External Quality Assessment (Vroeyenstijn, 1994).

* Mission, aims, objectives
* The programme: curriculum-
  structure, content model of
  delivery, assessment
* Dissertation and practical work
* The student: entry requirements
  and level. Selection rates for
  completion and drop-out.
* Study guidance, time for study,
  study advice
	* Facilities
	* Alumni
	* Staff
	* International contacts
	* Internal quality control
	* Organisation and structure
	* Modules and courses

Opportunities for comparative research in a harmonization context

With the perspective of harmonization, the following elements (figure 1) should be compared and analysed: (1) the student: incoming students, the students in different periods of study, the out-going students, access conditions, etc. ...; (2) the teacher: the professional from whom PETE receives feed-back and the orientation of the teachers' profile towards education; (3) the curriculum; the learning process to reach the aims and objectives. This very important element provides a lot of interesting information about modules, sequences, levels, etc. ... (4) the staff-members: their qualifications e.g. doctor degrees, their research output, etc. ...; (5) the institution: mission statement, objectives, organisation, relations (e.g. internationalisation), legal regulations, facilities, etc. :...; (6) research: education related research, publications, laboratories, etc. ...

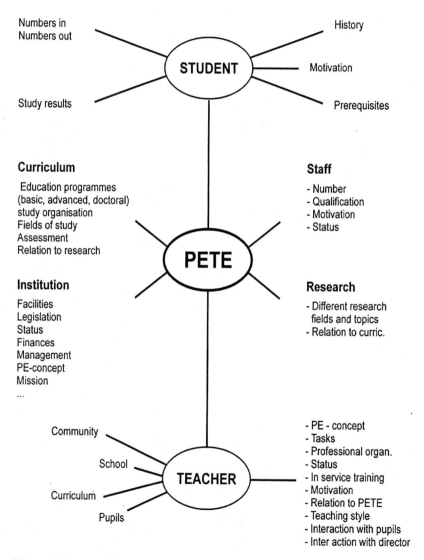

Figure 1: Opportunities for research in PETE

Conclusions

The cultural, educational and political diversity in the European Union on the one hand, and the necessity to coordinate all those diversities on the other hand, offers a lot of possibilities for comparative research. Moreover, the European Union needs coordination at several levels of society: in education in general, in Physical Education and in Physical Education Teacher Education. Coordinating a complete knowledge of the present situation is a first necessity. In the case of PETE, a lot of data are available at most of the four hundred institutions, but these raw data are yet to be compared and analysed. Such a comparative research in PETE can be very helpfull for the harmonization process and for quality improvement in PETE in Europe.

References

Crum, B. (1998). Conceptual convergences/divergences in European physical education teacher and sport coach education programs. De Lichamelijke Opvoeding (Netherl.) 86(3) 1998 p.100-104 and 86(5) p.204-207.

Laporte, W. (1997a). The physical education teacher for secondary schools in the E.U., Cahier of the Eur. Netw. Sport Sciences in Higher Education, Barcelona, ENSSHE.

Laporte, W. (1997b). Curriculum development in the European physical education Teacher Education, Cahier of the Europ. Netw. Sport Sciences in Higher Education, Barcelona, ENSSHE.

Ursprung, L., Freitag, E. & Schilling, G. (1995a). European Review of Institutes of Physical Education GFS-Schriften, Sportwissenschaften, 13, Zürich, ETH

Ursprung, L., Freitag, E. & Schilling, G. (1995b). European Review of Institutes on Physical Education. J. Compar. P.E. and Sport, XVII, 1,2-11.

Vroeyenstijn, A.I. (1994). Improvement and Accountability Navigating between Scylla and Charybetis. Guide for external quality Assessment in Higher Education. London, Jessica Kingsley.

Notes

[1] European Network of Sport Sciences in Higher Education.

[2] ECTS: European Credit Transfer System.

Chapter 38

PE teaching, ageing and the working environment.
The view of female and male PE teachers

Mette Krogh Christensen, Else Trangbæk and
Per Fibæk Laursen
University of Copenhagen, Denmark

> *"Becoming old is difficult when your identity has been closely linked with being physically active. But it is not concerned only with teaching, it has something to do with your whole life and life-form. Before, your body was just something you had and could trust!. Now it is more problematic. That can be hard to admit (female PE teacher, 43 years old)."*

This quotations stems from the research project, "PE teaching, ageing and the working environment". The focus of the research project as a whole is the relation between the development and change of PE and PE teachers' life history and experience. The purpose is to learn about and realise the significance of teacher identity in relation to the perception of physical and mental problems in teachers' working conditions, and to draw up wider perspectives with regard to training and in-service training. The central concepts are ageing and expectations, self-esteem and perception of competence. In this paper the focus is on the following problem complexes: (a) how do PE teachers perceive their competence and the importance of their own sports skills?; (b) how is it that ordinary ageing has an extraordinary significance for female teachers in particular in PE ?

The background and central concepts of the project

The research project looks at PE teachers' ageing, because today a trend can be seen that PE teachers retire from PE at a younger age than in other subjects. It has been an accepted situation for Danish PE teachers to retire around the age of 50, when it no longer feels "right" to teach PE. But now the situation is, that there will be very many PE teachers aged 50-59 in a few years. If they too are prepared to leave PE earlier than their other subject, the upper secondary school will be lacking PE teachers. So the solution must be that efforts are made to keep the older PE teachers for a longer time than has been the tradition until now, but that causes other problems.

In recent years, the reasons for retirement have been concentrated on physical wearing down and inadequacy in relation to the physical demands made by the subject of PE on the PE teacher. In addition, there is a tendency that women retire earlier than men. The question is whether the reason for the present situation can be found in the difference between male and female PE teachers' perceptions of self-esteem and competence in relation to becoming older in the subject of PE. The project will identify the extent of this question and possible sources to illuminate it.

In the problem complex around the retirement of PE teachers from the subject, the aspects of age and gender are so closely connected that it is necessary to analyse both in more detail. That there clearly *is* a difference between women's and men's career and competence is an idea that has deep roots in our culture. The life staircase is one of the icons for the idea of the course of life (Dove 1986). There is for both men and women a climax around the age of 50, but there are fundamental differences between the two life staircases. Today, some differences are still of current interest.

Age and gender are two concepts that are closely linked in this project. Ageing as a developmental psychological concept is connected to the theories of psychological adult development, both life-span psychology and life age psychology. In the project, primarily a life-age psychological angle of approach is used [1]. One of the front figures in early life-age psychology is the German-American development psychologist, Charlotte Bühler (1893-1973). She worked with the theory that the crucial factors that affect a person's life and work are the two resources, vitality and mentality. The lack of symmetry between a person's vitality and mentality creates the developmental changes in productivity, creativity and goals, which every person will meet. The Danish cultural historian and philosopher, Johan Fjord Jensen (Jensen 1993) suggests the concept of re-growth as the unifying designation for the theory and the ideal that life-age psychology represents, namely that mentality can develop independent of vitality. "Re-growth includes the actual nature of the growth processes that take place after the end of youth and before the real and final decline to old age" (Jensen 1993).

The expectations to a certain life age in relation to working life are precisely one of the dilemmas for PE teachers, female PE teachers in particular. The preliminary hypothesis of the project is that the PE teachers' expectations to work and their own proficiency are largely based on great vitality. An expectation that has been built up through their education and training and in the daily work with the pupils. That is why both a work crisis and a personal crisis can arise for the individual PE teacher when vitality decreases as a result of physical wearing down [2] or simply increasing age.

Facts about the upper secondary schools in Denmark

The upper secondary school, the Danish post-compulsory education, differs from that in other countries in several ways. The upper secondary school is a three-year general educational and academically oriented education for young people between the ages of 16 and 19, and PE is an obligatory subject all three years. The PE lessons are organised as two 45-minute lessons a week, but the lessons are held as one double lesson. The actual activities in PE have thus a time frame of 90 minutes, which gives completely different possibilities for organising the teaching than in other countries, where the time frame is much shorter. In addition to this, PE can be chosen as an elective subject at a higher level, and then the number of lessons is 3 double lessons a week for one year.

All teachers teach two subjects, PE teachers too. They each have about 4-5 double lessons in PE a week. The teachers' planning of PE teaching in addition must take into account that in practice they are organised as a three-teacher team, who together have two classes. Most often, the classes are divided into three sex-integrated teams, each with its own PE teacher.

Method and design

The research project has its origins in a series of courses, which, in 1996-1998, was a national in-service course for PE staff groups, i.e. all PE teachers in an upper secondary school. The answers to a questionnaire from the first phase of these courses have had two purposes: 1) to provide a background so the teachers on the course could base their teaching on the problems of the individual staff groups, and 2) to provide a background for collecting data for analysis in connection with the research project as they help to give a greater insight into the actual work situation of PE teachers (Trangbæk 1997).

PE staff groups from 76 upper secondary schools in Denmark participated in the questionnaire survey, which corresponds to half the number of these schools in Denmark. Thus, 722 questionnaires were sent out in the period August 1996 to April 1998 and 663 questionnaires were returned. The response percentage was 91,8%.

Table 1 : Structure for data collection

I	Questionnaire (I) to all PE teachers on the courses.	722 questionnaires. Response percentage = 91,8.	August 1996 - April 1998
	Qualitative interviews	12 interviews of 1½ hours.	February-April 1998.
II	Studies among former PE teachers	90 questionnaires. Response percentage = 70.	January 1997 - June 1998.
	Qualitative interviews	6-8 interviews.	June 1998 - December 1998.
III	Short interviews + observations	2 schools monitored during the courses and in daily life in the school.	January 1997 - June 1998.

The questionnaire survey is the basis for the preliminary results and trends. In addition, these results have been used as guidelines for making the qualitative interviews (table 1). It is expected that the research project will be finished in the year 2000, and until then, all the empirical material will be analysed.

Data and results

The age distribution among PE teachers shows a large majority aged 40-49. Fewer than 1% of PE teachers are aged 60 or over (table 2).

A not unimportant detail in the age distribution is that almost two out of three PE teachers up to age 39 are women. One could begin to speculate how this lopsided sex distribution can help to create the culture that surrounds PE [3]. Perhaps PE in the upper secondary schools is in the process of changing into a female-dominated subject (too), and then it will be interesting to see how the many female PE teachers will influence the subject in the future.

Table 2 : Age and sex

	24-39 years	40-49 years	50-67 years
Men, % of total	8 %	27 %	10 %
Women, % of total	16 %	31 %	8 %
Total, % of total	24 %	58 %	18 %

Qui2 = 0.002, N = 586, no answers = 77

The expected effect of age on PE teaching

One of the very central questions in the questionnaire survey was how PE teachers react to being older in the subject and if there is a difference in this regard between male and female PE teachers. The general impression is that the PE teachers expect changes caused by age in the actual method of teaching in the form of less physical activity on their own part. But it is not without cost to change teaching in this way. Every third female PE teacher and every fifth male PE teacher believes that reduced physical activity on the part of the teacher will lead to the feeling of declining professional qualifications and self-esteem, along with problems with maintaining respect from the pupils (table 3).

Importance of own sports skills in relation to PE teaching

Irrespective of gender, PE teachers in general attribute an important role to their own sports skills in relation to teaching generally (table 4).

Table 3 : The expected effect of age on PE teaching

	Men	Women
More instruction and starting functions, less physically active during the lessons. Fewer lessons.	37%	23%
Experience of declining professional qualifications and self-esteem. Problems with maintaining respect from the pupils. A wish to retire.	22%	33%
Verbalisation of the teaching, more pupil demonstrations and pupil tasks.	16%	21%
Necessary to keep in form and avoid injuries.	12%	12%
Age has no effect.	9%	8%
Irrelevant answers	4%	3%
Total	100%	100%

N = 497, no answers = 166

Table 4 : Importance of own sports skills in relation to PE teaching

	24-39 years	40-49 years	50-67 years
Great or crucial importance (8-10)	36 %	47 %	51 %
Some importance (5-7)	62 %	51 %	44 %
Little importance (2-4)*	2 %	2 %	5 %
Total	100 %	100 %	100 %

Qui2 = 0.035, N = 581, no answers = 82

The table starts with 2 points(*), as no one answered 0-1 point (= no importance).

Almost half the PE teachers believe that their own sports skills have great or even crucial importance in relation to the daily PE teaching. There is even a tendency that a higher age is connected with one assessing one's own sports skills as having great importance in the daily teaching. The PE teachers were asked to amplify their check-list answers [4]. The research team categorised the answers in the following way (table 5).

Table 5 :   What importance have your own sports skills in relation to PE teaching (text answers)

Good sports skills make the teacher self-aware and respected.	30 %
Good sports skills make teaching easier.	26 %
General teaching qualifications can compensate for the lack of sports skills.	21 %
Teachers with good sports skills motivate the pupils.	12 %
The teacher should be able to demonstrate as an example.	8 %
Irrelevant answers	3 %
Total	100 %

N = 345, no answers = 318

To have good sports skills generally for PE teachers is tantamount to the PE teacher getting respect and approval from the pupils, that the teacher feels competent and secure in the daily work and that teaching is easier.

However, there is a hint that women in particular find sex integration a problem in relation to maintaining respect. It is quite simply more difficult for female PE teachers to achieve respect and approval among the boys if the female teacher cannot manifest herself and her teaching role with the help of good sports skills.

Assessment of one's own professional qualifications

The questionnaire survey also shows clearly that male PE teachers as starting point assess their own professional qualifications higher than female PE teachers do (table 6).

Table 6 : Assessment of one's own professional qualifications

	Men	Women	Total
Very satisfactory (8-10)	66 %	46 %	56%
Fairly satisfactory (5-7)	31 %	49 %	40%
Not very satisfactory (2-4)*	3 %	5 %	4%
Total	100%	100%	100%

*the table starts at 2 points, as no one answered 0-1 point.
Chi2=0.000, N = 641, no answers = 22

Answers with 10 points, which applied to about 6% of all answers, were distributed with 80% men and 20% women.

The conclusion from these results is preliminary, that declining vitality affects the attitude to work of female PE teachers in particular. Unfortunately, the effect is negative, and the question is whether re-growth within PE exists as a possibility for these teachers.

Discussion

Well-being as a working environment term is a question of feeling comfortable at work, feeling adequate and experiencing pleasure and satisfaction with the work. The prerequisite for well-being in work is that one feels that one's qualifications are adequate in daily situations. As several studies show, burnout and mental wearing down are often caused by repeated disappointments and frustration about the experience of inadequacy (Hargreaves 1996). The result is failing self-esteem, both professional and personal.

The preliminary results from the questionnaire survey show that it is particularly the female PE teachers who experience problems with inadequate professional qualifications, anxiety about lack of respect from the pupils, and failing self-esteem as regards their profession in pace with increasing age. At the same time, the questionnaire survey shows that both women and men perceive their own sports skills as very important for the daily teaching, but that it is particularly women who experience a dilemma between the recognition that skills inspire respect for the PE teacher, and the recognition that lack of own skills is felt as a limitation in relation to motivation and self-esteem. In any case, there are indications that women pay more attention to how their professional qualifications affect the pupils and to their own motivation and self-esteem in PE teaching. This is shown by the following quotations from the study:

"(I have) an idea that it may perhaps be more difficult to inspire and motivate and, particularly, to demonstrate, when your physical form is not so good. Also an element of personal pride: I don't want to show an untrained body with a sagging stomach, it is (I presume) easier to involve the pupils when you go in front yourself (female PE teacher, 41).

Not so much with regard to going in front, but more with regard to how the pupils perceive you. You give or communicate a sports image - how will it be perceived in 10-15 years when I have to be young with the young people? (female PE teacher, 40)

Specially in order to win the respect of the boys, sports skills are good. It doesn't mean anything in relation to the girls (female PE teacher, 35)".

This raises questions: Is it the case that better sports skills give greater well-being as PE teacher? And is it the case that women are those who to a greater extent risk losing the well-being aspect in the work as PE teacher? On the basis of the results from the research project, the answer to both questions must for the time being be yes.

The present results indicate a connection between the importance of the PE teacher's own sports skills and the perception of professional qualifications. Sports skills are linked by PE teachers to self awareness as regards their subject and to the degree of difficulty in teaching: better and more skills = easier teaching. That is why, on the face of it, it seems that the problems linked to declining vitality can be seen as a reflection of loss in relation to one's professionalism and self awareness as a PE teacher - a loss that diminishes the PE teacher's feeling of well-being at work.

The Swedish PE educationalist Claes Annerstedt (Annerstedt 1991) suggests on the basis of a large study in Sweden [5] that a good PE teacher has the following abilities: 1. to create well-being and a good atmosphere, 2. to lead and plan the work, 3. to present the contents in the right way, and 4. to teach and get the pupils to learn. The PE teacher's personal sports skills do not have a central position in this description - actually they are not even mentioned. The results from "PE teachers, ageing and the working environment" seem to point in a different direction. In no way can it be ruled out that it is precisely the personal sports skills which the Danish PE teachers regard as the basic prerequisite for the abilities that Annerstedt suggests. On the basis of the results until now, it could be said that Danish PE teachers generally perceive personal sports skills as the actual source of their pride and commitment to the subject and as an essential prerequisite for being able to present the content in a correct way and create a good atmosphere. This perception is now creating problems of identity for some PE teachers, especially women, and especially older PE teachers.

But it seems that it is a perception that is changing. More younger PE teachers are prepared to experiment with other PE teacher roles than the front runner: the teacher role with the emphasis on physical presentation. They are preparing to alternate between a teaching form with great emphasis on the physical and a more verbal form even at the start of their career as PE teacher. In this way the focus on the PE teacher's professional qualifications will perhaps move a little further from sports skills as a prerequisite for satisfactory teaching. But does this development affect the fact that female PE teachers more than male PE teachers experience problems in relation to growing older in the subject? No unequivocal answer can be given on the basis of the questionnaire survey. We can only assume that a teaching form with less emphasis on the physical aspect in general will relieve some of the pressure of performance on PE teachers, and that for PE teachers, too, there will be a possibility of real re-growth in PE when vitality declines with age.

References

Annerstedt, C. (1991). Idrottslärarna och idrottsämnet. Utveckling, mål kompetens - ett didaktiskt perspektiv. Acta Universitatis Gothoburgensis, Göteborg 1991.

Bruun Pedersen, J. (1995). Kriser og valg i de ældre år. I: Månedsskrift for praktisk lægegerning, 3, 279-285.

Bühler, C. (1984). The course of human life: A study of goals in the humanistic perspective, 1968. I: Lauridsen, Peter: Personlighedspsykologi - en antologi, Nyt Nordisk Forlag Arnold Busck, København.

Dove, M. (1982). The perfect age of a man's life. Cambridge Univ. Press. Cambridge 1986.

Erikson, E.H. (1982). The life cycle completed. W.W. Norton & Company.

Fejgin, N., Ephraty, N. & Ben-Sira, D. (1995): Work environment and burnout of physical education teachers. Journal of Teaching in Physical Education, 15, 64-78.

Handel, G. & Lauvås, P. (1987). Promoting reflective teaching. The Society for Research into Higher Education.

Hellison, D.R. & Templin, T.J. (1991). A reflective approach to teaching physical education. Human Kinetics Books.

Hargreaves, A. (1996). Lærerarbeid og skolekultur (ori.titel: Changing teachers, changing time). Ad Notam Gyldendal, Oslo.

Jensen, J.F. (1993). Livsbuen. Voksenpsykologi og livsaldre. Gyldendal, København.

Melander, L.S. (1988). Undersøgelse af arbejdsmiljøet for idrætslærere i gymnasieskolen. I: GISP, 45.

Merriam, S.B. & Caffarella, R.S. (1991). Learning in adulthood. A comprehensive guide. Jossey-Bass Publishers, San Francisco.

Schou, N. (1994). "Nedslidningsstatus - i Roskilde Amt". I: GISP, 71.

Schön, D.A. (1983). The reflective practitioner. How professionals think in action. Basic Books.

Sheehy, G. (1974). Passages: predictable crises of adult life. New York.

Tennant, M. & Pogson, P. (1995). Learning and change in the adult years. Jossey-Bass Publishers, San Francisco.

Trangbæk, E. (1997). Idrætsundervisning, livsalder og arbejdsmiljø. I: Fagdidaktikrapport, Undervisningsministeriet, Gymnasieafdelingen.

Notes

[1] Among them Charlotte Bühler, Erik Erikson, Gail Sheehy

[2] Previous studies of the working environment of PE teachers in Denmark (Melander 1988; Schou 1994) and internationally (Fejgin 1995), indicated that it is not the physical wearing down, but on the contrary, other factors that are at stake for PE teachers. The project "PE teaching, ageing and the working environment" confirms that the physical wearing down is not the greatest problem for PE teachers in Denmark. Four out of five PE teachers do not experience any musculo-skeletal troubles, or very little (0-3 on a scale from "no trouble at all" (=0) to "worst possible pain" (=10).

[3] That the number of male PE teachers in relation to female PE teachers is a result of the number who are trained in the subject can hardly be the reason for so many female PE teachers. Because, until recently, equal numbers of male and female PE students were admitted and trained as PE teachers in Denmark.

[4] Only 52% did so, but nevertheless, the answers give a picture of the way in which sporting skills are important for PE teachers in everyday situations.

[5] The study comprised interviews with 15 university PE teachers, 15 PE teachers and 15 PE students.

Chapter 39

Olympism in the classroom: partnership sponsored educational materials and the shaping of the school curriculum

Kimberly S. Schimmel and Thimothy Chandler
Kent State University, USA

In 1992, International Olympic Committee (IOC) members received petitions from 160,000 school children in Australia asking that Sydney be chosen as the site for the 2000 Olympic Summer Games. As a show of "grassroots community support" 120 schools were paired with individual IOC members who were then lobbied in an attempt to bring the Games to Sydney. Whenever IOC members visited Sydney, they were taken to "their" school and presented with scrapbooks prepared by children that contained messages supporting the city (Booth & Tatz 1994). After Sydney was chosen as host for the Games, a complete "Olympic Schools Strategy" was released to the public. Part of this "strategy" included an Olympic Education Resource Kit which provided extensive and detailed instructions (primary grades through high school and inclusive of all subjects) for infusing Olympism and the Olympic Games into every classroom. Developed by the New South Wales Department of Education, endorsed by the Australian and International Olympic Committees, and sponsored by Coca-Cola and IBM, the kit was distributed to every school in Australia for inclusion in their curricula.

In this presentation we examine the context which has led to the pairing of schools with the IOC and private capital. In addition, we introduce a number of problematics which surround curricular materials which are produced and promoted by the "partnership" between corporate interests, government agencies, and not-for-profit foundations. We will highlight parallel processes: the expansion of the IOC's influence over the local populace by adding more linkages in its partnership model; and an expansion of corporate influence over school children by developing industry-sponsored "educational" materials. Both processes have their roots in the 1980's and in American market capitalism; but by the late 1990's both would be inextricably linked to a more globalized economy. On the one hand, the IOC's marketing of the Olympic Games and of Olympism becomes strengthened by teaming-up with local not-for-profit organizations and global corporate capital. While on the other, during the same time period, corporate advertisers begin to target (school) children as both a primary and future market group. We suggest that these parallel processes provide the necessary conditions for our problematic: The pairing of the IOC with local schools and the promotion of Olympism (and the Games as commodity) through corporate-sponsored educational materials.

Increasing power and profitability: the IOC's partnership model

On the first occasion that the Olympic Games were hosted in the southern hemisphere, the political credibility of the IOC and the economic viability of the Olympic Games depended upon Melbourne's willingness to support the ideals of Olympism and foot the bill for the Games. The inherent danger of this partnership model for organizing Olympiads was highlighted twenty years later in the serious, long-term problems of the city of Montreal following the 1976 games. The danger was then further exacerbated by the political issues surrounding the Moscow games in 1980. Such problems culminated in a significant change in the way that Olympiads have been organized and funded since the Games returned for a second visit to Los Angeles in 1984.

The original dyadic organizational model involving a partnership between the IOC and local government agencies in the host city became a more hierarchical partnership model in Los Angeles. On this occasion the IOC employed additional partners as its agents because the host city, or more precisely a majority of its tax-paying inhabitants, wished to invest as little as possible in the games. The Los Angeles Olympic Organizing Committee (LAOOC), a not-for-profit organization headed by Peter Ueberroth, took over many of the duties traditionally undertaken by the host city. More importantly, the LAOOC was responsible for finding the money to pay for the Olympics. Thus, the primary goal of the LAOOC became to encourage the march of capital into the Olympics, in order to ensure that there was relatively little fiscal drain on the host city. The LAOOC achieved this goal by going to the corporate marketplace for funding and support of the Games. The Olympic Program (TOP) was its major vehicle for achieving this.

TOP allowed the LAOOC to restrict the number of official Olympic corporate sponsors to 30 while raising the minimum level of sponsorship for each corporation to $4 million. As Gruneau and Cantelon (1988) have suggested, this was a very significant departure from the sponsorship model that had surrounded previous Olympics. TOP was the IOC's means of promoting exclusivity for the sponsors while exacting enormous sums of money from them. In other words, money was raised through selling the Olympic ideal. However, as we shall discuss later, commodifying the Olympic ideal exacted a (perhaps unanticipated) toll from the Olympic movement.

One example of the sea-change in the partnership model which TOP ushered in can be seen in the relationship between Coca-Cola and the Olympics. When boasting of its unbroken support of the Olympics since 1928, The Coca-Cola Company stresses its continuity of purpose in promoting the Games. The company's message is -- we've been supporters all along -- it's only our level of commitment to the Games has increased over time! By contrast, we wish to stress the difference between supplying the U.S. Olympic Team with 1,000 cases of Coca-Cola in Amsterdam in 1928 in order to help American athletes "feel at home," and paying for the rights to make Coke the exclusive Olympic soft drink of the L.A. Olympics in 1984 in order to strengthen a world-wide marketing strategy. The more recent pairing of Coke with the Olympics is in fact offering support of a very different order and for a very different purpose. Furthermore, the degree of influence which this new type of partnership has brought is also of a very different order. It bears mentioning that Coca-Cola's support of the Olympic purpose earned the IOC $176 million in 1996 in sponsorship fees --just from this one transnational TOP partner (Real 1996). Indeed, the Games became part of the global capital market and a product which needed to be sold to the global consumer. The IOC required that consumers developed brand loyalty *to* the Games, while its TOP partners were betting on consumers developing brand loyalty *via* the Games.

Coca-Cola, Chrysler, McDonald's, and all of the other global corporations that were part of TOP, were important players in the new partnership model of the Los Angeles games. Such a partnership model has been further refined and embellished in the Olympiads in Seoul, Barcelona and, most recently Atlanta, the "home" of the Coca-Cola Company. As an aside it is probably not coincidental that the TOP founder and LAOOC chairman Peter Ueberroth is currently on the board of the Coca-Cola Company!

The change in the partnership model which we have outlined signifies a transformation of the Olympics into an increasingly secular and market-oriented project where "a more fully developed expression of the incorporation of sporting practice into the ever-expanding marketplace of international capitalism" is now manifested (Gruneau & Cantelon 1988, p. 347). The IOC heralded the Los Angeles games as being successful. They were deemed successful because they were relatively uneventful in political terms (as compared to the Moscow boycott and the crises in Munich and Montreal) and enormously eventful in economic terms -- they made a substantial profit. Nevertheless, for many people the Los Angeles games came "to symbolize new heights in the corruption of sport [and]...any remaining vestiges of Olympic ideals seemed to vanish as a result of these 'Corporate Games'" (Gruneau & Cantelon 1988, p. 346). Many critics pointed to the IOC's choice of Atlanta over Athens as proof positive that the Olympics had finally lost all remnants of idealism.

Though successful in economic terms, the triumph of entrepreneurial capitalism and (American) consumer culture embodied in the L.A. and Atlanta games had an undermining effect: The IOC's new partnership model demystified the relationship between global corporate capital and the Games as a globalized, commodified product.   It seems likely that any loss of "Olympic mystique" (Nixon 1988) did not go unnoticed by members of the IOC.   Overt commercialism indeed has a price -- it threatens a legitimation crisis for the Olympic Movement and its buttressing Olympic ideals.   The problem then, for Olympic officials, became not so much about how to maximize profit; but rather how to recapture mystique.   If the Games were to be "successful" into the 21st century, they would have to both attract more global consumers and (re)create the notion that the Olympics are more than just another global (sport) commodity.   We suggest that one of the strategies employed by the IOC and its corporate partners was to mobilize school children to assist in the cultural and material sale of the Games.   Through the use of "Olympic Educational Kits," Olympism is recast as idealism and the Olympics (as commodity) are marketed to future consumers.   It is to the context of the schools that we now turn our attention.

Corporate-sponsored educational materials and the birth of Kid Konsumer

Beginning as early as the 1920's, American advertising campaigns have focused on children as influencers of consumer spending.   A few farsighted advertisers realized that in addition to marketing to adults directly, children could also be enlisted to help business sell products to parents.   Moreover, because schooling is compulsory, these advertisers recognized that schools provided a "captive audience" of millions of young advertising-assistants.   In his handbook for marketers (who target children), James McNeal (1992) provides the contemporary explanation for this strategy:

> *"[R]equesting items is a natural act for children. All that is necessary is to inform children of an offering and create a desire for it....Once the desire is present children will either try to buy the product with their own money or ask their parents for it....The marketer need only make sure of the availability of the product to the child/or parent "* (p. 85).

Thus, as Harty (1979) has expressed the point, industry enlisted a powerful foot soldier for their advertising campaigns: the nagging child. But rather than place overt product advertisement in schools, business provided "educational materials" with product or corporate names attached. Providing schools with free pencils and workbooks embossed with business logos, as well as material for classroom exercises related to specific consumer goods became common corporate strategies.

In later decades corporate attempts to advertise in schools accelerated. In addition to providing workbooks and pencils, the business community distributed videotapes, curricular packages, and free sample products to school rooms. Learning often meant learning about particular products. Companies provided schools with "free" commodities and accompanying "lesson plans" or filmstrips prepared by advertising agents -- product advertising packaged as pedagogy. A 1957 survey published in *School Executive* found that 97% of teachers surveyed used sponsored materials (Burk 1957). According to this report, few of these teachers used any "ethical standard" in determining whether to use the materials, and none of them received guidance from school administrators (Molnar 1996, p. 39). Given this scenario, it might be accurate to suggest that compulsory education had become "compulsory consumption." In fact it would take two more decades of rampant commercialism in American schools before any significant broad-scale public opposition was marshaled.

During this time marketers broadened their vision regarding the potential of school children to stimulate consumer spending. Not only were children to be viewed as influencers of their parents' purchases; but they became a target market in their own right. Instead of being the child of a consumer, Kid Konsumer had an identity all her own -- she could be presented with child-specific things to want now. She became Kid Kustomer. In addition, developing Kid Konsumer's "brand loyalty" became a coveted corporate prize. As Packard had noted:

> *"it takes time, yes, but if you expect to be in business for any length of time, think of what it can mean to your firm in profits if you can condition a million or ten million children who will grow up into adults trained to buy your products as soldiers are trained to advance when they hear the trigger words "forward march."* (cited in Harty 1979, p. 11)

It is the targeting of children as Influence Market, Primary Market, and Future Market (see McNeal 1992, p. 15) that accelerated corporate attempts to utilize schools as a commercial medium. Again from Packard who quotes *The Printer's Ink*, a publication for marketing communications:

> *"Eager minds can be molded to want your products! In the grade schools throughout America are nearly 23,000,000 young boys and girls. These children eat food, wear out clothes, use soap. They are consumers today and will be the buyers of tomorrow. Here is a vast market for your products. Sell these children on your brand name and they will insist that their parents buy no other..."* (cited in Harty 1979, p. 11)

So while industry-sponsored educational materials could be found in American schools in the early 1900's, targeting (school) children as consumers is a post-war phenomenon. From a marketer's standpoint, for children to be considered a viable target group they must "have wants," they must have money, and there must be a large enough number of them to "make marketing efforts worthwhile" (McNeal 1992, p. 4). The "baby boom" years following WWII provided all three.

In the five years following WWII, the number of American children increased by 50% and by the late 1960's children spent over $2 billion of their own money (McNeal 1992). Throughout the 1970's children were bombarded with kid-friendly advertising campaigns, both within and outside of schools. For example, Ronald McDonald became the standard bearer for the McDonald's Corp. and other cartoon-like characters were introduced to market products during this time -- including Tony the Tiger (cereal), The Burger King (fast-food), Geoffrey the Giraffe (toys), the Pillsbury Doughboy (baked goods), and the Campbell Soup Kids (soup). Interestingly, the first in a long line of kid-friendly Olympic mascots was introduced in the 1970's as well -- Waldi the Dachshund in Munich. Further, many popular cartoon characters were employed by corporations to "teach" children in schools about private industry. The American Iron and Steel Industry hired Disney's Donald Duck to narrate a school film about the US Steel industry. Exxon hired Mickey Mouse and Goofy to teach school children about energy; the resulting comic book was distributed free to all members of the National Education Association. The line between education and propaganda is blurred by corporate curricula that succeed as entertainment. Recognizing this, Great Britain's Code of Advertising Practices prohibits use of familiar cartoon characters (Harty 1994). No such code exists in the US.

Kid Konsumer meets globalized capital

It is the decade of the 1980's though that has been called the "decade of the child consumer." Children's advertising expert John McNeal instructs:

> *"In general, it appears that before there is a geographic culture there is a children's culture; that children are very much alike around the industrialized world. The result is that they very much want the same things, that they generally translate their needs into similar wants that tend to transcend culture. Therefore, it appears that fairly standardized multinational marketing strategies to children around the globe are viable. And they are advisable for those American marketers who want to avoid some of the intense competition domestically and are thinking of seeking profit and growth across the seas."* (1992, p. 250)

Though consumer's rights advocates certainly took notice, for the most part, competition in children's goods and services became so intense during the 1980's that marketing campaigns aimed at kids became an almost taken-for-granted aspect of American consumerist culture. This decade witnessed an explosion of media directed at school children: child-specific television and radio networks; magazines; and newspapers were all introduced or increased. In addition, children-based retail expanded beyond fast food and toys to include clothing, books, banking, and hospitality. What did attract public attention however, was a global marketing strategy aimed at schools. In 1989 Chris Whittle, a marketing executive, introduced the controversial Channel One which would advertise children's consumer products via television directly into classrooms. The concept was simple: Any school could access Channel One for "free" if it signed a three-year contract. In return the school guaranteed that a twelve minute Channel One program would be shown at least 90 percent of the days school was in session, that at least 85 percent of the students would watch it, and that advertisements would not be edited out. By 1991, Channel One could be seen in over 9,000 American schools. As Molnar (1996) has put it, Whittle's rallying cry was "give Channel One twelve minutes...and it would bring students the world" (p. 55).

Sydney's Olympic Schools strategy: some questions for discussion

What we have focused on in this presentation is the expansion of corporate influence over school children in the American context. What has yet to be considered is the history of corporate involvement in the Australian educational systems. If Australian schools have served as safe havens against the bombardment of corporate advertising, does Sydney's Olympic Education Kit represent a breach? If it is a breach then might this portend creeping corporate sponsorship of Australian curricular materials? If so, one wonders whether these strategies will spur public criticism. What we have suggested is that the processes we have sketched help shape the conditions through which a corporately-funded, IOC-sponsored curriculum made its way into every school and potentially every classroom in Australia. The inception of TOP in 1982, a partnership which has assured that global capital will sponsor the Olympic movement, coincided with an onslaught of corporate marketing campaigns aimed at children. And while the IOC likely pondered strategies to rescue the Olympic mystique from the overt commercialism of the increasingly corporate Games, school children were being socialized into becoming global consumers. Perhaps it should come as no surprise then, that Sydney launched the Olympic Schools Strategy to:

> "[P]rovide all school children with the opportunity to be involved with the year 2000 Olympic Games through ongoing educational programs

and special strategies which further the Olympic ideals whilst developing a range of understanding, skills and effective learning. (Sydney Organizing Committee for the Olympic Games)".

The Olympic Education Kit, which aims to "further the Olympic ideals", is literally framed by corporate logos. Even so, for our purposes here, the crucial questions have not been about how much corporate sponsorship is evident or explicit in these materials, but rather why these partnerships were formed to produce the Kit in the first place, and whose purposes are served by them. We would like to point out that although the IOC prohibits corporate signage in sport stadiums, they apparently have no problems with delivering corporate logos to schools.

The second problematic we would like to present involves the relationship between global and local interests who will likely benefit from the Olympic Games, and the role played by schools in constructing local consent to host them. Given the local resources that are required to stage this global event (construction of new facilities, reallocation of urban space, demands placed upon the urban infrastructure, etc.) the potential for public resistance runs high.   Therefore, are we witnessing the expansion of the IOC's influence over the local populace, in this case, through the coopting of educational institutions (and the children subsumed in them)? For as the IOC warns, "The Olympic flag, the Olympic symbol, and the Olympic motto are the exclusive property of the International Olympic Committee," and therefore cannot be used in or on educational materials without their permission. Thus, pursuant partnerships which have used these insignia (The NSW Department of Education/IOC/TOP) represent a bloc of vested interests of which these curricular materials are an expression.   In other words, the message contained in the Education Strategy is clear: The Olympics are wonderful, we are lucky to have been chosen as hosts, and we have the IOC and its corporate sponsors to thank. For even the most ardent critic of the Games, it cannot be easy to publicly oppose 120,000 enthusiastic school children. What is unclear is whether or not this strategy is an expression of a new partnership ethic or purely an idiosyncratic attempt to strengthen Australian nationalism. For example, again quoting from the Sydney Organizing Committee for the Olympic Games (SOCOG):

"SOCOG intends to make the celebration of ...[Olympic] values a distinctly Australian event. After all, Australians have a love of sport, a commitment to freedom and social fairness and live amid the friendliness and hospitality of a multicultural society."

Or perhaps, is Australian nationalism -- translated as Aussie Spirit -- a part of a larger agenda that encourages the local populace to share in the aspirations of local and global elites?

Finally, we question the notion that educating children about Olympism through a curriculum sponsored by the IOC is necessarily an appropriate endeavor for schools to undertake. With other corporate-sponsored educational materials, learning about a product is often synonymous with being socialized to consume it. Developing brand loyalty to a particular product is a coveted prize for marketers. What makes the Olympic product so different? Perhaps the Olympics are more capable of naturalizing, even mystifying, capitalist relations than are other forms of collective consumption. The cover page of the Sydney's Olympic Education Kit states:

> "Coca-Cola in Australia is pleased to be associated with the Olympic Education Kit....The Future of the Olympic Movement lies in the youth of today and with this in mind, the kit has been developed by the Australian Olympic Committee in conjunction with educational authorities to provide a valuable teaching resource."

Does the act of enlisting school children to help dramatize and (re)create the Olympic mystique strengthen the IOC's attempts to package the Olympic Games as the global celebration of the human spirit? Has the IOC's grasp been extended to include the world's youth as consumers of present and future Games and their "official" products ? Such suggestions put a different complexion on the President of the IOC's exhortation at the close of every Olympiad calling upon "the youth of the world to assemble four years from now ...". Might this be read as an ongoing attempt to perpetuate Olympism, socialize young global consumers, and ensure the "success" of future Olympic Games ?

References

Booth, D. & Tatz, C. (1994). Swimming with the big boys? The politics of Sydney's 2000 Olympic bid. Sporting Traditions, 11, 3-23.

Burk, D. (1957). Free teaching materials -- Assets or liabilities? School Executive, 76, (12), 55-57.

Gruneau, R. & Cantelon, H. (1988). Capitalism, commercialism, and the Olympics. In Segrave, J. & Chu, D. (Eds.), The Olympic games in transition. Champaign, IL: Human Kinetics Press, 245-364.

Harty, S. (1979). Hucksters in the classroom: a review of industry propaganda in schools. Washington, DC: Center for Study of Responsive Law.

Harty, S. (1994). Pied Piper Revisited. In Bridges, D. & McLaughlin, T.H. (Eds.), Education & the market place. Washington, DC: The Falmer Press, 89-102.

McNeal, J. (1992). Kids as customers: A handbook of marketing to children. New York: Maxwell Macmillan International.

Molnar, A. (1996). Giving kids the business: the commercialization of America's schools. Boulder, CO: Westview Press.

Nixon, H. II (1988). The background, nature, and implications of the organization of the 'capitalist Olympics.' In Segrave, J. & Chu, D. (Eds.), The Olympic games in transition. Champaign, IL: Human Kinetics Press, 237-251.

Olympic Education Kit.
    http:// www.australian.olympic.org.au/educate/

Packard, V. (1957). The hidden persuaders. New York: McKay.

Real, M. (1996). The postmodern Olympics: Technology and the commodification of the Olympic movement. Quest, 48, 9-24.

Sydney Organizing Committee for the Olympic Games.
    http:// www.sydney.olympic.org.au

Chapter 40

Selling the "Spirit of the Dream": olympologies and the corporate invasion of the classroom

Tara Magdalinski and John Nauright
Sunshine Coast University and University of Queensland,
Australia

As a part of Sydney's bid to host the 2000 Olympic Games, an 'Olympic Schools Strategy' was initiated in 1992 that paired Olympic Organising Committee members with schools across New South Wales. After Sydney was chosen as host for the Games, the Schools Strategy was released to the public. Developed by the Australian Olympic Committee, sponsored by Coca-Cola and IBM and with assistance provided by the New South Wales Department of Education, an Olympic Education Resource Kit was distributed to every school in Australia for inclusion in the curricula. According to the official press release, the kit was designed to 'create a greater awareness and understanding among our school children', and to 'encourage young Australians to learn about the values and the philosophy of the Olympic Movement' (http://www.australian.olympic.org.au/media/pr971205.html) This project represents part of a transnational research project that examines the ways in which Olympism is articulated in and through ongoing school-based programs whose aim is to foster an appreciation for the Olympic Movement among school children. To date, there has been little critical discussion of the Olympic educational strategies in Australia and the United States. While some public discussion has been present in Australia over sponsorship in schools and a Senate inquiry has examined the corporate funding of schools, analyses of the corporatising classroom have not been widespread.

Since the inception of the modern Olympic Games, there has existed a philosophy of 'Olympism' that purports to promote the ideals and spirit of sport as represented by the Olympic Games. Despite the homage to democracy expressed by proponents of the Olympic movement, the ideals promoted within this movement are rooted in Eurocentric, masculinist and elitist ideologies. These ideologies in sport centred on the doctrine of 'amateurism', an exclusive concept that gradually evolved to mean participation in sporting competitions for its own sake, or for success without direct material reward. In the past thirty years the ideologies of Olympism have diverged from this amateurist ethos to incorporate professionalism to form what Donnelly (1996) calls a global sporting monoculture centred on the values of success, capitalism and monetary reward for top level performances. In the present, these ideals, which he labels 'prolympism', are linked inextricably to a consumer culture that is divisive both in terms of class associations and economic status. The Sydney 2000 Olympics is representative of the incorporation of sport into multi-national advertising and marketing strategies. Such strategies are antithetical to those in sport that promote mass participation, physical education for lifelong health and the ideologies of sport that promote cooperation rather than those that foreground competition and victory. Thus the Olympic movement, centred on the activities of the International Olympic Committee, National Olympic Committees and organising committees for Olympic Games are now firmly entrenched in the global capitalist system and its attendant ideologies. In order to reproduce the global multinational corporatist system, large corporations have targeted children and youth in marketing strategies and through involvement in educational institutions through sponsorship, curriculum development and provision of free 'educational' materials to schools.

There is a long history of advertising and marketing that has been undertaken by capitalist corporations in order to sell their goods to the public. Between 1880 and 1930 a fully developed organised system of commercial persuasion and information emerged as part of the distributive system of large scale capitalism as Raymond Williams (1993) demonstrates. Companies moved beyond merely advertising their products, however, as they also seek popular legitimation by attaching societal values and institutions, such as the family or the nation, to their corporate images. The family, in particular is utilised as an ideal, an 'ideological totem', whilst also being continually developed as an *access* institution to the market' (Goldman 1992, p. 88). In the 1960s and 1970s families in general and children within families in particular were targeted by companies as diverse as McDonald's and Disney while a massive market in children's toys and leisure activities emerged after the Second World War. More recently, however, large corporations have moved from merely advertising their products and services to youth markets to direct involvement in educational programs and institutions, and this is a global phenomenon. In South Africa, for example, Coca Cola has sponsored schools in exchange for the placement of logo-bearing signs on school buildings.

The corporate invasion of educational institutions, particularly schools has developed over many years. More overt forms of sponsorship of school sport and the provision of educational packages with clear links to multi-national corporations are now well established and successful forms of advertising. To cite one example: the exposure, and thus advertising potential, generated for Pizza Hut through its 'educational department' is phenomenal. Twenty-two million school children in the USA participate in Pizza Hut's BOOK IT!® program annually. This program centres around the provision of free pizza vouchers for children who have met particular reading goals. The program also operates in Australia. McDonald's has also made a foray into the educational system and provides educational kits for under-resourced schools. For example, activities in the McDonald's Activity School Pack include recreating a McDonald's outlet in school with students role-playing various jobs and re-enacting other parts of the corporate structure, such as Head Office, suppliers, consumers. Other activities include visiting a local McDonald's to gather information about the store and then returning as a consumer to buy a meal; drawing plans of the store, making a model of the store using Lego, marking on a map the location of McDonald's stores that the children had visited, inventing words to 'Old McDonald had a store', to the tune of 'Old McDonald had a farm', and finally, selecting items from a list of McDonald's products to include in a diagram of what the child likes to eat (http://muu.lib.hel.fi/McSpotlight/company/publications/schools_pack.html).   (To link this with the Olympics, McDonald's official web site recounts the history of McDonald's involvement with the Olympics since it airlifted hamburgers to US athletes at Innsbruck in 1964). In Napanee, Ontario, Canada, Goodyear as part of integrating the town with their new factory there had industrial arts students devise projects applicable to Goodyear production and the school system went so far as to adopt a process of 'firing' and 're-hiring' of students who had performed poorly or misbehaved to link students with the industrial discipline of Goodyear (Palmer, 1994). In these examples we see some of the most clear evidence of corporate intrusion into schools and the mechanisms by which children are manipulated into becoming loyal consumers. Curricula activities are dictated by multi-nationals in order to instill brand awareness in children, and to introduce them into the world of corporate consumerism and (non-unionised) labour. Even more insidious than the Goodyear example was the case in March 1998 of a student in Evans, Georgia who was suspended from school for wearing a Pepsi shirt on the school's Coke Day. 'School officials say the shirt was an insult to Coca-Cola executives visiting from Atlanta and ruined a school picture in which students spelled out "Coke". . . Friday's Coke in Education Day was part of Greenbrier's effort to win a $500 local contest local contest run by the Coca-Cola Bottling Co. of Augusta and a national contest with a $10,000 prize' (*Cincinnati Enquirer* 3/26/98).

In the United States, the centrality of consumerism is such that leading analysts have suggested that the entire society is organised around 'themes' from Disneyland to Las Vegas to Shopping Malls and fast food restaurants. This theming of consumerism has invaded all sectors of society, but particularly targets youth markets in order to 'capture' the next generation of consumers (Gottdiener 1997). The Olympic movement is certainly using its theme of 'Olympism' as displayed in its global competitions to capture a global audience loyal to its brand of sporting competition. Thus, the Olympic movement operates clearly along the lines of many multi- and trans-national corporations in its efforts to create a consumptionist universality.

One example of how multinational corporations and the spectacle of the Olympics interact can be seen in an educational program developed by Sea World theme parks in the USA. Sea World, a group of theme parks owned by American multi-national beer brewing company Anheuser-Busch, has been one of the most active developers of educational materials for use in schools. Initially developed as part of marketing strategies, the educational programs have developed to include family and school visits to Sea World and Busch Gardens theme parks in California, Florida, Texas and Ohio, special educational camps and, most significantly, Shamu TV. Shamu TV, named for the killer whales that are the main attraction at the parks, is Sea World's educational television program that provides educational materials on nature to schools across North America. Shamu TV programs are now shown on the Discovery Channel Cable network that serves millions of households.

Sea World's Education Department lists its goals as instilling respect for living creatures, conservation of natural environments, increasing student competencies in science and other disciplines and to provide an educational resource for the entire community. Although these goals appear altruistic and community oriented with proposed clear educational benefits for students, it is clear that the real aim is to provide awareness of the Sea World's activities and the attractions at the parks. In its advertising material, Sea World urges: 'Join Shamu TV's student adventures as they visit exotic locations to investigate the world's habitats and many fascinating animals found there. You'll marvel at the animals of Sea World and Busch Gardens parks and learn from the people who care for them'. In another promotion of Shamu TV, Sea World states that

> *"Shamu TV brings the wonders of marine science right into your classroom. It helps your students develop a stewardship for the earth and its creatures. Each live, interactive, 40 minute program features the following:*
> *- live hosts from Sea World or Busch Gardens*
> *- up-close footage of animals*
> *- interviews with animal experts*
> *- a toll-free number students can call to have their questions answered by experts"*

Such material clearly illustrates that the programs are used to raise the brand awareness of Sea World and Busch Gardens through the direct linking of the nature-based programs with attractions at the parks.

In 1995, Sea World attempted to capitalise on the popularity and recognition of the Olympic Games in the United States as the 1996 Games were to be staged in Atlanta. It developed its *Ocean Olympians* educational unit that targeted students in grades 4-8, with the goal that 'Students will discover the history, ceremonies, symbols, and sports of the Olympic Games, as well as the adaptations that make animals everyday Olympians'. Upon completion of the unit, students would be able to describe the history of the Olympics, indicate the significance of the Olympic motto, compare and contrast human athletic skills to those of aquatic animals, name three ocean Olympians and describe adaptations for success, locate geographic areas where both human and animal Olympians live, and finally, to share these various learning experiences with their family and friends (http:www.seaworld.org/Olympians/oogoals.html). This unit seeks to make the unlikely connection between the Olympics and activities of sea animals. As a result awareness of the Olympics to be staged in Atlanta and awareness of Sea World were directly connected. The parent company Anheuser-Busch is also one of the largest sponsors of elite televised sports in the USA. Thus the Olympics can be learned and celebrated and ultimately consumed by children and their families through the educational experiences offered by Sea World/ Anheuser-Busch, without the company's involvement in the direct (and expensive) sponsorship of the Olympic Games. There is no direct acknowledgement of the IOC as an official part of the Sea World kit on the internet version of the program, though the IOC spends considerable time and effort to protect and defend its right to control Olympic 'education' and materials linked to the Olympic movement and Games.

Major sporting competitions, and particularly those sports with television exposure, have become increasingly commercialised over the past forty years. As the largest international sporting event in terms of global media coverage, the Olympic Games are no exception. Whilst professional sporting leagues and many international sports events such as the Soccer World Cup have been overtly connected with corporate sponsorship for decades, the Olympic movement has sought to control commercialisation on its own terms, deciding to admit only an elite core of major sponsors in their TOP program of Worldwide Olympic Partners, including Coca-Cola, IBM, Kodak, McDonald's, John Hancock, Kodak, Panasonic, Sports Illustrated/Time, UPS, Visa and Xerox. Nearly all of these companies are American-based multinational corporations and most have significant global brand recognition. These companies provide equipment and funding to the IOC and National Olympic Committees in exchange for being part of an exclusive group of sponsors to receive exposure during any Olympic-related activities and to use Olympic symbols and logos. The IOC closely guards the use of its images and protects the rights of its exclusive sponsors.

In the promotion of the Olympics as *the* major global sporting event and the Olympic Movement through an ideology called Olympism and as a movement that embodies the virtues of sport and sporting competition, the IOC has for a long time viewed education as an important part of its self-promotional activities. As Bruce Kidd (1996, p. 82) notes, the bulk of Olympic educational activities are 'technical in nature, aimed at improving the athletic performance or administration, or directed at schoolchildren, potential spectators, and others', in other words the programs are aimed at raising the Olympic brand awareness and the universality of the Olympics and Olympism in the minds of young Olympic consumers. This strategy has certainly applied to educational strategies surrounding the Olympics in the lead up to Sydney 2000.

Australian schools have been incorporated into the celebration of the Olympic movement and of the Sydney 2000 Games in a variety of ways. School children are encouraged to submit their artwork for a national art competition; the winning artwork will be featured on Sydney 2000 merchandise. A schoolgirl was used by the Sydney bid team to encourage the IOC to select Sydney as the 2000 Olympic destination, and more recently, the education arm of SOCOG has begun a national campaign designed to increase awareness of the Olympics amongst Australia's youth. Olympic Education Kits were sent to every school in Australia in 1995, and in early 1998, Winter Olympic Kits were distributed. In the near future, every Australian schoolchild will receive a copy of the SOCOG newsletter, a publication targeted at children that will contain a range of informational updates, activities and articles aimed at raising the consciousness of Australian children and to encourage them to 'share the spirit' of the Sydney Olympics. Of concern in this venture is the support that these supposed 'education' kits receive from those multi-national corporations who sponsor the Olympics, as well as the activities within the packs.

There has, to date, been a dearth of critical research into the Sydney Olympics. The little that has appeared has focussed on deconstructing the Olympic marketing representations of Sydney as a united city, employing research on class divisions, demographics and socio-economic status to demonstrate the marked division in Sydney's population (Waite 1998). There has been little public debate on the role of the governments in the provision of federal and state public funds to the hosting of the Olympics or the development of infrastructure. Further, any public criticism of the Olympics has been classified on many occasions by both SOCOG and government representatives as 'un-Australian', thereby reinforcing the links between uncritical nationalism and corporate consumerism.

Academic involvement in the Olympics has been primarily focussed in Australia on the Olympic centres, one at the University of New South Wales, and the other, unofficial centre, at the University of South Australia. Recently, permission has been sought and granted by the Queensland Olympic Council to establish an Olympic Studies Centre at The University of Queensland. The response of these centres to the Olympic Games has been overwhelmingly supportive, and the New South Wales Centre has actively organised promotional conferences such as the Green Games. Instances where academic criticism of the Olympics has been voiced has resulted in silencing (Holmes, 1997).

This paper is an initial part of a wider project on Olympic education materials distributed to schools in Australia and the United States as part of the 'selling' of the Olympic Games, Olympism and corporate loyalty to school children in the lead up to the Summer Olympic Games of Atlanta and Sydney and the Winter Olympics of Nagano and Salt Lake City. Specifically, we are interested in the content, framing and promotion of Olympism and global multi-national corporate capitalism as it appears in materials targeting primary and secondary school children.

We introduce a number of problematics that surround curricular materials that are produced and promoted by the 'partnership' between corporate interests, government agencies and non-profit foundations. Among these are: the pairing of Olympism and nationalism with consumerism in a context where children are a 'captive audience'; mobilising school children to assist in the cultural and material sale of the Games; the potential for incorporating teachers to assist in consensus building around the Olympic Ideology; the fundamental contradiction between internationalist and nationalist discourses; and the perpetuation/celebration of an agenda that encourages the local populace to share the aspirations of local and global elites.

We pay special attention to the ways that sporting and nationalist ideologies are intertwined with the ideologies of multinational capitalism and 'sold' through education. The package is not limited to physical education, but invades all sectors of the curriculum with student projects listed in each area of school study. Thus, the Olympic movement is read in the context of transnational organisations suggested by Macintosh and Cantelon (1995) and its marketing through 'education' is read in alignment with the strategies of multinational capitalism. Thus, Olympic 'education' as sold through the Olympic education packages seeks to capture adherents in their youth and create brand loyalty that will enhance the interests of the Olympic Movement's leader and their multi-national sponsors.

The Nagano Winter Olympic Education Kit

As a follow up to educational kits that were distributed to all Australian schools in 1995, the Australian Olympic Committee (AOC), the Sydney Organising Committee for the Olympic Games (SOCOG) and the Sydney Organising Committee for the Paralympics with the assistance of sponsors and the New South Wales Department of Education developed a Winter Olympic Education Kit to be used during the time of the Nagano Winter Olympics thus enhancing awareness of the Olympics in general in the lead up to Sydney 2000. As with the 1995 kits, the Winter kit, devised for primary and secondary school students, was sent to all Australian schools.

The connection between the Olympics, the education kit and corporate sponsors is clear from the outset as sponsors the *Sydney Morning Herald*, Sydney 2000, Berlei Sports, the Australian Olympic Committee, IBM and The

Seven Network (television) Sport. In the introduction to the kit, AOC President John Coates states that

> "the kit has been produced with the valuable support of Berlei, John Fairfax Publications, IBM and the Seven Network, along with the assistance provided by the New South Wales Department of School Education. It is the first of the National Education Program to be produced by the Australian Olympic Committee, the Sydney Organising Committee for the Olympic Games and the Sydney Paralympic Organising Committee. . . . [The kit] builds on the Olympic Education kits produced in 1995 and again will be distributed to all schools across the nation (1998 Olympic Winter Games Education Kit, p. 1)."

The 1995 kit was prefaced with commentary by IBM about their involvement in the production of the kit and the Olympics. While the Winter kit does not go as far as the 1995 kit in having students specifically target Olympic sponsors' signs (given the inaccessibility of Japan as compared with Sydney or other parts of Australia where such logos can be readily observed, the kit follows the original in its promotion of an idealised version of the Olympics, Australian nationalism celebrated in contemporary corporate capitalism and the Seven Network's presentation of these ideologies.

Conclusions: text, lies and videotape

Included in the Australian Olympic kits, American ones and the *Ocean Olympians* kit from Sea World are potted written and visual histories of the ancient and modern Olympic Games that are riddled with historical distortion and inaccuracies. Much history is mis- or dis-remembered in the construction of a history of an Olympic ideal – a history that is virtually free of politics and social inequality and one that provides isolated examples to illustrate broad assertions about Olympic ideologies or olympologies. Of particular interest is the manipulation of history to demonstrate the ideologies of peace and friendship and social equality that de Coubertin and the Games are meant to have had throughout the past century while downplaying or ignoring the gender, race and class exclusivity embodied in late nineteenth century conceptions of 'society' and 'culture'. Such depoliticisation of history is dangerous in that it teaches an idealised version of the past the never really existed. While there is no doubt that the goals of universal peace, goodwill and understanding are laudable as ideals, the uncritical writing of Olympic history that foregrounds myth and virtually ignores struggle and contestation serves to create the captive audience loyal to the ideal brand of ideal sports idealised in the Olympic Movement. As such, we as sports studies scholars and physical education practitioners must question the goals of such kits and the uncritical consumption they impart of decontextualised and dehistoricised sport disguised as a virtual religion of Olympism.

References

Babbie, E. (1998). The practice of social research 8th ed. Belmont, CA: Wadsworth.

Donnelly, P. (1996). Prolympism: sport monoculture as crisis and opportunity. Quest, 48(1), 25-42.

Goldman, R. (1992). Reading ads socially. London: Routledge.

Gottdiener, M. (1997). The theming of America: dreams, visions, and commercial spaces. Boulder: Westview.

Holmes, D. (1997). Conference Report. Sporting Traditions XI Conference. ASSH Bulletin, 27, 29-32.

Kidd, B. (1996). Taking the rhetoric seriously: proposals for Olympic education. Quest, 48(1), 82-2.

MacLachlan, G. & Reid, I. (1994). Framing and interpretation. Melbourne: Melbourne University Press.

McAllister, M. (1996). The commercialization of American culture. New advertising, control and democracy. Thousand Oaks; London: Sage.

Palmer, B. (1994). Capitalism comes to the backcountry: Goodyear's invasion of Napanee. Toronto: Between the Lines.

Waite, G. (1998). Playing games with Sydney: selling Sydney for the 2000 Olympics. Paper presented at the Commodification Conference, University of Wollongong, February.

Williams, R. (1993). Advertising: the magic system. In During S. (ed.), The cultural studies reader. London: Routledge, pp. 320-336.

Internet sites of Sea World and Sydney Organising Committee for the Olympic Games.

DATE DUE